RUSSIA'S MUSLIM HEARTLANDS

DOMINIC RUBIN

Russia's Muslim Heartlands

Islam in the Putin era

HURST & COMPANY, LONDON

First published in the United Kingdom in 2018 by
C. Hurst & Co. (Publishers) Ltd.,
41 Great Russell Street, London, WC1B 3PL
© Dominic Rubin, 2018
All rights reserved.
Printed in the United Kingdom by Bell and Bain Ltd, Glasgow

A Cataloguing-in-Publication data record for this book
is available from the British Library.

ISBN: 978-1-84904-896-5

www.hurstpublishers.com

CONTENTS

CONTENTS

PART THREE
VOLGA STOP-OVER

PART FOUR
CAUCASUS CONNECTION

CONTENTS

ACKNOWLEDGEMENTS

This book had its origins in two courses I taught at Dickinson College, Pennsylvania in 2013-2014: 'Religion and Communism' and 'Islam in Eurasia'. The invitation to come and teach for two years at Dickinson was due to Professor Elena Duzs, and it was also she who suggested I teach a course on Islam in the post-Soviet region, and so I would like to thank her for getting the ball rolling. I would also like to thank Dickinson College for giving me a grant to travel to Kyrghyzstan in 2013.

Back then, I had just finished a book on the Russian Eurasianist philosopher, Lev Karsavin, and I was trying to square the interest in the 'East' proclaimed by Russian Eurasianists with their perplexing lack of knowledge and real understanding of 'Eastern' religions and philosophies. As I commuted between Russia and the U.S., and started reading up for my new Islam course, I also decided to deepen my own knowledge of Islam and Muslims in Russia. Eventually, I began to see a certain gap in the literature. There seemed to be quite a number of books that were oriented towards the security angle, and quite a few histories of Tsarist- and Soviet-era Russian Islam; there were also books that gave sociological surveys of Muslims' beliefs and others that listed the multitude of rapidly shifting contemporary Muslim organizations. However, it was difficult to hear the voices of individual Muslims, or make sense of how being Muslim and being Russian were being combined at the individual level since the collapse of the Soviet Union. I thus decided to plunge right in and begin speaking to as many Muslims as I could meet, with the idea of writing down their views and life stories, and hoping that I would get some sense of where the Muslim community in Russia was going. After four years, this is the result, and I hope that the book does put a personal,

ACKNOWLEDGEMENTS

human face on the Russian Muslim community today. It will not replace the existing books, of course, but hopefully act as a useful supplement.

In the early days, I was beholden to Anna Gorbenko, my sister-in-law, for introducing me to her Tatar acquaintances; to Professor Marion Wyse, for putting me in touch with some of her Tatar and Dagestani students; to Ian Pryde and Ainura Maketova, for hosting me in Kyrghyzstan; to my good friend Leoscha Maslov, for sharing his knowledge of Islam with me, and putting me in touch with some fascinating people; and to Sergei Marcus, for introducing me to some wonderful Muslim contacts in Tatarstan and Dagestan. I would also like to thank each and every one of my interviewees for giving me their time so freely and generously: less than a third of their names appear in this book; as for the rest of them, many of their stories are still hibernating in my computer. Some of them have become good friends. I would especially like to thank Farit Valliulin from Kazan, Professor Magomed Ramazanov in Mahachkala, and Sirozhidin Abdusamatov[1] from Fergana, whose hospitality and generosity were quite humbling.

A word on the genre of this book. Before starting this project, I had been working for several years on Russian religious thought, which is a peculiar genre that mixes philosophy, theology, journalism, and public advocacy. I had also been living in Moscow and working as a teacher at various universities and theological institutes. In that sense, I was rather removed from the typical article-writing, publish-or-perish environment of Western academia. When I got back from teaching at Dickinson, I went back to my previous teaching work in Moscow, and continued teaching on inter-religious dialogue seminars. As time went on, I also lent a hand to the Russian muftiat's attempts to forge links with Western Muslims. My audience, as I came to see it, was thus not exclusively academic, and I had never intended the book to be a straightforward scholarly history or sociological study of Russian Islam. Instead, that mixed genre of Russian religious thought has left its mark on me: theology, sociology, and personal travelogue all ended up blending into a narrative account of my investigations. My brief time at Dickinson was enough to show me that such a genre is absolutely forbidden within modern academia (at least for non-tenured scholars), but as an unaffiliated individual I saw no need to make greater claims to omniscience and objectivity than were warranted by my status. However, I am highly grateful to Michael Dwyer of Hurst for taking on board this somewhat unconventional offering. I would also like to thank Bruce Clark for reading a nearly complete version of the book before that, and reassuring me that it was indeed readable and informative. I would also like to thank Professor Timothy Winter of Cambridge University for reading a first draught, and for deepening my understanding of Islam. Inevitably, given the complex and controversial nature of the subject, there are places where I have undoubtedly been naive and perhaps eccentric in my evaluations; I hope specialists can forgive this, while those new to the subject will find something to take away.

Finally, I would like to thank my wife Maria for once again supporting me wholeheartedly. In my previous bookish endeavors, this has been limited to letting me keep my nose in my books, but this time she also went out on a limb by letting me take off for distant parts, sometimes at rather trying times. Heroism indeed!

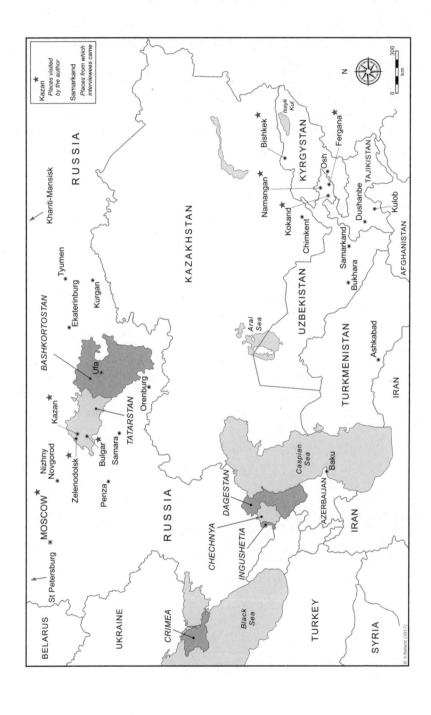

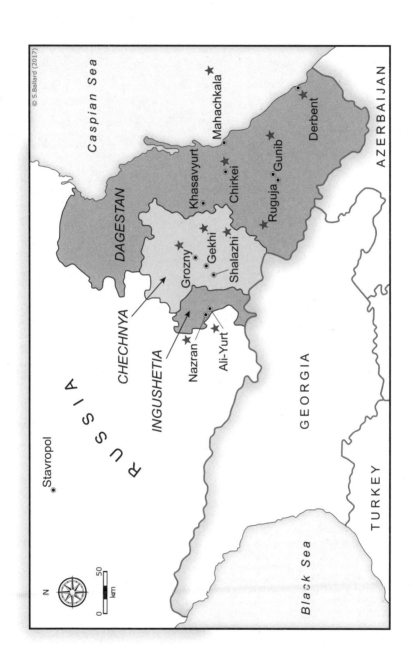

PART ONE

MOSCOW DEPARTURE

1

MOSCOW: MELTING-POT AND WOULD-BE MECCA OF RUSSIA

Muslim Moscow: ancient and modern

Moscow has its own Islamic geography and toponymy; some of it is ancient and dormant, some of it has come to life again recently. The Zamoskvorechie, or Beyond-the-river, region lies across the Moskva river within sight of the red walls of the Kremlin. It is one of Moscow's most picturesque and historic regions: the center of "golden-domed Moscow"; home to the world famous Tretyakov gallery; and dotted with sturdy merchant houses from the eighteenth century—a haunt for tourists and Muscovites alike soaking up their own past. But there are Islamic layerings to this past. The word Kremlin itself is a Tatar word meaning fortress. Two of the main streets in this beautiful district, are called Bolshaya Ordynka and Bolshaya Tatarskaya street. The word Ordynka derives from the Mongolian word *orda*, ("camp, headquarters") and refers to the Golden Horde that ruled Muscovite Rus from the thirteenth to the fifteenth centuries. The road heads south-east out of Moscow and used to link the Slavic capital with the Mongolian capital in Sarai, near the Caspian Sea. Bolshaya Tatarskaya, or Great Tatar street, recalls the district's long association with the various Tatar khanates; the embassies of the Nogai and Crimean khanates (the last to resist Russia's imperial expansion into the Eurasian steppe) were situated here into the eighteenth century, and from early on a Tatar *Sloboda* (district) sprang up in these streets—a regular feature of many Russian cities, where Tatar merchants, porters and restaurateurs lived somewhat separately from their Slavic neighbors.

Perhaps few stop to ponder the significance of these street names now, or of the Tatar origins of other Moscow landmarks, including Old Arbat, Moscow's "Oxford Street", not to mention the river that flows past the Kremlin, the Yauza. But these echoes of the Horde and Tatar khanates are not just ancient history. Today, the Uzbek and Kyrgyz embassies are located in Zamoskvorechie. There are tour agencies selling cheap plane tickets and phone cards to Central Asia, and several stores selling halal food.

On a Friday afternoon in late June, the pedestrian precinct that leads from the Tretyakovskaya metro past the enormous pink baroque church of Holy Martyr Clement Pope of Rome will contain some noteworthy visitors hurrying towards Bolshaya Tatarskaya street: an old bearded man in a turban and cotton gaberdeen, a dark heavily stubbled youth in a velvet skullcap, and two long-bearded, agitated and wiry men racing down the precinct in oddly short trousers (a sign of Salafist observance). In London or New York, such ethnic dress would not raise an eyebrow. But Moscow has not completely shrugged off its Soviet past—under communism, minorities were encouraged to be invisible and inaudible, and old habits die hard despite rapidly shifting times.

In winter, whether you emerge from the Tretyakovskaya or Novokuznetskaya exit, an Uzbek woman in a scarf and flowing floral dress will be selling green paper mats for ten roubles a piece, to the bafflement of most commuters. In the drugstore at the end of the precinct, a bearded youth gingerly avoids touching the female assistant's hand as she hands him back his change, and he snaps at a female customer to keep away from him: the two women are mystified, scared even, not knowing that the man is trying to preserve his ritual purity before attending prayers. Any contact, in his interpretation, and he will have to line up for half and hour and go through his ritual washing again—with freezing water. This is all connected to the presence of the Historic Mosque at 28 Bolshaya Tatarskaya street. The paper mats are for Friday worshipers to spread beneath them in the street as they do their prostrations on the surrounding snowy pavements and road; there is just not enough space inside the mosque and the mosque's courtyard for worshipers. Likewise, the bathroom where ablutions are made is so small it causes tailbacks into the yard.

But nowadays it is not the Islamic life around Zamoskvorechie that is really synonymous with Islamic Moscow in the imagination of most. For that, one has to travel fifteen minutes on the Metro north-west to Prospekt Mira where as the 1990s progressed, post-Soviet Russian TV became increasingly transfixed by an astonishing sight that replayed itself every year: the same sight as the Historic mosque on a Friday afternoon, but on an incomparably larger scale.

Just off Olimpisky Prospect, named in honor of the 1980 Olympic Games, and standing in the shadow of the Olympic stadium (now turned into a shopping mall) is the Cathedral Mosque, which has always been the biggest of Moscow's four mosques. By the mid-2000s the number of worshipers wanting to celebrate Eid al-fitr (called in Turkic languages, Uraza Bairam, and marking the end of the Ramadan fast) had reached between 80 to 100,000 people. The mosque capacity was a thousand. As a result, the broad avenues surrounding the mosque, including parts of one of Moscow's main arterial roads, Prospekt Mira, were cordoned off and became temporary prayer spaces for Moscow's now predominantly Central Asian Muslims. Helicopter cameras showed a carpet of prostrate figures, heads touched to the ground, and from high apartment windows the "hordes" of worshipers seemed to stretch to the horizon. This was Muslim Moscow at its chaotic, Malthusian extreme. It provoked anxiety and incomprehension, and not just among a predictable group like Russian nationalists, but among Moscow's native Muslims too, the Tatars.

The Prospekt Mira Cathedral Mosque is thus the place to start trying to understand Muslim Moscow, and even twenty-first century Muslim Russia. In late Soviet times, Moscow's Muslim population had consisted largely of Tatars, itself an ethnic category comprising different subgroups. In 1980, they numbered around 160,000 or 1.7% of the population (Moscow's Jews, for comparison, were more numerous at 175,000 at the time). By the early 2000s the Tatar population had not changed significantly, but by 2015 police estimates put the number of worshipers praying in the streets around the Cathedral Mosque on Kurban Bairam at 160,000. Together with the other three mosques, the number of Muslims in the streets reached 200,000—a record year. Experts estimate that only 10 per cent go to the mosque for this occasion, and this gives the generally accepted figure that Moscow's Muslims in 2015–2016 number around 2 million or 6 per cent of Moscow's total population (though others put the figure as high as 3 million). Thus in twenty years, Moscow has managed to turn into the largest Muslim city in Europe:[1] the next largest is London, where there were 1 million Muslims in 2015. But the internal demographic had changed radically, too: of these two million, the once predominant Tatars have come to comprise only 12 per cent of Moscow Muslims; on Kurban Bairam 2015 there were more Muslims on the street than the total number of Tatars in Moscow.

However, it is from this Tatar 12 per cent that the leaders of Moscow Islam are still drawn. After all, it was their ancestors who built the Historic and Cathedral mosques, and constituted in the Tsarist and Soviet period the capital's only numerically significant Muslim population. The Historic mosque dates back to after the Napoleonic wars when the tsar rewarded Muslims for their efforts in defeating Napoleon, the Bashkir cavalry providing special strength. The roots of the Cathedral mosque go back to the late nineteenth century when a group of wealthy Kasimov Tatar merchants, led by Hussain Baibekov (b.1857), organized a new parish in a north-western suburb of Moscow and began arranging for the building of the Cathedral Mosque. Kasimov Tatars were descendants of the Kasimov kingdom; one of the post-Horde formations that had good relations with neighboring Muscovy, they had been settled in Moscow as merchants for a couple of centuries. But the new mosque catered not for their needs but that of their peasant co-religionists from the Nizhny Novgorod and Simbirsk regions on the Volga, who, as the country industrialized, began flooding into Moscow as laborers, eventually turning the northern suburbs into more densely populated Muslim regions than Zamoskvorechie. In 1904, after negotiations with the tsar and Moscow officials, the Cathedral mosque was built.

The sponsors of the Cathedral mosque continued to be wealthy merchants and the parish and mosque building, whose design and bright exterior was reminiscent of an Orthodox church, were symbols of loyalty to the empire. In 1915, the Russian Word newspaper published a letter from Imam Fattahetdinov of the 2nd Cathedral Mosque of Moscow describing the patriotic mood of Moscow Muslims, who "are prepared with joyful hearts to make a contribution to the great and holy task of helping Russian heroes" fight against "the insolent and treacherous [Ottoman] enemy" and the "Turkish army which is under the command of leaders who are trampling down all humanity along with the laws of Islamism, that mainstay of Muslim existence."[2]

In the Soviet period, Moscow Muslims underwent religious persecution depending on the whims of the leaders, but wherever possible the mosque's imams tried to negotiate rights and privileges for their community, and continued their pre-Revolutionary position of demonstrative loyalty to the government. The mosque was the main stop-off for heads of foreign Muslim states visiting the Soviet Union and took part in many diplomatic initiatives to build ties between the USSR and the Middle East. H.F. Nasretdinov, the mosque's imam during the Second World War, maintained close ties with Central Asian, Volga and Siberian Muslim leaders throughout the Soviet Union, and in 1944 he received a telegram from Stalin, asking him "to convey to the believing Muslims of Moscow my greetings and the gratitude of the Red Army"[3] for the money the community had raised to build a tank division. In 1946, Stalin's Council for the Affairs of Religious Cults even mooted the idea of creating a single muftiat for all of the Soviet Union's Muslims: it would be based in Moscow, so turning Nasretdinov into a sort of Grand Mufti for the whole USSR. Due to Nasretdinov's close ties with the various regional Muslim leaders, this initiative received support from the three main Soviet Spiritual Boards of Muslims in Central Asia, Transcaucasia and the North Caucasus. However, after Stalin's death the idea was shelved, Nasretdinov fell out of favor, and Soviet Muslims continued to live under different, often competing, religious leaders.

Since the collapse of the Soviet Union, Muslim Moscow, like Russia and the former Soviet Union, has changed beyond recognition. The old bans on travel between towns, let alone republics, have been rescinded. The ailing corruption-riddled economies of Central Asia, along with years of civil war in Tajikistan and Chechnya, have created economic and political migrants across Eurasia. The most ambitious among these head for Moscow, where the real power and wealth of Russia are located, though every major town in Russia is also a destination for these Muslim migrants, with peak migration clustering around labor-hungry regions such as the oilfields of north west Siberia.[4] And this is why in a short span Muslim Moscow has turned from a quiet Tatar backwater into a bustling Muslim melting-point.

The city now has the largest Muslim population in Russia: according to some estimates there are up to 15 million (legal and illegal) migrants in the whole of Russia, the majority of them from Kyrgystan, Tajikistan and Uzbekistan, and of these, perhaps 3.5 million have chosen Moscow and its environs as their destination.[5] As well as being the eighth most powerful city in the world by economic indices,[6] Moscow is also the most populous Muslim city, not only in Europe, but including the former Soviet Union.. After all, Tashkent, the capital of Muslim-majority Uzbekistan, only has a population of 2.3 million. Perhaps naturally, therefore, Moscow's Tatars, who have maintained leadership of all of Moscow's four mosques despite being vastly outnumbered by their new fellow parishioners, have for some time begun to see themselves as the natural leaders not only of Moscow Islam, but of Russian and even Eurasian or CIS Islam. The bid for regional Muslim leadership received powerful symbolic confirmation when permission was given in 2004 for the rebuilding and expansion of the Cathedral Mosque. The foundation stone was laid in 2005 and the project went ahead under the supervision of the head imam of the mosque, Ravil Gaynutdin.

The reconstruction of the Cathedral mosque was as painful a process as this reshaping of Moscow Muslim identity. Gaynutdin was not a Muscovite, having been born in a village in Tatarstan, but he had excellent Soviet Islamic credentials: he graduated from the USSR's only Islamic institute, the Mir-i-Arab *medrese* (Islamic seminary) in Bukhara, where he studied alongside Ahmad Kadyrov (later president of Chechnya), Muhammad Sodik Muhammad Yusuf (post-Soviet Uzbekistan's leading theologian), and others who would become leading figures in post-Soviet Islam. Then, after a stint as the imam of a mosque in Kazan, he became the executive secretary of DUMES, the Spiritual Board of Muslims of the European Part of the USSR and Siberia, which was situated in Ufa. In 1987, during the years of *glasnost* and *perestroika*, he was made imam of the Moscow Cathedral mosque at the tender age of 28. Here he took advantage of the new freedoms to found an Islamic school to cater for the surge in interest in Islam. In the 1990s, he was actively involved in founding the Council for Inter-religious Relations and the Council of Muftis of Russia. Thus this attractive and eloquent figure (whose first education had been as an actor) became a symbol of Russian Islamic revival; it did not hurt that his family, cultural and educational roots lay in the Volga region and Bukhara—that way, he was equipped to build bridges with all the representatives of Soviet and post-Soviet Islam.

However, Gaynutdin's success also alienated people, Muslims and non-Muslim. For Muslims, Moscow had never been Islamically significant in Russian history. The first Russian-recognized Islamic body, in the times of Catherine II, had been located in Orenburg, a new garrison town near the Kazakh steppes; then it shifted to Ufa in Bashkiria, further north. Most scholarly activity had been located in Kazan. The vast bulk of Tatars had always been located in the Volga lands between these two last cities. Moscow was a big non-Islamic player, but even in the Soviet period its Islamic prestige was a reflection of the Cathedral mosque's accidental proximity to the Kremlin. All this was to say nothing of the fact that Caucasian Muslims had their own Islamic history; while they were not completely isolated, when Caucasian Muslims searched in Russia for Islamic links, they looked to Ufa, Kazan and perhaps Bukhara: Moscow could offer nothing Islamic at all.

MOSCOW: MELTING-POT AND WOULD-BE MECCA OF RUSSIA

Within Moscow, the project of Gaynutdin and his team to turn the Cathedral mosque into something all-Russian met with increasing dissatisfaction: the promised refurbishment of the mosque turned into a wholesale reconstruction that dragged on for an inexplicable ten years, with rumors of embezzlement swirling around the project.[7] For many Moscow Tatars the destruction of the 1904 building was the desecration of a historical memory: "School children used to be taken on tours to the mosque; it was a landmark, even for non-Muslims," they would complain bitterly, as the old building was dismembered, and the only area for worship for near on a decade was an outdoor marquee. Finally, among non-Muslims the resentment was based on ethnic–religious affront: how could the Muslims dare to claim the third Rome, the capital of Eastern Orthodox Christianity, as a bastion of Islam? Attempts were, and are, made to paint Gaynutdin's Council of Muftis as secret Salafist radicals with plans to undermine Russia. This, despite the fact that with four mosques for 2 million people, there is one mosque for every half million Muslims, compared to London's 5385 or New York's 3685 per mosque. Still, in July 2015 the new mosque was completed. It was twenty times more spacious than the old building: its new capacity was 10,000, supposedly the biggest in Russia (though the Chechens and Dagestanis claimed the same for their own capital mosques).

Again, its architecture proclaimed its special all-Russian nature: one minaret was designed in the style of the Suyumbike tower in the Kazan Kremlin, the other in the style of the Savior tower in the Moscow Kremlin. In the same year, the Spiritual Board of the European part of Russia, which, along with the more ancient Ufa, Kazan and Caucasian muftiats, was merely one muftiat, was renamed the Spiritual Board of Muslims of the Russian Federation (DUM RF) by an official stroke of the pen. Its headquarters were right opposite the new mosque. Bureaucratically, officially, politically, architecturally and demographically, Muslim power now seemed to be concentrated in Moscow. In a book celebrating the completion of the new mosque, Damir Khairetdinov, himself a third generation Moscow Tatar draws attention to the long buried fact concerning Stalin's plan for an all-Union muftiat to be based in Moscow. Now, under Putin—who patronized the project and made a speech on the opening day—that dream had come true. Moscow was the new Eurasian Mecca.

But, of course, there were anomalies, and reality does not move as tidily as the ideologues might wish. The new mosque had a capacity of 10,000 but that still left 150,000 or so Muslims praying in the streets come Kurban Bairam.

9

Most of these were Central Asians and to a lesser extent Caucasians. Inside the old unrefurbished administrative corpus just opposite the glittering new mosque, the imams, Arabic and Islam teachers, writers, journalists, press relations team and ideologues of the new all-Russian Islam are nearly all Tatars. Not only are they ethnically different, they are socially different: most of them have Masters degrees and PhDs, and, being Russian-born, are fully bilingual in Russian and Tatar. Many of the team are happy to help Central Asian Muslims adjust in Moscow: they liaise with the Central Asian muftiats and their representatives at the Moscow mosque who can help with the spiritual nourishment of their countrymen. But others share the same feeling as other Moscow Tatars of being swamped by aliens, and communication between the two groups is highly limited.

There is a certain element of self-defensive snobbery here. After all, a few generations ago some of these Tatars were also new arrivals from the provinces. Among some Slavic Muscovites, the stereotype persists that Tatars are all crude and semi-criminal market workers, porters, laborers or shady businessmen. As with Berlin Jews looking down their noses at new East European arrivals, some do not want to be tarred with same brush: We are Muslim like them, yes, but an integrated, middle-class and sophisticated type of Russian Muslim. Still, even where this snobbery is not present, if Moscow Tatars wanted to help their Central Asian brothers they could not: they speak different languages, both in a literal and metaphorical sense. The Tatar activists' Islam is highly liberal and intellectualized; the Islam of the guest-workers is rural, patriarchal and for many, especially the Tajiks, radical and fundamentalist. Even if it were not, how are these Central Asians to fit into the new vision of "Russian" Islam which the team at Council of Muslims of Russia is trying to work out?

This, then, is modern Muslim Moscow. But the crowds of worshipers on Kurban Bairam are only one way of looking at Moscow Islam. Each individual, prized out of the crowd, has their own story to tell. And, as the experts say, ninety percent of Moscow's Muslims are not to be found in those serried ranks at all. Some of them are not religious. Some of them are more religious than those in the streets: one Tajik worker confided that, in 2013, when he asked his fellow worshipers who had kept the fast, only a half of them had kept it in some form or another. Many will have kept the fast, though, and just wanted to avoid the crowds and possible aggravation. Others will gather in homes or the few licensed prayer-houses scattered around the capital. Some will observe it next year, and not feel like it this year. And still others, Tatars, will avoid the

Cathedral mosque out of principle now, since it has so transformed beyond recognition. The closer one gets to individuals, the more individual and idiosyncratic "Russian Islam" begins to seem, though each individual also carries within him a family, an ethnic, a national, and a Soviet story.

Muscovite Muslims: students, professionals and guest-workers

The Mustafin family: a Tatar tale

The Mustafin family live in a high-rise block in the new suburb of Butovo, right on Moscow's south-east edge near the ring road. Rais and Raisa, who are in their late forties, have four children, the oldest of whom is Rifat. Rais's elderly father is still alive and lives in the apartment with them. The three generations are a microcosm of history: the father is still a staunch atheist. Rais and Raisa grew up as self-conscious Tatars, but their identity was strictly ethnic not religious. In the nineties, they both found religion, and Rifat followed his parents in performing *namaz* from the time he was about ten. For the younger children, Islamic observance is the only thing they know.

For twenty-year old Rifat, "I am more a Muslim than a Tatar. Tatar culture is only valuable due to its Muslim content. My friends are not Tatars, but Muslims: I go to different mosques with my three closest friends: one is Chechen, the other Dagestani, and one is a Russian convert." But Rais, his father, has an almost encyclopedic knowledge of his Tatar roots; Raisa, too, considers her Tatar identity to be at least as important as her Islamic identity: "You know, if there had been classes in Tatar back then (in the early nineties), I would probably have taken those, instead of Arabic." She regrets being a Tatar who no longer knows her native tongue. It was not just religion that could not be freely practiced in Soviet times, there were also constraints on how minorities could express their language and culture. Some took that route after the collapse, learning Tatar and developing their ethnic identity. As one Russian, echoing this old skepticism about non-Russian displays of self, said about an old Tatar man who had started wearing a skullcap in her Moscow-region village: "He's Tatar. He's quite open about it, going around like that; he's not at all ashamed."

Rais's mother is a Tatar from the Nizhny Novgorod region, a *mishar*. Her family moved to Moscow before the 1917 revolution. His father was born in Nizhny Novgorod, but his father's ancestral town is Petrahi, which was also the

11

ancestral town of his mother. This is no coincidence: when the time came for the Moscow girl to marry, her parents went looking in their hometown for a spouse. In other words, almost a hundred years had passed since their ancestors had emigrated from the region, but the ties had not weakened at all. Nor have they today. Rais himself visits Petrahi often, and together with other Muscovites with roots in the village, he recently raised the large sum of money needed to rebuild Petrahi's central mosque, which was torn down in the 1920s.

Rais's mother grew up in the shadow of the Cathedral mosque just before the war. Though Soviet Moscow did not encourage ethnic enclaves, the area in those days was still full of Nizhny Tatars. On the great Muslim holidays, the men would gather in the prayer hall in circles. Each circle of men denoted a separate village: Petrahi, Sabazi, and so forth, little islands of the Tatar diaspora reconstituted in Moscow. It was more an ethnic than a religious act of solidarity, which is perhaps why the authorities allowed it. Now things are different in the Cathedral Mosque, Rais notes, with some regret. The Tatar "villagers" and their descendants have fled to the suburbs: central property prices soared in the nineties and everyone, Russians and Tatars alike, were forced out. The circles in the prayer hall are now made up of Kyrgyz, Tajiks, and Uzbeks.

Rais hardly ever visits the Cathedral Mosque nowadays. Instead, every Friday he attends a registered prayer-house in an apartment block down the road. The congregants have rented a premise of 250 square meters, and they pay the rent themselves, helped out from time to time by a wealthy benefactor. Here, as a Tatar, he is still in a minority. He estimates that 80 per cent of the worshipers are Tajik, 10 per cent are Tatar, and the remaining 10 per cent consists of other nationalities, both from Russian or "near-abroad" regions like the Caucasus and Azerbaijan, as well as other countries in the Arab world and elsewhere. Rais makes clear that he does not resent being an ethnic minority now; it is the rebuilding work rather than the repopulation in the Cathedral Mosque that he resents.

Rais is lucky to have a registered prayer hall so close by, but ideally he would like to see dozens more mosques in his city. He has been involved in organizing petitions for the building of a mosque in Butovo, so that a more permanent structure than the prayer-house can be founded. The committee approached different departments in the bureaucracy of local government and explained their situation. But they were passed from one department to another, each bureaucrat claiming that responsibility for planning permission, or registration, and so on, was not his remit. Finally, the answer was that no land had been set aside, and no one could discover who exactly was responsible for land allocation. The petition died a death in the swampland of Russian bureaucracy. "It's all part of the general hostility to Islam in the media nowadays," he laments, and recounts some aspects of his work trying to force media outlets to portray Muslims fairly and to retract untrue or unconfirmed stories about the terrorist activity of arrested Muslims.

Rais recalls how he moved towards Islamic observance. Both his maternal grandfathers had died fighting in the Second World War, on the Finnish front. The only person with some knowledge who remained was his paternal grandmother. She began to tell him about Islam, and about prayer in the nineties, when these questions began to be discussed. He started to go to the mosque on his own for *jum'a*. To begin with he didn't know how to perform *namaz*, so he just stood back and watched, impressed by this spectacle of men "communicating with the Almighty." He joined the rows when the time came for the imam to read his *khutba* (sermon). On one occasion in particular the *khutba* went to his heart: it was one of Gaynutdin's sermons. After that, he started to learn how to perform *namaz* for himself. He began to buy the Islamic literature that they had started selling in those days, and again, when he needed help in any matter, he would turn to his Grandmother for help. Since then, of course, Islam has become a major part of his life. However, he still can't read Arabic[8] and only reads the Qur'an rarely. To some extent, Rais feels he has found his level; he knows there is far more to learn, but he works long hours and can't set time aside for study of that sort, so he makes do.

Raisa's story overlaps with her husband's, except that her own family were wealthy merchants whose property was confiscated by the Bolsheviks, triggering their move to Moscow. Raisa's family, too, visited the Cathedral mosque on holidays in the 1970s, but as a girl she never went inside. Every summer, like other Moscow dacha-goers, they visited the Nizhny region, and then she might see a mullah, and the family would eat meat slaughtered locally. She was a good student and ultimately trained as a teacher. Being intelligent and headstrong, she had no intention of having an arranged marriage, but her parents wisely let her pursue a career, in exchange for which it was agreed she would have the right to choose among the range of Tatar boys her parents would present her with. Rais was the last of several candidates; she consented, and before long she had launched on the stressful business of being a wife and mother.

It was this that made her quest for spiritual support more urgent. After the birth of her second child, triggering questions of how to raise the next generation, she enrolled in a class on Islam taught at the Yasenevo library by Marat Khairetdinov. (Yasenevo, too, is a distant suburb far from her family's original north-western Moscow home). The Khairetdinovs came from a line of religious teachers in Tatarstan and Bashkiria and were close to the imams of the Cathedral Mosque in the Soviet period. Like Raisa, their own families had also moved south-west in the nineties; the brother Damir studied in Saudi Arabia and is now rector of the Moscow Islamic Institute, where Marat also teaches.

Her growing Islamic faith helped her through a life crisis and gave her a sense of peace and meaning. The bond of prayer grew to be important in cementing the family as well. Usually, after everyone has got home from work and college, Rais leads his elder son and Raisa in the evening *namaz* in the living room. This experience, and the respect inculcated for mothers in Islam (she quotes the hadith: "Paradise lies at the feet of your mothers"), makes her job as a mother far smoother. Another aspect of Islam that she adopted through her transition was modest dress. When she was in her teens, she wore tight jeans (new to Russia, then) and lipstick. Now, although she wears a trouser-suit at her teaching job, at home and outside she always wears loose dresses and a headscarf. This does not attract attention, as people often think she is just a pious Orthodox Christian. "Occasionally, people even ask me for directions to the church!" Raisa also has stored away a *paranja*, which she dons when she goes to the mosque or prayer hall.

Rifat is studying engineering at college and has won a prize for rally-driving, his obsessive hobby. When he has time, he studies Arabic, and he goes to *jum'a* prayer every Friday, not visiting one mosque in particular. However, he mentions that the Victory Park mosque, which was built in the mid-1990s, is special because of its imam, Shamil Aliutdinov. After *jum'a* prayers, Aliutdinov leads question-and-answer sessions and gives interpretations of the Qur'an. Rifat is perhaps an example of a new type of "Moscow Muslim", with his non-Tatar Muslim friends and his insistence on the priority of Islam over his Tatar identity. However, he is slightly anxious about the future. In principle, he sees no contradiction between being Muscovite, Russian and Muslim. In his room, he has hung two flags next to each other: one is the Russian tricolor; the other is the green flag of Islam emblazoned with the *shahada*. It is testimony to how he sees a complementarity between Russia and Islam. But he worries about the possibility of observance when he has left college: "Now, the caretaker gives us a key to a room where I can do *namaz*," he says (his father, too, prays in a disused room at the local clinic where he fixes the computers). "But I would need to find a job where I can carry on with my prayers and observances…".

Native foreigners: Central Asians and Caucasians

The Mustafin family are middle-class, college-educated professionals. Their level of Islamic knowledge is practical. They are the ideal audience for the new all-Russian muftiat; indeed their Islamic knowledge was deepened through their attendance at classes held by this muftiat in its early days. But Rifat's worries have some foundation: it is not clear whether it is possible to lead an all-Russian Muslim life in Moscow. In my travels, I meet Leila in Dagestan. She too is a Muscovite Muslim of Tatar–Bashkir heritage. As she puts it, however, she has "made *hijra* to Mahachkala": as she grew more observant, she found it more natural to be in an all-Muslim environment where the workplaces, and even the gyms, have places for prayer—Rifat's worry. Or there is Dilyara, who was born in Kazan. Her parents came to full Islamic observance while she was even younger than Rifat, and she has been wearing the hijab since the beginning of her teens, never encountering hostility in Moscow because of it.

But her own position illuminates a paradox about Moscow Islam and the role played in it by the Cathedral mosque. She actually works for the Council of Muftis in the administrative building opposite the mosque, but says: "I struggle to pray my *namaz* on time, I rarely go to the mosque, and I don't get any time to study my religion beyond the absolute bare minimum." Her Islamic communal life is almost non-existent: "There is a group of Muslim mums who meet in an apartment once a week, but that's really just so the kids can play together. Most of us are Kazan Tatars. I would say the ethnic link is stronger than the religious one." Pregnant with her third child, she and her husband are thinking of moving back to Kazan, where life is less hectic and it is easier to find the time and space to be Muslim.

How can this be? Even though she is two minutes from the glittering new mosque, she explains, the mosque is not for people like her. "It's not ethnicity so much as citizenship. They are all temporary residents. They have different problems from us. We simply don't socialize." Another Tatar working for the Spiritual Board of Muslims opposite the mosque jokes when I arrange to meet him "at the mosque": "No, no! Don't come to the mosque, God forbid!" He is making the same point with slightly blacker humor: the mosque is "foreign". Many of the muftiat workers express similar sentiments, boiling down to frustration at the unmanageability, and the low level of education of the real frequenters of the new mosque. They may be on different sides of a single courtyard but ideologically they seem to be worlds apart.

However, in some respects the distance between the muftiat Tatars and the Central Asian and Caucasian parishioners is not that great. I talk to some non-Tatars who frequent it: Odina from Osh in Southern Kyrgyzstan, "Zhora" (a self-chosen Russian nickname) and Muhammad-jon from Tajikistan, Ikhtior from Bukhara, and Isa from Dagestan. In many ways, in terms of Islamic knowledge and observance, they are like Dilyara and Rifat. A life crisis or the natural curiosity of teenage years, spurred on by help from a knowledgeable grandmother (grandfathers were always out working), caused them to start observing Islam more seriously. But they quickly hit a plateau, and their main accomplishment is to learn the Arabic prayers for *namaz* by heart. That is the be all and end all of observance for these migrant Muscovites. They may supplement this with gatherings with their compatriots, as Odina, who works as a live-in cleaner, does; an *otincha* (Kyrgyz wise woman) lives in her block, and she drops by once in a while to listen to her read verses from the Qur'an. To some extent this is all new for her, not something she did at home, where she had troubled relations with her mother-in-law, and eventually turned to alcohol. Islam is now something that gives her certainty, dignity.

Ikhtior's observance took off in Moscow, too, but he is content with his prayers. "There are classes at the mosque," he says, "but I am too busy to go. I have reached my level." I ask him whether, hailing from Bukhara, he is involved with Sufism, and he laughs in disbelief. He spends all his afternoons and evenings in the mosque after work, but generally it is spent snoozing or in conversation. It is a way for him to keep away from temptation: women and drink mainly. "I live with my cousin," he says. "And he spends the time I am here just sitting in front of the television with a bottle of beer in his hand." A Chechen parishioner at the Historic mosque, a former middle-weight boxer who also spends his time snoozing between prayer-times, tells me the same thing: "Here I am kept from temptation. I have ups and downs in my observance, though. Sometimes I go deep, and then I have cycles where I move away." He seems to be in deep mode when we are speaking; constantly muttering *duas* under his breath between answers, he cuts a striking figure, dressed up in a multicolored robe like a nineteenth century Khivan dervish.

Both Ikhtior and the boxer have taken on the role of advisors for some of the other parishioners. They know who is who among the different groups. Ikhtior points out to me a Tajik *sheikh* in a turban and gabardine, and another

Kyrgyz man who deals with the problems of the Kyrgyz. After *namaz* is over, these men attract their compatriots into circles around them. There is a duty-imam: a Tatar, who mostly answers questions about marriage, blessings and daily problems, but generally each community's needs are met locally. This can make getting a picture of the Cathedral Mosque regulars' real views and activities highly difficult.

Then there is someone like "Zhora" who goes to the Cathedral mosque once a year for Uraza Bairam, when he dresses up in a suit and tie and gets on an electric train to Moscow with hundreds of his compatriots. This infrequency, however, belies a deeper observance. For the rest of the year, he lives full-time in a small village in the Moscow region where he works as a security-guard, gardener, dog-walker and even baby-sitter for a rich Russian family. He comes from a small village near the Afghan border, where he did his army duty and struggled in vain to prevent heroin smugglers crossing the gorge into his country. He also fought in the civil war on the side of the communists, though he does not like to talk about that. The village in Tajikistan that he comes from boasts a reputation among Moscow Tajiks for being tough, full of bandits. He smiles: "I am a softie, really. But no one round here, especially those Uzbeks," he spits the word out—an Uzbek site-manager ran off with his pay—"would dare to break in to the house I am guarding."

Zhora prefers to go to Moscow for the big holiday even though, as with many Moscow region towns and villages, there is a small registered Muslim prayer-house in the next village along from his; every Uraza, up to fifteen hundred locals gather there. The leaders of the community are the head of the local Azerbaijani community and a Dagestani, the worshipers mostly Uzbek and Tajik market workers and builders. A dozen or so also gather on Fridays, but Zhora does not have time or transport for that. He is happy enough to pray by himself in his little hut on the edge of his employer's property.

A few years ago he got himself mixed up with the law when he lived in Moscow: first he lost money gambling big sums at cards, then he got into a fight on a building site and was deported. Needing the money, he came back a year later on new documentation. After that, he got a shock and started getting pious. Back home, an "Arab *sheikh*" has moved into his village and many men in the village are now religious. Gradually, he built up his own observance and can rattle off several hadiths, such as the one about those who feed animals being rewarded with Paradise: he in fact, takes scraps of meat to the half-starved dogs that guard the local farm. And when I visit him in June 2013, he completes the entire Ramadan fast in extraordinary conditions: the daylight hours last from 4 a.m. to 9 p.m. approximately and he abstains from food as well as water while digging holes, building fences and carting round building material in a wheel barrow. Every morning he rises at dawn to read the Fajr prayer. When the fast is over, he confides: "I feel like a new man, strong, lean. I can't wait to show my wife!" He does look skinnier, in his now loose T-shirt, which boasts a picture of Vladimir Putin: "He respects us. I respect him," he tells me earnestly, cutting short my cynical glance.

He finds time to share Islamic morsels with me: "Ibn Sina, 'a Fars', almost a Tajik, said he had found a cure for everything; only death he had not managed to cure. But God told him there was no cure for that. You cannot seal yourself in a vacuum and protect yourself from the world, a pin-size hole will destroy the vacuum. It's the same with death." He quotes stories he has heard at various *khutbas* about Ismail, Job (whom he confuses with Yakub), and Muhammad. He boasts to me of how Lenin plagiarized from Muhammad: "Lenin used to say, 'Read, read and read again.' But this was written in the opening of the Qur'an a thousand years ago. Lenin read the Qur'an many times and got strength from it. But it was not his strength; it was the strength of the Qur'an."

The story is a little wobbly historically, but it has a mythical import at least, and I will hear the theme of Lenin and Muhammad developed in different ways as I journey through the post-Soviet Muslim imagination. This is what scholars call Turkic (here Turko-Iranic) Islam's capacity for "nativization", that is, taking the universalist narrative of the Qur'an and transplanting it onto native soil. Scholars marvel at, and write tomes on, the Babla Tukhles epic poem, which has Adam accepting Islam in Central Asia. But they need look no further than one Soviet Tatar babushka's reply to her grandson's question: "Muhammad? Yes, he was born somewhere in the Nizhny region. Somewhere near the village of Pahili, I believe." Its thriving Christian-Eurasian counterpart is the Russian Orthodox conviction that Mary and Jesus were not—God forbid—Jews, but Russian.

Of course, there is only so much a foreigner can enter the world of migrant Muslims in Moscow: as becomes increasingly clear, it is a world that is fairly mysterious even to Muscovite Tatars. I am content to take people's self-descriptions of their observance and motivations pretty much at face value, merely weeding out obvious inconsistencies, obfuscations and self-aggrandizements. I want to get a human angle on the one hundred and fifty thousand prostrating figures that the helicopter cameras pruriently sweep over each year. I want to create a counterbalance to the media demonization that label these people as extremists, Islamic State supporters, a threat to Russia and so on, or else thieves, criminals, heroin smugglers. I don't want to scare my interviewees off by asking about extremism, revealing prejudices. The question of extremism always comes up, though: I don't have to ask the question. My interviewees anticipate it; it is part of their worldview, their psychic apparatus, a shadow cast over everything. And it will come to dominate my journeys, too.

The Question of Extremism: three attempts on Abdollo's life

The denial and avoidance of the extremist question, coupled with an obsession and fascination with it, is an odd dynamic. Isa, a Dagestani student at an American university whose family has settled in Moscow, tells me when I ask him what branch of Islam he belongs to: "My Islam is a religion of peace." I get a similar answer from Muslim, another permanent Moscow resident and a student at the prestigious Higher School of Economics, whose family is from Chechnya. (In passing he points out that he shares his first name with the famous Soviet–Azerbaijani crooner Muslim Mogomaev, so he never gets problems because of that aspect of his Islamic identity). Both Isa and Muslim know no Arabic, even though both read *namaz* five times a day, (although Muslim waits till the end of the day to read all the prayers, as there is no prayer facility at his institute). They tell me that, because of this, they have never read the Qur'an, which should not be read in translation. As a result, perhaps, Isa does not know who Ibrahim is, and Muslim is shaky on other core details. Instead, they seem to depend—against their will—on the media almost as much as non-Muslims for their picture of Islam. My question about Isa's Islamic "branch" was intended to elicit what denomination or even *madhab* Isa belonged to. But such "subtleties" were not on his radar. The question was interpreted against the background of the two main "Islamic sects" accepted by the world at large: good moderates and bad extremists.

Isa goes on in this vein, showing he has internalized the discourse: "Many people associate Islam with violence. But it is only the Wahhabis, the extremists and radicals that preach and practice violence. The victors write history, and in some sense the Wahhabis at a certain point were victors, and came up with sayings like 'kill all non-believers,' or 'kill all people who don't observe as much of the religion as them', interpreting the Qur'an in any way they saw fit. This is all wrong and anti-Islamic. There are recruiters who try to spread this sort of Islam. Generally, they only have success with young people whose minds are not yet fully formed, or who are psychically unstable."

All other subtleties are swallowed up in this distinction. I get a more self-conscious acknowledgment of this situation from Atiya, another Moscow Dagestani. Like hundreds of others he studied in Tunis for almost six years in the nineties and early 2000s, and there absorbed from his fellow Russian Tatars the Hanafite practice of folding his hands at navel level during *salat*. This was different from the native Dagestani Shafiite practice of holding the arms higher up and over the heart. His father saw him praying at home one day, and his parents confronted him later, wide-eyed: "Son, have you become an extremist?" they asked in terror. Confined to their own lands throughout the Soviet period, with religion a repressed affair, they had simply never seen non-Dagestani Muslims praying. Now they could only parse it through the increasingly dichotomous metric of Wahhabi/Sufi.

Isa's Islamic knowledge was far lower than Atiya's, and he is, of course, simply repeating what the government muftiats throughout the former Soviet Union are saying, down to the idea that it is only immature Muslims who can be taken in by Wahhabi rhetoric. But, Islamically, his own 20-year old mind is nowhere near "fully formed", as he has never read a line of the Qur'an. He admits that he has been approached by Wahhabi recruiters at the mosques in Moscow: "But they back off if they feel resistance or disagreement. They are very cunning and subtle." On the other hand, he undermines his own binary metric when he concedes: "I do know one clever, wise Wahhabi. He works for my father. He has a long beard, observes everything in the strictest way and is a good and wise man. But still, he does not push his beliefs on anyone." Isa often turns to him for help when he has questions about Islam.

Isa is about to complete a good degree, and speaks good English. I cannot imagine him, even though he is young and naïve about Islam, forming company with the extremists. But these things are difficult to gauge. A Dagestani medical student studying at the People's Friendship University tells me that a fellow student from her hometown of Buinaksk, who like herself was from a prestigious family and was studying to be a dentist, suddenly "went weird". He grew his beard, shaved his moustache, started wearing short trousers, and spent increasing amounts of time at the Cathedral mosque. She believes it all started when his professor began to give him a hard time. "Perhaps he didn't like Dagestanis," she speculates.

Muslim, whose family fled Chechnya after the first war, faces a similar situation. But his approach to dealing with potential recruiters is different: he simply never goes to a mosque, keeping his devotions entirely private. A fellow student, a cheerful Muscovite Azerbaijani girl who dresses stylishly and does not wear a hijab, tells me in even stronger terms: "I had a religious experience when I was ill as a girl. I started to pray *namaz*. But my parents categorically forbid me from going to the mosque. Too many extremists there, they said. They are worried for me." She, too, prays all her five prayers in a row at the end of the day behind the closed door of her bedroom. It is a common solution for many, and it is one of the strengths of Islam that it can shape itself to the needs and pressures of many different individuals.

A final detail of Isa's life fascinates me: his two closest friends at the American college are an atheist Ashkenazi Jewish student from Tashkent, and a non-observant Muslim from Kazakhstan. Together they make regular road trips together to the slaughterhouse in the Moscow region to get the meat that Isa prefers to consume. I chat to the Jewish student on another occasion: he tells me he feels that anti-Semitism has got worse in Uzbekistan since Islam started making a comeback. Back home, a friend of his at school even turned on him for being Jewish. But Moscow continues to be cosmopolitan in unpredictable ways, it seems. This melting-pot aspect of Moscow, this continuing Soviet-style "friendship of the peoples", is the best immunization against the misanthropism of the extremists. It is this quality, in fact, that the Tatar muftis are trying to bottle and sell as the peculiarly "tolerant" aspect of a specifically modern "Russian Muslim worldview".

Finally, in December 2015, I am introduced to a man who gives me a new angle on the Cathedral mosque, the state of Islam in Moscow and the vexed question of Islam and extremism. He is called Haireddin Abdollo.

There really is no hard and fast rubric for determining what is and what is not Islamic extremism. Everyone draws the line differently. The Russian government's easy identification of Salafism and extremism is highly problematic. There is a conservative Russian Islamic studies professor called Roman Silantiev who gleefully points to the Moscow muftiat's contradictory definitions of extremism as evidence that they are themselves secret Salafists, taking it for granted that "Salafism" *tout court* is equal to violent extremism. Damir Khairetdinov and Damir Muhetdinov, two key figures in the Council of Muftis of Russia, studied in Mecca; Khairetdinov worked for several years at the Saudi embassy in Moscow. That alone is enough for Silantiev to whip out the extremist label. But it is also Muslims from muftiats in Nizhny, Kazan and Ufa that reach for the conversation-stopping accusation, sometimes as a way of settling personal grudges. This is all not-so-friendly fire in the so-called "mufti wars". Still, Haireddin Abdollo can speak with more authority than most when talking of Islamic extremism in Russia and the CIS. When I meet him, he is only three months out of hospital: in the latest of three attempts on his life, six assailants sank knives into his ribs and left him to bleed to death on the street. Perhaps not surprisingly, it is his view that extremism is a big problem in Russia, the former Soviet republics, and especially in the Cathedral mosque itself.

When I meet him, the wiry and fast-talking Tajik pulls up his shirt to show me his wounds: he is still wrapped tightly in white bandages like a mummy. "They jumped me from behind," he explains, "six of them: each one of them stuck a knife in my ribs. They left me for dead. Later, they boasted about the attack on *Odnoklassniki* (the Russian equivalent of Facebook). But, *inshallah*, I am still here." He gives a broad grin. "Of course, they do not like what I am saying at the mosque. I have got a license to preach there. Not everyone is allowed to preach there," he says, proud of the distinction. "But I am the only one who tells it like it is, who says clearly what the mistakes of the Wahhabis are. The only time that happened to them was at the opening of the mosque. Ramzan Kadyrov, the President of Chechnya gave a speech. He laid it out plain and simple. He spoke against the *takfiri*s, and called the Islamic State satanic. They didn't like it. I could see them squirming. But they had to shut up and put up with it from someone like Kadyrov."

Abdollo is just under forty years old, but has already got degrees in law, accountancy and Arabic and Islamic studies from institutes in Cairo, Tehran and Moscow. His father's relatives were imams in Faizabad, and one of them was a *sheikh* in the Naqshbandi *tariqat* in Bukhara. He himself began learning Farsi at fifteen and devouring Persian literature and calligraphy with a Tajik *sheikh* who had moved to his city from Afghanistan. In the Cathedral mosque in Moscow, shortly after his arrival he was befriended by a Turkish hafiz who then introduced him to an Iranian scholar who had been a pupil of Ayatollah Khomeini. Together they studied *tafsir*, *kalam*, *falsafa*, history and politics. Later he perfected his Arabic at the Saudi academy in Moscow (where Khairetdinov and many other Tatars studied). Though himself a Sunni, he now teaches at the Moscow branch of the Iranian al-Mustafa university. Thus when he says that he is sure of the bankruptcy of Wahhabi thought and its feeble foundations in the Islamic tradition, he is not speaking from a position of weakness or ignorance.

Unlike Isa, Muslim, and their fellow Muslim students in Moscow, unlike Atiya even (who now works as a translator of Arabic for ITAR-TASS, a major Russian news agency), Abdollo defends a picture of Islam that does not deal in fearful dichotomies. For him shari'a and mysticism have the same ancestry and the same pedigree: it is not either/or.

He rehearses an old but convincing argument: "After all, all seven methods of Qur'an recitation contain well known Sufis in their chain of transmission; so do all the six reliable collections of hadith. We know that Ibn Taymiya (the hero of the Wahhabis) wrote works praising Sufism. If we omit all this, then we will get to the stage of doubting the *Sunna* and the Qur'an itself, God forbid." Having studied in Iran and Egypt, and with Turks and Persians and Arabs, Abdollo feels a deep and inherent unity in the rich historical Islamic tradition. His office mate is a Tatar from Ufa who converted to Shi'ism and made the first Russian translation of Al-Kafi, the authoritative Shi'ite hadith collection. He received a final degree in Arabic from the Moscow Saudi academy. None of this is contradictory for him: "We are being missionized from all sides in the former Soviet Union," he says. "We shouldn't get stuck in one rut. We can pick and choose." Then he tells me triumphantly: "If you just give me an hour with a Wahhabi, I will be able to bring him round to my point of view. He won't be able to stand up to my arguments."

I am not sure. I think of Atiya again, who also speaks Arabic fluently and studied Islam in depth. Now he has left observance completely behind. But to this day, he still holds fractured views about the meaning of Islam. He tells me how he first saw people in his hometown of Khasavyurt kissing the hand of Sheikh Said Affandi, Dagestan's leading Sufi *sheikh*. "Paganism, idolatry! I couldn't believe it. But it is best not to speak about these things. People are not ready to listen. It was not like that in Tunisia. Islam has become corrupted in the non-Arab lands, especially in the Caucasus." It is not as if Atiya is a Wahhabi; he no longer even considers himself a true Muslim, and he speaks with horror of a former classmate who told him the Shi'ites deserved it when extremists blew up their mosque in Khasavyurt some years ago. Nonetheless, it seems that Atiya had been studying at an institute in Tunis that kept him well away from the shamanistic aspects of Tunisian Sufism—things that go far beyond mere hand-kissing! And thus even after he has "burned out" on Islam and returned to his former secularist existence, he still categorizes Arab Islam as pure, and non-Arab Islam as tainted and paganistic.

Could Abdollo convince Atiya? Did he manage to convince his Wahhabi assailants from the Cathedral mosque? Later in our conversation, Abdollo reveals aspects of his life experience that cast more doubt on whether his own universalist approach could be a quick and ready solution. He knows his own Tajik nation well, including the Russian Tajik diaspora. For as with any scion of a poor and war-torn nation like Tajikistan, he has not been able to escape the fate of his countrymen and indulge only in literature and religious studies. There are no lavish academic grants to ease his path. From a young age he worked a bull on his plot of land and planted fruit and vegetables, and helped raise his younger siblings after his parents' death. He worked in the market in his hometown, and when he came to Moscow he did what many Tajiks, such as Zhora and Muhammad-jon, do: he labored on construction-sites.

"I have worked as a builder throughout Russia," he recounts, "and I have been to nearly every provincial mosque in Russia. And that's why I can tell you from personal experience on trust that extremism is a bigger problem in Russia than even the most worried people think. Speaking about Tajiks, I can tell you that a huge number of my fellow countrymen support ISIS either actively or passively. When I say actively, I mean they would be willing to offer support to it. And no one knows how to stop them. The imams in Russian mosques are hopeless: either they don't know how to stop these people or they don't want to. They are what I call imam–*shaytans*. If I had my way, I would drag each and every imam from around Russia down to Chechnya, to have a meeting with Ramzan. That is the man to stop them... Let me be more precise: I would say 30 per cent of Tajiks are devoted Wahhabis; 30 per cent understand nothing about their religion at all. And 40 per cent don't consider themselves Wahhabis, but by their beliefs and actions, you can see that this is what they believe: if you say to them, let's go to Navruz, the Persian New Year celebration, they will say: Oh no, that's *bid'a*. So in effect, they are Wahhabis..." He then goes on to praise Uzbekistan's president Islam Karimov for cracking down on extremists so brutally, noting that "in my experience, Uzbeks in Russia have been cured of the extremist bug."

Abdollo has gone from recommending an hour-long Islamic theology class with himself to an enforced audience with Karimov and Kadyrov. These presidents enjoy an unsavory reputation in the human rights community for good reason. But for the first time, listening to the freshly bandaged Abdollo, I at least understand where he is coming from. An hour long theology class really is not going to stop the murder and mayhem of violent extremists. Doesn't an imminent violent attack require a quick deflecting blow of pre-emptive violence? But here another paradox arises.

It is not just that state violence and repression foster more extremism. The fact is that Abdollo has been on the receiving end of violence not just from Wahhabis but from the Russian security forces. And this gives one reason to pause. In 2014, there was a high-profile mass round-up of Central Asian illegal migrants at the Sadovod market in the Liublino region of Moscow, and Abdollo's nearby apartment was broken into. "The police put a gun to my head and accused me of extremism. And not for the first time," recalls Abdollo. Which is odd, because the Moscow émigré paper he works for, the *Voice of Tajikistan*, had been publishing details of ISIS recruiters working in the Sadovod market. No doubt the security police were not going to listen to Abdollo's careful accounts of the Sufi treatises of Ibn Taymiya and admit their well-intentioned error.

This indicates that Abdollo's approach to Wahhabism and extremism cannot be taken completely at face value, despite his bandages. His own support for state violence reveals the twisted dynamic of "extremism". As several mainly Western scholars have pointed out,[9] many "extremists" are categorized as such not because of their dislike for the pagan Persian festival of Navruz—another theological nicety after all—but simply because the cohesion of their *jamaats* (communities) is seen as threatening by the Russian or Central Asian governments, or because members of such groups have engaged in protest against state corruption. It is well known that security forces plant drugs and weapons on otherwise harmless "new Muslims" (as the returnees to faith are sometimes called), who are then encouraged to leave the country, sometimes for Syria.

The fog of obfuscation is everywhere. Abdollo, the moderate Sufi–Sunni with tolerance for a broad spectrum of Islamic views, is himself accused of extremism. When the rector of one of the North Caucasus state-funded Islamic universities in Nalchik was killed in 2013, the papers reported that it was the work of extremists. I spoke to a Moscow imam who had visited him days before his death, and he was not so sure; like many, he thought it could be the work of the Russian security services, stirring up fear of extremism. In public, the imam adds his voice to those who denounce the assassination; in private, he despairs at this latest attempt to sabotage Muslim unity. Similarly, when Valliula Yakupov, the beloved "moderate" assistant mufti of Tatarstan was assassinated in 2012, the official version was that North Caucasus-style violence had come to quiescent Kazan; again, in private people had their doubts. Other natural suspects were the security forces, or criminal business organizations. In Russia, unfortunately the state and criminality still exist in not entirely separate spheres.[10]

So, as we will see, especially in Uzbekistan's Fergana valley, "extremism" is now a driving force in the lives and mental states of all post-Soviet Muslims. And in a country where "nothing is true and everything is possible", to borrow

Peter Pomerantsev's apt phrase,[11] it almost does not matter whether there is any fire behind the billowing smoke. The smoke is crippling enough by itself.

This is not to say that isolationist, violent forms of Wahhabism do not exist—Abdollo's wounds are far from imaginary. I had not set out to interview self-identifying Salafists or wished to "track down" those who had been categorized as extremists; I was seeking a different demographic. But in a great many conversations, my own demographic was so closely linked to the other brooding presence that it could not be ignored. "Valery", a Russian interviewee from Turkmenistan, for example, converted to Islam in his native Ashkabad after befriending old school mates who had found religion. They moved to Moscow together, where he eventually left Islam. One of the key triggers was an evening spent with his Turkmen friends: huddled round the computer, they viewed one video after another of ISIS executions, all the while giggling and joking "give it to the *kafir*". Another Russian, "Ivan", participated in a Sufi order in Tunisia while studying Arabic abroad. Coming back to Russia and wanting to go deeper into Islam, he was put off, not by any bloodthirsty hilarity, but simply by the crudeness of his new circle's approach to life. Thus, Valery and Ivan have joined Atiya in swelling the ranks of first-wave ex-Muslims, those whose expectations were not met by the religion.

In this atmosphere, with extremism on the one hand, and low levels of learning on the other, the question of how Islam should be lived in modern Russia is a hard but urgent struggle. In the following chapter, we will look at some of the muftis' definitions of *wasatiyya*, Islam's middle way, which is an attempt to live tradition in modern circumstances. The question, though, is how effective it can be in these conditions. We will also look at slightly different attempts to find a "middle way", not so much among the options presented by the Islamic tradition, but among the options presented by modern Russian or post-Soviet life. Meanwhile, the bogeyman of extremism should not obscure the rich answers being discovered on a daily basis by Muslims seeking to live out their faith in this corner of the world.

Picking up the pieces: a rich mosaic between Salafism and secularism

Russian Muslims have been synthesizing aspects of the non-Muslim majority culture for centuries. And Muslim life was fusing with modernity in fascinating ways from the mid-nineteenth century: on the Volga, in Bukhara, in the Caucasian mountains and plains. The first-wave *jadids* (discussed further in chapter 4) fused Islam with bourgeois capitalism, and then the second-wave *jadids* added socialism and nationalism. In the early Soviet period, using his usual sharply gauged method of winning over disparate audiences, Lenin promised "land and shari'a" to Caucasian peasants, just as he had promised "land and freedom" to Russian peasants, and, for a while, "red jadidism" was one Muslim response to modernity. True, these Muslim socialists were purged, but for many the Soviet experience and the Muslim experience ultimately came to be seen as complementary. Indeed, for some (see chapter 5) this sort of Soviet–Muslim blend is almost a type of "traditional Islam" that bears restoring.

For others, "tradition" has a different meaning, and they want to reach back to rituals, forms of dress, forms of mourning, that were never current in their own lives. The attempt to recreate an interrupted tradition is full of paradoxes. People who were born between the fifties and the seventies had a direct connection to "traditional Islam" as practiced in the Russian empire, and the words of their grandparents shaped their own identities in the 1990s. When the Soviet Union collapsed, a fantasy of recreating this still remembered tradition seized hold of the imagination of intellectuals. The same dynamic occurred among the Russian Orthodox intelligentsia. The link to the village was still there: the problem was that absolutely everything else had changed. The Soviet period had intervened. Thus, these recreated traditions do not always come out looking like the original. Instead, proxy forms have often been imported hastily from the Middle East, rather as much of traditional Russian Judaism has now been displaced by the uniform and rituals of Chabad Lubavitch Hasidism, imported from Brooklyn, New York.

This is partly the dilemma of the Tatar muftis at the Cathedral mosque and in Tatarstan today. They are working furiously to translate the *jadid* heritage that flourished from the 1860s to the 1920s (just as the Russian Orthodox are republishing Russian religious philosophers like Berdyaev and Bulgakov). They are even literally rebuilding pre-Revolutionary *medreses* across the Volga region. Often, though, even when they manage to restore *jadid* institutions and literature, they prove inadequate to the challenges of the late twentieth and twenty-first century. They have a slightly musty optimistic nineteenth century feel. And meanwhile, life has moved on.

This dynamic is not unique to Russian Islam, of course. Sometimes, too much is made of the difference between the Soviet–atheist Russian and the "traditional religious" Middle Eastern Muslim experience. But countries like Egypt, Syria and Iraq also experienced a strong dose of secularism throughout the twentieth century, in the latter part with Soviet help. In Egypt, the rise of Salafism and the return of the hijab (explored by Leila Ahmed)[12] were also reactions to modernity and modernistic attempts to paradoxically "create tradition". But there is an important demographic difference: Russian Muslims are a minority culture in a Christian or post-Christian environment. Central Asian societies are Muslim-majority but after long inclusion in the Russian and Soviet states, they also underwent a strong influence on the part of a dominant imperial Christian, or Christian-influenced, Western Enlightenment culture.

This means that Russian and Central Asian Muslims in the post-Soviet period have had a richer array of identities to choose from and, perhaps paradoxically, a more pluralist space in which to develop such identities. They are people who have been handed the label of "ethnic Muslim" by their parents and the Soviet state in the past. That label furiously insisted on the ethnic and secular limiting boundary of this identity. But now they are filling the label with religious content and handing it on to the future. And in some cases, the content they are filling it with is novel and unorthodox by the standards of the past. This novelty and creativity, while perhaps a minority option, makes Salafism look like only one option, and a pale, insipid one at that.

There is Ilshat Nasyrov, a Bashkir professor of Islamic philosophy at the Academy of Sciences. Reacting against the schizophrenic transformation of Soviet secularists into religious literalists, he "refuses to let anyone push me into believing medieval myths… or Sufi fairytales" and sees the Qur'an as a collection of Arabic folklore. Nonetheless, "even though I don't fully understand why myself", he prays regularly and observes the Ramadan fast— except when it would be impolite to do so, such as when he is visiting his father in a sanatorium in the countryside.

There is Farit Valiullin from Kazan, who trained as an artist in a prestigious Soviet school and did propagandistic work in the Soviet period. Now he belongs to a Sufi *tariqat*, but his favorite painting is Andrei Rublev's Trinity: "there you can see the Divine Love, the answer to why Hellfire, so admired by the icon-painter Dionysius, cannot be eternal." He reproaches Dostoevsky for not loving Christ enough: "he dissects his heroes with a scalpel; a far more religious writer, in my opinion is Chekhov."

Then there is Ildar Abulzyarov, a fashionable young novelist from Nizhny. He feels he has found his home in Kazan's archaic Muslim quarter, but he fights for the rights of the neighboring republic, Mari-El's pagans, and feels an obligation to them: "We can learn from them. And they were always loyal to the Kazan khan. It is not right for their identity to be attacked and diminished."

I meet Ismail, an ex-Salafist, who lives in Zelenodolsk, an hour from Kazan. When he studied in Mecca, he thought all *kafirs* were going to burn in Hell. Now he is still strictly observant, but he has mellowed. He has adopted two orphans, and wants to preach Islam gently, just to relieve the misery he sees around him daily: people sunk in alcohol, anger, puppets manipulated by their government. Midway through our conversation, he suddenly says: "Of course, the Qur'an is not all from Allah. It depicts the sun going round the earth. How could it be?" He shrugs when I gasp. But here is a Muslim not frightened of historical criticism. He loves the path of Muhammad. Historical detail cannot be denied, and it should not compromise faith.

Aislu van Rayn, married to a Dutchman, was born in a small one hundred percent Bashkir village in the shadow of the Ural mountains. Fifty years later she still remembers the Arabic prayers her pious grandmother uttered. Like all the most thought-provoking interviewees, she pushed off my offer to interview her with a firm, "I won't be interesting to you. I am not a Muslim." But then when I do not take no for an answer, she talks, and old memories keep flowing. Nowadays, in fact, she calls herself a Sufi and goes to Turkish Sufi ensembles at the Moscow Conservatory with her hippy Jewish friends.

There is also Rustam, a Tatar–Bashkir born in Moscow. He is a master at the Moscow branch of the Nimatullahi Sufi lodge, which was first brought to the West by the Iranian *sheikh* Javad Nurbaksh. Recently, the Order abolished the need for initiates to say the *shahada*. Twice a week Rustam leads musical *zikrs* in a killim strewn apartment in Kitai Gorod, downtown Moscow; the walls are covered with Arabic calligraphy, the chanting is in Persian. "Am I Muslim? It's difficult to say. Rituals like abstention from alcohol and fasting have never meant much to me. Look at the Wahhabis: they do everything just so, but they are spiritual corpses. But, on my Mother's insistence, I had a name-giving ceremony for my son where a mullah was present." Professionally, he studies Mongolian Buddhism. He has given his children bicultural names that could pass as Tatar or Russian. He also retains some interest in Gurdijeff and Eastern theosophy, which attracted him before his entry into Sufism. Of Muslim heritage, immersed in a Persian Sufism that prefers to see itself as "*taslim*" rather than "Islam" (due to its founder's negative experience of Iranian state Shi'ism), he makes definitions crack.

Close in spirit to Rustam is Russian convert, Valery-Ismail Emelianov, a sixty-year old businessman and writer. His first religious experience was with the Moonies. But then he quenched his thirst for Oneness in Islam, taking his *shahada* in front of imam Shamil Aliutdinov at the Victory Park mosque. He does not suffer from Rustam's ambiguity about calling himself a Muslim, but nowadays prefers the less ritualistic path of the Indian Sufi master, Hazrat Inayat Khan, and believes in the unity of the Abrahamic religions. He once caused a bit of a stir by wearing a *yarmulke*, or Jewish skullcap, to a Muslim event. "Well, it's a headcovering, isn't it?" he says mischievously to me.

Askhat, is even more definition bending. His father was a Tatar cultural activist in the 1970s, and the whole family suffered repression as a result. Like thousands of Russian and Ukrainian intellectuals, in the 1990s he joined one of the new Protestant charismatic churches. However, in recent years he has been seeking to combine a Muslim and Christian identity. Now he prays *namaz* from time to time at Moscow mosques. He even takes part in *zikr* sessions with the Chechens and Dagestanis in the basement of the Historic mosque. The ethnic ties are so strong, despite the conversion to Christianity, despite his ignorance of the Tatar language, that he is married to a Tatar woman. She tried Christianity, but her Tatar soul rebelled against it. Now she is a neo-Hindu, involved in spiritual yoga. But there's a twist: their son, although he writes Church music for Orthodox choirs, has "returned" to Islam. "There are many, many families like ours. I know that now. That's why interreligious dialogue and theology is so important for Russia," he tells me.

There is Sirozhidin from Fergana in Uzbekistan, who has spent years working in Turkey, Germany and mostly Moscow, one of hundreds of thousands of Central Asian "guest-workers". He went on *hajj* four times in the 1990s, and one of his sons memorized much of the Qur'an and studied in a local *medrese*. Sirozhidin himself studied Islam as a boy in the thaw after Stalin's death. When we meet in Moscow, he is happy to feed my curiosity about Islam, and talks earnestly about the "Eastern" morals of Uzbekistan, and how his own town is the most religious and traditional in the Fergana valley. And yet, I am confused as to why he stands through an Orthodox church service some Sundays, arousing the parishioner's speculation that he is thinking of converting, and avoids the mosque and his fellow Uzbeks in the northern metropolis. When I accept his invitation to stay for ten days in his home in Fergana, I find myself in a world where suddenly all talk of Islam produces nervous jitters. His attic is filled with dust-covered Arabic textbooks from the nineties that no one studies any more. His own Islamic observance seems to consist now in his fevered hunt for a traditional *paranja* that the daughter-in-law he is seeking for his son will wear on her wedding day.

Sirozhidin's sons, though, have different ideas about the *paranja*, as well as the "Eastern" morals concerning marriage that their father entertains. Sirozhidin's aunt, a Russian teacher, cheerfully mocks Islamic traditionalists, but also declares her own Muslim, Eastern pride: "Putin's lover is an Uzbek Tatar. Russians admire the traditional morals of Eastern women." There is a lot to unpack here.

Karina from Ufa, the capital of Bashkortostan, is of Bashkir and Tatar parentage. She knows only Russian, but her "Eastern" heritage and Arabic-derived surname somehow drew her towards the study of Arabic in Britain. Now she is married to a Palestinian she met there and lives in Istanbul, where she works long-distance for the Moscow muftis as a translator of Islamic articles from Russian into English. Of Russia, but neither strictly Russian, Tatar nor Muslim, she feels utterly rootless, a wanderer, whose most transformative cultural experience to date has been her immersion in liberal British culture. Some of this British–Russian snobbishness permeates her attitudes towards the "East": when she lived in Palestine, she could not help feeling it was slummy and chaotic compared to the more civilized Israel, where a lot of her former compatriots live. Still, by default she joins her husband's family when she feels like it in observing Ramadan, and she is picking up Turkish, a language cognate with the one not quite handed on to her by her forebears.

A little like Karina, there is Zuleyha, in her mid-twenties, whose family were high-ranking bureaucrats in Soviet Tajikistan and moved to Moscow to escape the civil war. She studied at an American college in Moscow, then moved to Barcelona. Now she lives in London and is married to a British comedian. She seems to have blended into multicultural "cool Britannia" without a trace. Lithe, fashionable, with model good looks, "people think I am Peruvian usually," she tells me in London-accented English.

I begin to believe she was right when she feeds me the usual line: "I am not Muslim, I can't help with your research." But soon, she is insisting on speaking Russian and confides how deeply she misses both Russia and the Russian language. The conversation winds on, and I begin to hear about her grandfather, the Soviet bureaucrat. In the nineties, he became a fully observant Muslim, "probably out of guilt for all the people he had sent to prison or their deaths". He remained in Tajikistan, but when he visited Moscow, they would all have to eat halal and say prayers, even though Zuleyha, who used to find spiritual comfort by entering cool, scented Orthodox churches and placing candles there, was not even aware that she was a Muslim until at the age of eight or nine her mother informed her. Now some of her Moscow cousins, erstwhile party-goers, have started wearing the hijab and observing Islam strictly. It turns out her own husband is half-Iranian. She does not quite know why, but they decided to be married in the *nikah* ceremony. Her father found an Afghan Tajik mullah to preside over the ceremony.

Other Islamic details emerge as Zuleyha talks. But the gist of the story is one that I will encounter again and again: the mirror of Muslimness shattered into a thousand fragments, and the "survivors" of the Soviet period were faced with a choice: to put the fragments back together somehow, to reconstitute an old identity, or to casually let the pieces drop and fall away. Zuleyha sees no attraction in being Muslim. Even being Tajik is a puzzle to her: she feels deeply uncomfortable with people like Zhora, Muhammad-jon and Abdollo who are reviving in their persons—in different ways of course—a Tajik–Muslim identity. Russian is her only language, cosmopolitan Moscow her primary culture. Her cousins, though, decided otherwise. They held the same pieces but made different choices about what to do with them.

So why are Zuleyha or Karina worth listening to? Did they not opt out? "My cousins would not consider me a Muslim," Zuleyha says, and on that basis is reluctant to be an interviewee. Nonetheless, she holds an important piece of the past. To some extent the reconstruction of the past that her cousins have chosen is false, or at least partial, a ready-made Salafist import. Her father was secular—so Zuleyha always believed. But then he took her to a mosque in Tunis that was filled with the prayers of saints, and for the first time she felt the spirit of the divine in a Muslim house of worship. He sat in the corner reciting prayers she did not know he knew.

And he would say odd things. He would justify eating pork and not fasting on Ramadan by reference to Ibn Sina (also known as Avicenna in the West), the "Tajik philosopher": "Islam is a rational religion. In those days, the Prophet believed such rituals had health value. Now we know better, we can observe the spirit without the externals." He was a Muslim by his own definition, which seems to have a dual heritage: Avicennan Muslim medieval rationalism, but also the reformist, modernist "anti-obscurantist" ideology of the Soviets. Like many, Zuleyha's father combined them into what for him was a satisfying whole. I meet several people on my journey who wed Soviet and Avicennan rationalism as a matter of second nature. Usually, this Soviet-style Islam is a cause for patronizing anecdotes: but does it not belong sociologically alongside the Muslimness of upper-middle class Pakistanis, who drink alchohol and embrace Western science, while at the same time considering themselves proud bearers of an ancient Muslim heritage? For many, it is a conscious construct, and not, as many think, Soviet intellectual impoverishment and ignorance.

So perhaps Zuleyha's "piece" fits into a different narrative, a narrative of transformed secular Muslimness, of post-Soviet Russian Muslimness. Ultimately, this depends on whether there are any "ideologues" out there to take up her emerging story. "Ideology" is a popular word in Russia today, where communist ideology has famously left a vacuum. The muftis at the Cathedral mosque like to use the word. Often such "ideology" is inward-looking or a loyalist discourse produced to keep the government off one's back. But if it is to be more than a verbal mirage, such ideology needs an audience of real consumers. Of course, the muftis know that: they are cut of the same post-Soviet cloth themselves, and they do have an audience: the Mustafins, and on a more intellectual level, people like Ilshat, Farit, and Ildar. But someone like Zuleyha?

Though she would probably find the idea bizarre, the muftis even seem to have her in mind, with their revival of the broadly tolerant Hanafite dictum that no ritual aberration can erase the core of one's faith once the *shahada* has been pronounced. And yet Zuleyha, along with Rustam and even more so Askhat, are an eclectic demographic that they cannot afford to pay too much attention to. If their journals, gazettes, interviews and books are too liberal, they will have the influential traditionalist–revivalist–literalist activists breathing down their necks. And under Putin, the "traditional" is encouraged to take precedence over the eclectic and the effetely intellectual.

Modern scholars talk of "Judaisms" and "Christianities" now, in the plural. There is also talk of "Islams" by scholars such as Mohammad Arkoun.[13] Likewise, Leila Ahmed defends the historic reality of a post-war Egyptian secular Muslimness that was eclipsed in the 1970s and onwards by the rise of the Muslim Brotherhood and the "quiet revolution" of the hijab's return. If we take an eclectic view of post-Soviet "Islams", we could see Zuleyha as a secular–cultural Russian Muslim, or if not that (as she has been convinced by Salafist definitions of Muslimness that she does not belong on the spectrum at all), as at least defining a possible point on that spectrum.

In my interviews, I deliberately spoke even with ethnic Muslims who had converted to Christianity, or, in the case of Rustam and Aislu, to a universalist Sufism. This was part of defining the extent of the spectrum of Islams. It was also an interesting experiment in determining the content of Soviet Muslimness once even the factor of religious self-identification with Islam had been removed. It turns out that the centuries-long blending of religion and culture meant that aspects of Muslimness could survive conversion to a different faith—as the case of Askhat and his family showed.

In chapter 2, I tell the story of the two Gulnaras from Bishkek in Kyrgyzstan. Both were born into an ambient, dormant Muslimness. In the freewheeling atmosphere of Kyrgyzstan in the 1990s, both were presented with the choice of rediscovering their ancestral faith, which lay only at one generational remove. But both were also presented with equally live and perhaps even more compelling options: New Age religion, Christianity and the widespread option of agnostic hedonism. One Gulnara became involved with Jamaat Tablighi, a Muslim missionary group that was targeting Kyrgyzstan then. The other Gulnara found her way to a Pentecostalist church. Both of them continue to live out their choices today, though each has added an interesting personal shape to their choices.

Why are the two Gulnaras interesting? They demonstrate graphically that Muslimness in the post-modern world is a choice, not a given. Very few people just return unproblematically to their roots anymore. This is true to some extent of the oft-idealized Arab Muslim heartlands, where the hijabs and gowns worn by women identifying with the Muslim Brotherhood are sartorial innovations that break with traditional peasant or urban women's garb— though part of the "modernist–traditionalist" narrative is to disguise innovation as tradition. This is taken as an uncontroversial truth in relation to the free, liberal, democratic Western world. But it is also powerfully true for Russia and former Soviet countries. This creative self-definition is sometimes overlooked; people assume that because the post-Soviet regimes are authoritarian people have less freedom to forge rich identities. Hence practitioners and researchers focus on the transmission of tradition as if innovation and spontaneity were not an option. The voices that appear in this book belie that assumption—some of them, at least. And even those who seem most cloaked in good solid "tradition" often turn out to be internally "eclectic", when one digs deeper.

Thus, the tapestry of Muslim identities in the post-Soviet space contains—in addition to Salafism—the subtler threads of secular Muslimness, and even the more marginal post-Muslim identities of Sufis and Christian ex-Muslims, which are critiques of emerging mainstream Muslim identity. But another far more dominant thread is neo-Soviet Muslimness. The nostalgia for the Soviet period is perhaps even more palpable in Central Asia and the Caucasus than in the Russian heartlands of the old empire. Under Lenin, all the Muslim republics of the Soviet Union were created out of whole cloth. The Caucasian ex-Christian Stalin hated Islam, but, as his letter to the "believing Muslims of Moscow" quoted above illustrates, he relented towards the religion during the crisis of the Great Patriotic War.

It has been said that the role of the hierarchical church in Christianity has often been played by the state in Islam, and Sunni Islam from its inception tended to venerate the state.[14] This and the "pro-Islamic" side of Lenin and Stalin, suitably digested and recast by the mythopoeic consciousness, is now producing a nostalgic idealization of Stalinist authoritarianism, where the "ideology of Communism" has been replaced by a scientistic, moralistic and statist "ideology of Islam". At first this looks eccentric in the Russian–Soviet context. Though neo-Stalinist Russian Orthodoxy exists among conservative–nationalist elements in the Russian Orthodox Church, "sanctifying" Lenin and Stalin is a bit of a harder sell there. Neo-Stalinist Islam, however, is probably better compared to the situation of religion under Chinese communism. There, "militant atheism" was far less militant, given the non-theist leaning of traditional Chinese religion. Likewise, Russian Islam was always a suspect, second-rate religion in the eyes of the tsarist government, so it never suffered the insult of demotion felt by Russian Orthodoxy. Communism-as-religion replaced Orthodoxy-as-religion in a new case of supersessionist theology. But for some at least, Islam and Soviet ideology could coexist. Dagestan today is a showcase for what that combination might look like, as we will see in chapter 5.

In the following chapters, then, I reproduce voices that reflect the different "Islams", or perhaps the different attempts to converge on a single Islam, now struggling to articulate themselves in Russia (the notion of multiple "Islams" may still be too pluralistic for the modern Russian Muslim sensibility.) I want the voices to be heard as the free self-determination of individuals and not just as illustrations of some theory. Understanding people's narratives rather than providing statistical generalizations was the order of the day. Initially, my choice of destinations was dictated by time, chance and finances. But eventually a pattern emerged of the different pieces that make up the Russian Muslim puzzle today and the links that snake between them: the Central Asian chunk that used to be part of the Russian and Soviet empires, and is today formally independent but economically intimately interwoven with Russia; the Volga region, emerging Russia's first Muslim heartland; and the Caucasus, whose most vital Muslim regions are Chechnya and Dagestan. And channeling and directing the energy from them all was Moscow, to which it seemed all roads ultimately lead, and my own place of residence to which I had to return after each journey. In Moscow, I could pick up the stories from the intervening places I did not have time to visit: Tajikistan, Kazakhstan, Crimea, Bashkortostan, and Siberia.

Being based in Moscow, it was tempting to think of Moscow as the "Mecca" of Russian Islam, the city that would eventually funnel all this diversity into a United Russian Islam that would be a dutiful counterpoint to Putin's optimistically named United Russia party. But even before I arrived at the end of my travels, I had to consider that there was at least one other contender for the unification of Russia's Muslims: the real Mecca, now located in the Saudi kingdom, and the center since the late Soviet period of powerful Salafist–Wahhabi influence in the region. So Mecca and Moscow were the first two axes I had to consider. Moscow dominates the post-Soviet space and increasingly its pulses are felt in Syria and Turkey. But Mecca is still the place to which all Muslims turn in *salat*, the Prayer, that powerful act of devotion which is the first ritual that new Muslims must master before they can enter deeper into their faith.

However, at the end of all my journeys I tried to step, in imagination at least, outside this "bi-polar" conception of Russian Muslims as lying between Moscow and Mecca, and to consider a more complex, and perhaps dismayingly chaotic, reality. After all, Russia is a place where simple unity is manifestly absent in so many ways. And according to the scholar V.N. Kalinin, the country occupies second place in the world for the number of Muslim religious organizations.[15] Unity, as often in Russia, conceals seething disunity. I did indeed arrive at some generalizations over my four-year journey into Russia's Muslim heartlands. But I had also started with questions. And it was with questions, albeit different ones, that I ultimately ended. That, after all, is the point of a good journey. For this investigation into Russian Islam was not just social science in the positivist sense, but was intended for the discovery of meanings, including spiritual meaning, a point all too often ignored when people begin to take the Islamists at their word and see Islam as just social or political. Thus, during the almost one hundred lengthy interviews I conducted, the point was not to tick off the answers to discrete questions, but also to empathize and enter into a new way of seeing and recounting the world, and to be pointed on the way of further knowledge.[16]

PART TWO

CENTRAL ASIAN COMMUTE

2.

SEARCHING FOR THE MIDDLE WAY:
BETWEEN KYRGYZSTAN AND MOSCOW

Wasatiyya: the muftis' way foward

It became clear to me early on that extremism exerts a collaterally distorting pressure on the identities of post-Soviet Muslims, as well as seeping into academic accounts of those who analyze them. A scholarly book by the American Martha Olcott called *In the Whirlwind of Jihad*, contains highly interesting sociological descriptions of Uzbekistan's Muslim communities in the Soviet period and far less about jihad and radical Islam.[1] It almost feels as if the author chose the title to pander to the expectations of the field, to lure in the far more numerous security studies readers who dominate the study of Islam, and not just religion specialists. After all, Islam and Central Asia are far more often covered in books with alarming titles.[2]

Still, the notion of extremism can be useful. It allows us to locate one end of the Muslim spectrum. Oddly enough, though, extremism is usually conceived of as in a binary relation with "moderate" Islam, even among Muslims like Isa and Muslim. But the moderate position by definition cannot be the other extreme. The term suggests a "middle" position. What then is the other extreme? That all depends on the perspective adopted: what is "moderate" for a certain group in a specific time and place can become extreme as mores shift. If one starts from a position of blanket suspicion towards Islam, from a position of Islamophobia as the widespread label now has it, there can be no moderate Islam, of course. As a useful metric, though, we can adopt a definition of moderateness that is being worked out by muftis across the post-Soviet region, and then see whether it really corresponds to the realities on the ground. Collating various sources, one can imagine a spectrum as follows:

LEFT OPTIONS:

Secularism

Universalism/individualism

"Spiritual" Sufism

MIDDLE OPTION:

Sufism–shari'a synthesis

RIGHT OPTIONS:

Ritualism (including *taqlid*)

Exclusivism

Political Islam

This spectrum gives schematic shape to the self-defined "view from the center" that several of the post-Soviet government muftiats now operate with, drawing on traditional and contemporary Islamic sources. The middle or moderate position is seen to be intermediate between two poles. The "far-right" pole is Wahhabi hyper-ritualism, which sees itself as a self-contained system, rejecting and demonizing all other options. It can merge into violent extremism and attempts to set up shari'a enclaves. The "far-left" pole is neo-Soviet secularism, which denies validity to any religiosity at all. For the sake of argument (and here I am fleshing out the system myself), individualist or universally "spiritual" religiosity, mysticism without ritual, would approach the left extreme. (In this scenario, Rustam Sabirov's *shahada*-less Sufism would be tending towards "left-extremism"). Ritualism, rejection of individualism with excessive dependence on authority, is already approaching the right pole. The "middle way" blends the individual and spiritual with the ritualistic and communitarian aspect. We have already seen that Haireddin Abdollo posits something similar as a definition of non-extremist Islam. He implicitly tries to find a "middle way" between Shi'ism and Sunnism; nor is he alone among post-Soviet Muslims in this openness.

In fact, roughly this approach to the moderate position was articulated for many years by Sheikh Muhammad Sodik Muhammad Yusuf, one-time mufti of Uzbekistan, and perhaps the most influential Muslim thinker in the post-Soviet area. Among several of his books, which have been translated from Uzbek into Russian and are promoted by the Russian muftis (whose conferences he attended till his death in 2015) is one called *Wasatiyya – the way of life*. Deriving from the Arabic word *wasatiy*, "middle", the term appears in the Qur'an: "We have made you into a just community [Arabic: *ummatan wasatan*, literally: 'a middle nation']." (Q 2.143). A hadith of Imam Ahmad ibn Hanbal (incidentally, judged *qudis* by Ibn Taymiya)[3] reports the Prophet as saying: "Avoid excess in religion, for your predecessors perished from excess in religion." Yusuf developed this concept in detail, using it to defend a blend of Sufi practice with ritual observance. Mufti Ravil Gaynutdin at the Cathedral mosque developed a similar option in a book called *Shari'a*, where he also devotes a chapter to *wasatiyya*, which he translates as "moderation", and sees as including concepts like pluralism and gradualism.

Ali Polosin, a renowned former Orthodox priest who converted to Islam in 1999, and now writes prolifically on Islam in the Russian press and social networks, quoted Yusuf to me in one of our conversations:

> Yusuf divides the Prophet's behavior into three classes. First, Muhammad's prophetic behavior: imitating that is obviously blasphemous. Second, there is common human behavior, such as the brushing of one's teeth. One is not obliged to imitate this, but if one does so it is allowed. Third, there is the Prophet's moral precedent, and this is the aspect that one definitely should imitate.

What Polosin takes away from Yusuf is that hyper-ritualism can be legitimately rejected: one need not necessarily wear one's trousers short, shave one's moustache, tie one's right-hand laces first, brush one's teeth with a *siwak*, and so on. If overindulged this is all undesirable *taqlid*, or blind imitation, and makes Islam incompatible with Russian society. Yusuf and Gayntudin are trying to open the way to a more ethics- rather than ritual-based Islam, which will be more attractive to their post-Soviet audience. In Gaynutdin's case, he ties this to the tradition of Tatar jadidism, or reformism, which sees *taqlid* as its own form of extremism.

A classic statement of this new centrism can be seen in a quote from assistant mufti Damir Muhetdinov in a recent talk. There, he attempts to defend an "intellectual" Salafism that is close to Tatar jadidism in its desire for Islamic reform, thus advocating a middle way between "bad" ritualistic Salafism/Wahhabism and "bad" ritualistic or hyper-spiritual (i.e. ritual- and dogma-free) Sufism. In his words:[4]

> the Islamic spiritual tradition...combines different points of view...but it does not admit extremes: neither extreme traditionalism that has degenerated into the archaization of life and patterns of thinking, nor extreme mysticism, that has degenerated into a rejection of the principles of faith.

This is all interesting and is part of the Muslim world's attempts to argue against extremism using the tradition's internal logic, rather than kowtowing to Western expectations. It is a useful metric. However, it is rather idealized and conceals certain problems which will be explored in more detail in later chapters.

Firstly, while the idea is that Sufism lends "interiority" to ritual observance, there can be a type of Sufi extremism, where Sufism too becomes repetitive, hyper-ritualistic and highly politicized (cf. chapter 7 on the Moscow Islamic university, and chapters 5 and 6 about Dagestan and Chechnya). Secondly, the notion of "political Islam" in this scale assumes that exclusivism emerges from ritualism and morphs naturally into attempts to turn Islam into an anti-state instrument through jihad. There is something to the argument that hyper-ritualism breeds dangerous isolation. However, ritualism can be non-political; meanwhile, "moderate Islam" can itself become political and indeed highly "neo-Soviet", as with the Moscow or Dagestani muftiat's attempts at different times to use state support to implement their Sufi-inclined version of Islam. Finally, as is now being recognized openly even among Russian Muslims, some Salafist "ritualist enclaves" or *jamaats* are unfairly demonized for political rather than theological reasons.

But there is another set of problems, too. The "middle way" depends on what is normal and average for a society. The problem here is that some norms are proclaimed *wasaty* according to bookish, medieval standards that do not hold today. If most Russian Muslims are far from the norms of *wasatiyya* proclaimed by Ibn Hanbal, Ibn Taymiya or Abu Hanifa (a key figure, as we will see), they cease to be "moderate", practically speaking, especially if even those propagating them do not observe them meaningfully. Furthermore, "moderateness" must take into account the norms of the ambient non-Muslim society, and this is often a calculation that Muslims on the ground have to take into account when negotiating their religiosity.

Added to this, the various parts of the post-Soviet space have modernized differentially. This results in the word *wasatiyya* being used unconsciously with quite different implications by different parties. Thus the Moscow muftis see women's rights as a part of "moderate", "traditional" Russian Muslim culture (Muhetdinov 2016, cf. chapter 6 of this book). Yusuf can likewise include women's rights in his description of *wasatiy* Islam. But Yusuf comes from a society where, as we will see in chapter 3, family mores—in some regions—are far closer to pre-modern norms than the contemporary or early twentieth century Tatar *status quo* that the Muscovites have in mind (cf. chapter 4). It is clear that his "average" uncontroversial notion of women's rights would be considered archaic by Tatar and Russian standards, as the following quote shows:

> The provision of a woman without a father or husband will be allotted to her brothers or their legal successors. In general, Islam does not permit a woman to remain without a guardian. The provision of a daughter rests on the father, of sisters on her brothers, of a mother on her sons, etc.[5]

So far, though, the Tatar Muslim definition of "moderateness" has not been articulated in as much detail as Yusuf's approach, which is closer to the norms that existed when the legal compilations of the different *madhabs* were formulated. A recent attempt has been made by the young Dagestani scholar, Ruslan Kurbanov,[6] to apply the relatively new "*fiqh* of Muslim minorities" to the Russian situation, drawing on scholars such as Yusuf al-Qaradawi and Taha Jabir al-Alwani. In trying to conceive of Islam as a minority religion, he thus tries to take into account the ambient Russian-European non-Muslim environment. But this approach often evokes disagreement even in the U.K. and the U.S. where it is being developed (some complain, for instance, that it divides communities and even families by leaving open to interpretation, for example, when to break the long summer Ramadan fast in northern climates.)[7] Kurbanov's book does not seem to have had any practical impact yet, showing that there is still a long way to go in turning abstract discourse about the desirability of *wasatiyya* into something concrete.

In this chapter, we will begin to illustrate some of these paradoxes, by looking in detail at the life-experience of some Muslims in Kyrgyzstan, a society where the Islamic, the secular, the modern and the pre-Soviet heritage are all intermeshed. Although Kyrgyzstan has been independent for twenty-five years, many Kyrgyz intellectuals still communicate in Russian, reference the same ideas, and face many of the same questions confronted by Russian Muslims; the continuing economic and political ties between the countries are also strong. In Islamic terms, the Kyrgyz case is also an interesting "control case" of how post-Soviet Islam can develop. Its status as an independent Muslim-majority nation is largely accidental: the small region was declared almost by chance a separate republic in 1936—for the previous ten years it had the status of an autonomous *oblast* (region) in the Russian Soviet Socialist republic; Tatarstan, by contrast, was given the status of an autonomous republic right at the beginning of the Soviet period. Today, though, Tatarstan remains within Russia, while Kyrgystan has been pursuing its own rocky path of independence. The sheer demographic fact of being a Muslim-majority independent nation powerfully influences how people imagine the prospects for Islam in the country.

The end of this chapter focuses on two Muslim voices from Kazakhstan and Moscow. It will quickly become clear that all this rather academic discussion of *wasatiyya* can be far from the urgent and chaotic reality on the ground, and the thorny question of how *wasatiyya* and "traditional Islam" is conceived and implemented in other regions, given this disconnect, will have to be taken up again in the relevant places.

Struggling to be moderate in Kyrgyzstan

Gulnara: certainty amid collapse

Gulnara comes from Bishkek, the capital. Accomplished, headstrong and independent, she received a PhD in Sociology in the 1990s and worked as the vice-rector at two universities in the city. Around 2005, she astonished her friends by starting to practice Islam seriously. The circle she belonged to were educated professional Bishkek natives who embraced the hedonism of the 1990s, living hard and playing hard: long hours in the office followed by long nights drinking and dancing in clubs were the norm. Her circle are not only indifferent to Islam: they actively detest the rising influence of the religion after the Soviet period. They may raise their hands in prayer to Allah before eating, but it is an ancestral reflex: the meal will contain alcohol, pork, and, if festive, horse meat and *kumys*, fermented mare's milk, along with lashings of good old Soviet champagne, *shampanskoe*. If asked to identify their spiritual belief, they will happily call themselves pagans, Tengrists, shamanists— referring to the beliefs of nomadic Kyrgyz. Unlike Osh, the southern Kyrgyz city which was part of the Kokand khanate, the northern part of the country was historically linked far more weakly to Islamic structures, and that division is felt in the country today.

The "wild nineties" were unstable, though. Cut loose from the Soviet Union, Kyrgyzstan's economy plummeted and crime rose. Things reached a head in the Tulip Revolution of 2005 when Kurmanbek Bakiev ousted Askar Akaev in a popular street revolution. Akaev suffered the same fate in 2010, and Roza Otunbaeva took his place. Despite the authoritarian nature of the Kyrgyz regimes, Kyrgyzstan's opposition and press have always been far more active than in Russia. This is true of the religious situation, too. In Kyrgyzstan, where 80 per cent of the population is Muslim (nominal or otherwise), the government has become increasingly lenient towards Islam and even used it to give a respectable veneer to its own authority; the White House (the presidential office in Bishkek) has its own mosque and imam now. Surprisingly, Tablighi Jamaat, the Pakistani *dawa* (missionary) group is legal in Kyrgyzstan—the only country in the region where this is the case. And it was this group that Gulnara eventually joined.

"I had been searching for something for a long time," Gulnara recalls in our long and emotional conversation. "I searched in Buddhism, in Christianity. And I never thought I would end up in Islam. I had nothing but contempt for Muslims and Islam." Work and play, it turned out, were not enough, and Gulnara is not the only committed secularist I meet who has trodden the path to Islam. For a start, as a woman in a male-dominated work environment, she was often subject to humiliation from her boss. And then job security and pay were bad. Ultimately her lifestyle was destroying her health. "After I became religious, I started my first Ramadan. I used to drink ten cups of coffee a day and sleep three hours a night. I thought I would never manage it—especially cutting out the coffee." But she did, and her health improved as a result.

It was Alexander, a half-Tajik and half-Russian friend from Kazakhstan, who nudged her towards Islam. He was the epitome of the nineties man: he had made a lot of money, "he was a glamorous guy, he used to go to striptease dances, and he drank Hennessey," apparently a sign of true decadence. But now he was telling her he had come to faith in God, in Islam. He would not leave her alone, kept calling her and telling her to repent. A while later, she bumped into another ex-hedonist, who was now going round in a hijab. This was followed by dreams warning her of disaster. Dreams are important for the Kyrgyz and Gulnara responded to them seriously. She began to think of her grandfather as well: "He was actually a mullah, who had several wives. He would get me to read the Qur'an when I was a girl, and I didn't know really what it was. I asked him: 'What is the Qur'an? What is God?' And he told me, 'It's a book about Paradise. Even the nails are golden there!' And I always remembered that, it always stuck in my head. Somehow it was a lovely image, a comfort."

It was those encounters and memories that made her buy a copy of the Qur'an in 2005. She also bought a collection of the hadith made by Valeria Iman Porokhova, a famous Russian convert to Islam and Islamic activist in Russia, which she would read occasionally (the choice of book once again illustrates the links between Russian-language Islam in now separated post-Soviet republics). And then one night, in a spirit of desperation, she took out that copy of the Qur'an. She took a shower to clean herself thoroughly, having some idea about ritual ablution but not knowing what it really involved. Then she put on a headscarf and turned to one of the shortest *suras* at the end of the Qur'an and read it. She prayed in her own words: "Lord! Please! Help me with all my problems..." And "somehow from that moment on my problems really did begin to solve themselves."

Strangely, I later meet another Gulnara who had reached a similar crisis point, and came to a point in her life where one evening she too took a "ritual shower" and asked God to show her the true path, which for her had boiled down to Islam or Christianity. But the "Muslim Gulnara" was also confronted by the Christian option, and as a former secularist it would probably have caused less shock among her friends. "An old friend of mine from Moscow came to Bishkek and we met up. He was a Korean, a Soviet Korean. He was a Christian by birth. We talked about religion, and I began to tell him about my thoughts on Islam. And he says to me: 'of course, you don't need to give up drinking completely. That's not the Christian way. Just do it in moderation. A little drink doesn't harm anyone.' I thought about that. And I thought, 'That's wrong.' I felt like he doesn't see how it is a slippery slope. You start with something small and it spirals out of control. He didn't convince me at all about his Christianity. It seemed very weak. I said to him: 'all that is Satanic stuff. I'm a Muslim. I can't have sex outside of marriage. Put it this way,' I said:

'If you let your child do a little thing, you blur the boundaries. Same here: one drink, next moment you'll be a drunkard.' My friend looks at me and says, 'Maybe you have a point.' That's it: God forbids everything that is harmful for his children. And it was after this encounter that I began to read *namaz* for the first time."

So Gulnara's final embrace of Islam, her first *namaz*, was also made against the background of Christianity. She gauged that Christianity was too weak to deal with the depths of her problems: the meaningless promiscuity, drinking, smoking, bad diet, and overwork—not to mention the national pessimism of a flagging nation. Above, we mentioned the muftis' search for *wasatiyya*, a middle path, and the problem of defining the mean when the extremes are fluctuating wildly. After she started praying *namaz*, which strictly regimented her day and threw up a barrier against her old lifestyle, she began to tread an Islamic path that she now sees as far from being "moderate".

A friend invited her to attend a Tablighi Jamaat meeting, and for over a year she took part in the group's activities. She now describes Tablighi with disdain: "Their teachings are highly simplistic, more appropriate for people who come from the slums of Pakistan and India. Everything is black and white. Islam is perfect, and Jews and Christians are wrong, evil, they have corrupted their scriptures. They are very proud: I have a cousin who joined their group: now he wanders about his village in Pakistani clothes thinking he is just like the Prophet." Again, it was not possible for Gulnara just to cast aside her Soviet Bishkek multiculturalism; as she puts it herself: "I am not a peasant" from a small village, unlike her cousin, who ultimately dropped out of the group and went back to his troubled ways. "If someone tries to fool me, I am not going to take it lying down." These blanket condemnations of non-Muslims tortured her conscience, but she was thirsting for meaning; she even swallowed her pride and bowed to the archaic patriarchal norms of the group. "As a woman I had to attend meetings separately, I could not ask questions, or mix with the men." But she was desperate, and remained with Tablighi. Slowly, in tears, she recalls just how deep she went into this exclusivist Islam.

She agreed to marry a man who enjoyed prestige among the group and pious Muslims in the city. "His hand was covered with gold rings. Later I found out he was a gangster. I didn't know what the rings meant at that moment." The rings, it turns out, were wedding rings. Unknown to her, she had become his fourth wife. "He prayed *namaz* five times a day. He wouldn't touch any food that wasn't halal. He followed the shari'a strictly. But he killed people. I know that now for a fact. And I had a dream about him, before we got married. We were both naked and having sexual relations. According to the shari'a, a dream in which you see your nakedness, or another person's, comes from the Shaytan—it's a bad omen. I knew that, even at the time. But I still married him. It was a bad mistake."

Eventually, she pulled out of the group and when she found out who her husband really was, she left him. Now she is married to a former student, and is happy: she had a dream before the wedding that foretold happiness, and so it has turned out. Her husband is not religious, and for Gulnara, after her seedy, not to say criminal, "non-moderate" experience with Tablighi, that is just fine. Nine years after her "reversion", she continues to pray *namaz*, and to observe Ramadan, though not as strictly as before.

She continues to be tortured by theological conundrums, though. At first, the strictness of Islam was just what she needed. "But now, I often ask myself: why does Islam go on so often about the fear of God? There is this big element of fear. But for me, essentially, Islam is a religion of love. I went to a good scholar that I know to ask him about this, but he didn't really help me here... He said to me: 'you must fear God as well; you are speaking like a Christian.' Then he made some sort of comparison with a traffic cop. If you don't obey the traffic rules and listen to the cop, you'll offend again.' I couldn't really see the point of that." She pauses at this point, and looks at me: "But actually, you know what. Just speaking to you here, I think I understand it for the first time. People need fear of God, because our love is not strong enough. I love God, but I still carry on doing sinful things: drinking, stealing, whatever it may be... And our lives are so short that many of us never have the time to develop that real love. God gives life and God can take it, and so we fear him and do what is right. It's the quicker path to righteousness. For instance, I love my mother, but I am afraid of my father, so I behave myself." (This will not be the last time I hear the theme of strong fathers, both in Kyrgyzstan and then Uzbekistan).

Nor can she stop thinking about the fate of the Jews and Christians; she actually spent a few months on a scholarship in Israel in the mid-nineties, and became quite conversant about the different Jewish sects, noting the similarity between how the ultra-Orthodox are trying to influence the government and what is happening with Muslim groups in Kyrgyzstan now. Again, when we speak on the phone for the last time, Gulnara uses our meeting to touch up her theology. "I would put it like this, regarding Islam and the Bible. All have one father, but the revelations to each of the sons become stricter and stricter each time. Islam is the strictest revelation. Why? Because after each revelation, Shaytan is working his business in the world, tempting people with new and worse temptations, and therefore God needs to protect people each time with stricter revelations...." For Gulnara, evidently, the "shaytanic" chaos of post-Soviet Kyrgyzia requires a strong spiritual medicine to resist.

Gulnara is still on her path. At times, she has serious doubts about Islam (she still is not sure exactly why Muhammad should be considered a prophet and not just a reformer). Her own *wasatiyya* involves maintaining sanity in a troubled world, but also establishing the position of Islam among the other religions that are live options in her region, mainly Christianity. That is, although Kyrgyzstan is nominally majority-Muslim, for someone who belongs to the intellectual elite like herself, it is natural to compare how Islam measures up to secularism and Christianity. Her path is now a lonely one. Outwardly, she does not dress like a Muslim: trousers, T-shirt, bare head. Her *wasatiyya* cannot include involvement in Tablighi. She even distrusts the imams at the mosque, seeing them as greedy for power.

She may recall her polygamous mullah-grandfather's "golden Qur'an", but as a modern Kyrgyz woman, the archaic attempt at a revival of his lifestyle proved spiritually suicidal—as bad as her uncontrolled hedonism. She has an affinity for Russian culture and jokes: "Kyrgyzia should declare war on Russia and surrender the next day." By this she is indicating that she is sick of Kyrgyzstan's chaotic independence, and wants to belong to a more cosmopolitan—but also firmly governed—whole. In many ways, she is like the Muscovite Bashkir, Aislu: her Islam is also "left wing", though due to her *namaz*, it is more "centrist". And, unlike Aislu, Gulnara seems to have retained from her Tablighi days a mistrust towards ritual-free spirituality, even in Islam: "It is heretical to neglect halal and *namaz* and just sit chanting the names of Allah," she says at one point. "That is all taken from Hinduism."

Gulnara's self-tailored *wasatiyya* is partly her own creation, and some of it, like the idea that Islam is a stricter revelation than preceding ones clearly contradict the Qur'anic idea that Islam is an easier path than Judaism; but a lot of it is rooted in a type of local *wasatiyya* being developed by the man she has been referring to as "her scholar", a Kyrgyz Muslim "moderate", to whom she still turns for answers, though not always successfully. I find out more about the roots of her belief, when she introduces me to him.

Kadir Malikov: building an Islamic State moderately

Malikov heads a center for the study of Islam in Bishkek, and among other publications has written a short book in Russian on Islam in Kyrgyzstan that is published by the American University of Central Asia.[8] He also appears regularly on television. "When I am presenting my religion program I wear Islamic garb and when I work at the center I wear Western clothing," he tells me, echoing exactly the words spoken to me by the former rector of the Moscow Islamic Institute, Murat Murtazin. The sartorial division is external evidence of an as yet unresolved secular–religious tension, a self-conscious uncertainty about how Islamic to be, when and where.

Malikov started off his adult life as a secular Kyrgyz just like Gulnara. "I was brought up in a good communist family," he looks over at me with an ironic grin. "My father was an engineer, my mother was a librarian. One of my relatives was a minister, and our family belonged to the *nomenklatura*. My grandfather, Kurban Nichbek Malikov, was a famous Kyrgyz poet. Of course the family was atheist, so I was brought up without religion. My first education was as a sculptor, and while I was at art school I also studied philosophy. That was what really led me to religion, to faith. I read a lot of medieval philosophy, Spinoza, the Bible. I also read the Bhagavad Gita at that time, which made a big impression on me. Finally, I started to read about Islam. One of the first books that moved me was *The Life of Muhammad*. It was written by a Russian philosopher or historian, Vladimir Soloviev, I think. Then there was a well known book by the American writer Washington Irving, also a life of Muhammad." Again, these non-Muslim Russian or Russian-language sources speak of the pluralism of early post-Soviet Kyrgyzia.

Having decided to embrace Islam, he embarked on a series of journeys. He studied in Peshawar and Islamabad in Pakistan, where he completed the forty -day preaching stint of a Tablighi Jamaat adept. Then he moved to Amman in Jordan. Finally, he ended up in Spain, where he wrote a PhD on Islamic life in the Fergana valley in the late Soviet period. Nowadays, he does not have much patience for Tablighi, echoing Gulnara's criticism to the effect that many young men join it as a way of avoiding the hardships of work and raising a family (they expect to be paid and kowtowed to for studying all day long.) On my first day in Bishkek, in fact, I had paid a visit to the Islamic University downtown, and had a long conversation with Sultan, a second-year student there. Dressed in a Pakistani kurta suit, he turned out to be a keen Tablighii, and unwittingly echoed this accusation when he told me that this family accused him of opting out of life by studying all day, something Sultan, of course, vehemently denied. He also proudly pointed to the Islamic University of Kyrgyzstan as the only "proper" one in the post-Soviet region: "In Moscow," he parried my query, "it's not a real institute: the men study alongside the women."

Instead, Malikov believes that Kyrgyzstan needs more of a Turkish model of Islam, though he seems to mean Erdoğan's sometimes controversial revival of Islam in politics rather than Ataturkism. "This includes an equal emphasis on the secular and religious elements, a respect for science. And there should also be a political role for Islam here. Not like in Saudi Arabia, but more like in Malaysia. Every group has a right to influence the law. I don't have in mind a lobby, really, but I believe the government should incorporate religious values, and citizens should have the choice to be Islamic. So if it comes to a punishment or a fine, a person should be able to go to an Islamic court. And politics can adopt good elements from the shari'a. Our secular law is stuck at the moment; it's not working, and it could certainly benefit from incorporating elements of shari'a." He offers the example of legal polygamy: many bureaucrats have lovers, who are left without inheritance rights. "Shari'a accepts the fact of 'lovers', legalizes them. It could add justice to this situation."

Again, *wasatiyya* depends on where you are standing. What Malikov is saying about a Turkish model attunes with Habermas' latest idea about "post-secular societies", where religion should no longer be artificially privatized. And the idea of the shari'a having an influence on a Muslim-majority state such as Kyrgyzstan is not surprising, even though, as noted, Kyrgyzstan's Muslim-majority status is somewhat accidental. This means that Malikov's ideas can just about be squeezed under the rubric of moderate. If he were to say such things in Russia, however, where the post-secular lobby competing for influence is Orthodoxy, he may well find himself declared an extremist, out to Islamize and undermine Russia. (On the other hand, Ramzan Kadyrov is implementing precisely such a program in the Russian Federation republic of Chechnya; although this is in contravention of the Russian Federation's secular constitution, and his Islamization of Chechnya is only grudgingly accepted by Moscow; more on this in chapter 6.)

But Gulnara's "moderate scholar" presents other paradoxes as well. A couple of days earlier, on another visit to the Islamic University of Kyrgyzstan, I had talked to Oroz Ali Adranov, a professor of Islamic ethics or *adab*. Adranov had uttered a paradox. Keen to distinguish his own position concerning shari'a and Islamic rule from that of the Islamic Movement of Uzbekistan or al-Qaeda, he had emphasized that he ruled out the idea of an Islamic revolution that would implement an Islamic state. Instead, he wanted Kyrgyzstan—"which is after all a Muslim-majority country"—to evolve towards full shari'a. "And would this state implement the *hudud* laws?" "Certainly. But it would be voluntary, you see." I put it to Malikov that a state where everyone was an observant Muslim would perhaps not need the *hudud* laws anyway, given the level of piety and fraternity, and asked him to outline his own position.

Evidently, Malikov had thought about this, as he rapidly laid out an answer. "This basically comes down to the question of eschatology, which is the question of how and when there will be a perfect Islamic society, or a Muslim state," he started. "There are three views on this. First, there are people who think we cannot have a Muslim state until the coming of the *Mahdi*, or Jesus. He'll kill the anti-Christ, just as David killed Goliath, and then he will introduce shari'a law for everyone. But until that time, we should wait passively and accept the status quo. Secondly, there are people who think we must put our hopes in a universal Caliphate on earth. And we should work towards it, rather than making religion a private thing and being passive. There is a saying that 'God will not change you until you change yourselves', which is fitting here. But this position excludes the idea of revolution: it proceeds through education and dissemination of Islam among the people. The third position is the radicals. Bring in the Caliphate now, by revolution, top-down, and impose it on the people. That's the position of Al-Qaeda, Jamaat Takfir and so on. There's one major problem here, though, which is very difficult to solve. Justifying your position depends on how you interpret the Qur'an. This means deciding what order the verses were revealed in, which verses abrogate other verses, and what is the intepretation of *maslaha amma*, the common good."

Ultimately, Malikov says, he is in favor of the second position: to disseminate Islam in Kyrgyzstan, to lobby for Islamic laws ("I would bring back the death penalty, for example"), until such a time as an Islamic state would emerge naturally. In the evening, I share these opinions with the secular Kyrgyz friends that I am staying with. There are mixed opinions. The women generally guffaw in disgust. But over the week I chat to two men in their mid-twenties, both married with children, both in the construction industry (so middle class by Kyrgyz standards), and I find that they passively support the new Islamic rhetoric now doing the rounds. One of them is called Bakyt Oktyabrovich: his patronymic, of course, attests to a devoted communist grandparent. But when I ask him whether it is not ironic to bear this patronymic and hold such religious views, he looks at me blankly. He is a good and friendly host throughout my visit, but it is clear that his knowledge of Islam is as rusty as his knowledge of communist history; instead the attraction of Islam, he says quite clearly, is that it encourages family, modesty, traditional values and the obedience of women.

Hence I am left perplexed by Malikov, Gulnara's "moderate scholar". He bemoans the Kyrgyz government's lingering Soviet mistrust towards religion, and sees his own activity as disseminating an Islam that will in the distant but real future make an Islamic state possible in Kyrgyzstan, replete with *hudud* penalties and polygamy. He eschews the notion of the Islamic state being only realizable after the *Mahdi*, and insists: "Islam, you see, is primarily about social justice." A couple of years later, I am reading Leila Ahmad's book *The Quiet Revolution*, and I realize that she defines the political Islam of the Muslim Brotherhood precisely by its correspondence to the concept of Islam as social justice. She also shows that Brotherhood activism spread to the U.S. in the 1970s and now accounts for the most vocal part of American Muslim activism. That is, the essentially radical and potentially violent position of political Islam can mutate into something more in keeping with Western notions of rights and justice. Adranov, oddly enough, had mentioned his trip to the U.S., where he marveled at how Muslims had established a presence in the White House. He took this as a role model for Kyrgyzstan. Malikov's vision also fits Ahmad's definition of political Islam perfectly, down to his rejection of old-fashioned quiescent "post-Mahdian" Islam. A few years later, I will meet a *sheikh* in Ingushetia whose position overlaps in many ways with Malikov's: in that part of the post-Soviet space, though, this *sheikh* self-identifies as a Salafi, and is labeled by his enemies as a dangerous Wahhabi.[9]

It is clear that Malikov sees himself as a moderate and is hostile to the extremists represented in Kyrgyzstan by the outlawed groups, Jamaat Takfir and Hizb ut-Tahrir. But now that Hizb ut-Tahrir claims to eschew violence, their own vision of a Caliphate which the people of Central Asia will evolve towards naturally seems to differ little from Malikov's vision. The most Malikov could do was accuse them of hotheadedness and vagueness: "They rant a lot, but in reality they have no idea of what structure the Caliphate will take, who will be in charge of what." Furthermore, when outlining the three positions towards the Islamic state, Malikov had also identified "a major problem...[it] is very difficult to solve [the choice]...[by] justifying your position...[through] the Qur'an."

Malikov as good as admitted that interpretation alone could not decide between peaceful evolution and violent revolution. Later on, he says that while Hizb ut-Tahrir claim to reject violence, they can act as a feeder group to groups that do espouse violence. All this makes it difficult to draw a clear line

53

between "moderation" and "extremism". Hizb ut-Tahrir is a legal group in countries like the U.K. and Australia: if Kyrgyzstan legalized it, perhaps Malikov would not have to expend such energy on differentiating their positions. Malikov himself remarks to me: "I don't like to talk about Islamic terrorism, as if the two are inherently linked. I talk of religious extremism. As I said, it's a question of interpretation. But this interpretation is not just about the logic of texts. It comes out of social conditions."

At another point in our conversation, Malikov had given me a wonderful example of the differences between *madhabs*, to illustrate the greater suitedness of the Hanafite *madhab* to Kyrgyz conditions. It revolved round a question someone had asked him on his show: "Should women be allowed to drive buses?" In sum, Malikov argued that the Saudi Hanbalite interpretation of a hadith forbidding women to travel equated riding camels and driving cars *tout court*. But a Hanafite would say that riding camels was forbidden due to the immodest posture of a woman spreading her legs to ride the camel. Since a car requires no such indecency, Kyrgyz women should be able to drive buses.

Here the problem of Malikov's *wasatiyya* seems to arise again in acute form. The Hanafite approach may be more moderate compared to the Saudi approach (which incidentally, he did not condemn, but approved of as a local variation). But given that the Soviets gave so much in the way of rights to Kyrgyz women, simply to take the question of whether one should contemplate firing female bus drivers with due seriousness would be to cause outrage to secular Kyrgyz women, and even to the now observant Gulnara. Such moderation can only look like extreme archaism and a type of ethical violence. I can see why the trouser-wearing, bare-headed Gulnara is often not satisfied even with Malikov's scholastic analyses. Evidently, she has developed a divergent notion of *wasatiyya*: not from the sources, but from life.

Despite all this, there is much in Malikov's intellectual approach that evinces sympathy, and I am left with the impression that, after all, a great divide separates him from the often desperate rhetoric of Hizb ut-Tahrir, or other more extreme groups. Nonetheless, the difference does not lie, as he himself had said, solely in "the logic of texts". Rather, the difference is that Malikov has chosen to work within realistic boundaries, both institutional and temporal: his forum is the university and the state media channels, his time frame for "Islamization" stretches for decades, not years. He is not a shallow utopian; his "Islamic state" is local, not meaninglessly global. True, he talks of the *hudud* punishments and the need to implement shari'a, but one gets the sense that hopefully, as in classical Islamic civilization, in his vision those punishments would have more of a symbolic value (remaining on the books to remind people of the literal meaning of "deadly sin"), and would be hedged about with sufficient barriers to prevent their theatrical abuse.

Likewise, his "generous" decision to let women drive is not as mean-spirited as might seem at first sight: it is, I would hazard, merely the attempt to bind a new Islamic discourse to an ancient, interrupted one, using the classical logic of the severed past. To unsympathetic ears, the ears of a pre-conversion Gulnara, and her old friends, for example, it will sound harsh and incomprehensible. For them, it goes against the only logic they know: that of the autonomous self and the market. But some such project is necessary, surely, if the Islamic past is not to be swallowed up entirely in oblivion.

Still, a lot does indeed depend on "social conditions", the other half of Malikov's equation, and Malikov is not entirely free of *ressentiment*. He ends our conversation with an anti-Western tirade. He may have lived and studied in Spain, but I hear more of Peshawar and Islamabad in his last words. "There really is a common enemy whom we are struggling with," he ponders. "And that is secularization, or what you could call in Islamic terms, Dajalization, or Satanization. You don't have to look far for examples. An American pastor recently burned a copy of the Qur'an in Afghanistan. There were all those abuses of Muslim prisoners in Abu Ghraib by American soldiers. The West is pressing an agenda of secularization. And often, the West promotes the division of the Islamic world on the grounds that it is promoting tolerance. So it argues for rights for Islamic heresies like the Ahmadiyya movement, knowing full well and hoping that this will lead to a division of the Muslim *'umma*. And then it engages in propaganda for homosexual marriages. None of this can be accepted in Muslim societies. It's a completely aggressive tendency, very powerful and intrusive. And the only way to fight it is with equally strong aggression. Otherwise you will be overcome."

Kyrgyzstan was for some years the only country to host an American and Russian military base, and in many ways it is perceived to be the most American-friendly of the regional states. However, this anti-Western rhetoric suggests that such a picture may not be fully accurate (Gulnara, too, criticized America for allegedly funding opposition parties to cause chaos in the country). But it would be wrong to trace these sentiments just to Peshawar; in fact, they have a dual heritage. They are also thoroughly native to post-2008 Russia, and in that sense this tirade would, for the regional context, be thoroughly *wasatiy*, or moderate. Indeed, one of the ingredients that makes the Islam of the Russian muftis "moderate" for the government is its ability to turn on this anti-Western sentiment when the occasion demands.

Oroz Adranov: lifelong believer

While I am in Kyrgyzstan, I meet other people who embody some of the country's Islamic history. Gulnara and Malikov are new Muslims, in effect, atheist-to-Muslim converts. But professor Adranov, who is about sixty years old and teaches at the Islamic University of Kyrgyzstan has been Muslim all his life. He represents those who maintained an unbroken link with Islam during the Soviet period.

"My parents were Muslims," he tells me, "and they instilled the faith in me. They started to teach me about the religion when I was already in the third class (about ten years old). In the holidays, we travelled to Uzbekistan to study the Qur'an. Of course, it was secret. But there were no borders in those days; it was one country. There was a stronger tradition there of observing Islam. And they had a lot of teachers who knew the Qur'an by heart. We went to Andijan, in the Fergana valley. Crossing over was much easier then. It was very important for my parents, especially my mother, to bring me up with a knowledge of Islam. She came from a strong Muslim family, her grandfather was a mullah: he had a collection of Arabic books, and I still have some of them today: one was printed in 1800 in Kazan. He had a big influence on our family, you could say. My mother was raised devoutly. She would read *namaz* five times a day, even in Soviet times, of course in secret. And during Uraza, she always fasted. My father was different; he wasn't so strict. He was an orphan. He lost his father in the war, so he didn't have a proper upbringing. But I was raised under the influence of my mother. My father worked as an oil worker, and he went to Uzbekistan looking for oil. While he was on his business trips to Uzbekistan, which lasted for fifteen days at a time, he would not pray *namaz*. But when he got home, he would say the prayers. So he wasn't as strict as my mother. But when he got older, he started to observe Islam more seriously."

But even so, the secular–religious divide also existed in his family. "I was the only one who spent the holidays studying the Qur'an. The others knew a bit, but not much. Perhaps it was because I was calmer than my brothers that my mother decided to choose me for this. My older brother was a bit of a hooligan, always getting into trouble. He was not inclined to religion at all. He was very good at secular studies, and he went to Moscow and did very well there. I also have five sisters. They are very religious, but they aren't very knowledgeable about Islam. They fast, and if they have questions about practice, they'll ask someone. Funnily enough, my brother in Moscow has started to become observant too. Before, he wasn't in Kyrgyzstan long enough to understand much. But some time ago he came back for a long stretch, and he began to look and see, and we explained to him what Islam is all about."

The gradual turn of his brother towards Islam is for Adranov a model of what he would like to see happen in Kyrgyzstan as a whole. He echoes Malikov's words about wanting his country to evolve towards being an Islamic state, and seems to be pessimistic and optimistic in equal parts that this will happen:

"We are a secular republic now, with a secular constitution. But we all know that 80 per cent of the population is Muslim. You wouldn't hear that mentioned on T.V., but in their hearts even government ministers understand that the majority is Muslim, and so this is a Muslim country really, not a secular country. So if our government permits freedom of confession and our religion develops at the pace it is developing at now, maybe it'll truly become a Muslim country, in the proper sense of the word. A lot of youth are now following Islam...."

I interrupt this optimistic prognosis: "But look outside," I say. "There's hardly a single woman in a hijab. Most of them are in totally secular dress." I also remember the guesstimate of Sultan, the student I had talked to on my first day, that only 5 per cent of the population are really serious about Islam— something that is confirmed by the families I have been staying with and meeting. "But that's the women," says Adranov. "Even that's changing, though. Women are bringing other women to Islam. And as for the men, go into any mosque, and you'll see hundreds of youngsters there, not just old people. They're spilling out onto the streets."

On the other hand, Adranov admits, "things are still slow. There is no government accreditation process for our Islamic University diplomas yet. We'd like to see that started. But it's not just the government that's dragging its heels; most of the religious institutions don't see the benefit and aren't interested yet. They want to be independent of the government. But the downside is that our diplomas are not recognized by state institutions." It is here that Adranov mentions America as a model to emulate. He was part of a delegation that traveled to several countries, including the U.S., to investigate how accreditation for religious colleges works. "Over here, when we went to our government, there was no department of religion at all, and they tried to stop religious education point blank. So when I was in America, I was amazed at the respect Islam had there: they held congregational Friday worship in Congress! Islam is a relatively small religion in America, but this could still happen there. While here, the country is majority Muslim and we're not allowed such public worship in government buildings. A Pakistani–American congressman explained it to me this way: since 9/11 the government wants to show greater concern and sympathy for Muslims and Islam. As a result, there are Muslims who are now very close to Congress and can make themselves heard."

This praise for America comes as an interesting contrast to Sultan's conceptions of Britain. With all earnestness, the 20-year old Tablighii had wanted to know: "Is it true that all British schools have a subject on the curriculum called Islamaphobia and that everyone must study it regardless?" However, as with Malikov, the soft-spoken and dreamy Adranov's desire to Americanize Islamic education in Kyrgyzstan still has a rather different goal in mind. It is all part of the move not towards a U.S.-style constitution, but once again towards an Islamic State. Responding again to my provocative questions about *hudud* punishments in this hypothetical Islamic State of Kyrgyzstan, Adranov says: "The country is secular now, and Muslims have to obey authority. So stoning is not permitted now. But eventually when, as I say, the majority of the population follows Islam of their own accord, there would be stoning, because that is the rules that Allah gave Muhammad in the Qur'an. It sounds strict, of course. But the crimes that people commit are also severe and mustn't be repeated."

Of course, given Kyrgyzstan's proximity to Afghanistan and Pakistan (home to two of Malikov's alma maters), it is not surprising that such statements worry secularists. Much of the population may passively support Islam, but it is a vague and blurry sort of support. When I talk to Gulgina Salimovna, the gap between the dreams of Malikov and Adranov and people who do not devote their professional lives to thinking about religion becomes evident again.

Gulgina Salimovna: caught between generations

Gulgina is a sprightly, stylish seventy-year old and a walking embodiment of the region's cross-cultural history, both its past, through her grandparents, and its future, through her grandchildren. She is the head of the Tatar community of Kyrgyzstan, and presents a Tatar-language radio show. But she is also the conductor of the Bishkek Soviet Military Choir. She considers herself a good

Muslim too, wearing a scarf round her neck that she can pull over her head whenever she needs to join in with a *bismillah* before food or some occasion demanding prayer. Tatar, Kyrgyzstan citizen, Muslim, Soviet nostalgist, woman... I learn throughout the course of our long, frank conversation that these things need not be contradictions.

We first meet in downtown Bishkek at a memorial meeting of Soviet veterans to commemorate the victims of the 1943 battle of Kursk. Different speakers take to the microphone. "Many comrades died in the struggle against the fascists," one intones, "but they had that feeling of being victors until the very end—something which is sorely lacking in our society today. We are all tired today. We need that spirit of the victors. Today is a time of peace: but there's also a war going on, a war of values, a war of ideology, for the hearts of people. I wish you all a great holiday! Remember! Remember and be proud of what we achieved!" There is clapping and then another woman takes the microphone, the daughter of one of the men who fell at Kursk: "Let us never forget that victory! And let us never forget that one in six young Kyrgyz men took up arms to fight the fascists. Many of them, like my father, lost their lives. Today we must not betray their great struggle to achieve peace." She goes on to read an emotional poem in honor of her father, "whose name is always engraved on my heart. The earth is one, all shall be at peace.... we had German children from the Volga staying with us during the war, and we took care of them...."

Afterwards, we find a quiet spot to chat and naturally, given the theme of the memorial gathering, the conversation first turns to the Soviet choir she directs. "We sing all sorts of songs. Oh, you must know 'I love my fatherland, Russia.'" I confess that I do not and am secretly disappointed, quickly giving up hope that we will get onto the subject of Islam. But I am mistaken. Gulgina's multifaceted story emerges eventually.

She was born in Kashgar, now in the Xinjiang Uyghur Autonomous Region of China. Her grandparents had first moved before the 1917 Revolution to what later became Kazakhstan, where they were part of the Tatar merchant community. When the communists began the collectivization process that resulted in the deaths of millions there in the 1920s, the family fled over the border to China. Later, they moved back to Soviet Kazakhstan and Gulgina, who had trained as a doctor, worked in Semipalatinsk. She moved to Kyrgyzstan in the late sixties; treating patients for radiation had alerted her to the fact that the controlled atomic explosions in the Kazakhstan desert were not as problem-free as the government claimed. Her home has been Bishkek for many years, but her family's peregrinations link her to a broad Eurasian Tatar history and make a mockery of national borders. Perhaps it is not surprising that she remembers the Soviet Union fondly, despite awareness of its dark side: as heir to the Russian empire it was the only entity that could geographically encompass her various homelands.

Her family eventually integrated into Soviet society, as her own career as a doctor testifies, but as with Adranov this did not prevent them from maintaining their Tatar and Islamic culture and practices. "My grandfather on my father's side was an imam, and a scholar. He also worked as an ethnographer. He went round interviewing people—like you. All his manuscripts are kept now in Kazakhstan. My mother's grandparents were also attached to Islam. But they didn't make a big song and dance about it. 'Look at me, I'm off to do *namaz* now.' They did it more in a whisper, behind closed doors. But still, they did keep the prayer up. They taught me that God exists, that He is One."

However, unlike with Adranov, Gulgina's family seemed to have had a more *jadid*, or reformist, approach to Islam: after all it was the Tatars who spread jadidism in Central Asia. And that *jadid* approach also seems to have passed onto Gulgina: "Religion was forbidden in the Soviet Union," she continues. "But we always observed Orozo. My mother's passed away now, but to her dying day, to her last hour, she fasted. She especially loved the Ramadan fast. She didn't understand it from the religious point of view so much, but as an organic medical thing. When it ended she still wanted to fast for another month! She was a believer in God, of course, but as a literate person, as an educated woman, she explained it from a rational point of view—it has a basis in health, for example, pork is very bad for you." These words echo those of Zuleyha's father, and Gulgina also mentions Ibn Sina's rationalism and medical wisdom. The only difference is that Zuleyha's father came through rational arguments to the idea that fasting and abstention from pork are now unnecessary, while for Gulgina's mother these customs were deemed healthy.

Gulgina today adds more reasoning of her own: "These customs were passed down from generation to generation in our family. We don't eat halal now, but we know what it is. The animal should be fed correctly, and treated right, and there are parts of the animal that you shouldn't eat. That's what its real meaning is. But today on Orozo, when they just take a lamb and cut its throat and then bring the meat to the mosque, you have no idea what the animal's been through. It's just a fraud. That's why my son-in-law only buys meat for the festival from Turkish butchers. He doesn't buy from 'our' Turks.

They are still too Soviet, they might deceive us. And I do the same: I can't buy bad meat and trick my children. In fact, my daughter is vegetarian, and I am sixty percent vegetarian myself; I eat less and less meat. But the main thing is that I keep a hygienic kitchen, which is the real meaning of halal." Again, the logic is a blend of the Avicennan and the Soviet-modernistic.

Interestingly, though, she has not been able to transmit this Soviet Tatar Muslimness to her children, still less her grandchildren. As regards her Tatar identity, her younger son mocks her gently: "'Look, there goes another one of your Tatars,' he will say to me. He himself feels part of Kyrgyzstan now. He knows he is not Kyrgyz, obviously, but all his friends are Kyrgyz Muslims, and it is the religion that unites them. In fact," she goes on, "my older son was something of a fanatic at one point. He got into the religion quite deeply. Praying, fasting. And we used to argue quite a lot about it. He was very explosive. I was never against his being religious. I just didn't see why he had to push it in everyone's face all the time."

Luckily, he has calmed down and seemed to find a balance, his own form of *wasatiyya*. This was partly connected to his moving to Thailand to work in the tour industry. "Since then, he's become much more mellow. Once I was making lunch, and called the children. I couldn't find Shukrat. So I asked his brother where he was. 'Oh,' he says, 'he's in his room praying *namaz*.' I didn't even know. And then we talked about it, and he quoted my own words back to me from before. 'Remember you used to say: faith should be quiet. It should be in the heart.' So that's how it is for him now, much quieter. But it's extremely important to him. He told me: When he is in Thailand, working there, he sees such nasty things. So much sin. And it's all for free, you don't have to pay for it. And then only the strongest faith can save you; only a quiet faith in the heart can save you from that."

Nevertheless, a significant gap remains between Gulgina and her sons. She still feels a bit nervous in Kyrgyzstan as a minority Tatar. I share Gulnara's joke that Kyrgyzstan should solve its problems by going back to being a part of Russia. She smiles, but says, "I feel a bit uncomfortable talking about that. The bottom line is: that couldn't happen. The Kyrgyz are different from the Tatars. They wouldn't let that happen. And I do get a bit sick of all this Kyrgyz pride, Manas this and Manas that," she says referring to the much adulated national epic poem and symbol of Kyrgyz identity.

Interestingly, her son has solved his "Tatar problem" by going deeper into Islam. And although he has become "quieter" about his Islam, he seems to share Adranov's and Malikov's quiet but determined dream to turn Kyrgyzstan into an Islamic state. Gulgina was protected by the Soviet state from being a minority in the Kyrgyz Soviet Republic: they all belonged to something bigger, and not to "Muslim-majority" Kyrgyzstan. But Shukrat seems to be seeking that "something bigger" in an Islamic state. Gulgina says: "I always say to them, you have to be tolerant. As Jesus says, You must turn the other cheek. But my sons disagree; they say to me: 'Tolerant about what? Tatar rights? What about Muslim rights? We can't be 'tolerant', we can't be pushed aside. We have to fight for our right to practice our religion now.'"

So it seems the family embodies a cross-generational clash that is brewing across the country between those like Gulgina, who sees no contradiction in calling herself a "secular Muslim" and those like her sons who want to dismantle the remnants of Soviet secularism. She is divided about what the best course of action is: "Faith depends a lot on your surroundings, on where you are, on the society," she says, echoing my own view. "If you are with haters of Islam, your faith is going to boil up in protest. You'll shut up, retreat into yourself, and start to believe really fanatically. But if you are surrounded by brothers, then you'll be moderate. I'm thinking, also, of what's going on there in Uzbekistan with President Karimov. He cracks down on the Muslims. But his own daughter is all over the place; people even make fun of her. And with his repressions maybe he's preparing some sort of explosion of Islam."

But on the other hand, she does not really like this new Islam. She gets up now off the bench to stretch her legs a bit and straightens her blouse. "You see," she turns to me. "I'm not dressed in the proper Muslim way, trousers and short sleeves, but still..." She sits down again. "But I'll tell you one thing," she goes on. "There's one thing I can't stand. And that's the hijab. I wear my scarf. If I know the canons, the suras, the rules and all of that... then how can I wear a hijab?" At the start of our conversation, I had mentioned the Christian Gulnara and Gulgina had launched unbidden into a justification of her desire to convert from Islam to Christianity: "I can understand the girl's decision. Especially for a woman. I think it must be difficult for a young woman to find herself in Islam. It's quite formal. There are a lot of commandments. And Islam is especially inaccessible for women. For a start, you have to read Arabic. Of course, in Central Asia all the alphabets were changed in Soviet times, and that makes it very difficult to read the books, the prayers. And the holidays can evoke a sense of protest: in Christian holidays, the whole family takes part, the women and the children included. But in Islam, everything's separate. In the mosque, if I want to go and pray, I have to go separately. That's particularly sad in the case of a funeral. In other religions, the sexes mix: but not in Islam. Women can only go later."

This speech uncannily echoes even the Muslim Gulnara's uneasiness with certain aspects of her freely chosen Islamic observance. In many ways, Gulnara and Gulgina are very close; they embody a secular Muslim identity, and a strong feminine identity, which is quite a contrast to even the moderate but steely-willed Islam of men such as Adranov, Malikov and Gulgina's own sons. It seems that the desire of the latter to press for more Islam in Kyrgyzstan will hardly be diluted by the soft-talking Gulnara and Gulgina. It might take the more vehement secularism of my *shampanskoe*-swilling friends to do that.

The other Gulnara: choosing Christianity

One of the last meetings I have before leaving Bishkek is with Gulnara. 16 per cent of Kyrgyz are Christian, and, as we have seen, the theme of Christianity is a constant hum in the background of religious choices, an "other" to contrast with oneself—as in the rebuke to the Muslim Gulnara's excessive emphasis on love: "You are speaking like a Christian now."

The main Christian denomination in Kyrgyzstan is the Russian Orthodox Church, which is seen by the government as a "traditional religion", following the classification of Russia. As such, it does not carry out missionary activity and is accepted as a natural Slavic religion by Kyrgyz Muslim activists. The main non-Orthodox Christian groups in Kyrgyzstan are the Jehovah's Witnesses, Baptists and Evangelicals; the Baptists date from the 19th century and are widespread in Central Asia, the others came to the country in the 1990s. The number of Kyrgyz Protestants is growing, and this has attracted the anger of Muslims, even though Sultan, the Islamic University student, is convinced that Tablighi comes off better in its missionary and polemic efforts among Tengrist and secular Kyrgyz. Especially in the more Muslim south, the Fergana valley, (where Adranov studied Islam in Soviet times), there is a real battle for souls going on.

I myself encounter Christian missionaries when I am staying on the shores of Lake Issyk Kul, the country's main tourist attraction. A hyper-zealous preacher screams out Biblical quotations and exhortations in staccato Korean to the backdrop of lively pop music, while a Kyrgyz assistant translates into Russian. There is hand-waving, yells of "Who loves Jesus most?", and boisterous singing. I speak to some of the Kyrgyz Christians in the group and they tell me they are already second generation. I also encounter quite a few

Kazakh Baptists by chance in a large Pennsylvania church in the U.S. run by Ukrainian Baptists mostly born in Kazakhstan. Thus Central Asian Protestantism is already a somewhat historical phenomenon.

Gulnara, though, is a convert of ten years, and much of her story overlaps (until the crucial choice of religion) with the other Gulnara. "My parents were not very observant. But they always said, 'We are Muslims.' Even when it was forbidden, we celebrated Kurban-Id and Orozo-Id. My mother observed the Ramadan fast, at least as far as I remember, for two years properly. My father was less observant. I have seven siblings, two brothers and five sisters. I remember when I was six—that was in 1982—I asked my grandmother, 'Is there a God?' She was quiet for a very long time. I thought she hadn't heard me or simply didn't want to answer. But finally, she answered, 'God exists. But don't tell anybody.' That's because she was afraid. Her father, my great-grandfather, had been repressed. He sang a comic song about Stalin. He was arrested and shot. In 1986, he was rehabilitated, under Gorbachev."

Gulnara's whole family went to Kyrgyz-language schools, except for herself. "I was the only one that went to a Russian school. That's because I had a speech defect, you see." She points to her face which still shows the marks of an operation. "I was born with a cleft palate, I was very severely disabled. They had to do serious surgery on me. And then it took me a long time to learn how to speak. The only schools that offered speech therapy were Russian schools." It was at that school that she first saw a Bible storybook, handed around by visiting Baptist and Jehovah's Witness missionaries.

"The next time, I began thinking about Christianity," Gulnara continues, "it was actually before I became a Christian, but it was an important moment. I was at college now, and I was doing a project comparing developed and underdeveloped countries. And I remember I came across a graph which gave all sorts of statistics comparing them. Two columns jumped out at me. In countries where 52 per cent or more of the population is Christian, the country is developed. In countries where 52 per cent of the country is Muslim or Buddhist, it's less developed. I think God showed this to me directly—that comparison between faith and economics. I can't have been more than twenty at the time. But what I saw clearly was that Christianity means education, enlightenment and success. Don't forget that I was living in a poor family, then, and we had lots of mouths to feed."

Gulnara's next steps on the road to Christianity were triggered by a series of jolts and disasters. Her elder brother went to prison. He had been leading a life on the edges of the law, and it had finally caught up with him. Gulnara took it very personally, seeing it as her personal failure that she had not managed to keep him on the straight and narrow. At about the same time, her beloved grandfather died. It was Gulnara who got the telegram first; she opened it and sat for a very long time crying. But worse was to come: a man tried to rape her on the street. A passerby heard her screams and rescued her. But she had been wearing glasses, and they had smashed, leaving some glass in her eye, so for a time she was nearly blinded. "All these things together crushed me, and put me in a deep depression. I said to myself: You were born deformed. Now someone has nearly raped you. On top of that my grandfather is dead. It must be a punishment. I must be a bad person."

Her next encounters were with a Russian Baptist woman who gave her a Bible and a Kyrgyz cobbler who refused to work on her shoes until she had listened to his preaching. Eventually she asked him to take her to a church and she began attending a Baptist church with him on Thursdays, unaware that Sunday was the main Christian day. Finally, in 2000, she converted, or "accepted Jesus as her Lord."

However, coming from a Kyrgyz family, she did not make this decision lightly and tried to see if perhaps her problems could be solved in Islam, a mirror-image of the crossroads at which the other Gulnara would stand a few years later (both of them, too, were involved in the hedonistic lifestyle then, and this was one reason why Gulnara chose a Baptist rather than a strict Pentecostal church).

"I did try to find something in Islam before I made that decision," Gulnara recounts. "As I said, my parents called themselves Muslims. But our Kyrgyz Islam is a mix of different things. When I was a girl, for instance, my Mum used to give me money in my hand, and we would bow to the moon for good luck. That's the shamanistic part. Then there's even some Russian Orthodoxy: we wait for three days and have a wake before burying the body. In strict Islam, the body should be buried straightaway, or as soon as possible. And we also observe 40 days of mourning, like the Orthodox. Then of course we had all sorts of Soviet holidays. Which is good, in its way, too," Gulnara adds, thinking aloud. "The Soviet Union saved the Kyrgyz nation. We might not have survived without it."

Hence as a result of family and national loyalty, Gulnara decided to observe the Orozo (Ramadan) fast in 2000, shortly before her final step into Christianity. "My mother told me to set myself three goals for the fast. I decided to ask God for two things: the first was to tell me who is the true God." (The choice seems to have been between Allah and Jesus at this point.)

65

"Then I asked God to stop my brother being bad." Next, she continues, "I washed my hands, prayed something from the Qur'an, said a *bismilla*, and asked God to fulfill my two requests."

But it was also at this time that her cobbler acquaintance gave her a copy of the "repentance prayer", whereby someone can accept Jesus as their Lord. The need for a choice thus reached crisis point. She kept the prayer for some time, and finally she decided she was going to read it. She held the prayer in her hands, and "I was actually terrified as I read this, this prayer asking Jesus to be my savior, that Allah would come along on a white horse and cut off my head." She laughs, and I laugh a little nervously too, rather stunned at the depths of fear her ideas of Islam have implanted in her. "But," she continues, "I read the prayer, and nothing terrible happened. So I lost some of my fear. It was an answer in a way to my question."

Throughout this transformation, Gulnara was still living with her family. "I wanted to leave home a long time before. But my father is very strict, he wouldn't let me. If you leave us and go and live on your own, he said, you can forget about your mother and father, and about your brothers and sisters. You won't see us again." Nor was her father happy when she started becoming interested in Christianity. Ironically, at that point, he wanted to kick Gulnara out of the house himself. It was only her mother's intervention that saved her. "I had a distant relative who had become a Christian. Her father actually took hold of her and started strangling her until she rejected Jesus. My father wanted to do that to me. But, again, my mother stepped in: 'She's stubborn,' she said. 'It won't work for her.' But I have a feeling that if he had done that, I probably would have rejected Christianity at that time."

Of course, Gulnara continues, it's a great shame for many Kyrgyz to have a relative who is a Christian. And Kyrgyz fathers are tough. "My own father was tough, and I respected him, I was afraid of him. Though probably, he was not as strict as some. I had a friend who got a bad grade, and her father beat her up over it." Despite this, Gulnara has normal relations with her family, and since she became a Christian her pride in her Kyrgyz identity has also increased. For many years, she kept trying to emigrate to the West, dreaming of a better life. After all, her first hopes for Christianity had been intertwined with respect for "Christian economies." "But," she laughs, "the Lord kept dragging me back. And now I realize my work is in my country. There is no nation like the Kyrgyz—perhaps only the Jews are such a special nation. And as for my father being strict, well, the Bible tells us to respect our father and mother as long as they do not tell us to go against the church. And my father is a necessary person in my life. And now, as the years have passed, my family have begun to respect my faith. Sometimes they even ask me to pray for them! You see, God overcomes all enemies if you have faith. It's become easier for me to live with Jesus."

Now she lives in Bishkek. She has taken in three teenage orphan girls, though one of them recently ran away, reverting to her life of crime and prostitution. She has been on mission trips to Osh, the tense southern city where there have been bloody ethnic clashes between Kyrgyz and Uzbeks. She preaches and distributes books with titles like "Muslim brother, God loves you." She is also an active member of her church. In an odd way, she is more integrated into her religious community, and even her country, than the other Gulnara, who, like many of my Muscovite interviewees, practices her faith behind the closed doors of her home as official Islam seems to have little to offer her.

Religious dialogue in the post-Soviet melting-pot

I fly back to Moscow the morning after my meeting with Gulnara. At the time, I am living in the Yasenevo suburb of Moscow. Apart from the searing heat and desert landscape of Bishkek, which contrast with my local forest's birch trees and pines, there is little architectural difference between my area and the Bishkek tower blocks. My next-door neighbors, "Dima" (the name is a Russian version of his Kirghiz given name) and Ainura are even Kyrgyz. They are renting a two-bed apartment; however, as is usual for migrants, eleven people live there, a panoply of post-Soviet nations who come and go: Tajiks, fellow Kyrgyz and Moldovians, mostly, helping Dima pay the rent. Dima comes from Osh. He is one of Moscow's "two million Muslims". And yet this much touted figure looks a bit meaningless when you take Dima's history: he gained Russian citizenship in the late 1990s, as did many Kyrgyz, who can avail themselves of a more generous work permit regime than citizens of Tajikistan and Uzbekistan. He visits Kyrgyzstan rarely now, as his brother—also a Russian citizen—lives in Vladimir; his four year old daughter goes to school in Moscow and does not even speak Kyrgyz. He has nothing but contempt for the Islamic revival in Osh ("Hypocrites! Bandits!") and is thoroughly secular. Dima represents an interesting demographic: it is quite likely that his grandchildren will be mixed Russian–Kyrgyz: for all purposes Russian, with typical Moscow melting-pot ancestry.

I mention Dima to show the tight interconnectedness of the Islamic post-Soviet space, to highlight again how moderate Islam can take on different meanings depending on place. Kyrgyzstan is different, of course, because it is not politically part of Russia, so the Muslim lobby there can develop a version of Islam that "golden-domed" Moscow and especially its new mayor, Sobyanin, will not tolerate. But in the spirit of interconnectedness, we will conclude this chapter that has mostly been devoted to Kyrgyzstan by considering two overlapping stories: that of Askhat, a Moscow-born *mishar* Tatar, and Ruslan, by ancestry a Kazan Tatar, but who was born in Chimkent, Kazakhstan, near the border with Kyrgyzstan and Uzbekistan. Their stories contain themes touched on in the stories of the two Gulnaras, Malikov and Gulgina.

Askhat and Ruslan have known each other for several years and are involved in a project called the March of Peace. The March of Peace consists of an Orthodox Christian, a Muslim, a Jew and a Buddhist marching together on a pilgrimage to demonstrate the harmony of the religions. Ruslan founded the project and leads the marches. Chimkent, like Bishkek, is multi-ethnic and multi-religious, and quite early Ruslan felt the need to use religion as a means of promoting harmony in the chaotic post-Soviet period. Askhat, as a Christian convert who still feels a devotion to his Tatar–Muslim roots, also devotes much of his energies to the March, as well as to hosting an interfaith stall at the annual muftiat-sponsored Halal Expo exhibition in Moscow.

But this is not quite interfaith as one might come across it in the West. For a start, Ruslan is an ex-gangster, who ran a criminal gang in the bleak city of Chimkent in the 1990s. They sold drugs and weapons, beat up hippies and other outcasts, and were not averse to wiping out their rivals. Askhat, by contrast, is a skinny 60-year old Moscow intellectual. He converted to Charismatic Protestantism in the 1990s, but at the beginning of the 2000s became Orthodox. He explains this not so much as a faith decision but as a political decision: "As a Protestant, I will always be marginal. As an Orthodox, there is some hope of changing things."

Both Askhat and Ruslan, though independents, actively seek government help for their project— just as Adranov and Malikov in Kyrgyzstan feel that the Muslim revival will be lacking until the government supports it. This is a common attitude in post-Soviet societies where the power vertical is important and "horizontal" civil society is lethargic. In the case of Askhat and Ruslan, it is noteworthy that only representatives of the "traditional" religions outlined in the Russian Constitution take part in the march. And the two of them are friendly with Vsevolod Chaplin, the controversially ultraconservative Russian church spokesman (who once declared that the Russian church could borrow some examples from shari'a, specifically shari'a interest-free economics). Finally, when they took the Peace March through Chechnya, they were attacked by local Wahhabis; four people were killed, but the group had Russian Special Forces soldiers guarding them, and this probably lessened the casualty numbers.

All this cannot but seem peculiar and paradoxical, and yet it vividly illuminates the sometimes bizarre conditions in which religion has to operate in post-Soviet Russia and its near abroad. The criminality and violence of the chaotic nineties have left their mark in all spheres of life and in all areas of the former Soviet Union. And yet despite these harsh conditions, the examples of Askhat and Ruslan contain much that is instructive in understanding Muslim identity in the region today.

Askhat Vafin: an Islamo-Christian chosenness?

Askhat is now a parishioner at the well known liberal–intellectual church of Saints Cosmas and Damian in the center of Moscow, and, like many there, is interested in Russian religious philosophy, a philosophy famous for producing thinkers like Nicolai Berdyaev, proponent of the Russian Idea. Berdyaev and other such thinkers saw Russia as having a special religious mission in the world, and promoted a form of Christianity straddling Eastern mysticism, best embodied in the otherworldly, hermetic focus of Byzantine hesychasm, and what they saw as Western practicality, as expressed in the social focus of the Catholic orders and the Protestant social ethic. As we will see in a later chapter, Russian Tatar intellectuals like Damir Muhetdinov have applied this to Tatar Islam, and one reason why they are ready to let Askhat have his stall at the Exhibition is because he promotes a similar idea. He too now sees his Tatar identity as a blessing, as it gives him a real link to the East. The Tatars, though, were always the most Westernized of Russia's Muslims, and thus they could also serve as communicators between the Central Asian East and the Western Russian heartlands.

Askhat also has a theological take on this: "Orthodoxy was for me partly a practical choice of confession," he admits, "but theologically, too, the *Filioque* makes Orthodoxy far more Eastern. The *Filioque* insists on the monarchy of the Father, on the idea that the basic foundation of the divinity is the Father, and not as in Catholicism, the Father and the Son. In that sense, Orthodoxy preserves closer ties than Western Christianity with its Judaic, monotheistic roots." For Slavophile thinkers, this crucial doctrine of the *Filioque* was always interpreted as a sign of Russian Christianity's ability to bridge the European East and West. For Askhat, it is the perfect bridge for him to become reconciled to his monotheistic, Eastern Muslim heritage. Likewise, Berdyaev's Russian Messianism becomes on Askhat's reading more of a Tatar Islamo-Christian Messianism, with Tatars leading the way to the reconciliation of the religions.

Thus, unlike Gulnara, Askhat's turn to Protestant and then Orthodox Christianity has not meant a wholesale rejection of his Muslim identity. For Gulnara, the Muslims breaking the Ramadan fast behind us in the Bishkek café where we were talking are quite simply damned, as "Islam is just a religion of works". For Askhat, Islam preserves the important principle of monotheism, and in some sense the Christ that he drew so close to, especially in charismatic sessions in his Pentecostal Church, is the Word of Allah. Quietly, discreetly, Askhat is embracing a daring sort of Islamo-Christian syncretism.

However, the path to this synthetic identity, his own form of *wasatiyya*, has been long and painful. Two of his grandfathers were mullahs in Nizhny Tatar villages. His family moved to Moscow just before the war, and initially his mother and grandmother lived in workers' barracks where the Russian workers would beat up minorities like Jews and Tatars. His mother thus always suffered from an inferiority complex about being Tatar. When Askhat went to school in the fifties, he recalls how the history teacher made him stand up in class and read the page about how the Tatar–Mongol yoke destroyed Russia. The accusing eyes of the Russian students bored into him; the experience broke something inside of him. "At school, as a result, my best friend was a Jew. We two minorities always sat together. Even though, many years later, I discovered there were several other Tatars in our class; they just hid it better..."

When his father finally finished a degree in engineering and got a good job he moved his family out of the barracks and into an apartment in the prestigious Taganka region. But unwittingly, he also contributed to Askhat's Tatar self-hatred. Just before he started school, he had Askhat repeat over and over again: "My grandfather was a government functionary, my grandfather was a government functionary..." The fact was that his grandfather had been a "religious functionary", that is, a mullah. Because of this, Askhat's father had been barred from studying anything other than engineering and banned from the best institutes. He did not want his son to suffer from the same stain of religious ancestry. However, even his strictly cultural Tatar activities in

Moscow led him to being hauled in by the KGB as late as the 1980s. "I had just read a *samizdat* copy of Solzhyntsyn's Gulag Archipelago at that point, and I was particularly terrified by Father's disappearance. I am ashamed to admit that I tried to persuade him to give up his Tatar activities completely."

It was a Soviet Korean (as with Gulnara) who first introduced Askhat to Christianity. Unlike the Muslim Gulnara, though, Askhat found peace and strength in Christianity, especially in the experience of glossolalia (speaking in tongues). His Tatar wife (his father had encouraged him to marry a Tatar) was baptized in an Orthodox church but nearly died three days later from flu. Her father, usually a quiet man, unexpectedly lashed out and beat her severely when he learned of her conversion. All this drove her away from Christianity. Askhat's own father, an atheist, kept tight-lipped about his son's conversion. "He didn't say anything to me openly. A bit later, when my father was already getting on, I bought him a book called the 'Life of Muhammad'. He began to read it, and saw that there was no necessary contradiction between Christianity and Islam. That was in about 1997 or 1998.... From that time on, actually, I began to see it as my life task to point out to people the similarities between Islam and Christianity. Just before that time," Askhat recalls, "he began to take Arabic classes as well, and he helped raise money for the rebuilding of the mosque in his village; the same one where my grandfather was a mullah, the one that was torn down. I'm not sure if he was a 'believer' as such—but there was something there."

This learning of Arabic and the rebuilding of his hometown mosque put his father squarely within the revival—not so much religious here, as ethnic—that swept up the Mustafins. But extraordinarily, Askhat was also pulled into this Tatar–Islamic revival, despite his conversion. "I taught myself to read *namaz* in Arabic at that time, as well, even though I am terrible with languages." Then, armed with his new knowledge, he started going to the mosque: "I go there and do the prostrations and read the prayer in Arabic: *bismallah arrahman arrahim*.... It's a wonderful feeling, being there in the rows among the believers, showing your utter obedience before God...." Nonetheless, he muses, "I am still a Christian. For me that is the most powerful connection to the divine—though I admit that to some extent you can find that in Islam: the Chechens have their *zikrs*, where they dance in circles and chant to a monotonous beat. The Hasidic Jews, I believe, have something similar."

Askhat's quest has gained added urgency due to his son, who has returned to Islam but is married to a Russian. "I have to think about my grandchildren.

They are half-Tatar and half-Russian. In my day, it was practically unthinkable to marry out. But now it happens everywhere. And what will they be? How will they think of themselves? The old categories don't apply anymore. So we need to start thinking for them."

Askhat's attempt to make sense of religious pluralism is not just a Moscow story. It recapitulates processes occurring from Kazan to Bishkek to Chimkent, and we will see similar processes in Fergana and Mahachkala. My conversations with the Muslim Gulnara and Malikov also covered similar ground. They had approached the question from an Islamic angle, justifying tolerance towards Jews and Christians in past and (implicitly) future Islamic states through the notion that Judaism and Christianity are not terms found in the Bible but are really later terms. In fact, Jews and Christians are really Muslims—and this is why Islam tolerates them. Of course, this Islamic–universalist approach suffers from not taking the Other's claims to identity sufficiently seriously, and we will look at this issue later. Meanwhile, Ruslan Abdullin, Askhat's collaborator, is putting forward his own take on the issue.

Ruslan Abdullin: harsh eclecticism

Askhat's motivation for interreligious dialogue is clear. With Ruslan the picture is not so obvious, given that he is a convinced Sunni Muslim. Going back over his words, however, I believe it might have arisen out of the violence he witnessed within his own religion, especially the explosion of extremism in Chechnya. In the course of our two long and exhausting conversations, he does tell me at one point, after all: "My marches also have the goal of creating peace within the religions."

But it is not easy to generalize with Ruslan. He is a storm of contradictions. The ideas he professes are one thing: some of them could even be rehashed and presented in the polite seminar rooms of universities. His life and lifestyle, however, come from a different sphere of existence. In his person, he is a grizzled sixty year old with a rough salt and pepper beard, a Muslim skullcap constantly atilt his head, and sharp challenging eyes—he embodies much of the violent energy, hunger and desperation of post-Soviet Eurasia. Ideas and stories spill out of him, some of them compelling, others repellent. In his life, the theme of violence and power constantly come to the fore. He has clawed his way towards a moderate, peacenik position, but it is easy to see how he might have ended up among the insulted and humiliated *takfiris*.

Unlike Askhat, he distrusts speech and discourse as a way of making sense of religious diversity and competition. Old forms of dialogue based on doctrinal and dogmatic comparisons have exhausted themselves. Ruslan therefore proposes, and is executing, a form of dialogue as spiritual action: a joint action undertaken by a Buddhist, a Jew, a Christian and a Muslim. So far he has led more than ten marches, some of them international, like the ones from Kazakhstan to Greece, and from Russia to Jordan. Ruslan absolutely prohibits any discussion of dogmatic matters between participants of the march. Experience has shown that they lead only to anger and vexed disputation. "Either you convert to my religion, or I stone you to death," is how he puts it in his typically blunt and austere manner.

Yet Ruslan does have his own eclectic way of theologizing about what the March is about. The marchers are transformed first physically, then spiritually. They spend enough time on the road that their bodily substances are replaced; that is, through the cycles of metabolic exchange the physical body of each participant is entirely renewed. This feeds into the spiritual transformation of the marchers, which is also effected by the rhythmic beat of their marching together. He dubs this "the unity of spiritual *zikr*", using the Sufi term *zikr*, or divine remembrance, to signify that the pace of the walking is a type of harmonious transformative meditative practice. While on the road, the Buddhist member beats his prayer drum and the Muslim recites Qur'anic verses: he is convinced the process can lead to the transformation of the marchers as well as the hundreds of curious and joyful bystanders who come out onto the road to witness the spectacle.

Ruslan has been through some transformations himself. He was born in Chimkent, a notorious dumping ground for Soviet exiles and prisoners. His extended family was shot in anti-religious actions in the Kazan region in the twenties and his mother was one of the few survivors, sent by her parents to South Kazakhstan, where she grew up as an orphan. His father's background was similar. Ruslan was raised an atheist, though much later he discovered that his parents came from noble Tatar families who could trace their lineage through Islam Bobo to the Prophet Muhammad. It was evident in his mother's gifts: she could cure people, knew about herbs, and could heal people from the evil eye. "Genetics is one third of a person's identity," Ruslan tells me with oddly categorical certainty, "and ultimately that came out in me."

But in his teens he was a member of the Communist youth. At school, he became the leader of a youth gang, modeled on the image of the SS he had picked up from Soviet war films—another strange detail Ruslan lets drop casually. "That was what Chimkent was like in those days," he goes on. "People punch you in the face and ask questions afterwards." After school, he was dragged into the army and sent to the Caucasus. "The bullying in the army was horrific. And they treated us Central Asians as *churbany*, blocks of wood... I lost my nerve in the army. People ganged up on me. Four people got me onto a mattress and raped me. But in the end I came out on top, I became a boss myself. Already, you could say, I'd grasped this truth in my last year at school, when I was charge of my gang: it's like Gumilev says, 5–6 per cent of humanity are leaders. The rest follow like sheep. I was made to be a leader."

Back in Chimkent, he started to head an adult gang. They sold drugs and guns, and aimed to be tougher than the Chechens who were coming in on this business. Then one day, his life changed. He was driving at 110 kilometers an hour to the suburbs. His goal was to put a bullet in the head of a close friend who had betrayed the gang. But his car crashed and he ended up in hospital, hovering between life and death. There, he had a vision of al-Khidr, the mysterious "green man" of Islam: "He was tall, very tall," Ruslan recalls, "with a gray beard, and a gray skullcap. He was wearing a striped robe. I was sitting, looking down, somehow, on my own body. He said to me: 'Ruslan, you are an idiot. You have a different path.'"

Against the odds, he recovered, left the gang and went into teaching—his father's profession. "It's the eternal choice in Tatar families: either a trader or a teacher." He moved to Leningrad to get away from his past, and there he founded a school in the mid-eighties whose pupils were mainly drawn from the supporters of a local football team. "But not everything was going as quickly as I wanted. I consoled myself that I was only twenty-eight years old. I recalled that Caesar, Hitler, and so on, had not achieved everything all at once. Allah showed me that it took them a long time to achieve what they wanted. And it took four more years before my schools bore any fruit."

Nowadays, these special schools are also a big project. He sees them as connected to the Marches, as they are "survival schools", where the pupils learn "how to control their internal energy. We learn how to live alone in the steppe, up in the mountains, at sea... how to survive while engaging in pilgrimage. It's a different order to anything that's been thought of before." His ultimate ambition is to found seven of these schools, one in each of the "seven spirits" of the former USSR, a list of cities he believes have spiritual potential.

But in the late eighties, he still had not articulated these ideas clearly, still less formulated the idea of a Peace March. He would have to go through more suffering for that. He ended up homeless in Moscow, living half-starving on the streets. It was then, he says, that he was visited by a mysterious Sufi figure who analyzed his life. Whilst living in a rat-infested attic, he had another vision. A voice told him to abstain from certain foods for five years, and to wear his skullcap constantly, which he does to this day. After that he sent out on a journey, spending a year in Chechnya. The year was 1998, between the wars. Ruslan crossed between the Russian and Chechen lines and was hauled before a death squad on both sides. The Chechen Wahhabi movement had solidified by that time, and they got to know of him, putting a price on his head. "But I wasn't afraid. I would have considered it an honor to die as a *shahid* at their hands."

After that he tried to drive to Mecca, but got stuck in the Emirates, where he lived in a mosque for a month. On the way back, he got delayed in Jordan, where he found himself a spiritual guide, a *sheikh*. That is when he began to seriously study Islam and to understand: "It's a terrifying, powerful thing to say the *shahada*, to be a true Muslim. But most Muslims have no idea. They repeat the words without understanding."

It was shortly after this that he began to lead marches, perhaps wishing to share what his own wanderings had given him with others. "I saw my marches as having one goal," he says at another point. "To break barriers, to clear away the old, to create the new." And a bit later, he quotes the Qur'an: "The Holy Book tells us, the members of the different religions, to compete in good deeds... it also says: 'there should be many ways to the Truth, and Allah alone will judge between men on the Day of Judgment.'"

These verses are often quoted by Muslims engaging in interreligious dialogue. Of course, they have to be harmonized with other Qur'anic verses that declare the superiority and uniqueness of Islam over other religions. Ruslan, too, swings between these poles, a few times mentioning that no other religion can compare to Islam, and also throwing in several castigations of the perfidious Jews, both in ancient Arabia and in world politics today— something that is unpleasant but often par for the course in post-Soviet Russia. I speak to his Jewish collaborator on the Peace March, and he shrugs: "What can you expect?"

But there is another contradiction, or parallel dynamic, lurking in Ruslan's attempt to live his new Islamic faith. It is a far more "Eurasian" contradiction. He sings the praises of Arab Islam, regrets the degeneration of Central Asian Islam (like Atiya from Dagestan, an almost unconsciously Salafist position), and refuses to countenance religious syncretism (which is why he dislikes interreligious comparisons and speeches). And yet in his own search, there seems to be, according to his own strict definitions, simply too much that is non-Arab and non-Islamic in his life experience for it all to be excluded. And thus, seemingly unaware of the tension, he talks about the importance of the Chinese year ("I am optimistic: we are entering a new age; the year of the fish is finished"); Hindu chakras; and at one point refers to a religious practice using the Russian Orthodox term *prelost'*—meaning something that gives emotional pleasure but is spiritually misleading.

It is with a skilful sleight of hand that he combines hadiths and chakras: "The Prophet Muhammad said: There are only two things that give physical pleasure: women and *namaz* [he forgets perfume]. Think about it. What could he have meant? Millions of people pray, but they wouldn't even think it possible to get physical pleasure from it. But when your chakras open on the March, everything tickles and feels pleasant, and you are bathed in exquisite pleasure. This is the pleasure of worship. You can see the same thing with Jesus, when he says, Turn the other cheek. It's equivalent to a hadith which says: If you hold your anger in, even if it is righteous anger, your heart will be cleansed. Holding your anger in fact opens up the fourth chakra; this gives rise to peace and faith. So there is a clear physiological meaning to Jesus' saying based in the science of the chakras. But," he concludes, "the Salafists and many Muslims reject this. They are idiots. I have been to India, though," he lets drop, "and I know something about Indian spiritual sciences. So it is stupid to deny the links."

It seems as if Ruslan has his own Islamic theology: it contains many New Age ideas that were circulating in the late Soviet period among spiritual seekers. Despite his self-image as an Arab-inclining strict Sunni, his theology is highly syncretistic. Are the marches then not so much a way of shutting down useless theological chit-chat, as claimed, but rather a way to keep the (somewhat arbitrarily chosen) "four traditional denominations" firmly distinct, in case, as with Askhat, they blend into each other and rub out firm identities?

If so, Ruslan's Marches are not a bad solution to the problem of maintaining a strong identity—necessary for harsh times—without forcing it on others. Ruslan, too, is struggling to be a moderate, (a *wasatiy*), caught between two different types of extremes.

On the one hand, he has steered himself away from gang violence, resisted the lure of misanthropic *takfir*ism, and even resisted the siren song of government money and support. It is true that he and Askhat are trying to firm up links with the muftiat, but I am surprised when Ruslan takes a call at the end of our conversation. "Meet me outside the Cherkessovskaya mall," he says. "I am selling newspapers there, trying to earn my way home." He is also sleeping on a friend's floor, a far cry from the lavish government-funded conferences and banquets put on by the muftis. You cannot say he does not have the courage of his convictions.

On the other hand, Ruslan is trying to remain true to his personal and family experience, to be a Muslim, a Tatar Muslim, absorbing the many arcane and esoteric elements in that experience and trying to fit them into a framework of historical orthodoxy, to create continuity with the Islamic past and his own Eurasian–Soviet–Russian Islamic present.

There is much that is disturbing in his vision, and even his fellow Marchers find a lot of what Ruslan says and does eccentric. In addition to the anti-Semitism (which he would no doubt deny), there is a thoroughly patronizing attitude towards women: "Leave us alone, dear. Go and do your job," he snaps at our waitress at the beginning; and then later: "Run along and bring us a coffee just as beautiful as yourself." He tells me at another point: "You could never be a Muslim. You have to make your wife obey you." But somehow, cerebral Askhat and his long-haired hippy Russian friend, who sits on the March's committee, can forgive all this, drawn by something powerful, compelling and hypnotic in Ruslan. As with many Russian intellectuals they have got to a point in their lives where they are sick of talking, sick of quoting Pushkin, sick of being on the wrong side of the government, of history. Ruslan's impetuous and occasionally mad actions (he marched right through the Donbass region in 2014 at the height of the civil war) fascinate them, hypnotize them, draw them in, as much by their symbolic boldness as anything else.

"Write, write," he commands me as our last interview comes to an end, and I am wilting with exhaustion at his intensity. "The professors and students of the West will hear my message and they'll go ahead and rule the world, but based on my principles. I remember very well an image from when I worked on a farm: the sheep refused to go to the shearing. So the farmer would get a goat, a proud billy goat with beautiful horns. The goat would go out in front of the sheep and walk ahead, and the sheep would follow him. It's the same with humanity. The leader leads by his extraordinary activity and energy and ideas. The rest will follow...."

It is another deeply post-Soviet idea: the need for strength, leadership, will, to combat the chaos, the descent into extremes, the need to hold the center somehow, when everything is tending towards collapse. In such circumstances, perhaps, paradoxically, to hold the Middle Way requires a certain measure of fanaticism.

3.

BETWEEN MOSCOW AND FERGANA: CHASING THE GHOST OF ISLAM

Sirozhidin: an "Easterner" in Moscow

My next trip takes me to Uzbekistan's Fergana valley, thanks to an invitation from a 62-year old Uzbek "guest-worker" whom I meet in Moscow towards the end of summer, 2013. His name is Sirozhidin Abdusamatovich Abdusamatov. A year later, I end up staying with his family for ten days. For his part, he invites me because he loves to receive guests, especially foreign ones: that is the "Eastern" way—although I am not a complete stranger, as we are introduced through a mutual Russian friend called Alexei. For my part, I accept the invitation because I am curious to immerse myself in the life of one of Moscow's "two million" and to find out about Islam in the notorious Fergana valley. The Fergana valley, of course, is the place where the Islamic Movement of Uzbekistan was launched in the mid-1990s, Islamic moderation morphing into extremism. It is the place where Islamic radicals on several occasions challenged Karimov's power; where Adranov and hundreds of others studied Islam in "open secrecy" in the Soviet period; and where illegal Hizb ut-Tahrir activists from Kyrgyzstan flee to escape arrest. It is on the radar of the CIA, the FSB (Federal Security Service of the Russian Federation) and other national security agencies. It is the Islamic lynchpin of Central Asia. How could I refuse Sirozhidin?

Our brief initial meetings in Moscow deal in stereotypes and idealized self-presentations on both sides. My ideas about the Fergana valley—admittedly derived from books—feed expectations on my side. But gradually, as he accepts me into his home and puts time aside to guide me round the valley, I begin to get friendly with his sons, his wife, some of his nephews, and his sons' friends. Some of the stereotypes fall away; some of the mysteries stubbornly remain. "Islam", that catch-all label for a hundred realities, takes on a ghostly existence, ever fleeing my prurient glance, rushing round corners in fear, never speaking its name, avoiding me. And as for my quite adequate but vague idea that the post-Soviet Islamic space is one, it turns out to be partially true, and partially false.

Sirozhidin, like many other Uzbeks and Tajiks in Moscow, does not quite inhabit the same skin he does at home. It is not that he has another wife or family in Moscow. That is common enough; some migrants have three wives and families in all, scattered over Russia and Central Asia. But a certain amount of self-invention goes on, nonetheless.

The first time I meet Sirozhidin, he is standing quietly at the back of an Orthodox church during the Sunday liturgy. He has been living in a spare room at Alexei's flat and when he is not working full days as a courier delivering medicine orders round Moscow, he babysits Alexei's son, helping to take them to church on Sundays. The two have become friendly. "Your son needs some Eastern discipline," Sirozhidin says often. Immediately, a surprise and a stereotype clash. Sirozhidin is *vostochny*, "Eastern". He can teach Alexei some of his wise ways. But what is he doing in a church? For several weeks Father Boris, the priest, has been giving him books to read about Christianity. There is speculation among the congregants that Sirozhidin is thinking of converting. Alexei, a keen Christian, toys with the idea. But ultimately he concludes that Sirozhidin, "in his Eastern way", is just paying his respects to the local authorities, or to the local spirits, and has no serious intent of giving up his own religion.

I meet again with Sirozhidin a short while later. It is July. I invite him to have a cup of tea and a snack in the café near the metro station. But Sirozhidin declines. "It's Ramadan. I can't, I am fasting." I buy him some bread to take home instead and then after our conversation I buy him medicine he needs at the pharmacy opposite, partly out of guilt. After our talk, the trembling Sirozhidin looks gray with fatigue: he has been working for ten hours and has not drunk or eaten all day. "See how God works," he says. "I didn't have any food at home, or this medicine. And now you come along." I am surprised. I too had gone for the version that he was contemplating conversion. It turns out he is a devout Muslim who observes Orozo and prays *Fajr* in the morning.

In that first meeting, he sketches some facts about his life for me. But later, like the statisticians counting two million Moscow "Muslims", or the hopeful Russian conservatives who claim that thousands are converting to Christianity, I realize my questions have only brought out the conventionally Eastern, Muslim Uzbek guest-worker in Sirozhidin. It turns out this is a mere fraction of his identity. Sitting opposite him in the café, I learn that he was born in 1952. Unlike his brothers, who were brought up during Stalin's repressions, by the time he grew up it was again possible to receive an Islamic education with a teacher that his father knew. He has four sons, "but I do not let them come to Moscow: it would spoil their Eastern upbringing". His mother is eighty-four and still alive, an *otincha* learned in the Qur'an. When he was growing up he would go to the mosque every Friday, he recalls. Proudly, he tells me that his city, Fergana, was the most religious city in the valley.

Moving away a bit from the Islamic theme, he reminisces about other aspects of his life. He worked in the tour industry in Fergana in the 1970s and 1980s. "I was good at it because I can speak to people in their languages. I know Tajik, for example, because we have lots of Tajiks coming to the Fergana valley and I wanted to speak to them. I also speak Turkish, because I lived and worked in Turkey and Azerbaijan for quite a bit in the 1990s." He is also naturally sociable and recently put up twenty Bukharan Jews from Israel who were returning to visit their homeland. Their leader, Bella, used to be a good friend of his. After this revelation, I feel less uncomfortable impinging on his hospitality.

In the East: everything is family

A year intervenes before I can take up his invitation, though. I have spent the year in the U.S. and it turns out that Sirozhidin himself has only just moved back home from Moscow—for good, it seems. "My sons want their father at home," he explains. Thus, having been away a long time in prestigious Moscow, when I arrive in Fergana, Sirozhidin insists on taking me on his wandering strolls round the town. Now, with me at his side, his tales of foreign derring-do are confirmed in full. Nostalgically, he uses me as a sounding board, uttering his thoughts out loud, pointing out buildings, taking me to the hotel where he worked for many years, inviting me to sit down with his friends outside one of their carpet shops opposite the main market. Abuzz with the delight of having returned home, almost a tourist in his own town, the main message he wants to relay to me in these first days is the Edenic nature of Fergana, and the superiority of its Eastern ways to those of decadent, cold and hostile Moscow.

I am treated to endless melons, grapes and apricots dried on the sun-baked flagstones of his large courtyard. We drive round the towns of the valley in his tinny gas-fueled Chevrolet (driven by 90 per cent of the population, a true Soviet equality of consumption) or in crowded *marshrutka* taxis. Towns that had been mere dots on a map and names in books—Namangan, Andijan, Margilan, Kokand—come alive. Occasionally, Sirozhidin will stop the car and hustle me across the road to a stranger's outdoor vine trellis. Hands are shaken, greetings exchanged. "Those grapes look amazing, you must try them. Do you mind?" Sirozhidin asks the beaming proprietor. He has many members of his family living in different parts of Fergana, and I am invited to taste and compare their grapes, too. The same process of tasting and appreciation is gone through for the different varieties of *plov* and *non* bread.

Bit by bit, I meet his family: his elderly mother; his one hundred and four year old grandmother; the family of his brother, who live in the center of town; an aunt and her family, who live on the outskirts; and more family, who live amid plush green orchards about forty minutes drive in the direction of the Kyrgyz border. But the three family members I become closest to are Sirozhidin's wife, Asmira, and his second and third sons, Shohruh and Shuhrat. They are still living in their father's house, which consists of a front courtyard surrounded by a spacious complex of rooms, a garden, and sheds for livestock round the back, including a cockerel that crows on the dot at 4 a.m. every morning. The eldest son, Sherzod, lives separately; the youngest son is working in Siberia.

For the first three days, I am kept tightly under Sirozhidin's wing, seeing the world through his eyes. On the fourth day, my host has to go off and do some business, and the two middle sons step in to entertain me. They take me swimming, to cafés, introduce me to friends, and we have long talks, some of them surprisingly frank. The business that has detained Sirozhidin, in fact, turns into a long-running theme of my trip: he is searching for a bride for Shuhrat. As he explains to me: "A good Uzbek boy has to marry a virgin. A good girl from a good family. And he will not choose himself. His father chooses for him. This is the Eastern way. He listens to me in complete obedience. It is not like in Russia, where you can just meet someone on the metro and be kissing the next day. Not here. We are not like that."

However, before the search for a bride really picks up pace—one negotiation is spontaneously initiated in the street on day two, when Sirozhidin bumps into a widow friend with an eligible daughter—I spend an evening with Sirozhidin's remarkable mother. She is sun-dried and frail, but crackling with energy in a bright green dress. To me she is all smiles, gently taking my hand, pouring me tea and conversing with me in broken Russian. But, ever impatient and whimsical, she is quite a handful for her family. Two days after I arrive, she decides that at all costs she has to go to Bukhara. She will not travel by plane, but insists on taking the fourteen hour trip in a hot, unventilated public bus. The temperature is now forty-five degrees, but she will not take "No" for an answer, and screams and waves her fists at Sirozhidin. The performance is repeated on several occasions, until she is hustled off to another son's house for a change of scenery.

The shouting is all in Uzbek, of course. But I am treated to an almost synchronic translation by none other than Sirozhidin. "You see," he tells me with slightly battered pride, "this is how it is with us. My mother screams at me..." Asmira, hurrying back and forth from the kitchen with new dishes in her hand, also chimes in: "She screamed at me too..." "Yes, and she screams at Asmira, too." "She said to me," cuts in Asmira, "don't you dare defend Sirozhidin. I said, Mother, I am not saying a word." "That's right," continues Sirozhidin. "She screams at us, and we have to take it. We cannot raise our voices, we must be absolutely silent. We are obedient. This is our Eastern way. Not like in Russia..."

On another occasion, having returned late from an engagement, Shuhrat is disciplined, loudly and without let-up by his father. But within seconds of the showdown, my host is at my elbow, putting a dish of *non* breads on the table. "You see," he says, equitably. "That is how it is. I can shout at my twenty six year old son, and he does not answer a word. If he said a word— a single word—he would be beaten, ah, so severely. He knows I would break his head. Not a word, you see." Equally, as we are driving to Namangan one day, Zuhra, the five year old daughter of Sirozhidin's eldest son, is treated to a volley of screams. With cheery, tourist-board sangfroid, Sirodzhin turns to me and explains the ruckus: "Zuhra was addressing her cousin using informal language. But he is her elder. She has to learn respect and address her 'o elder brother'. Since I have been away, the respect in this family has been crumbling. I have to set standards again."

All these are lessons in Eastern lifestyle, with "Eastern ethics" in action and on display for me—set up in clear contrast to the culture of Moscow. I begin, now, to understand that these displays of Eastern severity are something that Sirozhidin wants me to see: they are part of the Fergana valley's, of Uzbekistan's, bounty, along with the grapes, the melons, the plov and the *non* bread. They are something Russia does not have. Russia may be wealthier, it may consider itself more "progressive", but it has to import its fruit, it has to import its labor in the form of Uzbek guest-workers, and it will always have a deficit of Eastern ethics and harmony.

And yet there are tensions here. Cold, lawless Russia is Uzbekistan's immediate West, against which Uzbekistan gets to be "Eastern". But Russia, I soon learn, also symbolizes freedom, opportunity and escape.

"I would never let my sons come to Moscow: it would spoil their Eastern upbringing," Sirozhidin had told me quietly, humbly in Moscow, the gentle Eastern guest-worker struggling to feed his family in a hostile foreign clime. But then I discover that Shuhrat worked in St Petersburg and Nizhny Novgorod for four years. "The best years of my life, they were," he will tell me with painful nostalgia. "I had money in my pocket all the time. I had good friends. I had a girlfriend." The youngest son is currently working in Siberia. The eldest spent several years there. But it is the words of Shohruh, the second son, that sets me thinking. He is the only one who has not worked in Russia, having served in the army and subsequently gone into the construction business. For him, staying home is a matter of principle: "Why do Uzbeks work in Russia?! Papa doesn't need to work there anymore. He just does it to get away from the pressures here."

To some extent Shohruh is right. Sirozhidin in fact lives in a home six times the size of an average Moscow flat. The money he earns does not go towards basic necessities like a roof, food and basic living. It goes towards paying to build new houses for his sons in the countryside and towards the enormous dowries they need to get married. These may have become necessities, it is true, but Shohruh is hinting at something more: with their connections they can probably manage these requirements by working in Fergana. Indeed Shohruh is now setting up a restaurant business with his father. What he fears is that Sirozhidin will go off to Moscow again, not so much for money, but freedom. Being Eastern in Russia, it seems, can be more rewarding than being Eastern back home. There is something frivolous about his father's behavior, for Shohruh; it is almost like the crazy habits of Westerners to leave their countries and go on holiday abroad. No Uzbek would do that: after all, there is so much natural beauty beneath his feet.

"Ask no questions...": the sound of silence

And then there is the question of Islam: the Islam that I am meant to be studying, and observing, comparing and investigating. But I slowly—and belatedly, naively—realize that there is a big shadow looming over the Fergana valley, the shadow of another Islam: Islam Karimov (the leader of Uzbekistan until his death in 2016). I am new here, so it takes me time to realize that things are not quite right. Sirozhidin is determined to show me a garden of Eden and he manages to do this for one day, two days, three days... before the silences and omissions begin to get too loud, and he has to break into some stumbling explanations. I have a series of meetings where I bring up the subject of Islam and am promised the world: I will meet an imam; visit a mosque; talk to some teachers.

No doubt if I had gone through official channels all this could have been arranged, and talks on moderate Islam and its popularity been set up. But here I get the view from below, the view of people who know nothing of top-ranking muftis, for whom Muhammad Sodik Muhammad Yusuf is a vague name they only half recognize. Instead, every one of the promises to talk about Islam is quickly shut down, and I never go to a single active mosque (tourist mosques are okay) or meet anyone who can talk for more than five minutes on the subject.

Instead, I realize that I have already been given most of the meaningful information I will get about Islam from Sirozhidin in these lessons about "Eastern" etiquette. I come to believe that Sirozhidin's Russia-contrasting Easternness is also a codeword for Islam. Strong family, patriarchal values, the primacy of males, the obedience of wives, the hierarchical structure of the world: all these things are Eastern. But clearly they are Islamic too: unknowingly (or, perhaps as a fragment of his youthful studies) Sirozhidin is almost repeating the Qur'an word for word when he shows me how he behaves towards his mother:

> Thy Lord has decreed you shall not serve any but Him, and to be good to parents, whether one or both of them attains old age with thee; say not to them 'Fie' neither chide them, but speak unto them words respectful. (Q 17.23).

And yet, while in Moscow he was so keen to emphasize his Arabic studies under Khrushchev, and the Islamic knowledge of his sons, once I am in his home he mysteriously bypasses the opportunity to present this ethical perfection as Qur'anic or Islamic. Rather, it is Eastern, or perhaps Uzbek—although the notion of Uzbekness also contains its own tensions, it turns out.

It is on day two that Sirozhidin's brother arrives with his son: a twenty year old student. Sirozhidin tells me he is studying at an Islamic university in Tashkent. "You can ask him all the questions you want," he urges, keen to observe the laws of hospitality and cater for his guest's requests. The boy arrives; we sit down to tea on a rug in the courtyard under the stars. The family is chatting, so I propose that we go into my room in the innermost part of the house, so that we can speak more easily. I pose some general questions about the Institute he is studying at, and while I switch on some relaxing cheeriness, the boy suddenly becomes aggressively monosyllabic. He emphasizes that his institute has nothing to do with Islam and that he himself has not the least bit of interest in the subject. Four minutes later, his father comes in, and nervously takes over the reins of the interview. He wraps it up with a take it or leave it quotation: "Rasul does not say *namaz*... We have Islam now, just like in Soviet times... religion is free, anyone can do anything." Baffled, I say to Sirozhidin as the pair hurriedly leaves: "I think I might have upset him for some reason." Sirozhidin's own cheerful face is lined with worry: "Yes, you did. You really scared him. In future, let's just address all our questions to Zuhra," he says, referring to his five year old granddaughter. He says no more, not willing to admit to any abnormality in our convivial relations.

I am in a public park a few days later with Shuhrat, and we bump into some of his university classmates. I am presented with an opening that is not of my making. "Our country is doing well," an intelligent-looking youth says, after we have gone through talk of England and abroad. "But we have some problems. The biggest one is extremism. It's all about money you see. People get into these groups as they think it will solve their money problems." I steer the question towards their own thoughts on Islam and for ten minutes I manage to question two of the group about their levels of Islamic observance and that of their parents. It turns out that two members of the group pray five times a day. The other does a rough estimate: in their class of twenty, perhaps four to five are religious like them. "And now if you are under 18," one of them adds, "you can't go to the mosque." The most observant of the students says he is not sure whether that's a sensible law: but what can you do? The law is the law. He himself learnt Arabic from his father, who learnt it from his father, and he learned it from a teacher, back in the day when learning was not under a ban.

Gradually, the lads seem to lose their suspicion of me, and ask me what I think of Islam. I say something to the effect that I am a great admirer of liberal Islam, the type that sees Muhammad as having initiated change and reform in humanity, the starting point rather than the endpoint of new human possibilities. The observant student nods: "Yes, people are not fair about Islam. Take amputation, for instance. It is not as brutal as people make out. It is meant to be done incrementally. First the fingertip, then the finger, then the hand, up to the shoulder..." I nod, struck by how the *hudud* punishments seem to dominate the imagination so thoroughly in all discussions of Islam. Here the imagination only runs to defining non-extremist Islam by a gradual cutting off body parts rather than wholesale amputation.

Finally, the first youth even invites me to come and visit his uncle who is an imam in the medieval town of Margilan down the road. "I will even show you how to do washing." "You mean *wudu?*" I ask, but the term draws a blank. He promises to arrange the visit for Friday through Shuhrat and we part with all-round friendly handshakes. Half an hour later, I am surprised to see the same boys draw up in a car and troop into Sirozhidin's house. Sherzod, sitting in the courtyard with me, tells me they are discussing some money-making scheme, which they want his government connections for. After forty minutes they come out into the courtyard and without so much as acknowledging my presence, walk right past me. Our little conversation on Islam has frozen out all etiquette; I never see them again.

But the bathetic climax comes on our trip to Andijan. "I have a good friend there," Sirozhidin tells me. "He is an imam, very knowledgeable about Islam is Hojji. You can ask questions to your heart's content. He will answer them. We will be," he shiftily acknowledges the necessity, "behind closed doors." The old quarter of Andijan looks like a Middle Eastern city, East Jerusalem or Amman. I soak up the atmosphere. I am in a mood of anticipation, awaiting a scoop. We visit the historic central mosque, and Sirozhidin prods me to ask a man in a booth in the prayer hall some questions about Islam. "Go on. Ask him how many people worship here on Friday." I do. "Six to seven thousand," the man tells me. Sirozhidin looks at me as if, with such a nugget, we may not even need to see Hojji after all. We move on to look at a museum, where I squeeze out of the guide that the building used to house a *medrese* before 1917. "It was reopened as a *medrese* in the nineties," the guide says. "But then they closed it again."

Of course, the elephant in the room concerning this closure, as well as the ban on muezzins and anyone younger than eighteen visiting a mosque, is Karimov's fear of Islam as a challenge to his power. In Andijan itself there was a massacre in May 2005, when demonstrators in the central square that we have just passed through were fired on by troops. The government put the death toll at 187; others put it as high as 1500. Karimov alleged that the demonstrators were members of the Islamic Movement of Uzbekistan, which has ties to Al-Qaeda. Others maintain that the protestors were ordinary people, demonstrating against corruption and repression. In fact, driving along in the white Chevrolet one afternoon, the middle son Shohruh casually mentioned that he was doing army duty in 2005 and had actually been present on May 13 in Andijan. "It was a bit of a fuss, yes. But things have calmed down since then. Even that event was not as major as people make out. There are no extremists anymore." I had shared this with Sirozhidin, giving him more cause for worry. Finally, he said: "He is frightened. He can't say anything else." This was the strongest word he had used so far to describe the frozen situation I seem to have entered into.

We finally arrive at Hojji's. He runs a clothes shop, selling imported Turkish fashion items, and lives above his house. It takes Sirozhidin a long time to find the house, and he explains why. Recently, the government knocked down all the old wooden housing and replaced it with the soulless brick boxes that we are now passing. Instead of a winding old road, a straight highway aiding police force movement goes through the middle of the symmetrical brick dwellings. Hojji's old wooden house has been transformed into one of these clones. But finally, by carefully checking the street numbers, we find it.

Exhausted, we step into his air-conditioned premises with relief. Hojji offers us tea. When tea is finished, I get out my notebook. "All in good time," smiles Hojji. "Let me treat you to lunch first." Upstairs, his hijabed wife prepares plov in the kitchen. His sixteen year old daughter, engaged to be married next year, is veilless and brings us the platters. Russian TV blares in the background, some jiving half-naked female singer. Hojji and Sirozhidin watch as I shovel platefuls of rice into my mouth, burning to get my food obligations out of the way and onto business. Finally, sweating and bloated, I reach into my bag for my notebook.

"Oh Domingo," Hojji says, staring at me with baleful eyes, "I can't talk now. I feel so bad. I need to change my life. I can't even see you straight. I get these blackouts. I need to get away from here. Maybe you know of somewhere in Moscow where I could stay? I haven't been to Moscow for a long time. I would love to come to Moscow! So different from here, so interesting. Let's swap numbers. We should definitely meet up in Moscow."

And thus ends my third attempt to talk openly, albeit behind closed doors, about Islam. As we leave, Sirozhidin feels constrained to divulge one more drop of information. Part of the reason for Hojji's depression is that he is mourning his beautiful old house. He used to have a garden with an orchard. Now he has lost a considerable amount of garden and living space, and to make matters worse, the new house fronts straight onto a busy main road. The government has given him no compensation. Similar projects are afoot in Fergana. Sirozhidin's wife, Asmira, in one of her several paeons to the leader, and perhaps efforts to protect me, explains it thus: "Karimov loves us and is building big roads, big parks. He does everything for us; we are so lucky." Hojji, head throbbing, emanating a black wave of depression, was telling a different story, albeit without words.

Still, when I get back that evening the veil lifts a little. It is another starry night and we are all sitting under the sky in the courtyard. Sirozhidin is telling everyone how he found a *paranja* in the museum shop in Andijan that day (the *paranja* is another persistent theme that follows me round on my trip). Like a terrier, I seize onto this morsel and before Sirozhidin can express his disapproval, I ask his mother whether she used to wear the *paranja* as a child. "Oh yes, when I was little..." she answers. I probe a bit more. "And did you go to Islamic school?" "Oh yes..." The octogenarian brightens up and begins to tell us about her Islamic knowledge. We get onto the subject of Arabic and soon the mother is reciting a Qur'anic sura. She gets through about ten verses before Sirozhidin gets irritated. "OK, OK," he remonstrates, "it's time we close this subject, otherwise she'll never stop."

Asmira comes to the rescue and asks me if I would like to see the family Qur'an. The three of us retreat into the house and Asmira takes out a silk-wrapped Qur'an. I was expecting some old heirloom, but I was mistaken: Sirozhidin bought her this Qur'an when he made *Hajj* in 1993. Her own Islamic knowledge is just as recent: "I was literate in Russian," she tells me. "I could write Russian well. I was well educated, but it was embarrassing for me not to be able to read Arabic." She too made the *hajj* pilgrimage (once, to Sirozhidin's four times) in the mid-nineties, and when she came back, she started to pray *namaz* regularly and take Arabic classes. As far as *namaz* was concerned, her mother had taught her how to do that when she was a child. Now she prays five times a day, "when Hojji is away in Moscow. When he gets back though, I am too busy cooking and cleaning." Little Zuhra often mimics her prostrations, and "I am teaching her some of the *namaz* prayers in Arabic, too."

The three of us take turns reading the opening lines of Sura Ta Sin. When our recitations are over, Asmira puts the Qur'an back in its wrapping. As she does so, she boasts with maternal pride about her sons: "Our eldest, Sherzod has memorized half the Qur'an. Shohruh also knows quite a bit of the Qur'an. They both studied for a while. If you like, you can look at all their books. We still have them in the attic."

Skeletons in the attic: "we have Islam now, just like in Soviet times"

I take Asmira up on that offer a couple of nights before I leave, and this little trip to the attic seems to put a symbolic line under my unsuccessful attempts to find out about Islam in Fergana (or at least one way of approaching the matter). I tread the wooden stairs on the side of the house up to a dusty room. In the corner there are two large boxes with books spilling out of them. I rifle through the pile and find various Arabic grammar and exercise books. Flicking through them, I see work reaching at least an intermediate level. But when I bring up the subject with the two eldest sons, they shrug it off. The eldest in his usual taciturn and unreadable way, his eyes hidden behind ray-bans, murmurs: "That was a long time ago. I have forgotten nearly everything." Gamely Shohruh is even more dismissive of his youthful piety: "Arabic? No, no, I don't know any of that stuff. Religion is a crutch." I remember how on our trip to Namangan, we had stopped at a historic-looking mosque by the roadside. I asked if we could go in and look. Shohruh had got out of the car to investigate. "No entrance, I'm afraid," he had said on reemerging. "People are studying there. It's not for tourists." Asmira, who was sitting in the back, piped up: "That's the kind of place Sherzod studied at when he was learning..." We drove on, letting this reminder of the past dissolve in silence.

And so, the initial Islamic revival of the nineties, which Karimov had thought to integrate smoothly into his own neo-Soviet ideology for a post-communist Uzbekistan, is over—at least for the members of this family and perhaps other "first wave" enthusiasts. The idea that Islam could provide a new, popular platform for social and political life did not quite work out; the religion went back to being heavily policed and under heavy suspicion, as in Soviet times. For Sherzod, his brother, and to some extent his father, too, a limit was reached in how far they could go with Islam: some of that initial utopian enthusiasm is rotting now, gathering dust in an attic. It is not just Karimov, of course; the exigencies of making a living intervened, and perhaps the challenges that can dampen any serious pursuit of a demanding ritual life. The result for Sirozhidin's family, at least, is that attention has shifted elsewhere; meaning is not derived—not directly at least—from Arabic, the

Qur'an, the vexed question of hadiths and Islamic tradition, but instead, something more anodyne is acting as a stop-gap: it is safer and easier to talk of "Eastern values". Perhaps girls, women in an inner room with an eccentric foreign visitor, can "go on" about Islam. And those who reached a higher level or were more securely linked to family traditions can maintain their level; for others, though, a fog of worry obscures their access to the religion.

In Kyrgyzstan, moderates like Malikov are pushing slowly, as gently as they can, to find a form of Islam that will suit their country. Their notion of moderation, the scale it exists on, is partly defined by what has happened here. And what happened here was an attempt by a minority to use Islam as a political tool, to ratchet up the theocratic rhetoric—a naive, clumsy, and mostly imported rhetoric—and turn it on the neo-Soviet establishment. The establishment repaid the favor with harsh measures. There was an immediate blackout, a pall of smoke that clouded the entire issue, and has led to Sirozhidin's, to Hojji's, to Rasul's, intense and jittery nervousness, and indeed to a nervousness that is corroding the entire post-Soviet space. Whether Malikov will have more success in Kyrgyzstan is also far from certain, for the reasons we examined. That phrase of Rasul's father can be looked at from another angle, too. This jumping at shadows, this fear of religion—is it not indeed reminiscent of Soviet times: the bans on youth going to the mosque, the locked doors on *medrese*s and so on? In fact, as I will learn in Dagestan, in this part of the world the term post-Soviet is even a little premature. It is well known that Karimov and Nazarbaev were the last to want to leave the Soviet Union, and that unlike in Russia there was no regime change. But it might go deeper than that spiritually, religiously.

One night, Shohruh comes into my room as I am bedding down for the night. He takes up one of my books that are lying on the couch. It is a Russian book called "Religia posle ateizma (Religion after atheism)." He asks me: "What is atheism?" Thinking the Latinate word might not be in his vocabulary, I use a word with a Russian root, *bezbozhie*, (godlessness), to convey the concept. But this too draws a blank. I have a similar conversation with Asmira, when I ask her if she studied dialectical materialism at school, like most Soviet students. "Remind me again. I have heard the term atheism. But what does it mean?" Asmira had to leave school at sixteen to get married—that is her excuse for not knowing the meaning of the word.

So perhaps the term "after atheism" misses an important point. Soviet propaganda about the triumph of "militant atheism" was just that: often inflated self-deceiving pseudo-ideology.

Atheism simply passed many people by; they never practiced the new substitute religion. They understood it as poorly and ineptly as people now understand the tenets of the revived religions. So for Shohruh, for Asmira, there was no religion after atheism, because there simply was no meaningful atheism. One might say that Karimov is cracking down on Islam, as in Soviet times. Or maybe, the crackdown in Soviet times and the crackdown now are not about ideology, atheism or secularism, but about power. Maybe the crackdown is similar to that of the Egyptian, Syrian or Iraqi governments on certain forms of Islam, or the tsarist crackdown on certain forms of Islam. Maybe the dynamic is "Islam and power", not Islam before or during any so-called atheist regime. Neither atheism nor Islam were ever very orthodox here. Indeed, as countless stories confirm, Islam thrived rather well in the Fergana valley under "atheism".

Perhaps then, in this context, I am being as naïve about Islam as about atheism. Islam is partly about Qur'anic recitation, Arabic studies, *namaz*, ablutions. Those are its most concrete forms. But Islam here is also about the distinct and more intangible self-conscious "Easternness" that Sirozhidin keeps talking about. And here something much more important has been going on under my nose, something that also holds a key to a certain conception of Muslimness: Sirozhidin's quest for Shuhrat's future bride, and his peculiar obsession with the *paranja*.

Paranjas and promiscuity, projects and palaces

The first *paranja* that had elicited Sirozhidin's interest was draped over a mannequin in the museum of the palace of the Kokand emir. A week later I was to visit a museum in Namangan, where the *paranja*'d manikin was now crouching in a cart. In Andijan, the museum shop—a flea market collection of dusty items—actually had a faded old violet *paranja*, replete with eye-grille, for sale. Sirozhidin had asked excitedly whether they could get hold of any more, and the curator promised to contact him within the week. "I have one of these at home," he explained to me, "but I need another one." The appearance of a *paranja* was the most effective way to trigger reminiscences about the Eastern, and even the Islamic, past in Sirozhidin.

In different conversations with his mother, grandmother and other elderly female relatives, we tried to establish when exactly the last woman had been able to walk publicly in the streets of Fergana valley towns veiled from head to toe. Everyone was sure about the twenties: both mother and grandmother had been veiled themselves then. The thirties were a bit hazy, but in conservative towns like Margilan, there must have been *paranjas* on the street. Finally, there is disagreement: Sirozhidin's stubborn mother will not back down with her memory that even after the War women went outside in the *paranja*; she even stretches it to a memory of a *paranja*'d woman in the street in the 1950s. Everyone else is uncertain. But whether or not this is a false memory, everyone can agree that the *paranja* continued its life far longer indoors.

One afternoon we visit Sirozhidin's aunt, who is only a year or two older than him. She lives with her family on the outskirts of Fergana with Sirozhidin's grandmother. The grandmother stays indoors mainly, but is carried out into the courtyard in the late afternoon for some air. She has forgotten her Russian by now, and it is physically difficult for her to speak at all. Nonetheless, she contributes her whispered memories of wearing the *paranja*, as well as a few stories about sacred places and customs she remembers from her youth (the baker who went blind after swearing falsely in the direction of the tomb of Shaykh Mardani).

On that particular occasion, the usual legal *paranja*-talk had led into "nervous" territory again. As his aunt spoke briskly and cheerfully, answering all my questions, Sirozhidin's nose sank deeper and deeper into his cup. Finally, after forty minutes he had said in a weak voice: "I think that's enough. Please let's not have these conversations again. I fear for the children." The problem was that the aunt had strayed from reminiscences about the past to opinions about the present, from ordering a museum-piece *paranja* to speculating about who still wears the *paranja*, permanently and behind closed doors.[1]

"It all depends on what city you are from. Take Margilan, down the road— some of our family is from there. Even in the 1950s, it was very rare to hear Russian there. In Kirgila, it was all Russian-speaking. They opened a factory and lots of Germans came to live there. In Margilan, women never opened the door when visitors called. They'd shout to the men to open the door. Look at Mama over there: she started wearing the *paranja* at 9, and at 12 she got married. That's all considered savagery nowadays....

"Fergana is a Russian town. It was built by Skobelev on the tsar's orders, and settled by Russian soldiers. I went to a Russian school and all our kids finished Russian school. Then I studied in St Petersburg. So, in many ways I feel more Russian than Uzbek. And when it comes to religion, I know hardly anything about it. That's how it is here. It all depends on the city where you grew up. There are three cities where all the children will grow up extremely Islamic, with no exceptions: Namangan, Andijan and Margilan. In other places, it will be mostly atheists. Then you get a mixture: one grandparent will be an atheist, the other a firm believer. It's a fusion. My house is completely European. I am afraid to go into Namangan, to dress freely. My way of thinking is Russian; I get enraged by the Islamists in Margilan. I can't stand them. I don't like going there even to the market, let alone to have dinner with relatives. They're all hypocrites and slow-witted. Of course, you don't see the *paranja* openly there nowadays, but they observe it all behind closed doors."

I was treated to a visit to Margilan myself. On the second evening we went for dinner at the house of Abdul Aziz, Sirozhidin's dentist. The etiquette was to sit on the floor and eat with your hands— the company was all male. Now, listening to the aunt, I understand why: the women were in the back, and no doubt veiled. The aunt had continued: "After 1991, there were huge queues to get a visa to go on *hajj*. People waited for six or seven years. There were so many applicants from the valley. Every Muslim should do three things: pray *namaz* five times a day; observe *uraza*; and go on *hajj*. But I am seventy years old. I can't do *namaz*, because I don't know how to read Arabic. I can't fast, because I am diabetic. And I can't go on *hajj* because I don't have any money! So! But I am Muslim in my heart."

Her husband chipped in: "But not like the Arabs: they fight and kill each other." The aunt nodded and added: "Even most of our traditional Muslims are afraid of an Islamic government coming to power. They are in favor of Karimov. They don't live badly. They get a European education and they are free to practice their Islam. But for me there are too many rules; I am not going to keep that. But we have our Eastern ways; even the Russians admire it. Take Putin's lover, for instance: Alina Kabaeva. She's a Tatar from Uzbekistan: she has her family values. I heard a Russian the other day say: I want to marry a Russian girl, but she should be Uzbek Russian. That way she will be loyal, respect her elders, be hardworking and dutiful. You see: cultures give to each other. It's an era of mass migration, but it pleases me to hear of Russians who live here and admire our Uzbek culture."

Then the climax comes, triggering our departure shortly afterward. "Oh, Karimov is a tyrant, it's true," the aunt beams. "I don't like how he behaves, like he is the new khan. But think about it: we are the only country in Central Asia apart from Turkmenistan that has not had a civil war. Banning beards and so on has its effects: he has the extremists under his thumb now." The aunt adds some details: "The youth join all these Islamic parties, like the one you mention, Hizb at-Tahrir. I had a friend from Margilan. She told me her grandson went to Moscow. He called her up to ask for $2000 and she gave it to him, not suspecting anything. A bit later he called up and said, I have died to you as family. He had joined Hizb, you see."

Sirozhidin is not like his aunt, a fearless hyper-Russified secularist (she used to teach Russian language at Fergana university), whose Eastern pride includes praising Putin's choice of lover. Nor is he like Abdul Aziz, in whose town the *paranja* never had time to gather dust in the attic. Rather, he is limping uneasily between the two, romanticizing the Islamic past, but somehow through a Russian filter, so that it comes out "Eastern". But this odd interweaving of past and present, of Islamic and Russian, of *paranja* as symbolic museum-piece and living item, is observable at every turn.

This is exemplified the day Sirozhidin takes me to the palace of Kokand. The palace is a stocky but diminutive version of similar structures scattered around Afghanistan, Iran and northern India, a definite junior relative of the mosques and palaces in Samarkand and Bukhara. It now lies just on the edge of the town of Kokand. The palace and the town share the same name, but at first sight there does not seem to be much connection between them. One is a gleaming collection of towers and Arabesque-daubed tiles set in a large park; the other is a collection of ramshackle peeling Soviet apartment blocks intersected by honking traffic. But there is an odd subterranean connection.

For a start, the palace museum turns out not to be a museum in the classic sense; its glass-sealed past keeps seeping into the present. For every exhibit we walk past: costumes, pots, utensils, Sirozhidin takes my arm and explains that his mother or grandmother used these things, stored somewhere in their homes now. The courtyards, the vine trellises, the divans set under brick walls—it all seems familiar somehow. It dawns on me: there is no denying that the homes of Sirozhidin's relatives and this palace have definite, if blurred, congruities in their layout.

Then, after the museum, we are invited for lunch by Sirozhidin's friend, a former army buddy who served with him in Siberia ("we had to eat pork then; you couldn't avoid it"). He lives in the heart of Soviet Kokand's "projects". Dank walls, broken garish paint, crumbling concrete: it is all the typical urban immiseration of any provincial Russian town (since the 1870s, the Kokand khanate had been dissolved into one or another form of Russian rule, having to submit as well to its new architectural vagaries). But as we walk into the stairwell, a group of babushkas sitting on a bench in the entrance hurriedly get up and hurry away. I pay no heed, but Sirozhidin, as my cultural guide, excitedly whispers: "Did you notice that?" The older women were not stretching their legs, he clarifies, but rising in the presence of passing males.

Inside, the anonymous Soviet apartment blueprint has also been Easternized: there are no chairs or tables; we sit on the floor, the food on a knee-level dais. We eat with knives and forks, but Sirozhidin whispers that this may be for my benefit. He reminds me of dentist Abdul Aziz's truly Eastern freedom from cutlery. The wall behind us is covered with a rug depicting Mecca. So it seems that while the last native defenders of Kokand's, and Turkestan's, autonomy fled the palace in 1918 as the Red Army pounded the town, the new Soviet order could not immediately erase the habits of centuries.

But, still, what does Sirozhidin need this *paranja* for? Asmira does not even wear a headscarf, and his daughter-in-law (Sherzod's wife) works as a teacher in trousers and shirt. The answer lies in the ongoing hunt for Shuhrat's bride. The bastion of Sirozhidin's Eastern identity is his role as paterfamilias. While he had boasted to me in Moscow that Fergana was the most religious city in the valley, his aunt's explanations have cleared that up. Still, it is a matter of religious seriousness for him to marry off his sons to well-bred virgins. As I will see after visiting two wedding parties, the whole process then involves setting up a room within one's house for the new daughter-in-law, or even building a new house for a longer married son and daughter-in-law. An enormous quantity of clothes, embroidered spreads, and ornate covers must also be bought. Finally, even for a relatively Russified family, the wedding ceremony will involve the bride being draped in a *paranja* and kneeling before her husband in obedience. The difference with Abdul Aziz in Margilan is that the *paranja* will then be taken off, and the girl will join the guests in drinking champagne to celebrate the occasion.

The more I talk to Shuhrat and Shohruh, though, the more I discover that even this aspect of Sirozhidin's Eastern religiosity is being chipped away at. It is not just that the Arabic texts have been cast away into the attic to gather dust, so joining the *paranja*. Other breezes are blowing in from the north and disturbing even these Eastern family values the aunt had praised. Shohruh cheerfully and ironically tells me how his own arranged marriage went. He himself found a girl and was dating her. He then told Papa he had heard of a respectable family with an eligible daughter who he had heard was suitable. Papa threw his energies into arranging the match. The result was that the cunning Shohruh was betrothed with much fanfare to his own girlfriend.

It is a sign of Sirozhidin's gentle and trusting character that he had the wool pulled over his eyes. And there is a lot of wool to go round. I receive a few sermons on the purity of Eastern men and women, compared to degenerate Moscow (which, in turn, excoriates the degenerate West). But this, too, receives a few unwelcome blows from reality, when we are invited one day to drink tea with some of Sirozhidin's more mischievous friends. The conversation, to Sirozhidin's great discomfort, turns not to Karimov this time, but to mistresses and "bits on the side". Shohruh is happy with his wife, but he too lets drop that it is local custom to expand the playing field when the pregnancies lead to weight gain in the wife. To Sirozhidin's credit, he seems shocked by all this and whisks me away as soon as is decently possible according to the laws of Eastern hospitality.

One afternoon, I am driving round town with Shuhrat and for no apparent reason he carries on speeding down the road that heads out of Fergana towards Margilan. We pass his university without slowing down, and I am getting curious. "I have some business to do," he says mysteriously. A few minutes later, he takes a sharp turn to the left. We bump over a potholed road, and take another left turn into some dilapidated Khrushchev blocks. Shuhrat stops the car. "I'll just be a minute," he says, and slams the door. I look out the window: there's a rusting playground with grass growing out of the concrete play area. Dark children, who look like a mix of European and Uzbek, are kicking a deflated football back and forth. The minutes tick by rather uncomfortably.

Finally, Shuhrat comes back, face burning red, lips tight. He starts the engine. "Visiting someone?" I try. "That's my girlfriend," he says. "We just had an argument. It's like this—", he's speeding up over the potholes now, towards the main road, "we've got a baby together. She wants me to marry her. I can't marry her, of course. Papa would go mad. She's been married before, you see. She's half-Uzbek, half-Turkish. Not from a good family, no prospects. Her mother is dead; her father disappeared: he's living somewhere in Russia. It's not our child, actually. It's a friend's child. The girl gave birth to the kid in Russia and died in childbirth, and my girlfriend adopted it and brought it back here. I don't what to do. She's really pressuring me." I recall Shoruh's words about his brother: "A bomb waiting to go off." Even Sirozhidin had teased him a few times: "What'll become of our Romeo? I want to get him a position teaching in the college. But what will he teach? Love?" As we speed back to Sirozhidin's, he turns to me: "Don't tell Papa." I assure him his secret is safe.

This sets me thinking about another Fergana expert on star-crossed love. While at the Palace of Kokand I had bought a dusty Soviet-era Russian translation of the poetry of Babur, the founder of the Mughal dynasty in India, who was born in the Fergana Valley. Some of his love verses come into my mind: "The sanctimonious hypocrite, rubbing his head in the dust, bows to the *mihrab*; but my *mihrab* is your brow, I pray to you alone". No doubt the

Soviets had permitted the publication of Babur's poetry as a local example of anti-religious "secularism". But, of course, in Turco-Persian poetry, metaphors of wine and eroticism were also tropes for the intoxication and yearning brought on by love for the Truth, and the One, Allah. Babur alternated his drugs, drink and concubines with asceticism and piety, and refused to view it as outside of the Path to God. The Soviets had simplistically—rather like the Islamic fundamentalists after them—equated Islam with the observance of a fixed set of dry legal injunctions, and ignored that vaster, more paradoxical Islam that had seeped into poetry, dance and the unpredicatable pulse of everyday life. Perhaps that was my problem, too. I was going to have to look elsewhere for "Islam", to set my sights more broadly. This episode with Shuhrat was, I realized, also potentially Islamic, a dialectical twist in Shuhrat's movement along a more winding Islamic path.

Two evenings later, Shuhrat comes to my room. We chat for a long time. He has good and bad news. On the one hand, he has solved his little dilemma in the suburbs; on the other, there has been more shouting from Papa, who has found another prospective bride. The first issue was solved with audacity: Shuhrat called the girl's bluff and offered to marry her. He began to ring his father. His girlfriend turned out, as he had calculated, to have even colder feet than he did when it came to marriage, and hastily backed down. Meanwhile, the workmen in the courtyard I have been chatting to, friends of Shohruh making some extra cash by working for a friend, are getting near the end of their work. They have been turning two rooms in the wing off the kitchen into an apartment for Shuhrat and his bride-to-be. As is customary, Shohruh will move out, Shuhrat will move in, and when the little brother gets back from Siberia, he will move in with his wife and live with Sirozhidin and Asmira until the end of their lives.

The next hour is spent with Shuhrat complaining and reminiscing. "I am not happy with the work on the rooms. It looks cheap. But what can I do? I have no money here. They are going to press me into picking the cotton harvest again this year. Life in this town is miserable. It wasn't like this in Russia. I had a good circle of friends, mostly Dagestani. They even said I looked Dagestani, and we got on very well. I had no trouble with Russians. There was only one occasion when we were having a barbeque in the forest, and some guys attacked us. If I can persuade Papa, I'll go off to Russia again. Who knows: he might let me... Life isn't life here. And there is no way I am going to marry that girl he thinks he has found me."

I do not reckon his chances of escaping the match very high. But the next day, when the men are all out on business, I talk to Asmira. The conversation turns to this new bride. "Yes," she ruminates, "Hojji has found a girl for Shuhrat.[2] That is what the shouting was about the other day. But I am a bit sad about it, too. The girl's parents are good: one is a scientist, the other a doctor. But the girl wants to study. Shohruh's wife was also a student. She kept doing more degrees. And I had to take care of her children. It was worth it because she is now a head teacher at the college. But I feel too old to be a mother to Shuhrat's children as well. Still, if that is what Hojji has decided..."

Then she puts in a touching request: "I know Hojji wants to go Namangan with you tomorrow. Could you ask him whether he will permit me to come? I could help you to choose some jewelry as a present for your wife." Talking to her, I understand that while she may not wear the legendary *paranja*, the life she leads in many ways reflects a more ancient, a more "Eastern" or Islamic era—confined to the house for most of the time, and dependent on Sirozhidin's permission to go out and about on her own affairs. Sirozhidin goes to Moscow not just for money but for freedom, thinks Shohruh. Are Hojji's Moscow trips perhaps also a relief for Asmira?

I learn more of her life during our various chats: it turns out she was born in traditional Margilan, among what the aunt and Sirozhidin's mother call "the religious hypocrites". Her grandfather was a well known faith-healer. I have a "museum moment" with her, too, in Namangan; permission was granted to travel. Downstairs, there is a perplexing display of dusty cardboard dinosaurs. Upstairs is devoted to local history. There are photographs of Sufi *sheikhs* repressed by the Soviets and the ubiquitous mannequin in a *paranja*. However, it is not the *paranja* that triggers Asmira's reminiscences, but the cart itself: "I remember people used to come to our courtyard in carts like that. People would queue up to see my grandfather. He could heal the deaf, the blind, the lame, through prayer. He knew all the right prayers. Some of his gifts have passed to me. I heal through herbs...." When she was growing up, his family was dekulakized and that is how they fled to more secular Fergana.

In passing, she lets drop an extraordinary fact: that Sirozhidin's father was a Tajik from Dushanbe. I am perplexed. In Moscow, Sirozhidin had mentioned that he knew Tajik "because we have lots of Tajiks visiting Fergana." But in the full ten days we are together, despite all my questions about his origins, he did not mention the real reason for his fluent knowledge of the language. "Don't tell him I told you," Asmira urges. So now I have one more secret to hide from Papa.

I ponder why Sirozhidin did not tell me about his Tajik origins. Probably, in the atmosphere of Uzbek pride it is not something he wants to dwell on. The mutual contempt of the citizens of the five new "-stans" for their neighbors is notorious, each believing they are superior to the other. The Soviet division of Turkestan turned mixed Tajik–Uzbek cities like Bukhara, where bilingualism was the norm, into mono-cultural entities. Mixed origins, like excessive interest in religion, attracts suspicion and needs to be played down. The Soviet period injected new multiculturalism into Central Asia, flooding the area with exiled Chechens, Greeks, Meshket Turks, Crimean Tatars, Germans, Jews and of course Russians and Ukrainians. But after the collapse of the USSR, most of them left, and Fergana has slowly morphed into an almost Uzbek-only city—to the great regret of nearly all the older generation Uzbeks there.

Drinking at the well-springs of power

Asmira widens my perspective in other ways, too. On the last evening, Sirozhidin's nephew has a wedding party a few houses down along the back alley from Sirozhidin's, much to Shuhrat's dismay. It is another knell sounded for his own fate. Asmira leads me to a wizened old woman perched on a bench in the dark entrance way. This is her stepmother—who perfectly illustrates what Sirozhidin's aunt had been saying about the atheist–religious division that cuts through the Valley and the families living there. Apparently, she is a "character", somewhat of a battleaxe, and Sirozhidin generally confines his conversation with her to greeting and pleasantries. "But," Asmira tells me, "she is very clever. She used to be the Party secretary for the region and a teacher. She is still overseer of the *mahallah*. She was a communist, and she still is a communist. Recently, she began to get interested in religion, though. After Karimov came to power, he permitted us to have religion. It was a great gift. It is in people's souls and it will come out in the end."

The stepmother confirms what Asmira has said, and tells me, in much poorer Russian, that she taught herself to read the *namaz* prayers in Arabic recently. I ask her about Asmira's grandfather and his healing powers. Having just returned from a sacred shrine, I also ask her what she thinks of the healing powers of the trees, water and fish that people visit there. The old woman gives a long answer in Uzbek, punctuated by hilarious cackles and dismissive hand gestures. The message of contempt for these superstitious practices is unmistakable, despite my ignorance of Uzbek. Asmira turns stiffly to me and gives a monosyllabic answer that seems to bear no resemblance to what was said at all. I am left to contemplate the complications of a post-Soviet communist *mahallah* leader who reads *namaz* in Arabic and denounces saints and miracle healings: it seems to be another variation of the "Soviet–Avicennan" logic I have seen elsewhere.

At the shrine, though, I encounter a character who does not bother to resort to logic to explain his "religion after/with communism". The Satkek shrine is set in a complex of ponds and trees with healing properties in the shadow of the Alai-Pamir mountains. Pride of place is held by two enormous gnarly trees whose branches are draped in ribbons tied by supplicants, and there are various performers to entertain visitors who have made the pilgrimage there. There is also a museum. I wander in, and start looking around. On one wall there are agricultural artefacts and some costumes; on the other wall is a photographic display of repressed *alims* and Sufi *shaykhs* from the Soviet period. I chat to the curator, who turns out to be the founder of the museum too. He used to teach history and was head of the local Communist Party branch. I pose my usual questions and get plain and direct answers. "Are you religious? Do you pray?" He is, yes, and prays regularly. And in Soviet times? "Oh no, of course not. It was forbidden then. I was persecuting people who did that back then." There is no squeamishness here, simply a statement of fact: a rational transition from bowing at the altar of one great Power and source of life, to bowing at the altar of another Power.

Outside the museum, old ladies are soaking up metaphysical power from still another source. Throwing their arms round the trees, they mutter impassioned imprecations in Uzbek. Shuhrat, who has been let out for the day, translates for me: "O tree take away my pain, o tree bring me healing." He also tells me (perhaps stringing along the questioning foreigner a little) that his brother Shohruh visited this place when his daughter was suffering from jaundice, and the girl was miraculously healed. Shohruh had informed me authoritatively that Uzbeks (and unlike his father he is quite nationalistic, cheerfully insulting a "second-rate" Kyrgyz friend who overtakes us on the road one day) don't go in for tree-hugging: that is something the pagan Russians do. I kept my reservations to myself. But I had not expected him to have participated in this classic Turkic animist practice. Like the Arabic, like religion, it is something he prefers to keep silent about nowadays. Maybe it is just the diffidence of a practical man.

"Our Arabistan": hope and despair

My last night in the Valley arrives, and I spend it with Shuhrat's friends. They have all gathered to celebrate his cousin's wedding the next morning. He is in a dark mood again, as we make our way through the courtyard, squeezing our way past a crowd of embracing women. With a grimace, he says: "That's how they do it here." But he relaxes as soon as he is in the back room among his male friends. There are about ten youths, all of them extremely welcoming and curious. Russia and Uzbekistan are tied by a thousand threads; nearly every single one has worked or is working now in Russia. Some of them have even studied there. Abdul Aziz, the pious Margilan dentist, was seeing off a group of five youths, returning to Kiev to finish their last year at dental college. Mournfully, he commented on the civil war raging there: "It's sad, so sad. We feel it. In Kiev, they are good to our boys."

One of the lads here is studying economics at a college in Moscow and is quick to assure me that "Uzbekistan, Fergana is paradise for us." Another is a Tajik economics teacher, currently teaching at the high school he graduated. A third friend is a video-editor who speaks passingly good intermediate English; a fourth studies in Moscow and also works in a building team with a few of the others, doing European-style refurbishments for luxury apartments. They are curious about the UK and America, about the differences between their traditional lifestyle and that of the West. "Sometimes I would like to live like you," I say in all honesty, "more traditionally, but it's not possible to go back to that." "Yes, and sometimes we would like to live like you," someone answers.

The Moscow student brings up a clip on his phone: it shows the well known priest, Father Dmitry Smirnov, giving a sermon from the altar that praises Muslim immigrant taxi drivers for giving free rides to babushkas and for turning out in such full force for Ramadan: "Where do you find so many people in our churches on a holiday?" the priest laments, "That's why Islam will conquer the world as a religion." Smirnov and others may be flattering these Uzbek young men with their predictions of an Islamic takeover, but as in every other conversation I have had, it soon emerges that the young men are, like Shuhrat, strictly Bairam-only Muslims, who go to the mosque once a year on that festival. As the holder of the Smirnov clip himself admits: "I don't practice anything in Moscow. There's no time."

Still, the conversation crackles on. People throw around their opinions, but having been burned several times I know not to ask for any introductions or visits to mosques and besides, my time here is up. Speaking of Islam and Christianity, someone opines: "You go to the mosque. They teach you *namaz*; that's the goal of religion. I would never go to a church. That's Orthodoxy. I don't know what the difference is exactly. I'm not saying Islam is better. Everyone should believe in God. Russians believe in God too." Another chips in: "I believe in God. I watched this program which proved the existence of God very convincingly. It talked about the pyramids and aliens. How can scientists not believe in God with all these mysteries?"

With inexorable logic, one of the company eventually touches on the topic of extremism: "When I was in Petersburg, I was in a shop once and some guy invited me to a meeting. He showed me some brochures. He said, we just meet in apartments to discuss interesting questions. But they warned us in the army about Wahhabis, so I didn't go. I just tore up the brochure.... I go to the mosque once a year on Bairam. I don't do *namaz*. I'll do that when I am older. But now when you are sinful you can't do *namaz*. You shout at someone and then go off to pray. It's worse to be sinful and religiously observant. Better just be sinful and not keep the rituals. When I get to the stage of purifying myself of my temper, then I'll do the rituals. Also, I know that those people who approached me in the shop are not real Muslims: in Islam you do it when you want to. We don't go round forcing people to be religious, which is what they were doing."

Responsibilities are shouldered early for this group of young men. They have to sweat to gather together the dowry for their future brides, and to build the houses for their burgeoning extended families. There's no time for "variety", for self-discovery, for holidays in Spain and Turkey. The routine is simple: knuckle down in Russia for a few years. Let your hair down a bit, live it up perhaps, but not to the extent that it interferes with the main purpose of life. "We'd all probably like a bit more 'variety'," the Moscow student says, using what has become a codeword for a more morally loose and free lifestyle. "And lots of people do have some 'variety' on the side. But in our 'Arabistan', that's still considered a sin, whereas in the West, it's considered normal, not immoral. That's the difference." "Yes. You might consider our lives hard. But what else can we do? That's what we were born into; we don't know any other way."

Farewell: Russia and her East in anxious embrace

And so my visit comes to an end. Sirozhidin's "East" is seething with tensions. It is locked in an unbreakable embrace—economic but also cultural and spiritual—with its Russian West. People go to Russia to work, but they also go, like Sirozhidin, to find some freedom; it was Hojji's dream, in Andijan, to escape his blackouts and headaches, by spending some weeks in that great northern capital. But the love-hate affair goes both ways, too. It is not just Uzbeks that supplement their existence with Russian money and mores. As we will see in later chapters, there are Russians who look with admiration and longing to the East, seeing it as a source of traditional values, a hearth of Eurasian tradition that can lead Russia towards her own destiny. When I get back, in fact, Alexei asks me how my trip has been and sets out to stay with Sirozhidin two months later. Despite being an Orthodox Christian (with his own admixture of paganism and syncretistic interpretation), he has a penchant for traveling to Russia's East: he spent two months in Chechnya, too, where he admired the strict, patriarchal families and obedient children.

And what of Islam? It is, I had discovered, more intimately interwoven with these lives, than I had assumed. The Soviet dream had been to eradicate it by changing the Arabic script in which Uzbek was written first into Latin and then Cyrillic, by abolishing the *paranja*, by closing the mosques and *medreses*, and so on. But so much of Islam was oral, had already blended into customs and habits and seeped into the marrow of people's being, that it could survive this brutal hiccup. Far more tolerant than Christianity towards shamanism and local lore and language, Islam also found space for aspects of the Soviet project (to such an extent that its glaring atheism seems to have been overlooked by Asmira and those like her). Nonetheless, this resurfacing of Islam from underground to overground, its re-inhabiting of its old forms has been accompanied by trauma. And, as I would keep discovering in my conversations across post-Soviet Eurasia, the key trauma was the anxiety over extremism: the fear that oral, customary, instinctual forms would suddenly be substituted for the bookish literalism of the radical Salafi approach. And so the people I encountered seemed to be operating in a fog of anxiety and uncertainty, taking up the religion again, but uncertain of its ultimate limits, boundaries, and possible meanings. Some of the Uzbeks I had been meeting were still jumping at shadows, desperate not to offend Karimov's often arbitrary notions of what might and might not constitute extremism. Perhaps this explained the nervousness that I kept encountering. Indeed, when I get back to Moscow, Alexei confirms that the tension surrounding extremism even affected people's perceptions of me.

"Nobody believed you were an academic; they just couldn't square it with the beard. Only after a bit did they begin to warm to you." The implication is that I was after something else, a spy, perhaps, or, given my unruly beard, a secret extremist: beards have come under a strange ban in Uzbekistan, as yet another marker of extremism. This had its comic aspect: I had started my trip with a long beard. Sirozhidin persuaded me—rather forcibly, his nervousness rising again—to get it trimmed on day two, before we went to Andijan. On night five at dinner, after consultation with the other men round the table, Abdul Aziz the dentist had decided I was still too hirsute and practically manhandled me into the local barber, where by electric light, the whirring of moths and the curious faces of a dozen villagers, the man cheerfully stripped my face almost as bare as everyone else's—with a cutthroat razor.

This rhetoric of suspicion and fear constantly provokes troubling thoughts, unleashing censorship and self-censorship. The fear of extremism corrodes everything; the middle ground becomes interesting only as a potential feeder into extremism.[3] Even clinical psychosis begins to wrap itself in the spectral form of repressed Islamism. A year and a half after I get back from Fergana, Moscow and Russia at large is shocked to the core by the bizarre case of Gulchehra Boboqulova. A native of Samarkand, she worked as a fruit-seller and nanny in Moscow for several years. Then in February 2016, she beheaded the little girl she was caring for and spent half an hour wandering up and down the pavement outside the metro with the head in her hand before the police detained her. All the while, she was chanting monotonously that she was a terrorist who was going to blow herself up. In police custody, she was filmed explaining her actions: "Putin is bombing us with planes. Why are you bombing us Muslims, why no one saying anything? They also want to live." A male voice, she contended, the voice of Allah, had told her to take revenge for all this, and she was now going to travel to Syria.

Some nationalist voices cried, "We told you so!" in the Moscow press. But generally, the mood was one of shock and pity—Boboqulova was not really an Islamist terrorist but had, as the court acknowledged, a detailed history as a psychiatric patient—and the Islamist or migrant card was not played. For indeed, to succumb to the dark silences and suspicions is corrosive. Despite the shadows, I also managed to glimpse an Islam that refuses to let itself be swallowed up entirely by the anxiety of suspicion. As Asmira had said: "Religion is in people's souls; it will come out." There was the fear, but there was also the quiet attempt to go on seeking God, to go on drawing on the well of past tradition. There was Asmira and her granddaughter praying *namaz* together; Sirozhidin's mother reciting the Qur'an; Shohruh, affecting hard-bitten cynicism, reading his Qur'anic prayer by the healing tree for his daughter's health; even the eldest Sherzod, whose Arabic books are stacked in the attic,

RUSSIA'S MUSLIM HEARTLANDS

admits: "When the time comes, I will teach my son Arabic, of course." He, too, affects a worldly cynicism, but the memory is lodged—he had memorized half the Qur'an at one point, after all—and something sweet remains. Alexei tells me that when he visited, Sirozhidin joined in a long session of Qur'anic chanting with his mother and grandmother, while Alexei, looked on, touched, overwhelmed by this sudden display of the spirit. When I was there, he had told his mother to stop "going on". In my absence, his heart had opened.

It is good that Alexei was present at this family *zikr*. Russia and the East are not as distant as, say, England and India were. Before the Russians conquered Turkestan, the Mongols had ruled Russia; then the dynamic was reversed. West and East rub along side by side here, with no sea to separate them. If we invoke the notion of *wasatiyya* again, we can see a Russian–Turkic fusion precisely in Sirozhidin. He is negotiating two extremes: the stubborn ancient ways of Margilan, Asmira's birthplace; and the utter loss of identity in Russianness, which has almost swallowed up his aunt on the outskirts of Fergana. This, too, this negotiation of different combinations of Easternness and Westernness, their bleeding into each other, is undoubtedly, a part of Fergana's story, and also a part of Russia's. Fergana may have ceased to be just another Russian region more than a century ago, but mass migration makes a mockery of borders. In my brief visit, I had talked to about twenty members of Sirozhidin's circle. But their choices and dilemmas are replicated on a far larger scale: 2.3 million Uzbeks now work in Russia; some of them are semi-permanent residents, some have taken citizenship. And the different waves of identity will roll through these masses, producing all sorts of permutations.

One researcher[4] found that Central Asian migrants often head for Russia's Islamic regions on the Volga, where they feel more comfortable. There, as a migrant Uzbek woman worker said, "people respect us more." She also added: "When Putin visited Tatarstan [her new place of residence], the Tatars did not greet him in traditional costume and with *chick-chak* [a Tatar sweet]. But, *alhamdulillah*, our Uzbeks came out and did our dances and brought our cuisine for him." There is a pride in these words that echoes Sirozhidin's secular aunt: "See! we Easterners, we Muslims, even though newly arrived, can be more patriotic about Russia than Russia's own native Muslims."

And surely, in time, despite the prognoses of the pessimists and exclusivists, these Uzbek Russians, the ones who do not return home, who are a mirror image of the Russianized Uzbeks in Uzbekistan, will grow roots and gently reshape the native landscape of Russian Islam, of Russia's East, and even of Russia itself.

PART THREE

VOLGA STOP-OVER

4.

TATARSTAN: AMONG THE ARTISTS

"Scratch a Tatar..."

The following summer, I spend a week in Kazan, the capital of Tatarstan. My host is Farit Valiullin, a monumental artist who teaches at Kazan university and specializes in Tatar and Muslim architecture. Among his major works, he designed the interior of the Kul Sharif mosque and created a mosaic depicting the Volga Bulgarian king's acceptance of Islam (on show in the museum complex in the city of Bulgar). He is also designing a mosque in his hometown of Zelenodolsk. As he guides me round his homeland, he introduces me to other artists, as well as writers and cultural figures, my journey into Russian Islamic identity in Tatarstan taking on an aesthetic hue.

Kazan is a good place to explore the themes of Easternness, "moderation", and Russia's "Eurasian" identity. Naturally, it is also a good place to inquire about the nature of modern Tatar identity and Tatar Islam. The republic of Tatarstan bears both similarities and differences to Uzbekistan and Kyrgyzstan. The similarities include the fact that it owes its very existence to early Soviet power. Before Lenin, the region was known simply as the Kazan *gubernia*—just as the Kazakh steppe and parts of the Fergana valley emirates were also swallowed up into Russian administrative districts. Kazan was a Russian city par excellence, the home of the Kazan icon of the Mother of God, and host to numerous famous students such as Tolstoy and Lenin. Its non-

Christian subjects were simply Volga Muslims; the term Tatar was too broad, referring as it did to Turkic Muslims in the Russian empire all the way to Azerbaijan. Eventually, the term Tatar became part of the new republic's name, but it was a compromise choice. Many argued that the term Bulgar would have been more accurate, and the ruins of Bulgar two hundred kilometers south of Kazan are still viewed as the place where Volga Muslims' roots and identity really lie.

Unlike Kyrgyzstan and Uzbekistan, however, Tatarstan did not gain independence after the collapse of the USSR. Geographically and culturally, the Volga Muslim regions form the northern tip of central Asian Islamic lands stretching from Bukhara to Kazan, and taking in Ufa and Orenburg. But today in Bashkortostan and Tatarstan, Bashkirs and Tatars comprise only 35 per cent and 52 per cent of the overall population respectively, and they are surrounded by other Russian republics. This made it difficult for Tatar nationalists to realistically fight for independence, despite efforts in the nineties. Instead, the Tatars settled for autonomy. Unlike Kyrgyzstan, therefore, the accidents of geography, along with human gerrymandering, mean that Tatarstan has only a weak "Muslim" majority, and is surrounded and intertwined with Orthodox Russians as well as pagan Mordvins and Udmurts.

The result is that ties with Russia, Christianity and non-Muslim ethnicities are far more intimate than across the southern "Asian" border. Malikov's dream of evolution towards an Islamic state would look revolutionary here. There is also more than a grain of truth in Shuhrat's statement: "I wouldn't recognize Tatars in the street. They look Russian, don't they?" Napoleon famously said, "Scratch a Russian and you will find a Tatar", and the Russian aristocracy often liked to play up their Tatar roots. But one might reverse the saying: "Scratch a Tatar, and you will find a Russian." All this was brought home to me in my conversations and travels with Farit.

Farit: new Muslim, new art

Farit's life is deeply intertwined with Kazan. He grew up in the shadow of the eighteenth century Azimov mosque in the Tatar *sloboda* (quarter) in the 1960s. The house had been built by his grandparents who, due to successive expulsions of Kazan Tatars by Russians, had been born in the Siberian Altai region near Mongolia.[1] Ironically, it was thanks to Soviet dekulakization of Siberian peasants that they ended up fleeing back to their ancestral city. Farit's parents, like most people in the district, were factory workers, who labored ten to twelve hours a day, leaving them little time for family. It was these rough circumstances that contributed to Kazan becoming one of the criminal capitals of the Soviet Union. "Our sort had no time for family. It was work and then drink," he recalls. Indeed, onlookers thought it would be Kazan rather than Grozny in Chechnya, that would explode into separatist violence. Farit himself remembers attending nationalist rallies in the early nineties:

"There were crowded halls, with everybody standing up in their seats and waving their fists, shouting 'Freedom, freedom', but the way they said the word it sounded like Hitler's fascists. They too were criminals. Then we had delegations of Chechens coming over and stirring things up. I was glad I got out of that." He has only praise for Tatarstan's first president, Shaimiev: "He's balanced, he's a centrist: we have to help our neighbors, we can't just cut ourselves off from Russia. That's nonsense."

In the late seventies he moved to Moscow and studied art, turning out the social–realist works that were expected of Soviet artists in those days. In his twenties he married a half-Indian woman, by whom he has a daughter. Recently he attended his granddaughter's baptism in an Orthodox church—a common instance of Tatar–Russian interaction, due to the high rates of intermarriage. His second wife is Tatar, but like most Tatars she is very secular and Farit's turn to religion only occurred five years ago.

This turn was precipitated by a life crisis and, as with Kyrgyz Gulnara or Moscow Askhat, Christianity was certainly on the table as an option. Farit defaulted on a business deal due to the bribes his partners had to pay to corrupt officials, and nearly suffered a heart attack. He was in Kiev at the time, and went to the main cathedral there and lit a candle, praying to God to save him. "But I never had any need for praying to Jesus, to a man. What would be the point of that?" A sense of pride in his ancestors' struggles to preserve Islam pushed him to investigate this option more deeply. For the first few years after his "return" to faith, he gradually increased his prayers, but he did not fast during Ramadan; he was too frightened. In time, however, that too came, and now he belongs to a Sufi brotherhood and performs the five prayers scrupulously, as well as avoiding all non-halal foods. All this gives him peace of mind, and helps him avoid the trials and traumas of what he sees as the Americanization of post-Soviet Russia.

The Tatar *sloboda* is the first place Farit wants to show me. In 2015 the district is a striking contrast to the rough neighborhood of Farit's youth. It boasts newly paved, gentrified and flower-bedecked streets. Its whitewashed, restored mosques and intimate cafés are frequented by fashionably hijabed women, and stores selling Islamic books entice strollers to come in and browse. In tsarist times, it functioned as a pale of settlement for the Tatars, keeping them on the other side of the river from the main Russian town, but now it has become a symbol of revived Islamic identity and testament to Shaimiev's successful negotiation of real autonomy for his republic. Farit takes me to visit the three restored stone mosques on its main street, and then we walk past the Muhammadiya *medrese*, before eating lunch at a café and then visiting the Qayyum Nasiri museum. In the coming days, I return to this quarter several times, with and without Farit. I meet there with several people who add to my appreciation of the city: Ramil, another Tatar artist who specializes in original calligraphy; Ildar, a novelist from Nizhny Novgorod who has relocated to Kazan; and Vladimir Popov, a nationally famous ninety-two-year-old artist, whose work and life blurs the boundaries between Russianness and Muslimness in extraordinary ways.

On the first day, as we walk past the Muhammadiya *medrese*, Farit is keen to tell me a little of its history. It was a center of learning for Volga Muslims before 1917, and was converted back into a functioning Islamic school in the 1990s. But for Farit, perhaps its most significant meaning lies in the fact that Baki Urmanche studied here. Urmanche, who lived from 1897 to 1990, became Tatarstan's first nationally prestigious artist and Farit later takes me to the house museum where his works are exhibited, as well as introducing me to a friend of his who was his student and assistant.

Urmanche began life as a pious Muslim boy, and as a teenager studied Islamic law and Sufism in the Muhammadiya *medrese*. However, his artistic interests took him away from religion (the estrangement began when his orthodox father broke the violin that the artistic youngster had carved out of a piece of wood), and this was a story repeated across the board. Several leading Tatar writers and artists started their intellectual lives as Muhammadiya *mudarisses*, and then left religion for culture, contributing to the new Soviet Tatar identity. But in the 1980s, as religion and Islamic culture began to make a comeback, Urmanche also began drawing Islamic calligraphic works again and praying *namaz*, so coming full circle to his early Sufi training. For Farit, Urmanche's mystical Islamic sensitivities, his original art, and his bridging of pre- and post-Soviet history hold the key to how he himself can combine the role of artist, Muslim, and Tatar, and his name crops up often in our conversations.

The other building Farit wants me to see is the museum of Qayyum Nasiri. It sits further along the same street as the *medrese*, and is a stout wooden house with two floors that recalls a typical Russian merchant cabin. Nasiri (1825–1902) represents an earlier stage on the path to modern Tatar identity: he was a *jadid*-reformer even before that movement had really got off the ground. His activities included setting up a Russian-language school for Tatar peasant children, where they studied from textbooks, atlases, grammar books and compendiums that he himself had composed in modern Tatar. This emphasis on secular knowledge outraged the traditionalists, and in his last years he led an isolated life in the house, busying himself with his herb and flower garden, as well as devoting himself to cooking and writing recipe books. Nasiri also wrote the first grammar of the Kazan Tatar dialect, a doubly distasteful achievement for the traditionalists. Firstly, they could not understand why anyone would write a grammar of a language spoken by the common people. And secondly, Nasiri used this grammar to teach Tatar to Russian students at the Kazan seminary set up by the famous missionary Ilminski: so, in effect, he was helping the Russians to convert Tatars to Christianity.

But the missionaries were never very successful, and Nasiri set a famous precedent: he found a way to translate medieval Arab–Islamic ideals of literacy into vernacular European ideals. His post as a teacher in a Russian institute was among the very first occasions when Eastern scholarship gained Western recognition; Hussain Faizkhanov (1823-1866) taught at St Petersburg university, and also wrote Tatar history using the latest methods of European historical scholarship. The achievements of these pioneers are still celebrated today. "There is no such thing as an uneducated Tatar," Farit tells me in the museum, and Gulsina, our hijabed guide, smiles and agrees. It is men like Nasiri that built the foundations of this modern literacy, and Gulsina proudly quotes me the words of Karl Fuchs, a German historian who lived in Kazan, that "the Tatars are more educated than many European nations", a quote that is engraved beneath his statue in one of the city parks.

Walking through the dark-beamed rooms of Nasiri's house, where his "missionary" grammar and children's encyclopedias are on display, and then wandering into his kitchen and garden, evokes comparisons with Tolstoy, who also liked to alternate his literary activity with teaching children and leading an active life close to nature. When Farit takes me to meet Ramil Harimau the next day, I feel that Nasiri's combination of craftsmanship, secular knowledge, Tatar pride and religiosity is still alive. There are also echoes of Baki

Urmanche, as I discover when Ramil tells me he is a keen woodcarver—except that unlike Uramanche's ill-fated violin, Ramil makes bows for archery.

Ramil lives in a new tower block opposite the Azimov mosque, not far from where Farit himself was born. A gangly man of forty-odd years wearing a gray skullcap, he seems kind but nervous as we shake hands for the first time. Farit later explains that he is suffering from exhaustion, having just finished a big calligraphic commission for the Tatarstan muftiat. Unfortunately, and it is not the first time, they have not paid him for his work, and he is struggling to make ends meet. As we chat, it emerges that his discovery of Islam has brought him not only spiritual contentment, but also trouble and sorrow. The shadow of suspicion and anxiety that hung over the Fergana valley is not entirely absent here, either.

To begin with, Ramil shows me samples of his work on the computer. As with Nasiri and Urmanche, he combines the ancient and the modern. One work is a Qur'anic verse that will hang over a technical college in an Arab country. Ramil has made the letters look like an engineering circuit board. "No one else does calligraphy like that. He's unique," Farit says with almost paternal pride. However, his originality is firmly rooted in the traditional science of Arabic calligraphy: Ramil trained for eight years, between 1989 and 1997, to become an Islamic calligrapher in Istanbul, sitting at the foot of a well known master while studying Islam as well, and eventually getting *ijaza* from him (the traditional name for the degree that is passed on down a strict line of transmission).

Ramil's story of how he moved towards Islamic observance departs from the frequent narrative of refuge from life troubles. "When I was in my late teens," he recalls, "I started doing Chinese and Japanese martial arts. I began to get interested in the culture, including the music. It was the music that first made me think about the similarities of these cultures with Tatar music, and then I began to get interested in my own culture. I started to trace how these links were formed, often through the Mongols, and that eventually led me into finding more out about Islam. Chinese culture is much higher than our culture; we lost a lot of ours, although some of it is preserved in the villages. In the sixteenth century we had very advanced and beautiful calligraphy, but then it degenerated. We need to rediscover that level, to raise the culture again."

The music and the martial arts also extended into his hobby of making bows. Leading us into the small bedroom of his cramped apartment (which he shares with his wife and small daughter), he reaches up onto the top of the wardrobe and pulls down two specimens in progress. "There are four different types," he explains: "Tatar, Indian, Chinese, and Persian." Then he shows me the five parts into which the bow is segmented from a smooth piece of birch, with all the pieces bound tightly together with glue made from the sturgeon. He bends it back and forward for me to show me its strength. All this artistic heritage, it seems, comes from and was encouraged by his parents: both of them are architects and his mother draws for pleasure, while his father works in wood. Ramil tells me that there are strict limitations on what you can do within the canons of calligraphy. "You can take an *alif*[2] for example, and bend it this way, or that way, but not this way." Again, rather like one of his bows. He traces for me the shape of an *alif* snaking a way through one of his pieces.

The talk turns to his Islamic life today, and here more shadows begin to emerge. Although he lives within walking distance of Kazan's beautiful historical mosques, he does not spend any longer in them than his religious duties require. His dealings with the muftiat are minimal, too. Corner-cutting, broken promises, unpaid work, interfering bureaucrats are a constant blight on his dealings with them. Farit nods his head fatalistically. This is Russia, after all. What else can you expect? Religious officials are still bureaucrats; they indulge in the same sins as their secular counterparts.

But Ramil had even worse problems in the past. When he moved back to Tatarstan from Turkey, he had a stint in jail. Farit tells me the details after we have left. The authorities saw an observant Muslim who was also showing a heavy interest in martial arts and concluded he was an extremist. In the 1990s, as elsewhere in Russia, many of the revived *medreses* were funded and manned with Saudi assistance, leading to the rise of a primitive Salafism that often combined with or sometimes replaced Tatar nationalism. As recently as 2012, a group claiming links with the Caucasus Emirate shot dead the assistant mufti Valiulla Yakupov and laid a car bomb under the vehicle of chief mufti Ildus Faizov, who was wounded but not killed. Ramil was lucky, in that his mother is a well known figure in Tatarstan. She went to the police station and kicked up a fuss, and they eventually released him. But, as Farit says: "He was fortunate. A lot of people go into prison and never come out. They just disappear into the system."

How the authorities could have taken the softly-spoken, wiry Ramil with his Turkish calligraphic education for a Salafist is a mystery. But, along with everything else, it has left Ramil shaken and isolated: "It's easier to be a Muslim in Turkey," he reminisces mournfully. "I try not to mix with Muslims here, even in the mosques. There's always the possibility of problems with the authorities. They might suspect that you are a Wahhabi. I try not to talk to the muftis either. But that's me, I suppose. I am quite isolated. I only have two friends. One of them reads *namaz*, the other doesn't. It's hard living like that, but that's how it is." Farit nods sympathetically. Later he tells me that he also avoids praying in mosques, only attending the local mosque once in a while out of respect for his local imam, "because I belong to a Sufi order, and we are forbidden from going to the mosque, we have our own *jamaat* (community)."

After the meeting with Ramil, Farit drives me back across the river to his studio, which is just outside the inner ring of Kazan city, near a park. This is where I am sleeping: on a truckle bed amid his finished and unfinished canvases. The building is a concrete 1960s structure that contains various exhibition halls and galleries. The walls of the corridor where the artists' studios are located are covered in strange papier mache 3-D Qur'anic calligraphy that looks like an unsuccessful early attempt to combine post-Soviet freedom with new religious sentiments. Each evening, I lie back against the wall and read from a book Farit has put in my hands. It is a collection of essays about Urmanche, edited by his daughter. "If you want to understand how I see the role of the artist, that is where you should look," he assures me. It also turns out to be a useful insight into the mind of another artist I will meet in the coming days, Vladimir Popov.

Urmanche was particularly fired by an aphorism from Goethe that Farit too likes to quote: *Sapienti sat* (the knower knows). The artist is said to go beyond the philosopher in reaching the principles that underlie the world. Philosophers use reason, but art transcends reason; in this sense, art is a science which gets to the real essence of the world. I read in the book: "Precisely for this reason the artist–thinker is necessary for society. He is called upon to draw other people after him, who have only passed through the school of rational understanding of the world... *Sapienti sat*: the knower knows... in the language of the seer means that only he who is initiated into the mysteries of sacred teaching can attain a true understanding of what been said."

Urmanche, it seems, thus managed to survive as an artist in the Soviet period, as the Goethean approach allows for the artist to serve and beautify the state—though this was not entirely unproblematic: Urmanche spent ten years in Solovki, the Soviet prison camp. This neo-Soviet Goethean aesthetic mysticism also permeates Farit's worldview. He tells me on one occasion that he "believes in an optimistic, life-affirming, joy-giving art, which is thus true to the spirit of Islam." At another point he invokes a technical get-out clause for his painting of the human figure: "It is acceptable to paint portraits in Islam," he argues, "as long as they do not cast shadows, and then they are considered

116

'conditional' portraits, more like symbols than representing the reality. Unlike with Christian icons, we must not idolize our art; our work must not provoke passion or adoration. Those are the principles I try to follow." Later he shows me the sketch for a mosaic of the acceptance by the Bulgars of Islam, and it is true that the figures of the Bulgar chiefs and Arab visitors cast no shadows. He continues: "I draw to express my love for Allah: that is my credo as an artist. I draw the line at sculpture, as sculpture obviously casts a shadow and can encourage idolatry." As if to bear testimony to his words, on the floor of the small canvass-stacked room that abuts the main studio, Farit's prayer rug is laid out, permanently tilted in the direction of Mecca.

On our second day, Farit takes me to a retrospective exhibition at a gallery near the Kremlin and the question of how Farit survives as a devout Muslim in the art world comes up for me again. A good sprinkling of Kazan's creative elite are gathered there, artists and writers, and even a few politicians. After the speeches, there is a buffet for the artist's friends; the atmosphere is one of slightly boozy bonhomie, and I wonder amid the wine-sipping camaraderie what his long-haired colleagues make of his piety. "Artists are free souls," says Farit. "I don't jump to make judgments. I made a decision not to be a short-trousered freak. Talgat Tajuddin, who is a Sufi, came to our mosque and gave a sermon about a devout Muslim who prayed all day but did not support his family, leaving that task to his brother. The Prophet reprimanded him: your brother has chosen the right path. So I don't believe in isolation. Of course, I don't socialize too much with that sort of crowd but I don't wall myself off somewhere."

On the other hand, listening to the speeches and looking at the canvases, I realize that it is probably easier for Farit to fit in here than, say, with the Damien Hirst brigade in Shoreditch, London: there is still a strong whiff of social realism in the paintings and in how people talk about the duty of the artist to contribute to Tatarstan's civil society. So Farit does not sound that off base compared to the general tenor of the gathering when he tells me that, "An artist must remember he is an artist and not just be a painter, a dabbler. He must contribute to his culture, and remember which Republic he is living in, and what he will leave behind."

But the Goethean romantic approach, mixed in with Urmanche's Muhammadiya-inspired Sufism, contains a strong Romantic pantheistic element that also resonated with certain aspects of the Soviet worldview. Despite the regime's ideological atheism, Soviet cultural and even scientific figures were far more open to the occult, the esoteric and the mystical than

Western figures. Urmanche's daughter formulated these links in her own way; for her, the Muhammadiya *medrese* of her father's youth was not just a dry religious academy but a school for the soul, which in her essay she likens to the training undergone by the ancient Greek philosophers: like the ancient pagans, the pupils in the strongly Sufi-oriented *medrese* were taught to break through the barrier of the "I" into universal consciousness and creativity.

Urmanche seemed to have retained Sufi elements in his worldview, mixed in with overtly pagan elements—again, features that I detect in Farit's own worldview, and then even more strongly in Vladimir Popov. At the age of forty, Urmanche claimed to have had a vision on the banks of the Volga, recording the strange event in a poem, which I translate into my notebook:

.... Looking down...I saw rising out of the water

And lying on the bank Someone

To be more precise, if I am not mistaken,

The Water King

Looking like a warrior of old, gray old man Korkut.

He spread his great body on the amber sand

In the form of a person, but without arms and legs;

The upper part was human, the rest like a fish,

Though the face and beard were true Adam.

A mysterious vision, only the outward appearance of the creature —

But who was this, what was he doing here?

What sort of soul was his, dangerous or not?

I don't know the truth.

This vision would serve as a guide for Urmanche's artistic vision in life, and was, his daughter writes, his first stage onto the path to clairvoyancy: from then on he used the faculty of the imagination to penetrate the true forms underlying reality. It was due to this creativity and sense of unity with the world that Urmanche discovered the inner strength to survive the harsh fate the befell him during the Stalinist years, when he was imprisoned in Solovki. Oddly enough, it seems that Urmanche's time on Solovki overlapped with that of Pavel Florensky, an influential Russian Orthodox priest and philosopher, who also combined a Goethean religiosity with an interest in the occult, the pagan and the esoteric. Attempting to see the positive side of the new Soviet regime, he remained in Russia rather than emigrating, out of a mystical attachment to his motherland. The two Solovki inmates, one Muslim and the other Christian, bear witness to the strange congruities and paradoxes of Russian religion in conditions of Soviet existence.

I find out more later about Farit's own spiritual path, but in the meantime the theme of Russian Christianity and Islam and the odd spiritual ecumenism of Soviet artistic creativity arise in sharpened form when I meet Vladimir Popov.

Vladimir Popov: Lenin—genius—Islam

A Moscow acquaintance had urged me to look up Popov if I was ever in Kazan, promising he would illuminate for me the nature of Islam in Tatarstan. Farit, too, is acquainted with Popov, and hands me an album of a recent retrospective exhibition to look through. Popov is now ninety-two and began his work in the late 1950s. The early pages of the album contain socialist realist works: a combine harvester turning the soil in the newly developed farmlands of Kazakhstan, the construction of a new plant in a Siberian city. In the 1980s there are canvases depicting landscapes in a style that echoes the sacred, cosmist sensibility of Nicolai Roerich. In the 1990s, Popov seems to have moved from depicting Siberia and Kazakhstan towards ancient Uzbek cities and landscapes in Turkmenistan.

In the early 2000s, though, form and figure disappear entirely: the final pages are all filled with dynamic Arabic calligraphy. A portrait of the artist in the front shows him in his late eighties, smiling, and sporting a long beard and shaved upper lip, seemingly in Muslim style. I know, too, that his calligraphic works are displayed by the Moscow muftis at various exhibitions and even adorn the offices opposite the Cathedral mosque. Thus I am burning with curiosity to know how a young Soviet artist has gradually metamorphosed through Roerichean mysticism into an Islamic artist.

Popov invites me to his home for dinner. His apartment is situated opposite the main Bauman precinct, and while I am waiting for his assistant and favored student, a young Tatar artist called Gulnaz, to bring me up, I notice a large bust of Lev Gumilev staring out across the traffic. Gumilev was a Soviet historian who studied Turkic languages and peoples, but his fame rests mainly on his status as a Eurasian thinker, who conceived of Russia's destiny as a blend of Asian East and European West. It is a serendipitous encounter, and I circle the marble head and read the inscription: "I, a Russian person," it proclaims, "have spent my whole life defending the Tatars from slander." Later I find out how the quote continues: "They are in our blood, our history, our language, our worldview.... the Tatars are not a people who are outside of us, but within us."

Gulnaz arrives as I am pondering this, and leads me down a narrow alley and up into a cramped apartment that seems little changed since the 1970s. While Gulnaz, wrapped in bright and flowing Middle Eastern dress and tightly pinned hijab is quite reserved, Popov grasps my hand warmly and talks fluidly with childlike frankness. The shelves and floor are spilling over with canvases, both landscapes and calligraphy, that Popov has hauled out to show me. First, however, we have dinner: Gulnaz has cooked some Tatar specialities, and as we eat she pours the tea and then, bowing, offers to withdraw while the men converse.

It is an odd cultural moment: Popov, now beardless, is entirely the down to earth Russian in his manner and for most of our conversation, the theme of Islam will remain distant. His relationship to it turns out to be refreshingly eccentric. Gulnaz, I learn, has been living in Turkey, and like Ramil, studying calligraphy from a master in Istanbul. In her occasional contributions to the conversation, she gives answers designed to show that her own Islam is thoroughly orthodox, and that her heart really lies in Turkey, "where real Islam is,"—in contrast to Tatarstan. Mischievously, I ask whether the influence of Ataturk might not have corroded that, and I am not too surprised when she does not recognize the name. Still, while Gulnaz's dress and Eastern comportment seem somewhat mannered and *nouveau*, presenting an odd contrast to Popov's blunt secular demeanor, it is hard not to detect in her features a similar free spirit to Popov's. And Popov himself explains, when dinner is over that he saw something unique in her that made him break his own promise not to take on any more students at his late age: "It is my duty to hand everything I have over to her great talent. It is my parting gift. She will go far in the world, believe me."

Gulnaz is young and going through her own transformations. Popov, though, has made transformation an art form and been doing it for decades. "I was never a commission artist," he says, "I was always looking for new possibilities, new forms." He surprised himself as well as others, not least with his last leap away from representational art to pure calligraphy. He has a worldview, but is like a bubbling spring: from the height of ninety years, distinctions seem to have fallen away, old forms have been shed. Most people manage one or two transformations in a lifetime, and struggle to rationalize them. Most countries do the same, trying to find the link between the tsarist, the Soviet and the post-Soviet, the Eurasian and the neo-Eurasian, the pre-Islamic and the post-Islamic. But Popov seems to live in the moment, and maybe in this he encapsulates all his, and all his country's, pasts into one present.

This is not mere theory, on my part: Popov tells me about his experiences during the Great Patriotic War. He actually lost his memory completely on the front due to shellshock. "We were chasing the Germans into the Caucasus across the salt flats: they moved by day, we moved by night..." He spent a couple of years in and out of hospital after this, but his memory never came back completely, and he had to write notes to himself to remember things. Extraordinarily, he tells me that due to his poor memory he has not learned the Arabic script, and someone has to write out the Arabic words before he takes them and converts them into art.

During the war, he had his own religious transformation. His mother ("she was a Catholic, I think, from Cracow; or maybe she was a Protestant"—that distinction, too, is lost) had been praying for him as he fought on the front: "And I thought, yes, I was in such situations, where everyone else had died and I survived. The Almighty saved me.... In 1942, after close escapes, I sat down and thought about it: I realized that the Almighty exists, He is one and the same for all people. And I recognized only Him...."

Still, he was always a patriot of his country. The amnesia, the impatience with pedantic distinctions (Protestant or Catholic), means he focuses only on what matters to his vision and concentrates on that. Recognizing the Almighty, being a theist in an atheist country, did not seem like a contradiction, just as, perhaps, it was not a contradiction for Asmira and Shohruh in the Fergana valley, who had likewise forgotten or never quite learned what "atheism" was meant to be. Or like Bakyt Oktyabrovich in Kyrgyzstan, who encompasses the Soviet, the Kyrgyz and the Muslim without the batting of an eyelid. Instead, Popov's socialist realist depiction of the Eastern landscapes of the Soviet Union, either in their untouched beauty or being settled by Soviet pioneers, was shot through with a sensitivity to meaning, to the divine—rather like the Sufi-tinged work of Baki Urmanche.

I love my country. I was born here, I was brought up here. I may be unsatisfied with one or another thing but this is where my life has been. The USSR did much that was positive in the world. I think Lenin was a genius: before 1917, the West and America were engaged in exploitative capitalism. After 1917, the West suddenly had to be on the lookout: if you don't share what you have got, you'll be in trouble! My Dad was chasing Petlurans until 1926; he was not a Party member but he supported them strongly and I joined the Party when I was on the front. When I was born he named me Vladimir in honor of Lenin, and my sister was called Ninel [Lenin backwards]. The only thing that Lenin was lacking was a recognition of a higher force. If Lenin had recognized God, the whole Soviet project would have been even better, it would have been done in a godly way.

Now, he tells me, "I can best express these ideas of mine using an Islamic platform." Is this, too, a stripping away of details, leaving only an intense focus on the One? But again, Popov has found a highly distinct way of expressing this: through drawing *tugras* for public leaders. A *tugra* in Ottoman times was the ruler's official stamp or seal (and the word goes back to the mark that Turkic nomads branded their livestock with). It is a highly ornate Arabic rendition of the ruler's name and perhaps qualities or titles. One of the first *tugras* that Popov made was for Vladimir Putin.

"I have done four for him in total," he boasts proudly, in an entirely endearing way. "And I was also developing my idea of what I wanted a *tugra* to be. Usually, they just include the name, patronymic and family name of the individual and then one or two verses from the Qur'an. But I decided to take this form further. I wanted to use all the possible power that is inherent in the calligraphic form and pour it into the *tugra*. I wanted to use the *tugra* to capture the character, the personality of the subject: is he pessimistic or diligent? What is his hobby? It should all be readable— like a rebus. When I was at the Qur'an Forum in Iran in 2002, I made a *tugra* of the leader and the government and brought it with me, as a sign of respect, you see. It turned out, and this is usually the case, that the media make a big deal of my *tugras*. So far I have had twenty different exhibitions, in the Arab and Muslim world, and two in the West: one in Belarus and one in Madrid at a conference on Islamic art..."

He did three more *tugras* of Putin, each one tracking the ascending ark of the leader's destiny. And then he did one for the president of Tatarstan, which was also prescient. He did another *tugra* for the Tatar surgeon who saved Yeltsin's life, and then began to expand the form to people he did not know personally: "I did *tugras* for the leaders of the Group of Eight and the Group of Twenty. I studied the papers to find out about them. They are very important; they influence the earth enormously..." Going back over his words, I recall another of my interviewees who was similarly enamored of leadership and its propensities: Ruslan from southern Kazakhstan, whose ancestors hailed from Kazan.

By this time, we have moved into his living-room to view the canvases scattered on the floor and sofa. Popov continues with relentless energy to talk, also emitting Ruslan-like sparks: "I don't feel I have lost anything by leaving behind painting. I have always had a simple theme in my art: peace. So too, now, my theme, you could say, is that we all live on one planet, we are one boat sailing in the sea, and if we fight the boat will sink. I specifically chose an Islamic platform to convey this message, because it is through Islam that you can best understand the oneness of humanity, we are all earth-dwellers, fellows on one earth: earth is our birth mother...."

The Goethean pantheism with a paganistic edge is particularly evident in two works he holds up for me now: one is of the planet earth (wrought out of Arabic letters) whirling in space, and the other of the sun. Each one has an inscription below it in Russian, rendered fancifully in Old Slavonic script, and in Arabic. He tells me he has been looking to translate the inscriptions into English, so I oblige, writing down the English version on a piece of paper for him. The one to the Earth proclaims: "Love and gratitude to Mother Earth for her care for humanity." The one to the sun is similar: "Love and gratitude to brother Sun for his actions that help humanity." Popov gushes boyishly as I write out the translations: "Can one live without the sun? As soon as the sun comes out, don't we all leap up and say, Ah! The sun is out, let us go outside...?" The Slavonic script and the English translation are, again, a means to reach out to as wide a stretch of humanity as possible. We move into the corridor to look at other pieces, and Popov shows me on the walls various awards and endorsements, all of them in Arabic from the Arab and other parts of the Muslim world. "I have been factually accepted into Islam," he tells me proudly. "I even have a document testifying to this. One needs just two signatures to confirm entry into Islam and make it official, but I have the signatures of Dr Butt, a famous theologian from Pakistan, and a Tunisian *sheikh*. They signed the document in 2012." This Soviet reverence for bureaucratically stamped documents puts me in mind of an atheist colleague who hoards his two baptismal certificates, one from the Orthodox and one from the Baptists, claiming: "That way, I am covered." In Popov's case, the boasting is entirely good-natured and charming, and after ninety-two years on earth and all that he has lived through he is thoroughly entitled to it.

Still, I am a little perplexed: despite Popov's admiration for the prophets' messages of peace (Muhammad, Jesus and others), he does not strike me as a

Muslim. I get the impression that a Soviet- or Russian-style cosmism: Lenin, mother earth, astral energies and so on, seems to constitute his views just as much as, or even more than, Islam. So I put it to him with blunt pedantry: "Do you pray *namaz*, then?" He looks up at the ceiling as if searching for an answer in the beyond. "I pray," he answers finally, "without the need for all the prophets. Just straight to God."

There is no doubt that Popov is an unapologetic eccentric. However, the host of Arabic-language endorsements that cover his wall suggest that the Muslim world really does seem to have taken him as one of their own: he has given exhibitions in Tehran, Beirut and Cairo, selling out in cities in Morocco and Syria. Maybe there is something in Russian–Soviet Cosmism that speaks to Arabs and Iranians, too.With his flamboyant disregard for details, in the eternal present of his near amnesia, Popov seems to have fused contradictory strands and clashing meanings into a whole. And yet, in his context, Popov is not so eccentric: he is a nationally recognized and awarded artist whose works hang in respectable galleries. His vision repeats and amplifies the voices I have been hearing across the Eurasian steppes and valleys. And remarkably, though he is handing his heritage onto Gulnaz, who is Islamically far more readable and conventional, it seems that he still has a lot left in him. In fact, I end up flagging before he does, having to politely excuse myself near midnight, while Popov carries on gesticulating, explaining, and recounting.

Bulgar: our mystical center

I spend a few days outside the city with Farit; the last couple of days he hosts me in his apartment in Zelenodolsk; and mid-week, we drive the two hour trip down to Bulgar.

Bulgar is now little more than an archeological site. A restored minaret and monastery lie amid state-of-the-art museums, and the whole complex sits snugly on a bend in the Volga river. Here the Volga is swollen, and stretches lazily to the hazy horizon; it is seductive, dream-like. One can fully imagine Urmanche's water king, old man Korkut, rising mistily out of the flood and parting the curtains of reality for a mesmerized poet. And Bulgar itself occupies a hypnotic place in the Tatar imagination, and in the Russian Muslim imagination in general. Putin, with his canny Eurasianist ability to find a place for non-Russian ethnicities in the new Russia, gave a speech here in July 2012: he pinned a medal to the chest of Ildus Faizov, the mufti of Tatarstan, who had survived a jihadist car bomb only a month earlier, and talked about how he would do everything to prevent North Caucasus-style radicalism taking root on the Volga. Bulgar is connected in everyone's imagination with a deep-rooted native Islam, a well-spring of local identity.

The Volga Bulgarian kingdom, for a start, long predates Kazan. It lasted from the seventh century to the thirteenth century. It was the center of a mixed Turkic–Finnic principality that stretched across the entire Volga region and traded with the Vikings to the north and the Arabs to the south. Its ruler, Almush, received a delegation of Baghdad Muslims led by Ibn Fadlan in the tenth century and his people converted to Islam a few decades before Vladimir of Kiev converted the proto-Russian people to Christianity. By comparison with Bulgar, Kazan is a mere youngster: it was only after Bulgar was destroyed by the Mongols in the thirteenth century that Ulu Muhammad founded the Kazan khanate in the north. Ivan the Terrible then conquered Kazan a hundred years later, razing the mosques and expelling Muslims beyond the city. The Kazan khanate became the Kazan kingdom, a part of Muscovy, and then simply the Kazan *gubernia*.

These brief facts contain an important message for Tatar identity. I had seen how the Moscow Tatar Askhat was forced as a child to read about the Tatars' perfidious role in subjugating Russia to the famous "Tatar–Mongol" yoke. In the Soviet period and to some extent even now, this schoolbook view of the Tatars prevails; Askhat's experience is common. But an alternative view holds that the Tatars are really "Bulgarians", and that they were just as much a victim of the Mongols as the Slavs were. In the modern period, the attempt to demonstrate this in a scholarly manner goes back to Hussein Faizkhanov (1825–1866), a Nizhny Tatar and early *jadid* who was a contemporary of Qayyum Nasiri. He showed that there were important continuities between Bulgar and Kazan, and that the language and ethnic composition of Volga Muslims have ancient Finnic and Turkic roots, while the Mongol input is late and secondary. Strikingly, after the 1917 Revolution there were plans to create an Idil–Ural republic, which almost succeeded. 'Idil' is the Turkic word for the Volga; the Ural part referred to the famous mountain chain which cuts through Bashkiria. The republic would have united the Turkic Muslim "Tatars" and "Bashkirs" into one people living on the territory of the ancient Bulgar kingdom. As in Central Asia, though, the combination of Soviet fear of large non-Russian entities, coupled with disagreements among non-Russian ethnicities themselves, put paid to that plan. Idil–Ural, like Turkistan and like the united Caucasian republic, remained a dream—a dream that has sometimes been taken up again by nationalists, or Islamists seeking to define the boundaries for their "emirates". Today, there are plans afoot to build an all-Russian Muslim academy in Bulgar. Time will tell whether it will go the same way as the Idil–Ural republic, and if the Moscow-centric Spiritual Board of the Russian Federation has its say, such a shift of gravity away from Moscow is unlikely to occur.

Rinat: "We were converted by water and steam"

My guide when we arrive at the museum is Rinat, an ingenious and underpaid doctoral student who is writing his dissertation on the runic scripts of the ancient Iranic and Turkic tribes. Like Ruslan, Rinat's family was exiled to Kazakhstan in Soviet times, and only recently moved back to Tatarstan. It is clear that his work as a tour-guide in Bulgar holds a deeply personal meaning for him, as for others; Bulgar may lie in ruins but its legacy lives in people's hearts. Rinat is more of a secular Turkophile; so far he has escaped the Muslim revival sweeping—unevenly, sporadically— over the region, as I learn quite quickly when I ask him what he thinks of the Krashens (Tatar-speaking Muslim peasants who converted to Russian Orthodoxy over the centuries but preserved their language and customs). Most Tatars, especially serious Muslims, do not consider them Tatars at all—a Christian Tatar is as anomalous as a Jewish Christian or a Protestant Irishman is for some. But Rinat, with his deep historical knowledge of Jewish, Buddhist and Christian Turkic tribes and kingdoms, does not see what the fuss is about; for him Tatarness is based on culture and language—religious commitment cannot exclude belonging.

Rinat may be a secular-leaning Turkophile, but he is not indifferent to Islam. In fact, there is much in ancient Turkic culture that for Rinat seems to pre-empt Islam. As we walk through the museum, he comments on the glowing artifacts, illustrating this to me. There are the ancient pitchers, for example: "This is a *kungan*," Rinat explains, "a tall pitcher with a lid. When we lived in Kazakhstan, we had never seen them. But when we moved to a village in Tatarstan, all the villagers had them. If you haven't washed from a *kungan*, you haven't washed properly at all: every Muslim has five of his own *kungans*; it's a sign of wealth and *barakat*." The pagan Turkic relish for cleanliness then, mapped onto Islamic *taharat*, ritual washing. It is an interesting throw back to the Kokand museum, where Sirozhidin was able to name and claim many of the "ancient" objects, so demonstrating the persistent continuity of the past. Another artifact that draws Rinat's attention are the buttons found in ancient

Bulgaria: "Their circular shape symbolizes heaven, or Tengri, in Turkic culture: outside you have the world and within you have God. The Romans and other Indo-Europeans had three gods, but the Turks always had only the One God. They were ready for *tawhid*," Rinat comments.

Some of the other objects do not have a direct religious meaning, but they feed Rinat's pride in other ways. Of the remains of grain found in Bulgar, he comments: "The Bulgars cultivated five types of grain, while in Northern Europe they only had three. And people say the primitive Bulgars did not know agriculture!" When we pass a case displaying weighty hooks, he explains they were for fishing: "The Tatar word *balyk* means fish, in general now, but back then it referred only to the best fish, sturgeon. You can see by the size of these hooks that the Volga was full of sturgeon the size of sharks: it would have been dangerous to swim!"

As we come out into the open and walk towards the minaret and restored monastery wall, Rinat enlarges on the virtues of this ancient city. "As a sinful Muslim," he ponders ironically, "I always point out to tour groups that when Bulgar was in its heyday churches were allowed here and there was even a foreign quarter and something resembling the institution of an embassy. In other words, Islam was very tolerant. But nowadays, we can see an irony: this is the spiritual heart of Muslim Russia, but it's also the most Orthodox part of the Volga region: it is the area of the Spassky diocese with thirteen parishes, which is an extraordinarily high number. The Church is frightened that the Muslims will take over this area. It has always been like this: right from the beginning when Ivan IV conquered the Kazan khanate, they settled colonists here and kicked out the Tatars and even the local Russians. To this day, you won't find a Tatar village 40 kilometers north of the Volga: Tatars were forbidden from settling there. It is all Russian villages."

As for his own attitude towards Islam, he speaks in more detail about this, outlining his own vision: "I don't pray *namaz*. My family was completely secular, but still, my father bought me a Qur'an when I was young to introduce me to the idea of Islam. I have read several different translations, and now I am reading the translation of Kuliev for spiritual reasons, and I hope it will lead somewhere. But I don't like to be told what to do. I don't like it when people say, You need to wear Muslim clothes. Why? What are Muslim clothes, anyway? Arab clothes: but that's just a form of nationalism. Once I was leading a group of Malaysians around and the ambassador asked me, Why are the girls dressed like that? He was pointing to a fourteen year old in a hijab, with a long dress and gloves. He wanted to know whether they were married.

For them, women only dress like that if they are married. I just told them it was fashion, pure and simple, and a sort of imported Arab nationalism."

A bit later, Rinat has a chance to describe his own hopes for Islam—a non-Arab-dominated, local, Turkic, Tatar Islam—when we pass a large iron sculpture depicting a turban, an inkpot and a staff. The sculpture gives visual form to a famous legend concerning how the ancient Bulgars came to accept Islam. It is a legend that still forms a powerful lynchpin of modern Tatar attempts to define their own form of Islamic religiosity, and it has influenced Rinat strongly too. According to this legend, the Prophet Muhammad sent three of his companions to convert the Bulgars, giving one a turban, one an inkpot and one a staff. The turban, which will be unwrapped and used by the believer as his shroud, symbolizes the believer's mortality and constant dependence on Allah; the inkpot symbolizes learning; and the staff symbolizes how Muslim leaders are a shepherd to their flocks. The legend goes that when the companions reached Bulgar, the khan's daughter had fallen ill, so the companions placed the pen in the inkpot and it turned into a tree. From the tree they plucked a branch with which they cured the daughter (using it as a switch to beat her skin in a steam bath). Respect for medicine thus also enters the legend by the backdoor.

Tatars see in these elements the ingredients of a peaceful Islam; while in the Caucasus the dagger or sword is a popular symbol of Islam, in the Volga region it is the shepherd's staff that predominates. Rinat goes further in his reading of the legend: "We can say that Christianity came to Russia by 'fire and the sword'," he says, referring to the famous phrase which describes the forced conversion of the Kievan Russians by Vladimir, "while Islam came to Bulgaria by water and steam. At least that's how I like to see it." An important element that Rinat omits to mention, but which also plays a powerful role in Tatar Muslim identity, is the fact that the Bulgars' conversion took place before Kiev's: hence Islam is the oldest religion on the territory of the modern Russian Federation. There is also the fact that Vladimir refused the Bulgars' attempts to convert him to Islam, on the grounds that "Rus loves wine". All this fuels the modern Tatar Muslim self-image of the Tatars as an ancient indigenous, clean, God-fearing, sober and orderly people. Farit himself often highlights how the Tatars are industrious, clean and honest. Depending on the mood, or the period under recollection, he will sometimes contrast this (for the worse) with the moral fibre of the Russian people, while at other times, attributing to Russians similar virtues.

As we are saying goodbye, Rinat shares one more legend with me, the story of the 'reappearing minaret'. Local monks had tried to destroy the remnants of the ancient mosque, but whenever they tore the monument down it would rebuild itself. Rinat laughs and informs me that he tells this story to every group he leads, and recently people from afar afield as Chelyabinsk and Samara pre-empt him with their telling of it. Obviously, it seems that as with any good legend, its ability to spread is fueled by the need it satisfies in people's souls. The idea of the minaret, or Islam, constantly sprouting despite oppression—whether by the Mongols, or the current Russian government—has its appeal. While Tatars are not like the Bashkirs or Kyrgyz, who remember their family genealogy to the seventh generation, Farit and others I meet have a keen awareness of their family's past and put special value on their heroic preservation of Islam in the face of oppression, as well as the religion's constant ability to spring back in new and fresh forms.

Farhat: "I first read the Qur'an in Russian"

On our way back to Kazan, we pass through another Bulgar: this one a small Soviet-era village. Farit stops to pray *namaz* at the local mosque, a small wooden building at the end of a dirt road. Here, too, on a more humble scale from the reconstruction going on in the eponymous ghost city, there is a tale of Islamic revival, as I discover when I talk to the iman, Farhat. When I learn that he used to be the local communist party boss, I am inclined to think that his story is going to fit the model of the ex-communist museum curator in Satkek (in the Fergana valley): a seemingly opportunist neo-Soviet new Muslim. But as we talk more, it appears that his beliefs really do go deeper than the skullcap and Pakistani kurta suit he now wears. He admits that there have been many unthinking "reversions" to Islam, but explains that his path involved a thoughtful choice. It was his reading of the Qur'an that set him on the path to religion: "I had always been told that it taught hatred, and I was very afraid of religion. All my friends were Russian, and I could see no difference between them and Tatars, so this separation that religion would want seemed to me a bad thing. I thought the Qur'an must be 'extremist'. But then I got hold of a Qur'an, it was just like this one," he drags one off the shelf and hands it to me, "and found it was quite the opposite. I read it all in one go, just like that, quite by chance, and in Russian—there were no Tatar translations around in those days. I was about 40. There was no hostility, no contradiction, no violence. The message was: if you want to keep the religion, keep it. It's entirely up to you."

The village is mixed Russian and Tatar, and Farhat insists the two communities rub along well. "I have a very good relationship with the priests here, too. We all help each other. We have round tables in our local House of Culture, we explain each other's religions to people who come to listen, and we cooperate on common challenges, like drug abuse among the young. There's no competition. You see, if a Tatar women converts to Christianity, I am not angry with her but with myself: why didn't I explain the religion better? There can be no question of force. People choose freely."

Tatarstan's inter-religious tolerance sometimes suffers from being the subject of so much government PR that one wants to poke holes in it. However, that ancient Bulgarian model of monastery and (reappearing) minaret standing side by side, now famously reproduced in Kazan with its adjacent Kul Sharif mosque and Russian Kremlin, does seem to be a feature of many people's lives. Nevertheless, Rinat's reference to the fourteen year old in gloves and full-face veil, and his anger at the "Arab nationalism" of such costumes, are a reminder that extremist Salafism has left its trace here too.

Alsu: "I am no longer a good atheist"

On the other hand, the demographic and geographical factor plays its role in making this Bulgar–Turkic freespiritedness a natural choice. Intermarriage is so high that many families reproduce the mixed religiosity of the republic in their own fabric. Farit, with his Orthodox granddaughter, is a case in point. Another small example is given to me by Alsu Tarkhanova, a woman in her late fifties, who is now Chair of the Executive Committee of an organization called "Tatarstan—New Century". She grew up in a village similar to the small Bulgar. Of her nine siblings, five are married to Russians. Her own first husband was half-Jewish and half-Russian; her second husband was Russian; and her mother-in-law was devoutly Orthodox. Both her mother-in-law's children, though, had married Tatars and when she was nearing death, fearing there would be no one to pray for her soul, she asked Alsu to light a candle for her every year. "So every year, I go to the church. I don't cross myself and I don't do the prayers myself, but I light a candle and I give some money or buy some food for the Sunday school and I ask the children to pray for her soul. You don't have to be Orthodox to do that. I do something similar with the mullah. I know some Muslim prayers but not all of them, so I ask the mullah to pray for our dead relatives."

Other reminiscences from her youth throw light on Gumiliev's belief that the Tatars are a people internal to the Russians, and that even before she "intermarried" she was already somehow interwoven with Russianness. "When I was at university, everyone thought I was Russian. You weren't allowed to speak Tatar then at university. And everyone always called me Alya, short for Alu, in my case, but everyone thought I was Alyona. One of my girlfriends was very surprised when she found out I was Tatar!" In her village there was a similar blurring with traditions: "The Tatars and Russians would both give each other painted eggs when spring started. At five or six in the morning you would go from house to house giving eggs, sweets and other things. The Russians called it 'Christing' and we just called it Red Egg day. It was only later that I found out about Easter, that it was a Christian holiday. I don't even know which came first." In the Bulgar museum, Rinat had mentioned a similar custom: he assured me that the tradition of giving eggs in Tatar villages goes all the way back to pre-Christian and pre-Islamic Bulgaria.

Alsu now works for a Tatar political–cultural organization. Like Farhat, though, she used to be a communist, and her offices today are in the former buildings of the Communist party in Kazan. She too lies on that strange and backward-looping trajectory that goes from religion to communism and back again. At the outset of our conversation she insists: "I am an atheist." Later, she tells me about her mullah grandfather, and her devout cousin who became religious after her mother's painful death. She sees her cousin often and she has taught Alsu some prayers; she even recites the *fatiha* for me in flawless Arabic. She sometimes attends prayer circles that her cousin holds; they are also attended by her cousin's *shakirds*—the term usually used for the disciples of a Sufi *sheikh*. It seems her cousin has become a spiritual figure in her village. Alsu rounds this off: "So I am religious. I know I am a Muslim. I don't have to convert to Islam, I am in Islam already."

And she sheepishly concludes when I ask her why she described herself as an atheist: "I suppose that I am not a pure atheist anymore." Often people criticize the nominal nature of ethnic Muslims' religious identity, but this a reminder of how nominal many atheists were. Probably, too, as a public figure, Alsu has not shrugged off the Soviet habit of affixing one label on the public office-door, while using a different label for the inner door.

Young muftis

Imam Ilfar Hasanov

Back in Kazan, I meet two people who are at the forefront of public Islam in the republic. One is imam Ilfar Hasanov, the imam-khātib of the Qul Sharif mosque. The other is Rustam Batrov, assistant mufti of Tatarstan.

Hasanov used to be the imam-khātib at the old Marjani mosque in the Tatar *sloboda*, and was catapulted into his new prestigious position at the heart of Tatarstan Islamic life due to a chain of events that is still sadly familiar for the different Russian muftiats: the previous incumbent, Ramil Yunusov, who was also director of the Kazan Kremlin museum, was accused of embezzling funds. There were protests by his enemies and supporters, and—at the same time as Kazan was being rocked by the assasination of Yakupov and Faizov—Yunusov suddenly disappeared from public life and was rumored to have emigrated to London. Hasanov, unlike another mooted candidate, made a smooth transition into his new position due to his evident skills, both personal and scholarly.

When I meet him, he has just finished reading the Friday prayer sermon. Among the worshipers are twenty foreign athletes: the swimming Olympics are taking place in Kazan's newly built stadium (I overhear a group of burly Australians comparing their performance in a café that afternoon) and they line up to shake hands with him. A young Egyptian lingers and Hasanov chats to him in the Arabic he perfected during his studies in Medina.

Alone with me in his spacious office, Hasanov gives me a recap of the sermon he delivered in mellifluous and rhetorical Tatar. Then, he talks about the role of the Qul Sharif mosque. Begun in 1996 and completed in 2005, it was a replica of the mosque that used to stand in the center of Kazan during the Kazan khanate. As such it is a symbol not only of Islamic revival, but also of Tatarstan's success in negotiating a high degree of autonomy from Moscow. Hasanov also underlines that "it has become the symbol of the Tatar nation, not only in Russia, but around the world. Tatars come to visit it from Finland, China, and many other countries." It is also a place to showcase Islam for non-Muslims: there is a third balcony where tourists and the curious can come in and look at the mosque.

The conversation turns more personal when Hasanov talks about his own Islamic experience. He is not a returnee to Islam, but grew up in one of those families which managed to sustain observance throughout the Soviet period.

This was due to his grandmother's experience: during the war, she lost her husband and, looking for spiritual support in the hard task of raising her family, turned to Islam, guided by a neighbor. Her own parents and grandparents had passed her down Islamic books written in Tatar, thus escaping Russian censors. "We have old Arabic manuscripts in the family, and so do many other families. We just need the scholars to catalogue them and translate them: there is a whole treasure awaiting discovery!"

Mufti Rustam Batrov

Batrov, who is in his mid-thirties, grew up in a superficially observant family in Nizhny Novgorod and became interested in Islam due to the well known Nizhny mufti Umar Idrisov, a fellow student of Ravil Gaynutdin and Muhammad Sodik Muhammad Yusuf in Bukhara. After studying at the Moscow Cathedral mosque *medrese* in the nineties, he then served for ten years as mufti of Yaroslavl.

Recalling his time there affectionately, he offers a snapshot of small Muslim communities outside of the major Muslim population centers. This most Russian of all towns was settled by Tatar merchants in the nineteenth century, and at the turn of the twentieth century they had gathered the funds to build a mosque. After a long struggle against Christian opposition, which involved the tsar's personal intervention, permission for the mosque was granted, and in the twentieth century an aura of miracle surrounded it: it survived Stalin's attempts to shut it (the order was strangely not followed up on) and a bombing attempt by the Germans. When Batrov was there, a Russian youth tried to set fire to the building but the petrol bomb did not explode; later he repented before the community.

While serving as the Yaroslavl mufti, Batrov completed a biography of Abu Hanifa and edited a cutting-edge Islamic journal. Having tired a bit of Yaroslavl's backwater status, he was pleased to be offered his post in Kazan. A Nizhny native who received his Islamic training in Moscow and now serves in Kazan, Batrov represents an interesting breed: a Muslim cleric who was educated entirely within Russia. I thus decide to ask him to explain what exactly is meant by "traditional Russian Islam". It is a question, not surprisingly, that he has been thinking about deeply. Rather like Malikov in Bishkek, he lays out his answer with the speed of one who has rehearsed his position. Unlike with Malikov, though, there is no mention of an Islamic state.

Batrov traces four main senses of this shifting term. It was probably the strongly pro-government mufti Talgat Tajudin who first used it, and then the term was taken up during Medvedev's presidency as a synonym for pro-Russian Islam. But Batrov speculates that Tajudin himself, who is Islamically very literate, had probably used it as a convenient shorthand for the Arabic term *ahl al-sunna wa-l-jamaa*, i.e. the people of the prophetic tradition and the Sunni consensus, which is often how mainstream, non-sectarian Sunni Muslims identify themselves. After the assassination of Kazan's assistant mufti Yakupov in 2012, people once again turned to the term in an attempt to specify what exactly non-extremist Islam should be like. It then emerged that there was no equivalent in Tatar; it had remained a purely Russian term.

Batrov then outlines a second use of "traditional Islam" by ethnic Muslims: for them it refers to the "Islam of my grandparents", and is something thus inherently good, bearing the seal of nostalgia. For its opponents, it is "*babai* Islam", the Islam of the old folk leaders, the *babais*, and thus is associated not with positive antiquity, but with ignorance and lack of authenticity. Its defenders say that it is, indeed, not bookish Islam but the Islam of real life. Often it is seen as an alternative to foreign, Arab, imported, or indeed Wahhabi Islam: *babushka* never wore a hijab, why should I?

Then there is a third meaning: traditional Islam is national Islam, more precisely here it is Tatar Islam. This is more systematic, less nostalgic. It is a way to preserve the Tatar nation from assimilation and disappearance. But the emphasis is on the nation, rather than the religion. Batrov here mentions the name of Rafail Hakimov, a Kazan engineer and academic, who in the nineties proposed that Tatar Islam was a torchbearer for what he called Euro-Islam: this was an updated version of jadidism, which argued for the compatibility of European and Islamic values, and saw Tatars as being able to practice and disseminate this sort of Islam not just for Russia but for Europe as well. From my conversations with the Moscow muftis I get the impression that this approach is now very much discredited at the official level, probably for being too Tatarocentric as well as insufficiently grounded in Islamic tradition and wider international Islamic currents. Batrov does not express strong criticism of Hakimov, but emphasizes that such ideas are of merely "historical interest" now. It certainly seems that such a style of thinking is distinctly out of vogue now that people have matured into a deeper knowledge of their religion, and the thesis that modernity and secularity should be mutually exclusive has come to be disputed not just in Russia, but worldwide.[3]

Finally, there is a fourth position, "the position I take," says Batrov. "For me, 'traditional' Islam is orthodox Islam. It's getting back to that original phrase, the Islam of *ahl as-sunna wa'l jamaa*, the Islam of *'aqida* (theological doctrines), *fiqh* (jurisprudence) and *tasawwuf* (Sufism). The figure who best represents this in history is the scholar Maturidi, who restated the Asharite position. He made peace with the Shi'ites and the Sunnis. He emphasized the doctrine of the *ahl al-rayy*, people of the opinion, which gives a license for scholars to use reason to adapt to the times. For example," Batrov says, "when I served at the Yaroslavl mosque, the Caucasians would give grain to the poor at the end of Ramadan. They were following a hadith and the Shafi'i *madhab* doesn't allow one to depart from the exact wording of the Prophetic tradition. But I said to them: what is the point of giving grain to poor people in a modern Russian city? It's completely useless. In fact it shows a lack of consideration. It will cause these recipients of charity more trouble trying to turn the grain into money. So the Hanafite school, to which Maturidi belonged, updates this by analogy: we just give money.

"So," he summarizes, "I see 'traditional Islam' as consisting of three principles. The work of Maturidi, which is full of peace and a spirit of reconciliation. The heritage of Abu Hanifa, which is permeated with a spirit of reason and rationalism. And finally, there is the Naqshbandi school of Sufism, which infuses all this with mysticism. Still," he goes on, "these four interpretations of 'traditional Islam' can be combined, they do not contradict each other. I am also a patriot, I am devoted to my Tatar 'traditions', I respect our customs, such as the forty day mourning period. This is how the custom of mourning has developed in this land, and it is a matter of tradition, perhaps in the nostalgic sense to follow that number and not, say, some other number."

Batrov accepts that this notion of "traditional Islam" is still an umbrella for a lot of diverse concepts. He also accepts my observation that post-Soviet Islam on the ground is highly fragmented and individualistic. But he sees this as a virtue and a cause for celebration. "I don't see Islamic unity in that way, namely that people need to have exactly the same worldview. It is like the blind men and the elephant: each one feels a different part and has his own idea of what the entity is. I don't actually want to impose my understanding of Islam on anyone else. We have a secular government and this allows us to have plurality of religious belief. As a result, Islam is turning into a subculture of people with special interests. One space is intellectual, another is where guest-workers gather and feel comfortable. Each one finds his own answers..."

He also dismisses the idea that such plurality and fragmentation might lead to radicalization. Extremism, he believes, has other roots, and he quotes a recent study from Kazakhstan: "The one thing that these disparate people had in common," he notes, "was that there they had no role model of a father: their fathers were absent either literally or metaphorically. They were alcoholics or workaholics or had left the family. For example, even the son of the chief prosecutor had become an extremist. So diversity is not the problem."

"We have only just emerged from a totalitarian society," he says later, "where we all had to think alike. So I am in favor of freedom of thought. It's a reaction against the collective ethos. I don't want one canon of behavior and thought; it goes against people's natural diversity. But perhaps you can say that our unity is that we have one Qur'an, one Ka'aba. As for loneliness, we live in a different society, we form communities ourselves, we find like-minded thinkers and create our own groups, perhaps on the internet. That's a way of overcoming loneliness, in fact. I don't see a problem with that. There's a saying from the Prophet: At the end time, my 'umma will divide into seventy-three communities. In one version, it finishes: only one will go to paradise, the others will go to Hell. But there's another version of the hadith: only one will go to Hell, the other seventy-two will go to Heaven. That's the version I embrace! In fact, it is the version that Imam al-Ghazali adopted. I am all for plurality."

Batrov's approach is recognizably close in spirit to Gaynutdin's and Yusuf's *wasatiyya*—an attempt to formulate an Islamic worldview for Russian Muslims that is grounded firmly in Tatar and Central Asian sources (Maturidi, Abu Hanifa and Naqshbandi are all Iranic or Turkic thinkers from the Iranian or Central Asian area). In many ways, it is similar to the traditional Islam formulated by Turkish Muslims, who draw on the same sources. One could say that Batrov's thinking comes out of the Nizhny–Moscow–Kazan triangle. It certainly gives space for "ethnic Muslims" to slowly enter into some form of Islamic observance that will not alienate them from secular post-Soviet society, as I learn from the example of Ildar Abulzyarov.

Ildar Abulzyarov: "it is hard being a Tatar novelist..."

I meet Ildar Abulzyarov, a novelist in his mid-forties, through Batrov, a fellow Novgorodian. At first glance, he seems to have little to do with Islam: his Chuvash ancestry make his blonde appearance indistinguishable from a Russian's. He also seems to be living the trendy creative life to the full: one of his novels is being filmed in Kazan, and as the recipient of the prestigious

Pushkin prize, he has received government help to buy an apartment in the city. But in fact he turns out to be an interesting embodiment of Batrov's "Islamic pluralism".

The novel for which he won the prize is called *Khush*, a Russian acronym which decodes as: "I want to die a shahid (martyr)." It tells the story of a shadowy Islamic terrorist group operating out of the historic mosque in St Petersburg, and carrying out a series of attacks in the city. "I spent a long time," Abulzyarov tells me, "hanging out at the St Petersburg mosque myself. And I got friendly with a bunch of Tajik and Uzbek migrants. The story arose out of that experience." His second novel is set in Kyrgyzstan during the Osh riots. He also reported as a journalist from Tahrir square during Egypt's revolution. So Islam and his creative work are deeply linked for him.

The combination is not easy though. "I got quite a bit of stick for *Khush*," he tells me. "A lot of people thought I made the 'shahids' a bit too sympathetic. It wasn't published in book form to start with, but appeared in a journal in installations. And people's reactions were bad: they stopped inviting me to stuff, to book fairs and things like that, I was just dropped from various events. Somehow being a Tatar novelist isn't so easy. In fact, my publisher advised me to adopt a pseudonym. It was hard, very hard. Essentially, it's chauvinism. No one respects non-Western literature, that is, Eastern literature..."

His Tatar and Islamic identity are important for him and worth defending. As far as Islam is concerned, I hear echoes of Batrov, who is perhaps a bit of a spiritual mentor to him. "I do pray, actually," he says, "though not on the dot. I actually used to go to the mosque every Friday back in Moscow, but then I stopped: there was just not enough space. Nowadays, I do *namaz* when I feel like it, when my soul feels like it. That was how it was in the time of the Prophet: back then there were only three prayers. It all evolved. Of course, I am very secular and no doubt the fanatics would want to cut my head off for saying this! Likewise, when it comes to Ramadan, my mother keeps the fast now in fact, and I keep a few days. I am a Hanafite: in this *madhab* it is enough to say the *shahada* and to have faith and God will take care of the rest. Though of course a lot of people would call me a *kafir* for saying so!"

His move to Kazan had a spiritual aspect. "I feel like I am at home here, like this is my spiritual home. I love the Tatar *sloboda* here. This is my city in a way that Moscow and Petersburg could never be. Here it is easier to be Muslim. Even though the Orthodox are trying to dominate here, people like Batrov are fighting back and insisting on a more pluralistic way: when the Orthodox wanted to impose the 'foundations of Orthodox culture' course in schools, the muftiat managed to stand up for the rights of Tatar Muslims." He also mentions the recent Kazan scandal that concerns the newly appointed Metropolitan of Kazan, Feofan. In his first public appearance, Abulzyarov tells me, Feofan gave a jingoistic speech proclaiming that Tatarstan was Russian land, that new churches needed to be built, that public land on the territory of the Kremlin historical complex should be "returned" to the Russian Orthodox church—including the mosque. Again, more provocations that put Tatars on the defensive. "But thanks to our muftis and local campaigners, Tatarstan has generally achieved religious equality: if they build a church, they have to build a mosque too. That is something it took struggle to achieve here... still, outside Tatarstan, this equality stops. There, the struggle has not been won."

He continues on an interesting note: "That's why I feel a responsibility towards the minorities living among the Muslims here in the Volga region. I mean the Maris and Udmurts, who are pagan. Sometimes Muslims act towards them as the Orthodox act towards Muslims. I find that very unjust. The Maris, Udmurts, and the Magyars too, were native peoples during the time of Volga Bulgaria. They helped the khans, both then and under the Kazan khanate. And the Kazan khan protected and rewarded them—their fate is very much tied in with the fate of us Tatars. Now they are losing their identity and I feel a duty to help them. I have taken part in some of their ceremonies and rituals and I read a lot about their history and customs in research that was carried out before 1917... we are all interwoven. I mean, undoubtedly I have Chuvash ancestry, you can see by looking at me. And my ancestors lived in villages where people all had Russian names. Usually they had been baptized as a way to get out of a tight situation: if they were arrested for stealing, they would either go to prison or could get off the hook by becoming Christian. So they were nominally Christian but they still went to the mosque."

I am touched by this broad-minded approach. After all, for all that the Tatars complain about Russian Orthodox imperialism, there can be a sort of Tatar Muslim imperialism. I discover this first hand from an Udmurt acquaintance of mine who is studying at an Orthodox university in Moscow. She grew up not knowing her native Finno-Ugric Udmurt tongue but is now learning it with her husband, and tells me that Orthodoxy encourages this expression of their roots. "But when our girls marry Tatars, they become Muslims," (she mimes a hijab), "and start speaking Tatar. They become Tatar, in fact." Some academics have shown how similar small Siberian peoples were also "Tatarized" out of existence in the nineteenth century.[4]

During our meeting, Abulzyarov spontaneously offers to show me round his beloved adopted Tatar *sloboda*. I have seen most of it already, but he locates an out-of-the-way Tatar café where I am treated to Tatar *lagman*, a dish I had believed existed only in Uzbekistan. He also insists that I visit the new Jewish school that has been built down the road from the Azimov mosque: "It's a great school," he tells me. "They built it a few years ago, and everyone wants to go to it. My dream is to move to the quarter near the school and send my son there."

This pluralism is second nature for Abulzyarov, and he has absolutely no problem with Tatars choosing different religions. But he ponders the strange currents which can govern such choices—a lesson I have absorbed from Askhat in Moscow and Gulnara in Bishkek. "A lot of my Muslim acquaintances have converted to Catholicism, or Protestantism, or even Orthodoxy," he informs me. "The beauty of the churches attracts them, it is very compelling. But it's a mysterious thing how people choose their faith. I knew one guy who converted to Orthodoxy, but whenever he tried to pray to an icon or in church, he would be overwhelmed by black images, by darkness. He couldn't take it anymore, so in the end he had to go back to Islam!"

Conversion, of course, is a sensitive issue and can quickly turn into a political football, with both muftis and metropolitans trying to talk up the numbers of people joining their fold and abandoning their old "errors". But there is room for a less polemical approach, as Rinat at Bulgar had shown in his attitude to the Krashens, those Tatars who converted to Orthodoxy over the centuries, while still clinging to their Tatar language and customs (rather like Abulzyarov's forebears). After all, the Volga region is *de facto* an Islamo-Christian space, and back in Moscow, Askhat had wanted to combine that side-by-side Islamo-Christian fusion within his own self.

In fact, sometime after my trip to Tatarstan, I stumble across the case of Dinara Bukhareva, a middle-aged Tatar woman originally from Nizhny Novgorod, but now resident in Moscow. Her case throws new light on Abulzyarov's comments about the conversion of Tatars and the tension between Orthodox and Muslims on the Volga today. Bukhareva adds a further meaning to the notion of Volga coexistence. She has converted to a rather conservative form of Russian Orthodoxy, but like the Krashens is trying to combine Orthodoxy with her Tatar language and culture, seeing the two as complementary. To this end, she has investigated the history of Christian Tatars in the medieval period and even turned up a Christian Tatar ruler, an ally of Moscovy, who was canonized as a saint. However, in an interview with the conservative priest Father Georgy Maximov on the Orthodox *Spas* TV show, she went a step too far, and claimed that her ancestors from the village of Safanjani were crypto-Christians who built a church in the village. Bukhareva thus pictures herself as returning to her Tatar–Christian Safanjani roots, rather than betraying her people, as many Muslim Tatars would have it.

But her *Spas* interview caused a scandal, as it turned out she had her facts about Safanjani wrong. Bukhareva was swiftly shot down by Damir Khairetdinov, a Muslim Tatar historian, who pointed out that the village never had a church and was solidly Muslim. Nonetheless, the spat between Bukhareva and Khairetdinov merely confirmed the Islamo-Christian Volga synthesis in a different way. Unlike Askhat, who does not know Tatar and is not consciously seeking out a community of like-minded Tatar Christians, Bukhareva has joined together with other Tatar converts and they have formed a little parish in Moscow where services are held in Tatar. More remarkably, she has made an effort to carry on taking part in the meetings of the Moscow Tatar community center, and the center has agreed to let Bukhareva and her "neo-Krashen" fellows attend their events. Thus the passive individual tolerance of Abulzyarov, Rinat and Askhat has taken on a concrete communal form in Moscow, where the Tatar community is now—after a bit of stress and name-calling—a collective Islamo-Christian space. Even Khairetdinov, the head of Moscow's Islamic University, was not objecting to Bukhareva's choice publicly, so much as entreating her to ground her identity in the facts.

Towards the end of my meeting with Abulzyarov, the talk turns to the new attempt by the Moscow muftiat to create an all-Russian Islam. He knows many of the Moscow muftis from their Nizhny Novgorod school days, and perhaps this is why he is more skeptical than he is with regard to the Kazan muftis. He distrusts the amount of Kremlin money being poured into the lavish conferences and events held in Moscow. And he lays into some of the discrepancies of Moscow Islam with a sharp sense of humor, recalling one typical event he attended: "It was an *iftar* meal in Moscow," he recounts. "It was at a fancy hotel just off the Kremlin, and the dining-hall was packed with all sorts of Middle Eastern VIPs. Just after the symbolic breaking of the fast, they had a show on stage. It was a nice Russian girl in a fetching mini-skirt whirling and spinning about to some racy music. Then the chief rabbi chimed in with a humorous speech. *Al hamdulillah*," he laughs, "the fast is broken— Russian-style. I found it all deeply embarrassing," Ildar continues, "but who knows: maybe it was a hit. Maybe they'll be coming back for more...!"

I laugh: such incongruities seem to be the order of the day in Russian religion. But, on the other hand, eccentricity can also throw up interesting instances, like Bukhareva and her little community.

Zelenodolsk: Islam in a Dostoevskian clime

On the way to his hometown of Zelenodolsk on the day before I leave, Farit insists on stopping off at the famous Raifsky monastery. He wants to introduce me to Father Sergius, an elder, who "has a truly Christ-like" spirituality. The monastery sits amid ancient forest on the shores of a sparkling lake. Farit, like many other Tatars, sees the monastery as a source of spiritual power, and has often had conversations with Father Sergius, whose patriarchal sermons about morality, the importance of sobriety and family life, evoke no contradiction for this newly observant Sufi. Although Father Sergius turns out to be unavailable (he is suffering from cancer and confined to his bed now) I am introduced to another artist friend of Farit's called Tukhtar. Every Sunday, he sets up his easel and paints in the shadow of the monastery walls, as well as selling his work there. Farit and Tukhtar guide me through the monastery complex, and as we walk through the churches they gaze up at the various frescoes and icons with deep interest: they are discussing the artistic merit of the restoration work; in several cases they know the artists personally, having graduated from the same Moscow art school.

Tukhtar: "the Russian language is a pure delight"

When we arrive in Zelondolsk, Tukhtar invites us to his apartment for tea. It is located in a very battered Khrushchev block not far from a street named after Tukhtar's uncle, a famous Soviet Tatar writer. Tukhtar has not left his hometown, unlike the more ambitious Farit, who reproaches him for being a lazy-bones. He is also trying to get his friend to become more Islamically observant: "He's like a cat," he jokes. "He lives like a Sufi in the present, never planning, climbing everywhere—and, of course, getting into trouble." Part of that trouble included a phase of alcoholism; now, due to Farit's efforts, he goes to the mosque once in a while. His Russian wife looks on with amused tolerance.

But Tukhtar's cat-like spirit makes for sparkling conversation and he picks up on ironies that pass the more serious and devout Farit by. Over the entrance to the monastery there had been a banner in red archaic script that read: "Russia is strong and will forever be strong." This mixing of religion and nationalism had only evoked a non-committal grunt from Farit, who had pointed out a Lenin statue to me in downtown Kazan and remarked: "This is part of our heritage, too. We are not like the Ukrainians who are trying to destroy the past." Tukhtar, though, laughs at this latest neo-Soviet "Orthodox propaganda", and recalls his own days painting banners for the Party: "One time, I painted a banner that said: 'Lenin lived, lives and will live'—you know, the quote by Mayakovsky. But I was half-asleep and wrote the attribution as V. Lenin. As if Lenin was egotistically proclaiming his own immortality. Another time, I messed up and wrote: 'The CPSU is the heart and soul of the party.' That is, the Communist Party of the Soviet Union is the heart and soul of the Party." These unintended sabotages went unnoticed: the small town bosses in both cases did not know their catechisms well enough to detect the errors.

Still, Tukhtar has his own Sufi miracle stories. In fact, he is the product of one. His parents were barren for years, and travelled to a *sheikh* in the Caucasus for a blessing. "You will have a son next year," promised the *sheikh*, "but someone will die in his place." A year later Tukhtar was born; his father died some months afterwards. His mother was a pious Muslim throughout the Soviet period. Farit had already told me the story of her deathbed confession. With tears in her eyes she told Tukhtar of a great sin that she had committed, which had haunted her conscience all her life. During the famine that ravaged the Volga in the 1920s, she had stolen a piece of bread. For Farit, it is testimony to the extraordinary conscience that Islam can foster in people even in the most chaotic and immoral of times.

But Tukhtar is too mischievous to stick to moralistic stories. Commenting on his mother, he ponders: "It is as Dostoevsky says: the line between good and evil passes through the heart of every man." The Dostoevsky quote is a prelude for Tukhtar to launch into one of his favorite themes: the beauty of the Russian language and the depths of Russian literature. "I don't want to insult Tatars or our native Tatar tongue," he says, glancing at Farit with a glint in his eye, "but the Russian language is so much infinitely richer. Russian is my second language. I didn't start learning Russian till I was seven, at school, and then all my classmates teased me for my accent. But after that my Russian became better. When I was growing up in the 1960s, they no longer had Tatar schools; we would just have one class of Tatar a week. The Russian kids would go outside to play, and of course, we wanted to play too, so we didn't take a big interest in it. It was a way of getting rid of the language, I suppose. So I shouldn't praise Russian too much. Our Tatar language has contributed to Russian, but that's the thing: so have many other languages, so it is a universal language. The Russian language is a pure delight; its sounds are so extraordinary..."

This puts me in mind of a Moscow Bashkir I have met, Aislu Van Rayn (before her marriage to a Dutchman, she was Abubakarova). Also from a family who, two generations ago, observed Islam piously, she began learning Russian only at the age of seven, but quickly overtook her classmates (one of whom, she recalls, asked her in all good faith: Are you not ashamed to be a Bashkir?). Now she teaches Russian at a Moscow university, and her family's Islam has been distilled down to a modish cosmopolitan Sufism. Tukhtar, too, seems more inclined to Dostoevsky than the Qur'an, and the rest of the visit is spent discussing Russian fairy-tales (we both agree that with their happy-go-lucky heroes they seem to preach a message of fecklessness) and reciting Russian verse.

Ismail: "Let the Salafists stew in their own juices, I have my own way"

That evening, Farit introduces me to another of his Zelenodolsk friends, Ismail. A stocky, good-natured forty year old, he was a Soviet army kid who grew up on bases. His father was Russian, his mother Tatar, but as the wife of a Soviet officer she repressed all mention of her Tatar identity. He had always been spiritually inclined, and his yearnings found a mentor in the late eighties in the person of Valiulla Yakupov. Yakupov, a popular Kazan mufti assassinated in 2012, engineered much of the Islamic revival in Kazan in the 1990s, including the opening of Baki Urmanche's Muhammadiya *medrese*. Ismail speaks affectionately of Yakupov, recounting how he would spend evenings studying with him at his home, sleeping the night there too: "This was the late eighties. Kazan was still a criminal city. You stood a good chance of being knifed if you went out late," he explains.

With Yakupov's help, Ismail went to study in Tajikistan: "There was no institute in those days. Yakupov found a man who had preserved knowledge through the Soviet times and I studied with him. This was before the Civil War [in 1992], so things at that stage were peaceful. The classes were conducted in Russian, so I had no difficulty with that. It was really the best option for me in those days; this was before radicalism had spread in Central Asia. We studied the Qur'an, Arabic and the foundations of faith. When the civil war started, we left. Tanks were already appearing in the streets, and the shooting was starting. That was in 1991."

However, when he came back to Kazan, religious education had changed in a sinister way, without anyone really suspecting it: "I continued my studies in Tatarstan by attending Muslim youth camps. For the most part the teachers there were Arabs. We didn't know what they were teaching us, but basically it was Salafism. We only found that out years later. After that I started to work at the Muhamadiyya *medrese* as a teacher, which shows you the level of knowledge back then! There was nothing, it was all completely from scratch. I taught what I could, according to my knowledge. And then came the next step, completely unexpectedly: the Arabs would reserve places for Russians at their universities, and they would find people to sponsor the Russian Muslims, who had no money back then. I submitted an application to study abroad, kind of off-handedly. And then I forgot about it. Two years later, out of the blue, I was summoned to the Saudi consulate and given an invitation and a visa to travel to Mecca! And that's how I spent seven years in the *um al qarra*, the mother of cities!"

For about a decade Ismail held strongly Salafist views: "Everything had to be exactly by the books. I believed that all non-Muslims will burn in hell; only Muslims will be saved. You feel awful for the non-Muslims, you want to convert them, but that's your belief—that's what fanaticism is." Along the way, some of his classmates turned to violent extremism, and even Farit nods in recognition: he has been on mosque youth trips, he confides now, and heard misanthropic Salafist rhetoric blaze up all of a sudden as the picnic is being laid out by the banks of the Volga. Still, fortunately, Ismail never went down that path. Instead, due to his own natural curiosity, he worked his way out of Manichean monomania towards something wider: "You grow up," he says. "Life throws what it does at you... When I was a fanatic, though, I have to say, it gives you a buzz. It's exciting to live like that, with that certainty. But deep down there's a part of you that knows it's wrong. My dreams were telling me that I was stuck, that I needed to move on to something else. But it's tough to get out, to go through the steps you need to get out of it."

Still, based on his own experience he does not believe there is a formula for distinguishing between his own present-day "reasonable Islam", as he calls it, and fanaticism. In this, he repeats Malikov in Bishkek, who had said that the question of extremism goes beyond the "logic of texts". Ismail has no patience for the truism that Islam is self-evidently "a religion of peace". Far from it, he says: "From the point of view of the Qur'an and the *Sunna*, everything that ISIS are doing now has a justification. There are indeed verses saying that you must kill the *kafirs*. There are hadiths about slaves. I know, because I have read all these sources and can quote it all to you in Arabic. So from an Islamic point of view, ISIS are irreproachable. Where they go wrong is in taking the Qur'an and the hadith as completely inerrant."

I glance over at Farit and do a double take at Ismail. Has this "moderate", devout and observant Muslim just questioned the inerrancy of the Qur'an? He confirms that I have heard him correctly. "I wouldn't say such *fitnah* [heresy] to a Muslim in public, of course. Let them boil in the juices that I once boiled in! But over the years, yes, I have come to the conclusion that there are things in the Qur'an that cannot be from Allah. I can't believe that the true God does not know that the earth is round. And there are other facts that correspond to the time of Muhammad but not to the eternal knowledge of the Creator. So the Qur'an is all from Muhammad, but there are things which are human in it."

I have heard this position—overtly stated, rather than merely hinted at— from only one other Muslim, Ilshat Nasyrov, a renowned Bashkir professor of Islamic mysticism, member of the Russian Academy of Sciences, and translator of Al Ghazali's monumental "Revival of the Religious Sciences" into Russian. In our conversation, he had told me that he views the Qur'an as partly "a collection of Arabian folklore: all its rhetorical devices, its metaphors and expressions are all from that time and place". Like Ismail, Nasyrov is religiously observant. But he quotes the Russian writer Ivan Bunin to me: "My own soul is a mystery to me." That is, while his academic side insists on the historicity of the Qur'an, his spiritual side thirsts for ritual and God. The two are not yet reconciled, although Nasyrov whimsically likes to refer to himself a modern-day Mutazilite rationalist, who believes in the createdness of the Qur'an. He, too, echoed Ismail's words: "I would never express this belief to any of my relatives. They would think I was a *kafir*. Some of them have a very simple approach to religion. They don't even know the Bashkir language anymore, nothing. My wife's sister started to wear the hijab not so long ago. And her husband believes in all the Sufi legends. For him all those fantastic miracles are absolutely true, in the literal sense. So I try not to shock them with my beliefs."

Ismail is not an academic with Nasyrov's encyclopedic knowledge of the entire Islamic tradition. But their spiritual struggles are similar. For Ismail, Islamic devotion is able to exist without a belief that the Qur'an is the literal, eternal word of Allah, because the fruits of the Islamic lifestyle and the change in his heart bear witness to its power. His faith, stripped of cast-iron "proof", is free to soar. His devotion to the figure of Muhammad plays a role here too, and for the second time that day, I am put in mind of Dostoevsky:

the writer said that if he were forced to choose between Christ and the Truth he would choose Christ. Is Ismail's choice also a Dostoevskian solution? To choose Muhammad over the dry Salafist 'truth' of inerrancy? To skate over the shackling claims of Islamist "sola scriptura" for a more mysterious solution? To choose love and life and Muhammad, over an unchanging and all-dictating literalism?

Ismail's and Nasyrov's orthopraxis combined with a critical approach to the sources is monumentally significant. Batrov, Malikov, Gaynutdin and others talk of a "moderate" or "traditional" Islam. But their post-Soviet attempt to revive pre-Soviet Islamic beliefs still bypasses the leaps and bounds made in critical Qur'anic scholarship, and it still contains within it the seeds of a fundamentalist belief in the unproblematic inerrancy of scripture and tradition. Of course, this is not just a Russian Muslim problem. But these two voices show that, as with Judaism and Christianity, textual fundamentalism can be relinquished without loss of spirituality.

In fact, Ismail now says, all these problems concerning the definition of Islam do not interest him so much. He lives Islam, praying regularly and attending the same Sufi circle as Farit. But now he is more concerned with bringing the Islamic message, as he sees it, to the wider world. He has adopted two children from an orphanage. He gives lectures to the curious. He believes Russia needs Islam, but not in the sense that people must be brought kicking and screaming to the faith, or that there must be a mass conversion. "No, I don't think the masses will come to Islam. Not everyone needs to convert. But those who are sincere Muslims can show a better direction. Perhaps in forty or sixty years, there will be enough wise Muslims to set an example, a critical mass, you know, to avert Russia from its old disasters, from the old dilemma of revolution or war."

Phrasing it differently, he says Islam can give meaning to the lives of those masses who live a life of "beer, sleep and Putin." Orthodoxy has a role to play here, but Islam is more suited: "Russians have no meaning in their lives. They would look at life differently if they knew Islam. They wouldn't take bribes for instance. Orthodoxy helps somewhat. But when you see those services on T.V., it's clear that it's mostly old women who attend, and it's not the aged who are going to transform society. It's young people who change the world. And the mosques certainly attract young people...."

TATARSTAN: AMONG THE ARTISTS

Farewell: the greatest painting in the world is The Trinity

On my last day, Farit and I have breakfast and then he drives me to the airport. Our last conversation in the car in many ways recapitulates the Islam of "artistic Kazan" and of this Russo-Tatar republic on the Volga that I have been exploring during this rich and intense week. Kazan passes on our right as we skirt it for the airport, and Farit points out a final sight to me: "That's the monastery where the icon of the Kazan Mother of God is held. It's a pity we did not have time to go there." He then proceeds to tell me the story of the icon's wonder-working powers during the first few weeks of the Great Fatherland War, how Stalin flew the icon round Moscow when the Germans were invading, and how this was the beginning of their defeat.

I listen in silence. Finally, I can resist no more: "Farit," I retort, "I don't understand. This icon was painted as a memorial to the crushing of Tatar Kazan; it is a symbol of Russian and Orthodox victory over Islam and Tatars. It is one of the four icons that mark out the four corners of Holy Russia...." I leave aside the urban myth of Stalin flying the icon around Moscow: it is something easy to sneer at, but it shows again how the pervasive omnipresence of Soviet iconography (Lenin's picture, even if depicted by the likes of a cynical Tukhtar, looming large at every life event in the growth of the citizen from child to adult) has soaked deep into the soul of all citizens of a certain age, leaving indelible prints no matter what worldview they later choose. But Farit surprises me. After a moment staring over the wheel, he has gathered his thoughts and replies.

"*Allah tagalah*," he says carefully (*tagalah* is the Russian or Tatar pronunciation of Arabic *ta'alah*: May He be exalted), "has a program that is beyond us. We see only the flat landscape but if we go up in a plane we will see hills and valleys and all the other fuller dimensions of real life. So it is with the defeat of Kazan. There was some meaning in the Russians coming here and conquering this land. As a result we Tatars and Russians have fused into each other. Look, you and me are speaking Russian. Not everything can be understood immediately. Out of defeat something rich, something deeper probably arose."

He recounts a story from his youth that, Tukhtar-style, illustrates the depth of the Russian soul. He was painting a snowscape on a freezing day in a village. An old grandmother came out to him and invited him into her poor hut for a crust of bread and tea. "This is Russia at its best. True, from one minute to the next, you don't know whether they will beat and berate you, or call you their brother. But in the Russian people, there really is also this quality of *soperizhivanie*, the ability to empathize, to enter deeply into the life of another."

The Kazan Mother of God also sets him talking on another theme. "You know what the greatest painting ever done in the world is?" he asks after a pause. "No," I say. "Andrei Rublev's *Trinity*. In that painting you can really see the divine love. There is no more beautiful representation of God's love than that. Whenever I am in Moscow, I go to the Tretyakov gallery to stand in front of it and admire it." He then asks me if I have ever watched Andrei Tarkovsky's film about Rublev. The Soviet director's masterpiece about the medieval icon painter is a classic of world cinema and I have, of course, seen it. "Then you will remember," Farit says, "the scene where Rublev argues with Dionysius, the older monk. Rublev cannot accept Dionysius' fierce depiction of Hell. For him the main thing is love not justice and suffering. For him, the apocalypse will end in light, all will be saved. The fire is only a means to purify sinners. You can see this in the message of Jesus. Jesus Christ is truly amazing: when he is on the cross, he does not condemn sinners. He says: 'Father, forgive them, for they know not what they do.' He is talking about the thieves: because of course, for killing such a man, they will go straight into the boiling waters of Hell. But Christ's doctrine is to forgive, while the warrior's instinct is to strike back and kill. Really, there are so many things that we do not understand."

The talk of hellfire arises from one of our earlier conversations. Now Farit is solving it with reference to the Russian Orthodox Andrei Rublev, as filtered through the Soviet Tarkovsky, and, as with Vladimir Popov, he feels not in the slightest bit self-conscious mixing these sources (though, strictly speaking, orthodox Islamic *tafsir* denies the crucifixion of Jesus). Oddly enough, the Moscow muftiat has recently translated and published a work of the early twentieth century Tatar theologian Musa Bigiev, where he uses diverse sources ranging from Ibn Arabi to Ibn Qayyim to argue that the punishment of the wicked in Hell is finite, and that the divine mercy will encompass even the wicked in the end. But Farit and Popov do not know this. Instead these questions and the solutions arise naturally out of the circumstances of their interwoven life lived side by side with non-Muslims at every step. Their theology, like Ismail's, is spontaneous, and original in a way the representatives of the official muftiats cannot risk.

Farit surprises me further. As with Tukhtar, the conversation moves on to Russian literature. But Farit disapproves of Tukhtar's adulation of Dostoevsky: "Honestly speaking," he argues, "I prefer Chekhov and Tolstoy. I associate Dostoevsky with a painful episode of my youth, so he is problematic for me. I had just split up with a girl in Moscow, at the Institute. I don't think I have ever, even since then, experienced such pain in my life. My world was falling apart. I couldn't concentrate on my studies. And on top of that, I started reading *Crime and Punishment*. Dostoevsky dissects his characters and looks at them through a magnifying glass. He's a great writer, but he is not full of joy and spontaneity, like some of our great Soviet writers even, and like Baki Urmanche. Dostoevsky didn't really believe in Christ. He was a doubter, a tortured soul. So I don't read him." And there we have it: a Muslim critique of Dostoevsky's insufficient Christian spirit—a spirit that for Farit is one strand in his own Sufi vision of joy and love. Given Dostoevsky's cult status among Orthodox believers, it is an irony to ponder.

Farit has ferried me faithfully between Kazan and Bulgar and Zelenodolsk, and in the process opened up his soul to me. His and his fellow Tatars' artistic, humanistic vision of Islam has added a new dimension to my understanding of Russian Islam. The accurate and bespectacled Farit has also opened up to me unstintingly about his own life and views. In all of this, as usual, I have been the neutral observer, jotting everything down endlessly. So I feel an implicit and quite justified reproach in his final quiet words to me, an edge of frustration I have heard when he talks to the carefree Tukhtar:

"You can read and read, and talk to all sorts of different people, but you won't learn anything unless you accept the truth with your heart," he says. "I could tell you many things, but you wouldn't be able to believe them; you wouldn't want to believe them. For example, a *sheikh* who said to a man: Go into that library and you will find the answer to your question, and he opened the first book he saw and found just that. Or a Sufi who can recite *zikrs* under water for an hour. Or a *sheikh* who recites the names of Allah until his skin becomes red-hot. People have told me I should publish these things. But why? If you told people that there are men who can fly without any aid through the sky, would they believe you? No? Exactly."

My curiosity is aroused, but as an academic fence-sitter, I have probably plummeted all the depths I can manage for now. For me, my return flight to Moscow will have to be achieved with the help of a plane.

PART FOUR

CAUCASUS CONNECTION

5

DAGESTAN: SHEIKHS, STALIN AND THE SPIRIT OF THE MOUNTAINS

Laughing in the heart of the storm

Six months later, it is January 2016, just after New Year. A screaming wind is blowing outside the Central Mosque of Mahachkala and clouds have scudded over the sun. The Said-hajji Abubakarov Islamic Center, a pale green brick building, stands surrounded by mounds of snow and ice opposite a busy roundabout that filters traffic out of the city and into the watchful Caucasus mountains. Ten years ago, near this very spot, Said Abubakarov, the young mufti of Dagestan, his brother and his driver, were blown to pieces by a car bomb. I am watching Khas Muhammad, the boys' now childless father, a stooped elderly man in a velvet robe and skullcap with a sheepskin coat thrown over them, talking to two other wizened elders. There is a burst of laughter; Khas Muhammad slaps his interlocutor on the back, and the two other old men convulse into giggles too.

This is the odd thing about Dagestan. It is Russia's most corrupt federal district. It is a hearth of terror, with gaudy stories constantly burning in the media. Only four days before my visit, ten men are mysteriously shot dead outside the gates of the Derbent fortress. I stand at the spot a week later, before crowding into a small parlor to have a tasty *shashlik* dinner with my hosts. Armed special forces police man the junctions downtown and in the hills. And yet, completely unexpectedly, I seem to have entered into a milieu where banter, badinage and ribbing know no let-up. This is the funniest place on earth, it seems.

I am spending the week with Magomed Bagaudinovich Ramazanov, a professor of education and director of an Islamic primary school. It is he who makes the first joke, as we roll along the frozen highway from the airport in a hefty jeep driven by his nephew Temurkhan. An explosive device is thrown under the vehicle from the side of the road: "They're trying to kill the English spy," he cracks. Not getting the humor at first, my heart skips a beat. But it is only a firework, the remnants of some New Year jollities. A towering New Year fir tree flashes by our right as we hit the main street of the city, confirming that Mahachkala, like any Russian city, runs according to the usual post-Soviet calendar of secular festivities. The jokes, though, going off like Christmas crackers at every turn, are punctuated by longer serious moods: another New Year tree standing proudly in the square opposite the republican parliament is surrounded by unsmiling blue-camouflaged police with machine guns. There have been several attempts by Wahhabis to topple the pagan monstrosity. Black humor might be Dagestan's answer to living in the shadow, just as polite silence was the answer in Fergana.

Mahachakala is a small city. Bagaudinovich,[1] as I will affectionately come to think of the astrakhan-hatted, square-spectacled professor, quickly establishes a routine for my first few days: nights are spent in the Leningrad Hotel, days in the complex surrounding the Central Mosque. Apart from the Said-hajji Abubakharov Memorial Institute, this includes the headquarters of the Dagestani muftiat, an Islamic radio station, the Dagestan Humanities University, the vast Risalat Islamic articles-and-books store and a stylish restaurant called Madinat, where we have our meals regularly and my mood is lifted by apricot *kasha* and other delicacies.

The Leningrad hotel and the Mosque complex come to symbolize for me the two poles of Dagestan. Looking out over the now frozen Caspian sea, the Leningrad is a relic of the 1980s, a sixteen-floor crumbling holdover with worn carpets, rusty taps and flickeringly lit low-ceilinged corridors. The heaters are stone cold; a stench of tobacco hangs in the air. On my second night, I find the canteen on the tenth floor. An apologetic Avar woman in a headscarf serves ersatz food, and a proud Caucasian man, still wisely wrapped up in coat and hat, finishes off his chicken and takes his last swigs from an accompanying bottle of wine. He gazes stone-faced as the results of a dance routine are announced on the TV. But the Leningrad is still seen as the pride of the city, its name and concrete majesty a memory of good times, a beacon of aspiration.

The Professor tells me as we ascend in the creaking lift that first evening: "We are going up, *inshallah*! We are all believers here." Turning to the Russian concierge, he jokes again: "There is no difference between Russians and Avars. We are all believers here, all together." It is more Soviet friendship of the peoples, than Abrahamic brotherhood—and does not quite ring true given the dominance of Avars here and the flight of Russians (the Avars are the most populous of Dagestan's twenty-odd ethnic groups.) A bit later, speaking of his own work in Dagestan's Islamic revival, he comments: "We are trying to inculcate the norms and values of behavior at our school. We want to develop a new ideology. Spiritual ideology is not alien to our tradition: we had it in Soviet times. Of course, it was not openly religious. But we need to recreate something to replace it." Here even more than with Vladimir Popov's Lenin-tinged Russo-Islamic fusion, the question of whether the Soviet era need exclude the new Islamic era is mooter than ever. In the coming days, Bagaudinovich will outline for me his own vision of where Dagestan is going, drawing on his own rich personal history. He is well-placed to do so, as he turns out to have a foot in both the Leningrad past and the new Islamic present.

And then there is the Mosque complex, dynamic, fresh and energetic, but somehow not completely out of the shadow of the Leningrad. Here is where a new generation of Muslim teachers, imams, writers and other cultural figures are spearheading an Islamic revival, or rather the second wave of an Islamic revival begun in the nineties. Among the figures I meet are Magomed Yusupovich, the thirty-four year old rector of the university, Leila Husseinova a radio presenter for Dagestan's Islamic radio station, and Magomed Abdurahmanovich, the minister of religion. A Dagestani representative in Moscow had arranged for Abdurahmanovich to meet me, and I had anxiously envisioned a stooped, bemedalled dignitary. But I bump into him in the Madinat café, and discover that he is a boyish-faced man in his thirties—as is the minister of sports, a recently retired boxer enjoying a coffee at the same table. The Madinat is a gathering-point for these new movers and shakers: as with many spaces in Dagestan it is equipped with prayer rooms and ablution facilities, so that one need not interrupt meetings to walk the five minutes to the mosque to perform all the prayers.

The reason for youth in these positions is not just precocity. In the last ten years, fifty senior religious figures in Dagestan have been gunned down by extremists and youngsters have taken their place. This is brought home to me when I meet one of the old survivors, Khas Muhammad Abubakarov, who now heads the institute that commemorates his two slain sons. Bagaudinovich hurries me over to the mosque when the second *azzan* sounds, boasting along the way that its 15,000 capacity makes it the biggest mosque in Russia (a dignity both Grozny and now Moscow claim). Somewhat to my surprise, he does his ablutions and performs the prayers. His eighties-style business suit and playful red tie stick out in the ranks of track-suited youth in velvet skullcaps. But he will tell me later: "Ahmad-hajji [the present mufti] always says to me: we need you at the mosque—*especially* in your suit and without a head covering." An esteemed professor sends a signal that religion is not just for the ignorant. When the prayers are over, he pulls me into the peaceful, thickly carpeted side-hall, where Khas Muhammad, small and moustachioed, greets me with twinkling eyes. In his purple velvet gown, he emits a wise, peaceful aura. The tall Bagaudinovich holds us both in his embrace: "Meet the grandfather of Dagestan," he beams.

Khas Muhammad Abubakarov: father of martyrs

Before we go up to his office, Khas Muhammad gestures to a wall of forty-odd portraits in the lobby of the institute. I have only just digested his own tragic story, and now the old man tells me who these people are: Islamic activists killed in the last ten years. Dagestan may not have gone through the annihilating war that raged in Chechnya or Tajikistan, but this is a low-level war of sorts. The dynamic is broadly similar to that in Chechnya and Central Asia: early post-Soviet social or ethnic grievances were spiced up with Islamist dynamite to produce a fatal and low-burning concoction.

Here, there was never a successful separatist movement as in Chechnya, mainly due to Dagestan's patchwork-quilt ethnic diversity: the republic is home to four major ethnic groups, and up to thirty smaller ones. Instead, the economic collapse that Russia suffered in the nineties hit Dagestan particularly hard, exacerbating these interethnic and social tensions. The ruling circles, where majority ethnicities such as the Avars and Dargins were heavily represented, failed to bring off economic reforms, and the Avar-dominated republican muftiat was seen by some of its disgruntled opponents as complicit in the government's cronyism and corruption. As in Tajikistan and Chechnya, Islamic opposition groups who at the start of the nineties had embraced democratic visions as an alternative to neo-Soviet stagnation in society and politics, drifted increasingly towards theocratic Salafi solutions. The late Soviet era had also seen huge population shifts, with different ethnicities streaming into the cities from their mountain villages. This uneasy melting-pot, with a muddle of identities and languages, fostered a climate where Wahhabi internationalism could seem like a panacea to some. The targets of the radicals[2] were "traditional Muslims", often Avars, who were seen as too cozy with the corrupt government, and as the war in Chechnya progressed, such radicals hitched their bandwagon to their (far more homogenous) neighbor's independence-turned-Islamic liberation struggle. The ultimate goal was now to create a Caucasus-wide Islamic emirate that would solve ethnic and social tensions with one foul blow.

Bagaudinovich and Khas Muhammad themselves were both born into this Avar elite. However, over the coming days as we travel round together, I observe the two interacting and their versions of the past differ on important points. Bagudinovich, whose father was a decorated tank commander, praises the Soviet legacy unabashedly, while Khas Muhammad has strong reservations. Just before going to meet the old "grandfather", in fact, the Professor tells me "a secret" about his past: "My mother was Ukrainian, you see. And she converted to Islam in the Soviet period."

He is piling on the paradoxes, and also kidding me again about the "secret": in fact, a leading film-maker in Russia turned his mother's story into a prize-winning documentary. Bagaudinovich tells me part of the tale now, and on my final day we sit down to watch the documentary together. "Intermarriage was quite usual," he says, "between Russians and members of the Dagestani elite. The Russians ran the factories and high ranking Dagestanis would interact with them and they would fall in love." The details of his story are a little different, though. I learn later that his mother was a Ukrainian peasant-girl whose whole family was annihilated in the thirties by Stalin's forced collectivization policy. Finally obtaining permission to leave her homeland, she followed an uncle to Mahachkala and met Bagaudinovich's father by chance in a mountain village. However, even before learning that the horrors of Stalinism are so intimately woven into his own personal history, I am having trouble squaring his cheerfully recalcitrant Soviet "ideology" with our regular visits to the mosque (I observe a smiling Victory Day portrait of Stalin on the portico of a college that lies on one of the main roads leading to the mosque itself).

As we take our seats in his office on the fourth floor, Khas Muhammad unfolds some of his own story in between the renewed cups of tea and steaming meat dishes served by his assistants. He was born into a prestigious Islamic family which fought to preserve Islam in the Soviet period. "My grandfather was Hajji Murtaza Ali," he reminisces in his gentle voice. "He and his son Abu Bakr helped spread Islamic learning in Ingushetia and Chechnya. They were great scholars; Chechens respect them to this day. My grandfather had real charisma: he never raised his voice, but people strained to listen to him, and they did everything he said. During the thirties they practiced Islam in secret, they kept it alive. Even the KGB couldn't stop them. In one village, they were going to close the mosque. A friend of my father's climbed up the minaret and proclaimed the 'azzan at the top of his voice: *Allahu Akbar, Allahu Akbar.* The KGB understood: there's no point closing down this mosque. They'll just pray in the street!"

And yet, despite this, the family gradually entered the Soviet system, so that Khas Muhammad was able to study medicine in Leningrad. "I had only top marks in my studies," Khas-Muhammad recalls now. "Physiology, genetics... I was the brightest in the class. I walked with a real swagger when I got to Leningrad. Look who's here, I was saying to every building as I walked down the street. Khas Muhammad has arrived! And now I am suffering for all those A's I got. What nonsense they were teaching us: Soviet genetics. It was all a complete lie. Even then, I disagreed with Lysenko's theory.[3] I pointed out the errors. I was lucky I wasn't sent to prison!" In fact, when he returned to Mahachkala from Leningrad, he was arrested as he got off the plane—but it was another case of Avar black humor: "I had met our chief of police in Moscow and he decided to see if I would be scared or not! I wasn't scared! I went along with it. The officers took me straight to a welcoming committee!"

Khas Muhammad may look down on his youthful Soviet self. But he still teaches medicine at the university. All this makes Bagaudinovich's little interruptions pointing out that Khas Muhammad benefited from the system not entirely beside the point. But for the moment, the Grandfather does not want to dwell on this and loses himself in more reminiscences of his family. "My father was a *hafiz*. I remember listening to him reading the Qur'an. His shirt would be soaking wet with tears. Soaking." He closes his eyes and softly recites some *ayats* of the sacred book, chewing over the syllables in his mouth with child-like delight. "In the eighties, I started to work myself to revive Islam," he resumes, his own eyes moist now. "I went to the village of Akh-ti, which has the most beautiful mosque in Dagestan. I found six strong Lezgins, ready to give their life for Islam and I started teaching there. They wanted to keep the mosque as a museum. The museum keeper said to me: I am half-Avar, please leave me alone. I said to him: I am even tougher on my own kind. One of the Lezgins showed me what he was reading: the Qur'an—in Lezgin! That's it, I said. You have to recite and study it in Arabic. So we began Arabic classes...."

As the conversation continues, Khas Muhammad tells us some miracle stories about his *sheikh* of the sort that would rival Farit's in Kazan. This is followed by a genre I soon become familiar with: the gentle ethnic put-down. A Kumyk berated Khas Muhammad for receiving too many guests at home and so putting strain on his wife. "But I just smiled at him. That's what we Avars are like. My wife loved guests just as much as I did. She was happy. The Prophet Muhammad, peace be upon him, loved to receive guests. I said to him: 'I don't smoke, I don't drink. I don't chase after women. It's just the guests: that's my only habit!' The Kumyk had to agree...!" Bagaudinovich and Khas Muhammad look at each other and laugh: it's a moment of Avar complicity.

At the grave of Sheikh Said Affandi

Eventually, the name of Said Affandi of Chirkesk comes up, as it does in many conversations with those connected to the Dagestani muftiat. Said Affandi's speeches, writings and sheer personality were the fuel behind much of the "traditional" Islamic revival in Dagestan in the eighties and nineties. He too was killed in a car explosion along with six other people in 2012, but his name and memory are still fresh. Affandi was a *sheikh* in two Sufi orders, the Naqshbandi and Shadhiliya (the mixing of orders is common in Dagestan). In his youth he worked as a shepherd and fireman, as well as serving in the Soviet army in Lithuania, before devoting himself entirely to Islamic studies and gathering *murids* round himself. From pictures, he cuts a not dissimilar figure to that of Khas Muhammad: short, wizened, good-humored and sympathetic. He looks just like one would want a "traditional" Sufi *sheikh* to look.

In many ways, Affandi provided something that other regions of Russia or Central Asia (with the exception of Tajikistan) could only dream about— some genuine link to the ancient Islamic past. In Kazan, Batrov was trying to reinject Islamic content into the Russian-language term "traditional Islam" by conjuring a trio of Maturidi philosophy, Hanafite law, and Naqshbandi mysticism. But in the Volga region, the Sufi orders had been crushed by the thirties, though one academic I talk to mentions that loose Sufi structures existed into the Khrushchev period. In both Chechnya and Dagestan, however, Sufism (strongly linked to ethnic and political identity) survived throughout the Soviet period.

And so Sheikh Said Affandi's activity after the collapse of the Soviet Union attracted not only Dagestanis: I meet two Moscow academics who made the trip down to Dagestan to take vows of allegiance to the *sheikh*. Affandi gave them easy spiritual exercises to do, the recitation of a few short *du'as* a day, judging that these cerebral heavyweights would find anything more rigorous beyond their capacities. He made similar allowances for busy, secular Dagestanis: his belief was that even if a person was seemingly far from religion, a little bit of devotion and belonging was better than nothing, and might lead to more.

Naturally, Khas Muhammad and Bagaudinovich revere Sheikh Affandi, and the present mufti of Dagestan has taken over his role as head of the Naqshbandi order. However, the situation with Affandi is not entirely straightforward. Atiya, a Kumyk from Khasavyurt who has lived in Moscow for several years, had also mentioned Said Affandi in our conversations. He spent six years studying Islam in Tunisia at ez-Zitouna university. When he first saw Affandi, he was shocked: a queue of people was lining up to kiss his hand. His father's friend, a police officer, went crazy—out of joy and regret at the missed meeting—when Atiya told him what he had just seen. But Atiya, proud of his "genuine Arab" Islam, had a different reaction: "It's idolatry, kissing a man's hand. But you can't speak to people who won't listen." Another student, also Kumyk, tells me that her family views Affandi as a pseudo-*sheikh*, who merely played up his role but had no real Arabic learning, unlike their own Ilias-hajji. Still others viewed with distaste the corrupt officials who considered themselves Affandi's *murids*. Such disagreement is natural, of course, and the overall impression of the Dagestani brand of "traditional Islam" being built up round his legacy is favorable. Still, there are contradictions in this legacy, as I learn the very next day when, at Bagaudinovich's suggestion, he and Khas Muhammad take me to Affandi's village in the mountains to visit his grave or *ziyyarat*, and then to visit the Sheikh Affandi institute, where about two hundred youths are studying in an institute set up by the *sheikh* in his lifetime.

It is day three and my first trip out of the city. We follow a series of hairpin bends into the hills, leaving the Caspian sea below us, and emerge onto a rolling snow-blanketed plateau. Before transferring to the road that leads to the village, we are flagged down by a machine gun touting helmeted soldier. Murad, our driver, insists with Fergana-like deniability, that he is merely checking that our car is road-worthy and hoping for a bribe if not. Half an hour later, the car turns down a small bumpy track and stops before a green metal-fenced enclosure: the grave of Said Affandi and other martyrs to the extremists. We get out and I breathe in the pure, chill air. I tramp on ahead through the snow, soaking up the mountain view, the weak sunlight, the icy wind, letting it wash the tiredness off my face. When the others catch up, we line up opposite the grave of Said Affandi. Khas Muhammad recites verses from the Qur'an in his careful, gentle Arabic, and whispers down the line to me to pray to God for some blessing. As we are filing out, some other visitors arrive and seeing the Grandfather in our midst, approach him for a blessing.

Next, we travel a looping road to the Said Affandi Institute on the other side of the valley. It is housed in a magnificent five-story building whose vast windows afford a breathtaking view of the mountains. We arrive in time for afternoon *namaz*, and I notice that the fifty-odd students performing their prostrations are doing them with athletic speed, barely pausing between cycles. A table is set up for the honored guests to address the students and Khas Muhammad begins his speech with a severe denunciation of this hyper-athletic prayer pace. Slowly, deliberately, he berates them, quoting hadiths and shari'a on the correct tempo of prayer, once again dreamily enunciating the correct elongated pronunciation of the Arabic words. Later, out of hearing of the students he declares fiercely: "It was terrible. I wouldn't let a student so much as touch a book before he had learned how to pray *namaz* completely correctly." On our tour of the building later, he picks on one or two students and tests their pronunciation of prayers, tutting disapprovingly at the slip-ups and errors. But he turns to me later and gives his rich old chuckle of yesterday: "I know these boys, you see. They ask me up here quite often to teach...."

Put on the spot, I give a little speech of my own about how lucky these students are to be born into a culture that straddles East and West, and the opportunities this can afford them. When we reconvene in the office with the institute's vice-rector, however, Murad, asks me my impression of the students and I have to admit that I am not sure whether our words really got through to them. Cannily, he comments that this undermines my message that language is a tool of communication and enlightenment. But he is right to detect skepticism in my impressions. Our speeches had taken up quite some time, and when the floor was thrown open to questions, not a single one was forthcoming. As we are guided round the classrooms, library and other prayer halls, Bagaudinovich points out to me the Russian literature section and expands on the secular–religious mix in the curriculum. But it is plain to see that the boys' knowledge is very weak: one of them cannot name the date of the Russian Revolution and Bagaudinovich's hurried explanation that he is shy does not fully convince me. Murad tells me later that he finished the institute himself and comments: "I enjoyed it, but the boys are all from local villages and don't like studying." Murad's own work as a driver also begs the question of what these graduates will end up doing after their studies.

A couple of days later I buy one of Said Affandi's most popular books, *The Treasury of Blessed Knowledge*. It has been recommended to me by the rector of the Humanities University, who says it single-handedly put him on the path to Islam. One section, however, alarms me and throws unfortunate light on the clash between "traditional" Sufi Islam here and Wahhabism. Several pages explain the nature of Wahhabism. Lengthy reference is made to a work called "The Confessions of an English Spy", (which in fact is a late Ottoman forgery) in which the spy confesses that he found the simple pagan-living Abdal Wahhab in the Arabian desert and proceeded to indoctrinate him with a wicked bunch of superstitious practices that he hoodwinked Wahhab into believing was Islam. Abdal Wahhab himself and his later followers did not pray regularly, they consumed alcohol and held that belief in God alone was enough to gain salvation. The English spy persuaded Wahhab that the latter had all the qualities of Muhammad, leading Wahhab to see himself in this manner. Elsewhere in the book, Said Affandi assures his readers that the Wahhabis will burn in the very center of Hell.

The store-assistant who sells me the book in the Risalat bookshop assures me that it flies off the shelves, and that the young people especially love it. It is an unfortunate sign that Sufism and Wahhabism in Dagestan are engaged in a symbiotic mutual distortion which is fueled not just by politics, but also by low standards of education. For, of course, the so-called Wahhabis accuse Sufis of the same thing, namely that the *tariqatists* have abandoned the shari'a for the personal practice dictated by their *sheikhs*, that they attribute idolatrous Muhammad-like status to their *sheikhs*, and that they are lackadaisical about ritual observance.

This conspiracy-fueled mutual demonization muddies the waters when it comes to ascertaining how Islam should really be practiced today. But Said Affandi and his followers also encourage a literalism when it comes to believing in the truth of Qur'anic and Sufi legends. As Ilshat Nasyrov had commented about his Bashkir relatives, it is a case of people brought up in an atheist vacuum whose return to religion has a desperate modernity-rejecting edge to it. The readiness to accept the forgery of the English spy shows that credibility and despair are not just features of the extremists who are lurking in their mountain retreats not far from the Sheikh Affandi institute.

However, despite these faults there is still much that is positive in Said Affandi's legacy, especially on an emotional level. Before we leave, the students gather again to sing various songs in honor of the Prophet's birthday, as it is Rabbi al-Awal, the month of the Prophet's birth. These *mawlids* are in Avar and were composed by Said Affandi himself, who had a reputation as a talented Avar poet. They are beautiful songs and the students' faces are evidently also absorbed in their rhythm and meaning. And there is a touching democracy to this society: as we are putting on our boots to go outside again, three old men arrive. Their faces are glazed red by the cold, but the wrinkles come from sixty or more years of hard mountain labor. They have come to listen in to some lectures, Bagaudinovich tells me, as the institute also serves as a *medrese* for the locals of this village. Peasants, perhaps, or kolkhoz workers, they approach the venerable Khas Mohammad, professor of psychiatry in the capital of Dagestan, and without ado, slap him on the back and are soon engaging in the usual loud jokes and ribbing. Perhaps it is something in the mountain air that produces such hilarity, I speculate.

Stalin's ghost is alive and well

The drive back starts off in daylight, but darkness falls suddenly even before we have started the descent to Mahachkala. The company stops off at a roadside mosque to pray the fourth prayer of the day. I wait outside, deciphering an Arabic banner hanging over the road: "there is no strength or power except in Allah". As we nose our way down the hairpin towards Mahachkala, I am sitting up front but I keep my ears pricked to eavesdrop on a conversation between the Professor and Khas Muhammad in the back—at least those stretches that are in Russian rather than Avar. It is a continuation of the one that flared up briefly the previous day about Lenin and Islam.

"But Lenin was against Islam," Khas Muhammad is insisting softly, "he persecuted it, didn't he? He killed thousands of *alims*." "Lenin did us a favor," replies Bagaudinovich. "He cleansed our land of those *sheikhs* who were just deceiving people, while pretending to give them Islam. Lenin did great things for the Caucasus. I believe he was sent by the Almighty to save Dagestan and Islam. Those German tsars would have had the Caucasus without Caucasians, they would have killed every last one of us. Under Lenin and the Soviets, we had more children. They built houses and schools and hospitals. Our own family, *subhana Allah*, has sixty members: I counted them recently! Infant mortality decreased in Soviet times: my mother never tired of saying that. And Stalin, too, was a decisive leader. Do you think we would have all the chaos that we have now under him! Impossible! People were too afraid to cheat or steal. The Soviets had ideology, you see. They had their own type of spiritual ideology: it was patriotism, respect, helping people. Things that are scarce on the ground now. Now we need to use religion to raise up people's morals, to introduce it in the schools..."

The conversation winds on. Khas Muhammad seems to be nodding, and occasionally he grunts assent, and occasionally Bagaudinovich cedes a point: "There were bad things, of course," he admits. "And I'll tell you this: they should never allow public access to the archives from those times. The names of the denouncers are all written in there, from nearly every village. In my father's village, though, no one was deported. But if people found out, grandsons would take revenge on grandsons for what happened to their ancestors. It would be a bloodbath."

They move on to speak of other things, and Bagaudinovich talks for a long time about the history of the Mongols and other topics. As the Professor's impromptu lecture comes to an end, Khas Muhammad sighs: "Ah, and all that suffering [from the Mongols] because they did not have Islam." He pauses, and some moments pass. Then he sighs again: "Yes, life is brief and when I look back, I can remember very few happy moments. Perhaps, once or twice, I was happy, sitting at the feet of my *ustadh*, learning *tajwid*. Those things gave me happiness. But all else is just struggling for existence, and going through the tests that Allah *subhana wa ta'ala* sends to us. People are stupid to worry, to be afraid. It is especially silly to be afraid of those cowards who attack us, those atheists...."

Back in town, we drop off Khas Muhammad at the mosque, where he spends much of his time nowadays, engaging in the *sunna* prayers that supplement the obligatory *fard* devotions of a devout Muslim. He is also, Bagaudinovich tells me, one of those who fast two days during the week, despite his friends' protests to take care of his health. He also "preserves his *wudu*" between prayers, that is, keeps himself in a state of ritual cleanliness throughout the day. He may have a sharp tongue with the students, but I cannot help feeling that, despite all the tragedies that have befallen him, he emits a comforting light.

Bagaudinovich insists on treating me to dinner in a restaurant, and between courses I decide to take him up on his admiration for Lenin and

Stalin. But while he admits to certain brutalities, such as the purging of the army before the war, all in all he remains firm that this was justified and does not cloud the overall good. Finding an Islamic justification, he comments: "There is a hadith that says you should find seventy ways to excuse a person's behavior rather than attributing a bad motivation to them. And that is what we should do with Stalin." The figure of seventy triggers a memory of Batrov in Kazan, justifying his pluralism with reference to an alternate reading of the seventy-three-schools-and-Hell hadith. Here the Eurasian thirst for "strong leadership" has coupled Stalin and Islam. On the plane back, I sit next to a student who also tells me: "I don't see any contradiction between Stalin and Muhammad. They were both strong leaders, weren't they?" This fusion, too, in an odd way is also a regional form of "traditional Islam" or even "moderate" Islam—at least from a Russian, Kremlin-based perspective: it is an Islam that encourages absolute obedience to the government and, supposedly, enhances the stability of a fissile border region.

There is another aspect to Bagaudinovich's worldview. I have seen it elsewhere but, once again, in Dagestan it is all more intense: the Soviet–Avicennan rationalist fusion. In Bagaudinovich's version, it comes off looking like extreme scientism. He is an admirer of Yahya Haroon, the Turkish creationist who retails American Protestant fundamentalism for Islamic purposes. The pseudo-science of finding modern (Western) scientific discoveries such as embryology or geotectonics "predicted" in the Qur'an is popular in parts of the Islamic world and is a symptom of grossly undeveloped educational and research institutions. Bagaudinovich is a pragmatist, though. In the Soviet period, Dagestan was actually incorporated into a modern scientific community, so institutional science is not alien to the region; Bagaudinovich is not miracle-hunting like the Egyptian or Saudi engineers— or even the Uzbek mufti, Muhammad Yusuf, whose works are also saturated with the miracle rhetoric.[4] Still, the crumbling scientific past (funding has dried up, standards have plummeted) is morphing into something more mythical now.

"I came to religion through science," he explains, referring to his two years at a medical college before he switched to humanities. "I remember when I first gazed at a neuronal cell down a one-million-strong microscopic lens in a laboratory in Leningrad: my mind was blown away. It was as if I was face to face with the creator. And what especially fascinates me is genetics: the genetic program that we are unfolding now is a miracle. Everything is strictly determined by genetics. You can see it in families, their traits, and in whole peoples, like us Avars... our history is in our genes. So I take what I can from genetics, psychology and biology and use it for inspiration. It is good material to increase students' belief in God."

Science, then, is not a methodology or technical tool, or critical apparatus, as it is for secularists. But nor is it a secondary bag of facts that is far inferior to the Qur'an, as it is for the miracle hunters. Rather it is a religious–political tool, useful material for inculcating citizenly religiosity. It is another ingredient, along with Soviet values, in the slowly-rising dough of a new Dagestani Islam.

My surprise at Bagaudinovich's scientism is not as great as my surprise at his unabashed Stalinophilia. It is a topic that I will ponder over the coming months, and in fact almost two years pass before I finally begin to make sense of what I am seeing. I find the key to the paradox when reading a seemingly modest article by one of Russia's leading experts on Soviet Islam, V.O. Bobrovnikov. It is called "the creation of Islamic traditions in the Dagestani kolkhoz,"[5] and consists of his own twenty-year old meditations on the nature of Soviet and then post-Soviet Islam in the republic. His main conclusion is that Islam in Soviet Dagestan was not a pristine and ancient "traditional" system that engaged in a long underground resistance to Soviet ideology, but rather an evolved modern hybrid of tsarist- and Soviet-era policy decisions and Islamic practices. The picture of Islam as an ancient and unchanging reality was held by certain Soviet ideologists, who thus saw it as a backward entity to be abolished. But it was also held, for more romantic but equally political reasons, by the West's leading expert on Soviet Islam, Alexandre Bennigsen, who conceived of a pristine underground Islam engaged in eternal opposition to Soviet power.

Bobrovnikov's conclusion is that Bennigsen's data was all derived from second-hand sources. The reality, which this approach distorted, was that the Dagestani rural and urban communities which practiced Islam had been created quite deliberately, first by tsarist bureaucrats incorporating the Caucasus into the Russian empire and then by Soviet bureaucrats restructuring the region for Soviet purposes. A host of Soviet Orientalists and administrators also selectively encouraged certain local Islamic traditions that they felt cemented the new modern farming communities, thereby creating quite new Soviet–Islamic communal realities. Thus "Soviet Islam" and its "Islamic traditions" go back for the most part only to the mid-twentieth century or, in very "ancient" cases, to the mid-nineteenth century.

Bobrovnikov's conclusions throw light on Bagaudinovich's and Khas Muhammad's views. Khas Muhammad's memories dwelled on the intense anti-religious crisis moments in the Soviet period, and his stories implied that Islam was indeed something pristine and separate from the hostile Soviet reality. And yet, chatting in the back of the car with Bagaudinovich, he could not deny that in some logic defying way, Bagaudinovich's defense of Soviet benefits were also true to his own experience. By clearing away the idea that Islam was always different from and opposed to Soviet modernity, Bobrovnikov had made the paradox unravel, for me at least: the Islam which both men had inherited and were now transmitting was not some timeless entity, as old as the hills. Rather, it owed much to a deep convergence and cooperation between communitarian aspects of Islam and Soviet ideology. The Islam that both hoped would rescue their republic from the doldrums was indeed "traditional", and so a panacea for modern ills: but it was traditional in a thoroughly Soviet and Russian, and modern, way.

How to celebrate a wedding: lezginka *or* nasheed?

The following day, the theme of science comes up again, when I actually meet some Dagestani scientists at a wedding, and get a chance to see how Bagaudinovich's views fit in with other people's. At my table, every one of the eight guests is a mathematician or scientist, and some are heads of their departments. The make-up is ethnically diverse: a Lezgin, a Tabarasan, a Dargin, three Avars and a Russian. Quite a bit of the conversation is taken up with ethnic kidding: a drunk Lezgin is like a sober Dargin, and so on. The tables are also gender-segregated, and judging from the cafés I have been out in, it seems that this is not an Islamic arrangement but just part of the local patriarchal culture.

But Bagaudinovich confides that events such as these are still in search of a solid format. Many people no longer feel comfortable with the old boozy wedding celebrations, but they still do not know quite how to behave Islamically. "It's clumsy," he says, and today's event bears him out. At our tables, the drinks are tea and juices—the vodka and Soviet *shampanskoe* are out. Instead of the usual wild dancing and thumping traditional Caucasian songs with boys doing the *lezginka* dance, (and we pass such a reception spilling out of a banquet hall on our walk back into town) this couple wanted something more Islamic: so a handful of religious students have been brought in to provide the Islamic content. From time to time, a quiet thoughtful youth will get up and take the microphone to recite some *ayats* from the Qur'an. Or, after the rash of speeches and congratulations has died down, the music system will come alive with the latest Middle Eastern *nasheeds* in Arabic praising the birth of the Prophet.

"Personally," Bagaudinovich tells me in between the din of speeches, *nasheeds* and toasts, "I don't like this mixed sort of event. I think you should either have a *mawlid* or a secular wedding reception—without the drink, of course. This is neither one thing nor the other." The science professors are uncomfortable for their own reasons. At first, they observe a patient silence when the Qur'an reciter starts reading, but soon they are back to their whispers. Bagaudinovich chides them as the reading is coming to an end: "Be quiet, you atheist rabble!" The tone is light-hearted, but there is a slight undercurrent of seriousness. After a decent interval of an hour, the more senior professors get up to leave, having put in their stint.

After the table has emptied, I am left alone with Bagaudinovich and the lone Russian. He moves down to sit opposite me, extending a hand to introduce himself as Sergei Nicolaevich. His Russian face, plump, with a shock of white hair and rheumy blue eyes, makes me nostalgic for my in-laws and I chat naturally to him, feeling now that I am at a Moscow family gathering. The crisis of Russian universities is a natural talking point, but eventually I ask him what he makes of all this, the increasing tempo of Islamic observance.

"The way they do it here is quite natural. It's gradual, bit by bit. That's their culture. I have no objections. I mean, strictly speaking, I am a *kafir* and I shouldn't even be here—it's a religious celebration after all. But no one makes me feel like that." Nonetheless, although some Russians admire Dagestan's "Eastern" culture, Mahachkala—like Fergana—has gone from being a half-Russian city to being almost entirely Dagestani. Sergei Nicolaevich explains that Russians here do not really have a strong sense of community; the only time he sees his relatives is on the day of the dead: "We tend the graves together. That's how our family keeps in touch." It is a wonderfully Russian custom. But it seems symbolic, too: amid a vigorous and contradictory revival and renegotiation of customs among all the bickering ethnicities surrounding this Caucasian Russian, the only bedrock ritual left is to celebrate the gradual death of the tribe. Unlike in Tatarstan, the interaction between Muslim and non-Muslim is far less rich.

That is not to say that the same "friendship of the peoples" ideology and the evolving "peace of the traditional religions" do not exist here, too, at least rhetorically. It is just that the southern Muslim heartlands on both sides of the

Caspian are *de facto* leaking their Russian populations. Bagaudinovich, with his Ukrainian roots and gentlemanly Soviet cheerfulness, is constantly expressing good will to non-Muslims: he calls up a Russian friend on January 7 to congratulate her on Russian Christmas, and of course, jokes: "Have you converted to Islam yet?" And he insists we make a visit to the synagogue on Friday night.

I had also visited the synagogue in Fergana with Sirozhidin. About ten native Bukharan Jews remain in Fergana, all elderly. Here too, we are greeted by only four members of the community. If the Russian people drain is serious, the Jewish one is catastrophic. We chat amicably, until the pleasantries are interrupted by an incident. Ninety-year old Shimi suddenly pulls out a heavy pistol and starts screaming for blood, and the two youngsters attempt to calm him down. He is reacting to a blurred, long-bearded figure on the CCTV screen. It turns out Shimi is not letting his imagination run wild. There have been several threats to the synagogue by Wahhabis, and the gun in his belt is there for good reason. Most of Mahachkala's Jews, to Bagaudinovich's genuine chagrin, have now left the city along with the Russians.

The ethnic wise-cracking and people's friendship wears a bit thin in Derbent, too. In theory, Russia's oldest city and Russia's oldest mosque are the scene of Shi'ite–Sunni harmony. One side of the mosque is for Sunnis, the other for Shi'ites, a setting that would delight Russian Muslims citing Maturidi's peaceable attitude to Islamic sectarian differences. But, as in Fergana, I get the feeling that the jollity is a bit forced when I meet with the Azeri caretaker of the mosque. In the presence of our Avar company, he seems tight-lipped and unwilling to open up about his past; the meeting proceeds quickly and superficially. Afterwards, Bagaudinovich mutters something about the low number of Avars in the city compared to Azeris.

Young leaders

Back in Mahachkala, I have a rapid-fire series of meetings. The first two are with the rector of the Dagestan Humanities University and the minister of religion. The next three are with charismatic women: Patimat Abdullaeva[6], the wife of Ahmad-hajji Abdullaev, the current mufti; Khadjia Shikhalieva, the founder of a women's Islamic organization; and Asiyat Buttaeva, a professor of philosophy.

Magomed Magomedovich: know your roots

Magomed Yusupovich Magomedov is charming, and again, surprisingly young for a rector. It was he who had recommended Said Affandi's *Treasury of Blessed Knowledge*. Before reading that he had been leading a carefree, hedonistic life and was searching for something more—the classic trajectory of Islamic return. He is thus very much a part of the Said Affandi-driven religious revival here. However, as a historian he is also seeking to revive other aspects of Dagestani Islam, just like Batrov in Tatarstan.

"Eighty per cent of the people in our institutes and mosques are young people," he says, "so that is our main demographic. We have to educate them, to inculcate in them a proper, sophisticated Islam. Many youths have lost their roots; they no longer speak their grandparents' native languages, only Russian. We want to revive our pre-Revolutionary Dagestani traditions; men such as Saipulla Kadi Bashlarov espoused a sort of Caucasian jadidism. He combined Islam with secular knowledge; he wrote on Islam but also wrote medical works in German. His mentor was the Tatar spiritual leader, Zainulla Rasulev; he supported the *jadid* reformers but was also a Naqshbandiyya *sheikh*: this, for us, is a very attractive model that combines our Sufi traditions with openness to modernity. And the Rasulev connection is also interesting because, of course, it shows that Dagestani and Volga Islam are connected: there can be a wider Russian Islam. In fact, there are plans to create an Islamic academy in the city of Bulgar, and we want to create a Shafi'i institute within that institute to host the teaching of our Caucasian *madhab*."

Rasulev is also a figure admired by Nizhny and Kazan Tatars and is sometimes known as the "Tatar king". The head of the Moscow Islamic university, Damir Khairetdinov, tells me Rasulev is a distant relative of his. This partially contradicts those who maintain that there is no such thing as "Russian Islam", that it is too ethnically fragmented to constitute a meaningful whole. As my trips have shown, there are real links, loops and feedbacks between the different Muslim Eurasian regions. But in a quieter aside, Magomedov expresses skepticism about the new Spiritual Board of Muslims of the Russian Federation, centered in Moscow. Dagestan, with Muslim roots stretching back to the Prophet's companions (who reached the Caucasus in the 640s), is too proud to take these bickering and power grabs seriously. Not that they do not have a similar desire to prove their Russian patriotism: "The Moscow muftis talked a lot about how they helped persuade the Crimean Tatars to join Russia. But we also made trips there. We just don't hug the limelight." At one point in our conversation, when we are talking about American excellence in various fields, Magomedov expresses offense: "I can't accept that America is the leading military power in the world. Russia is."

He also talks about the problems of reaching youth and, of course, extremism. "Our tradition is immensely rich. But unfortunately, most young people don't know about it. Instead, they know about Caucasian dance and song—the *lezginka* and all that. I find that sad in a way. The youth are being told that this is all it is to be Caucasian: dancing, singing, being romantic and merry! That is your culture. But there is so much more."

It is an interesting observation. Often the picture of Dagestan is of a place that is uniformly Islamic. Sociological surveys stagger people when they present almost 100 per cent levels of belief in God. But Magomedov's words indicate that this is misleading—Dagestan is, after all, part of post-Soviet Russia where ignorance and indifference about religion dominate. Hirach-Gajji, another of Bagaudinovich's drivers with whom I become friendly on our various trips, also puts me right about levels of Islamic observance: "Some people just go to the mosque as otherwise they would be the black sheep," he tells me. "You know, everyone else is going, so I'll go. And you wouldn't believe what they get up to in the meantime. Drink, women and worse." Bagaudinovich also adds his own contribution here. He did a survey among 150 of his students to find out who could translate the *fatiha* word for word. Not a single student knew its meaning in its entirety. Hirach-Gajji also muddies the picture when he exclaims contemptuously: "A lot of youngsters will only come to the mosque once a week. They won't pray regularly." The reasons for their Friday attendance may be social conformism, I think, but that still puts their observance light years ahead of Russian Orthodox observance, where yearly church attendance is the norm.

Magomed Abdurahmanovich: Syria beckons

Magomedov speaks a bit about extremism, and believes that they are finally winning the battle. The issue of extremism is taken up in more detail by Magomed Abdurahmanovich, the young minister of religion. He has been in the thick of the fight against Wahhabism, having worked for several years as an imam in a village where the local extremists tried to assassinate the previous imam.

"He was severely wounded, but he survived," he recalls. "However, he moved to another village... But," Abdurahmanovich continues, "things are getting better. We have been working hard to change people's mindsets. I invited all the parents of boys who had gone off to Syria to the town hall. I wanted to talk to them, to find out their worries, and also what is driving their children to do this. Usually, you know, they go off because they have been promised a car, a house, money—it's a way to get rich for them. A lot of them also have this idea that, you know, 'we can't live in the Russian Federation, it's *dar al-harb*'. So we got Qaradaghi down here to explain to them about *dar al-silm*. We had a conference with muftis from Moscow and Tatarstan. Putin also came. He said: 'Allah has deprived Erdogan of reason.' He used the word Allah! Muslims were amazed!" In his own village, he has had some success. "I have tried not to alienate those who are inclined to Salafism. I want them to come to our mosque. With some, it is all or nothing, us versus them. There were Wahhabi representatives in the mosque. I let them be; I told them I don't want to make differences with you. And things have been peaceful so far."

This attempt to reconcile Salafists and "traditionalists" has been tried across the board in the last few years. In April 2012, the leaders of the "non-traditional" Salafist community in Dagestan met in the Central Mosque with mufti Abdullaev and the mosque's imam Magomedrasul Saaduev: it was one of several meetings where both sides shook hands, agreed on unity, and foreswore violence. However, shortly afterwards Said Affandi was assassinated, and relations broke down again. The republican authorities stepped in and closed the Salafist mosque on Kotrov Street. I drive past it with Bagaduinovich and see that it is still closed; the usual coterie of blue camouflaged soldiers are guarding it.

That is not to say that in Dagestan, as elsewhere in the North Caucasus—mostly in the less volatile western Kabardino-Balkharia—there has not been a renunciation of hostilities between "tariqatists" and Salafists. Theologically, an agreement to disagree seems to be possible, though "English spy" rhetoric on both sides does not help. I watch a YouTube clip by Mufti Ahmad-hajji Abdullaev where he delivers a Friday sermon in the same Central Mosque that I have been spending so much time around: his rhetoric is still positive, and he says that no matter the color of your headwear, green or otherwise, you are welcome. (Green is the color worn by members of the Naqshbandiyya *tariqat*.) "Both are good," says Abdullaev, making it clear that tariqatists and, presumably, Salafists both serve Allah.

One can only hope that this conciliatory, inclusive trend will continue. But, of course, it is not just theology, or the crude desire for "money". As in Fergana, there have been deep and violent provocations by Russian forces and

Russian-friendly local government cliques, whose corruption, nepotism and arbitrary justice have marginalized many. In addition, the definition of Wahhabism has often been politicized from the beginning: as with Andijan 2005, defenders of civil rights or opponents of government corruption have been smeared with the label of Wahhabi to shut down dissent and change for good. As Denis Sokolov points out, some Muslims who leave for Syria or the Middle East do so not for extremist reasons but to escape corruption; they are then barred from returning. It is a case of funneling dissent out of the region.

It also occurs to me that the young minister's delight at Putin's populist use of the name "Allah" is hardly likely to placate the "insulted and the injured" on the fringes of the Avar-Dargin pie, or detract from the Russian government's support for the heterodox Alawite dictator, Assad. And not everyone believes that the Moscow-sponsored Qaradaghi has enough theological authority to change attitudes.[7] However, a couple of months after my visit I see that Abdullaev wins an informal text-in vote for honorary "president of Dagestan", that is, the most popular social figure of the republic. It seems, then, that the mufti and his helpers may slowly be gaining souls and achieving a unity that can transcend the ethnic, religious, political and economic differences that have split Dagestan.

Muslim women forward!

Patimat Abdullaev: the rebel tamed

The first of my woman interviewees is, in fact, the wife of mufti Abdullaev. I have been invited to say some words to Magomedov's students and she slips onto the podium as I am speaking. Things do not get off to a good start: when I finish she objects to my statement that there can be different types of Islam. I am about to clarify my position when Bagaudinovich leans over and whispers to me: "That is the wife of the chief mufti of Dagestan." I choose my words carefully, therefore. It probably would not do to go on record as picking a fight with the mufti's wife. She is waiting back in Magomedov's office after the talk and I brace myself for a tense encounter. However, I am completely wrong-footed. Patimat Abdullaeva turns out to be both charming and gracious. Full of humor and critical spirit, she listens sympathetically to my own impressions of Dagestan and other matters, and then opens up with refreshing honesty about her own life and views.

Patimat was another secular rebel, who for a long time resisted her elder brothers' turn to religion, and instead pursued a successful career as a TV journalist. When she did finally turn to religion, she says, "most of my so-called Muslim friends had a terrible reaction, especially at the TV station—they began to avoid me. The only person who encouraged me, would you believe it, was the mother of my best friend, who was Russian: I went round to visit and Auntie Valeria greets me at the door: 'Oh,' she says, 'you look so lovely in that scarf. I wish you could persuade my daughter to wear a scarf like that....' Later, I heard Said Affandi say something that resonated with me. A Russian girl who had converted to Islam came to him and asked how she should relate to her family: 'they are not believers,' she said. 'They are Christians.' The *sheikh* was very displeased, and told her: 'You should never say that: Christians are believers too.'" Patimat adds a similar story about an elderly Russian woman who followed her family to Stavropol, but later returned to Mahachkala: "I missed the sounds of the *azzan* every morning," she said. It is a story about "our Russians", "Eastern" Russians, similar to those of Sirozhidin's aunt on the outskirts of Fergana.

She talks a bit more about her family: as is common in Dagestan, her own family reveres their Arab genealogy, tracing their roots back to the different waves of Arabs that came to the Caucasus. Her grandparents spoke Arabic and continued their regular life of prayer behind closed doors during Soviet times. The subject of Arabs leads to Arabic and how she studied it. We then find common agreement on the need for religious people to be linguistically and literarily talented, to understand the nuances of language and texts. I also put it to her that the status of women in Islam leaves something to be desired, mentioning the shabby and cramped conditions of the women's section in mosques in Moscow, as a case in point. Patimat agrees: "It is unacceptable. But that is changing. In Chechnya they have an enormous, clean and very beautiful section of the mosque for women. Sometimes husbands do not understand the rights of women. I can say that I am lucky. My husband positively encourages me to continue with my career and to get out of the house a lot, as you can see today!"

Pursuing this theme, I ask her about polygamy, which is an often discussed topic among Russian Muslims. I do not know it, but I have pushed a button. "Don't get me started on the topic of polygamy," she heaves. "It's a painful, painful thing. I will tell you, polygamy is worse than death. It is a great mystery. You know, history has turned to tragedy because of polygamy. Think of it: the whole unhappiness between Jews and Muslims," she brings up an earlier theme we have discussed, "is due to polygamy. After all, it was the quarrel between Hagar and Sarah that led Ismail to grow up estranged from Isaac. And from that came the estrangement of two great nations."

After our conversation is over, Bagaudinovich reveals two surprising facts that throw a completely different light on her comments. The first is that Patimat is in fact the second current wife of mufti Abdullaev. And the second is that her first husband was Said Abubakarov, Khas Muhammad's son, the mufti who was assassinated in a car bomb. I am astonished. Her words come back to me: "Polygamy is worse than death." This was not an empty phrase. She had had direct experience of both, and still felt the former to be worse than the latter. Later, I was unable to find confirmation that Abdullaeva was indeed the mufti's current second wife.

Khadija Shikhalieva: a woman's mosque by any other name

Khadija Shikhalieva heads an institute called *Muslimaat* on the edge of town. It is another initiative inspired by Said Affandi: a meeting and learning space for women who may not feel comfortable in the mosque, either for the reasons Patimat mentioned or because of a general mistrust of religion. Shikhalieva tells me that when she founded it in 1995 she was as lacking in knowledge as her students now are, and its early participants—rather like Ismail in Kazan—were pulling themselves up by their bootstraps, both learning and teaching at the same time.

Shikhalieva also throws in an interesting detail: "One of the models that I had in mind when I founded the institute was the Institute for Noble Girls that existed in St Petersburg before 1917: it was for girls of the aristocracy, where the students would learn four languages, secular knowledge, but also subjects that a wife needs to know. I liked that model very much. Not that marriage is the automatic be-all and end-all: some of our girls get married on graduating, but some go on to further studies. The point is that there are many women's organizations now in Dagestan, and we fill one particular niche: we offer spiritual values and education about how to raise a family. On Thursday evenings, women can come here to pray *zikr* together and read blessings for the Prophet. They learn *nashids* and how to make *du'a* in Arabic."

At first, Shikhalieva thought about calling the place a mosque, but Said Affandi advised her against the term. Dagestan does not have a tradition of women's mosques or female imams, such as parts of China do. Although that Chinese idea has been adopted in some other parts of the Islamic world, it was controversial enough setting up a women's center. But the *sheikh* threw his weight firmly behind it, and it evidently filled an important need: not just uneducated girls and women came, but journalists, public servants and intellectuals also flocked to get an Islamic education there.

I speak to some of the girls, who have just had an oral exam on the Prophet's life. They range in age from fifteen to eighteen and all are dressed in a uniform of flowing green *jalabiyya* and white headscarf: as elsewhere in Russia (I think of Gulnaz in Kazan) the return to "traditional religion" is expressed by adopting an idealized form of pious garb imported—somewhat paradoxically, as the garb is not "traditional" for the region—from the Middle East. At home, these girls will probably change out of these uniforms. And even now, two or three of the young women are keen that I don't get the impression that they are docile marriage-fodder. They jostle forward to answer my questions about what they intend to do in future: "Don't get the idea that we all want to get married off," one lectures me firmly. "I want to go to medical school, for instance."

After the meeting, I tease poor Hirach-Gajji who is on driver's duty today: "What do you think?" We have become friendly in the last few days, and he takes my meaning: his unmarried status is hanging over him now that he is pushing on for thirty. But though he started to become religious five years ago and now prays and fasts regularly, he shakes his head with a grimace that reminds me of the willful Shuhrat in Fergana. "No, no. I wouldn't look for a wife there. Too traditional for me. They let you have one meeting and then—bang—that's it, you're married. A lot of people in Dagestan do that, but not me. And besides, they can pretend to be all modest and pious when you meet, and then it turns out they have a rotten character. No thanks!"

Back in Moscow, I stay in touch with Hirach and find out a few months later how his own romantic situation unfolds: that summer he gets married to a young teacher at Bagaudinovich's school. And as if to prove that cosmopolitanism is not entirely a thing of the past in Dagestan, it turns out that his new wife's father is a Mahachkala "mountain Jew", and her mother Russian. Hirach tells me he has attended two Passover meals at his father-in-law's. "All religions are true for me," he comments calmly. Another year passes, and Hirach is already a father. When I see him on another brief trip to Mahachkala, he explains earnestly: "But I want to have four or five children. Strong families are important. I missed that when I was growing up. My parents remarried, and I wasn't close to my half-siblings. Besides, all my relatives have moved away; they live all over Russia now, so we don't see each other." Again, Islam will be the powerful glue, I think, that will bind Hirach and his (gradually Islamizing) wife into a unit that will resist these centrifugal impulses.

Asiyat Battaeva: "We are neglecting our boys..."

My next meeting is with Asiyat Battaeva, a professor of philosophy. Having read an article she has written expressing criticism of aspects of the religious revival, I am hoping she will provide me with a different perspective, one that will take me outside the inner circle of the muftiat. But although she is a Kumyk by ethnicity and not religiously observant, her views only confirm for me that the Islamic revival mostly enjoys across-the-board support.

She lives in a beautifully decorated house on a hill in the suburbs, whose walls are hung with antique Dagestani artefacts: some years ago a Serbian friend expressed regret that he had never seen a traditional house and Asiyat and her husband decided to rectify this. Given the artistry of Asiyat's house, and the fact that she is a philosopher and her husband a physicist, I anticipate that she will have reservations about religion. However, though she says with straightforward honesty, "There is no point beating about the bush: I was a keen supporter of Soviet power. Why lie?", she goes on to say: "I completely support the Islamic renaissance in our republic. I would become religious myself, but after a whole life of living as a Soviet person, I just cannot do it. I cannot start praying. The old ideology still lives in me."

As for Bagaudinovich, state-supported implementation of Islam is unambiguously desirable. What the Western imagination, with its notions of church–state separation, might interpret as cynical manipulation of religious symbols, she sees positively. She attended the presentation of the Uthman Qur'an at the Pushkin museum in Moscow before an audience of Middle Eastern dignitaries, and she follows the attempts of the Moscow muftis to develop a government-friendly Islam. This all fills her with pride. "I want to help replant the tree of Islam that was uprooted in Soviet times," she says. Perhaps the only difference with Bagaudinovich is that they disagree on whether Islam was completely destroyed by the Soviets, or whether there is continuity. The Professor opines that Islam survived pretty well under the Communists; Battaeva sees the need to start from scratch. Probably, each is drawing on different experiences of their family and larger ethnicity—and perhaps even definitions of Islam.

Still unclear about how her views hang together, I ask what she thinks of a traditional Islamic institution like Shikhalieva's *Muslimaat*, and she again surprises me—after all she is an educated career woman—by expressing her whole-hearted approval. Things become a bit clearer when, as we sit down to dinner, I learn that the woman serving us is her daughter-in-law: as in Fergana, there are big families and the youngest son continues to live with his parents. Even though the Battaevs reached the pinnacle of the Soviet academic ladder, they preserved their traditional family structures. In fact, during the meal the husband tells us of his own family. He counts eighty-six cousins, putting even Bagaudinovich's sixty-strong clan to shame. In such an environment, Battaev goes on, it is easy to pick a wife whose compatibility you can be sure of. Thus, as in Fergana, although the family's Islamic customs were partially stripped from them, the patriarchal family structure, whose justification is so easily linked to an Islamic rationale, has preserved the conservative norms that favor a rediscovery of traditional religion: hijab, *jalibiya* and all.

Battaeva is contributing in her own way to the Islamic revival: she teaches a free class in ethics at a religious school. Reverting to the subject of the *Muslimaat* institute, she expresses a different worry, which she sees as contributing seriously to the problems of Dagestani society. Unlike for a Western liberal, she sees the problem not in terms of freedom but in lack of structure. As she puts it: "At the moment we are neglecting our boys. They are neither Eastern nor Western. They have lost a lot of what Iranian or Afghan men have, that is, the ability to go out and trade and make money and support their family. They have come under the influence of the Russian model. They don't do their duty by their wives. And so you get families splitting up. All the best students, in fact, are girls. So they have to do everything. And since the times of Brezhnev the Dagestani extended family has been breaking down."

The echo of ancient church bells…

I do not succeed in finding an alternative opinion to the government-sponsored religious revival. Kumyks and Avars may differ about the allocation of resources, but the fundamental model of mosque-state fusion is uncontested. I hear a divergent voice, but it is from a Lezgin academic who has lived a good part of his life in Moscow, far from his native republic. This is Alikber Alikberov, Russia's leading expert on the ancient history of the Albanian kingdom that covered the territory of southern Dagestan and Armenia. In his work, he has shown that the early Lezgins were Christian and that among their cultural achievements were church-building and bell-ringing. "Fellow Lezgins who used to find the sounds of church bells abhorrent to their

Islamic sensibilities," he grins, "now find that they quite like it." His academic work thus feeds into questions of contemporary identity.

Alikberov wants to separate the notions of nation, ethnicity and religion, and disapproves of Russianness being linked to Orthodoxy. He considers himself Russian in a broad, liberal sense and objects to the idea, tacitly promoted by the government, that to be truly Russian you have to be Christian, just as he objects to the tacit idea that to be Dagestani is to be Muslim, an equation his academic work overturns. "I am a European. Yes," he insists, "Dagestan is part of Europe, and in Russia we have got to build a civic nation that's independent of ethnic belonging; everything should be organized according to the civic, non-ethnic principle. The idea of the 'Soviet *narod*[8] was an attempt to move in that direction... but it was still ethnic in conception. We can't let people monopolize Russian culture; for that matter, we can't let people monopolize European culture. I am a European Dagestani: it's Europe with an Eastern culture. We had our Christian literature, too, you know, written in our native languages all the way back in the fourth century. We were part of Europe once, and we want to return to it..."

Alikberov admits, though, that since the Crimean debacle in 2014, Russia's "Eastern turn" is taking the country further from that cosmopolitan dream. He lives in Moscow. His wife is half-Ashkenazi Jewish and half-Georgian. One of his children identifies as Jewish. "I am a *liberast*," he chuckles sarcastically, using a not very flattering Russian insult for liberals.[9] In our rolling, humorous conversation, Alikberov had even highlighted the Jewish influence on Dagestan, due to the Jewish Khazar kingdom which ruled the area in the seventh century.

However, Jewish or not, Alikberov's vision of a European-style Dagestani civil society does not resonate with Battaeva or Bagudinovich, and it is they who are shaping that society now. When I meet Leila Husseinova at Dagestan's Islamic radio station, this is confirmed: she was born in Moscow to Bashkir and Tatar parents, and grew up in an environment similar to the Mustafin family. But after becoming religious, she "made *hijra*" from Moscow to Mahachkala. Leila, and other non-Dagestani new Muslims like her, is thus replacing emigrants like Alikberov, or Atiya, the Arabic translator who now lives in Moscow and makes trips home rarely. And when he does, he tells me that he shaves his trendy goatee and takes off his beret: "People just wouldn't understand it down there."

For Leila Husseinova, the reverse is true, as she explains: "My husband and I have built a house in Mahachkala. We just feel at home here. The Dagestani mentality is very attractive. It's extreme, yes: if people get angry they get angry! But they have also drowned us with love. And being a Muslim here is so much more comprehensive." She tells me of her surprise at the public swimming pool: there is a women-only swimming day, and a prayer hall near the changing rooms. Women slip out, get dressed, pray and go back to swim again. There is also a prayer hall in the local library.

She also takes active part in a Sufi *tariqat*, and mentions Patimat Abdullaeva as the woman who got her involved: "It happened when I interviewed Patimat in Moscow. You cannot resist her enthusiasm and love for the *tariqat*, and I joined it thanks to her influence." I ask her what the *tariqat* added to her faith. She smiles. "That's like asking: why do you live? You can write a million words and still not know." She is not, then, in a hurry to move back to Moscow with its four mosques for two million Muslims. On this she agrees with Atiya, whose six years of Tunisian study have left the merest of traces: he still puts his right shoe on first, eats with his right hand, and if he sees a woman standing in the metro, he will give her a seat. "But there are too many temptations in Moscow to be a real Muslim," he says.

Magomed-Mikhail: "We Muslims will end up protecting Christianity."

On day six, Bagaudinovich wants to take me out into the mountains again. We have breakfast at the Madinat café and another quick visit to the Humanities University. Whilst there, the rector's assistants delay our departure by ushering me down to the basement. To my surprise there is an archery range there, and everyone insists I fire a few arrows at some targets from different bows. "Archery is a *sunna* of the Prophet," one man explains to me, and I remember Ramil in Kazan, the quiet bow-maker. I am not a very firm shot, but I can see the symbolic attraction of the sport for the religious mind: erring neither to right or left, one must avoid sin and hit the target of righteousness. In the mosque, I have met several cauliflower-eared ex-boxers. One of them has told me: "I have given up boxing since I became Muslim." Dagestanis lead Russia and the world in boxing and martial arts; for those who have become religious, archery is the best way for them to channel their prowess, while obeying the *sunna*.

We drive for an hour and half until we come to Akhulgo, the site where the Russians finally overcame Dagestani resistance to their conquest in the nineteenth century. It is a tall crag topped by a stone tower. At its foot is a small mosque, and three memorial stones to the heroes of the Caucasian war.

Some gnarled trees are festooned with ribbons. One plaque reads: "Here on October 17, 1832, in unequal combat with the tsarist army, there died the heroic leader of the mountaineers' fight for freedom and independence, the 1st imam of Dagestan and Chechnya, Ghazi-Magomed." At the foot of the (reconstructed) tower, another plaque reads: "Here is where imam Shamil landed, after jumping from a rock on the day of Ghazi-Magomed's death." Another one commemorates the sixteen fighters who were walled up in the tower and fought to the last against the tsarist soldiers.

Bagaudinovich brings the children from his school here, and Magomed Yusupovich had told me the place was important in instilling Dagestani identity. Given that there are people in the hills further north who still consider that Islamic resistance to the Russians is an ongoing duty, I wonder how Dagestanis interpret this monument. Hirach-Gajji gives me his own take on the matter: "This is all history for us. It's important to see how our ancestors fought heroically. But we have been part of Russia for almost two hundred years now. We are part of Russia; there is no problem there." A bit later on, however, the usually genial Bagaudinovich allows himself a darker thought: "The Caucasus wars have still not ended," he ponders. "And they never will. The Caucasus is the thorn in Russia's side...."

After soaking up the atmosphere, Bagaudinovich and Hiraj pray in the small, warm mosque and we move on. Half an hour of snaking through canyons and skirting a large reservoir that supplies half the republic with water brings us to another site from the Caucasian wars. There is a half-built mosque here which has not opened yet: the money ran out before it could be finished. The name and date of the battle are carved in large letters on the side of the mountain. Again, his darker mood over, Bagaudinovich impresses me with his openness: "They should build a monument to all the Russian Christians who died in the war, too," he believes. "After all, lots of mothers lost their sons here and we are all together now. I mentioned this idea to [mufti] Ahmad-hajji, and he liked it. But it hasn't been taken up, because of the lack of funds."

Climbing back into the car, we drive even further up into the mountains, passing through an arch into the sizable municipal town of Gunib, perched midway up a steep flank, and then follow more hairpin bends until we stop at a quiet spot from where the valley stretches out far below and you can see the answering flanks of the opposite mountains. Here, set back off the dwindling road in a little orchard, is a marble rotunda. It is built over the rock on which Shamil was sitting when he finally handed himself over to General Barytinsky on 25 August, 1859. We are tottering on the top of the world here, and the silence is audible; I am not surprised to find out that there is a Soviet-era guest-house nestling further up the road, which still does a good business in providing rest for those escaping the pollution of the big towns. I even start planning a retreat for myself the following summer.

But now is time to turn back; we have reached the end of the road—our own, and Shamil's. On the way back down, Hirach-Gajji is inspired to take a detour to his father's ancestral village of Ruguja. So, after winding through Gunib again, we turn off the already perilous tarmac road onto a rutted earthen track, and drive carefully along for twenty minutes. A few vehicles bump past us, heading in the opposite direction, and the drivers all beep us. "Either we know them," laughs Bagaudinovich, "or they are honking just in case we do." In most cases, it turns out that Hirach-Gajji does know them: he may never have set foot here, but he has met them at different family gatherings of the Ruguja "diaspora" down in Mahachkala and other towns.

One more bend, and a cluster of weathered white stone houses crouching into the hill looms into sight. Soon we are revving precariously up and down the narrow lanes of the village, and it is not long before an old man leans in through the window, and discovering Hirach-Gajji's ties to the village, takes it upon himself to introduce us around. We spend the next hour strolling through Ruguja, pushing a way through lanes overhung by crumbling houses and Arabic-scripted door frames. Across from the graveyard, where a funeral is in procession, Bagaudinovich shows me a long, low building: the old Soviet "house of culture". The iron statue gesturing in front of it, he explains, is of Abdurahman Daniyalov, the man—says Bagaudinovich—who saved the Dagestani peoples from deportation during the war. In 1944, when he got wind of the plans for the Chechens, he flew post-haste to Moscow and met with with Lavrentia Beria, whom he successfully persuaded to make Stalin reconsider his tragic plans.

At the time, I am so charmed by the romance of the mountains and the old world charms of the village that I soak up this information uncritically. But back in Moscow, I poke about a bit, and discover that most historians consider Daniyalov's saving of Dagestan, an account keenly promoted by the current (Avar) president of the republic, to be a myth. It seems Daniyalov would have been too young to intervene, and too unimportant even to be privy to advance information about the deportations. Later on in his career, he supported Stalin's initiatives for the North Caucasus, and according to his critics, launched the policy of ethnic discrimination against the Kumyks and Lezgins.

Once the mountain vapors have dispersed, I also begin to rethink our winding pilgrimage round Imam Shamil's various sacred sites. His handsome and stern bearded portrait seems to have become, for Bagaudinovich and many others, an anodyne symbol of Dagestani pride. But a bit of digging reveals a different picture: Shamil, another Avar, was after all not just a national hero, but a fiercely Islamic mujaheed, whose battle was not just with the Russians, but also happy-go-lucky *munafiqun* (the Qur'anic term for hypocrites)—that is, Dagestani Muslims whose observance of shari'a was lax, and who saw no sense in fighting the far stronger Russian forces. Some of the villages we had been traveling through would have been stormed not just by the Russians back then, but also by Shamil and his *ghazis*: once taken, Shamil imposed strict shari'a on them, including amputations, summary executions, and confiscation of property from "hypocritical" Muslims on the grounds that "Allah created everything in the world for the believers." In effect, his imamate was a strict Islamic caliphate, justified by literalistic references to medieval Shafi'i law codes, but without any of the constraints on the rule of an imam so carefully put in place by medieval *fuqaha*, or jurisprudents.[10] In other words, Shamil's imamate was arguably far closer to the model of his modern Dagestani namesake, Shamil Basaev, and his dwindling followers today, than to the comparatively lackadaisical Islam of Bagaudinovich.

Bagaudinovich is not alone in his re-appropriation of the original Shamil, though: in his youth, the world-famous Dagestani writer, Rasul Gamzatov, accepted the Stalinist excoriation of the old mountaineer warlord, and wrote a poem called "Imam" that opened:

The English enthusiastically wound a turban round his head

And the Turks diligently daubed his beard with henna

And gave him a Koran, and more importantly, a saber of steel:

'Here's your imam, mountaineers—the representative of Allah on earth'...

After the collapse of the Soviet Union, Gamzatov did some rethinking, and came closer to Bagaudinovich's position of hazy admiration for the national hero, writing now of his earlier condemnation:

"What can I say in answer? Before him, and before you,

My people, I am unforgivably guilty..."

So Shamil still lives in the mountains, I discovered. Like Daniyalov, his image shimmers behind a haze of myth, shifting with the winds of ideology. But it was ever so from the earliest days: after all, did not Hadji-Murad, Shamil's chief naib, immortalized for Westerners in Tolstoy's novella of that name, first fight against Shamil on the side of the Russians, and then switch to the imam's side, before finally abandoning him again?

Back down in Mahachkala, night has fallen, and I am invited to dinner with Bagaudinovich and his family. We are back in the twenty-first century now—or rather, the twenty-first century as propped up firmly on the twentieth century, and especially that part of it dominated by the loving shadow of another Caucasian strongman, Iosif Vissarionovich, about whom Bagaudinovich suffers no ambiguities of affection.

The company consists of Bagaudinovich's wife and sister, two aunts, and daughter, as well as one of his nephews, a recent graduate who is now a lawyer with the public prosecutor's office. The apartment is situated in a block that was built just before the Second World War. In theory it is possible to walk through the entire building on each floor from the first flat in one wing to the last flat in the wing on the opposite side of the tree-lined courtyard: this was a measure included by the architects in case the building needed to be turned into a hospital. Air-shelters were also built in the basements. Given that it was constructed in 1934, Bagaudinovich points out, this shows Stalin's readiness for war with the capitalists.

There is a late Soviet feel to the décor and as we pass back through the rooms, I cannot help noticing a calendar in the kitchen celebrating the anniversary of the Great Patriotic War, replete with a portrait of a smiling avuncular Stalin, or the photograph in the study of Putin shaking hands with a local official: "my former student", Bagaudinovich explains. In contrast, the living-room is dominated by a large painting of the family's ancestral village: it is a giddy vista of craggy stone houses perched on a mountain's edge, even more breathtaking than Ruguja. "Most of those houses are in ruins now," Bagaudinovich tells me, "and the villagers have moved up the slope to build new ones. But a lot of people have moved down into the towns." A few feet across from the picture, the windows of the living room open onto a balcony with a grand view over the port, where shipments of oil and fruit are docked from Kazakhstan and Iran.

The talk over dinner barely touches on religion. Islam here is merely the Professor's eccentric hobby. When the topic is raised, it sounds like a breach of politesse, and is accompanied by slight distaste. Bagaudinovich's daughter, a quiet, intelligent ophthalmologist in dark spectacles, who has just returned home after ten years in Moscow, remarks: "There are too many mosques being built in Dagestan. What we need is schools." It is a sentiment that Alikberov would no doubt applaud. Still, when Bagaudinovich later gives me copies of the children's magazine he edits, I notice she contributes a health column for the publication, which aims to give children and their parents a mix of Islamic history and holidays, along with secular and general history and information. Her secular Muscovite leanings must be wrapped in Islamic packaging to reach an audience down here.

When dinner is over, Bagaudinovich steers me back into his study. He wants to show me the film about his mother, which he told me about on the first day. It is called "I found my happiness in Dagestan". And here I am face to face again with the mystery of how Stalinism and Islam can continue to exist side by side in these parts. The film begins at a family gathering in the Ramazanov ancestral village, which looks much as it did in the painting. Bagaudinovich's mother, Elena Vasilievna, her hair partially covered by a light scarf, is celebrating her birthday at the head of a table, surrounded by her Avar family and many villagers. There is dancing, (alcoholic) toasts, and an endearing shot of a younger Bagaudinovich engaging in a very nimble rendition of the *Lezginka*. Slowly, Elena Vasilievna recounts her story.

She was born in Ukraine before the war. Then, nearly her entire family was dekulakized, dying of starvation or being deported to Siberia. She and a brother ended up in an orphanage. When she was sixteen, somebody advised her to write to Stalin for permission to travel. Every day, she ran barefoot for a kilometer to the post office, awaiting a reply.

One day it came, and she was given a passport and the right to travel. She followed an uncle to the Caucasus. Once there, she was sent to a village to help teach accounting. But then she was roped into teaching Russian to the villagers: "They couldn't understand me, and I couldn't understand them." An imposing, fiery-eyed young man called Bagaudin met her on the road and was smitten by her. His family accepted their son's decision to marry this foreigner, and for the next eleven years, Elena Vasilievna slowly absorbed the village's customs, language and ways. "I took on Islam too. Why not? These people were good to me. I trusted them fully, and there was no reason to doubt their religion either."

In 1942, Bagaudin went off to join a tank corps; his wife stayed on teaching in the village, enabling the Avar villages to enter the wider world of Russian and Soviet reality. She put the village on the map of the Soviet Union, integrated it, and helped drag it into the twentieth century. Eventually, she herself was awarded the medal of Mother Heroine of the Soviet Union. "We agitated for fathers to send their girls to study. We organized a boarding-school where girls could learn," she recalls. The results are all around her: her former pupils now look just as aged as she does; one old lady in tears tremblingly grasps her old teacher's arm, recalling her days on the school bench. Elena Vasilievna's own voice breaks as she summarizes: "I am so grateful that I have such a big family. May God always permit you to remember your family. Never forget your family, never!"

And so there it is, the question of Stalin: not black, not white but—as I enter further into Bagaudinovich's worldview—increasingly grey. Here is a woman whose family was wiped out by the tyrant. But then she writes an entreating letter to him, and he grants her the gift of freedom and forgiveness. In the eighties, it seems, though I cannot ascertain the date from the film, Elena Vasilievna went back to Ukraine and tried to have a memorial built out of Dagestani marble to her fellow villagers who died in the famine. But the authorities would not permit it. She tried to have the church restored, but received the same answer. She was lucky, in fact, to have moved places and changed identity, because for fifty years she slipped off the radar as a *persona non grata*, the vilified "child of kulak parents". How else would she have received a medal from the state? And yet, she bore a great gratitude to Stalin—for the new freedom, the award, the Great Victory in '45—and this gratitude has passed down to her children, including Bagaudinovich.

The Professor is not the only one who has continued in education: his sister is also a teacher. Together they are continuing a project of modernization begun by their mother and the regime she lived under, only now they are weaving Islam into the mix. I see now the intensely personal roots of Bagaudinovich's defense of the Soviet period, and how, for him, there is not the slightest contradiction between Soviet values and Islam. Judging by the film, however, it seems to me that the Islam of Bagaudinovich's village was not the underground Arabic classes and Qur'an recitation taught by *alims* in old barns, the type that Khas Muhammad remembers. It was, rather, a legacy of strict patriarchal traditions, village customs, perhaps a pantheistic gratitude to the local divinity, all mixed together and morphing into something new as Russian language and Soviet traditions joined the blend.

On my way to the airport the next day, we stop off at Bagaudinovich's Islamic school. As everywhere, there is a tacit reminder of violence: a woman's portrait hangs over the staircase; she is the owner of the building. Her husband is in prison on corruption charges, and his first wife was assassinated over a business deal. We wander around the shiny new premises. Bagaudinovich had told me at the wedding that people were still very much making it up as they went along as regards the format of public events and their Islamic content. Here, too, there is an odd pick-and-mix flavor. One little girl in a hijab and short sleeves makes the Professor bend down so she can whisper a secret into his ear. Bagaudinovich chuckles to me: "Her parents are Russian converts. They insist on dressing her up in this hijab, even though she is wearing a T-shirt." The hijabs are optional, however, and the curriculum follows Russian state standards. But as in Fergana, though less so, Islamic endeavors attract suspicion: a few years ago, people accused the school of Wahhabi leanings. A group of strict parents were forced to move from a suddenly banned school and sent their chidren to study here for a while, attracting gossip in Mahachkala society. But they moved on when they understood that Bagaudinovich's venture was too liberal for them.

I chat to some of the teachers, two of them Arabic-language graduates of local universities, and watch as the children name objects in Arabic. While we are in the director's office, a new parent comes to enroll a child: he turns out to be a Syrian with Dagestani ancestry who moved to the Soviet Union in the eighties. "Over here I am an Arab; back home in Syria, I am a Caucasian. It's tough. The cultures are so different. Here you see things that you just couldn't see in a Muslim country." It is a common reaction of non-Russian Muslims to Russian Islam, but people forget that it applies even to this most Islamic part of Russia, as well. The Syrian's wife, who is with him, finished medical school and is now retraining as an acupuncturist. They seem very pleased with Bagaudinovich who, hearing of their straitened circumstances, tells them of the interest-free loan system the school offers parents.

The road from Mahachkala to the airport goes on for about ten to fifteen kilometers, and looks like an extended building site. The birth rate here is high, and people are still pouring in from the mountains, settling in places like this. To me, these new habitations seem grim, wild projects, but Hirach-Gajji and Bagaudinovich have a different view. As in Fergana, "It's a father's duty to build a house for each of his sons. These houses will be occupied by good families, who will help each other in the traditional way," says Hirach-Gajji. The Professor, too, is optimistic about the demographic boom, and repeats a sentiment he has aired several times during our travels:

"We Muslims will end up outnumbering Christians. And our faith is strong, so we will also end up protecting Christianity, stopping it from dying out." He mentions the new mosque being built in the other direction towards Derbent: "That's why we are going to call it the Isa Center, in honor of their prophet." I remember him articulating something similar in the film about his mother: it seems his Ukrainian roots have produced a soft spot for Christianity, an Islamic–Christian fusion. However, this Islamic–Christian fusion is the opposite of Askhat's in Moscow. Here Islam is the dominant element. As with his other siblings, Bagaudinovich even bears this dual identity in his name: Elena Vasilievna gave her five children both Avar and Russian names. Magomed Ramazanov is also Mikhail, the guardian angel. Perhaps Bagaudinovich sees himself as the guardian of a dying Christianity, or at least a Christianity, that, like his mother, will be finally comfortably absorbed into the new Islamic–Soviet narrative rapidly spreading here.

Kadir Malikov's words keep coming back to me. The moderate Kyrgyz Muslim was dreaming of an Islamic state in his eighty per cent Muslim republic. In Dagestan, the muftis seem to have attained a rapprochement with the government that is far more successful than in Kyrgyzstan. And an hour or so up the road in Grozny, the capital of Chechnya, a *de facto* Islamic state practically exists already as an odd mirror-image of Putin's fantasized Orthodox Russia. But could this happen in Dagestan, which is after all the mother of Islam in the Caucasus and Islamically far more venerable than the lately converted Chechnya? Oddly enough, it seems, the Chechen model is not something Dagestanis necessarily want or are able to emulate.

A passing comment during one conversation has stuck in my memory: "In Chechnya, they have totalitarianism," one person had said round the table. I had leapt in for clarification and got the sense that perhaps I was not meant to hear this comment about the feared Chechen leader. The person who made it seemed to be back-pedaling furiously: "I meant totalitarianism in the good sense," he clarified, and given the general admiration for Stalin, perhaps he was sincere. He went on: "What Kadyrov has created there is enviable. Russia, and especially the Caucasus, needs strong leaders. Caucasians are an energetic people: that's why they are so good at sports, boxing, martial arts and so on. But that can get them into trouble too. And besides, Dagestan is too diverse to implement Kadyrov's style of leadership. It's easier if you have just one nation to control." At this point, Bagaudinovich had chipped in: "Yes, the Kumyks, Tabasarans, Azeris and so on all want their cut. And the Nogais: maybe we should just cut them loose...!"[11]

Thus Dagestan's patchwork quilt of diversity means that a Chechen quasi-theocracy is an unlikely outcome. Dagestan is doomed to compromise, to democracy, in fact. Those who dream of purity and homogeneity and the Islamic revival will have to leave, for the mountains that border Chechnya, or Syria perhaps. As for the others, as one Moscow Muslim with links to Dagestani Sufism put it: "Dagestanis already have their caliphs and their caliphate—it's right in front of their noses. The Sufi *sheikhs*."

Still, even the Sufi *sheikhs* are not single-handedly going to solve Dagestan's huge economic and social problems. The clans, those huge "genetic" conglomerates that nurture the identities of Bagaudinovich and Battaeva, make implementing the secular liberal order that Alikberov dreams of very difficult. Here, landing jobs for one's relatives (like Bagaudinovich's lawyer nephew) is a virtue. Giving the jobs to strangers is a vice. But that is bound to create discontent. And so, while things are improving on many fronts, the future continues to look uncertain and cloudy.

6.

CHECHNYA: THE AVATAR IS SLEEPING...

Ground Zero: everything's normal

A year later, January, the Caucasus: it seems like *dejà vu*. Hirach-Gajji, Bagaudinovich's friendly driver, had encouraged me to ask his boss whether we couldn't take a detour to Grozny and spend half a day there: "It's a good place to hang out," he assured me. But we had other things to do. Now, in 2017, I am going to get a chance to check out Chechnya's "good totalitarianism".

It has to be said: Chechnya—or more precisely Grozny—is Ground Zero, in the imagination of many, at least. The anxieties and suspicions, the accusations and psychoses, the nightmares that crawl below the surface everywhere else were made utterly plain here. Here was the place where you shouldn't let your feet take you: "one of my friends went off to fight in Chechnya, and never came back," as Ismail had said in Kazan. "It was just luck that I didn't go too." Another Moscow interviewee had told me that he used to dream of "escaping to the forest", as one of his friends had: there, life was pure, simple and without worldly temptations.

The process that occurred in Chechnya had a sleek and swift logic: in the mid-nineties a secular-nationalist struggle for independence led by a former

Soviet general wrested a quasi-independence for the republic; its leaders then rapidly read up on Islam and started to implement shari'a: public whippings and amputations were the theatrical symbol that their homework was paying off. Next, a group of militants slipped over into Dagestan and set up two shari'a enclaves, where beheadings were added to the list. On the surface at least, it seemed as if Sufis and Salafists had achieved a consensus, with the secularists left behind. All that remained was to install the next phase of the program on the rest of the Caucasus with the help of Arab mujahedeen fresh from Afghanistan, Bosnia and Tajikistan, as well as local Caucasian sympathizers. But then in 1999, the Kremlin, with its new leader Vladimir Putin, unleashed another wave of annihilation; the brief but brutal second Chechen war ended up with Grozny being bombed out of existence into a blasted wasteland. Out of the rubble emerged Ahmat Kadyrov, a Sufi mufti, and his son Ramzan. By force of persuasion and persuasive heavy force, many militants switched over to the growing Sufi theocracy; those left behind dwindled as the 2000s progressed, until all that remains now is a grand-sounding Caucasus Emirate, which numbers between two hundred to a thousand fighters, still launching attacks from their hiding places in the mountains.

Now everyone, it seems, talks about how Chechnya has become perfectly normal. That at least is the message relayed constantly on Russian television, where features on Ramzan Kadyrov and his charming family alternate with programs showing the natural beauty of the republic's snow capped mountains. Much of the Western media presents a grim antithesis to this view, dwelling on the human rights abuses and the dictatorial tendencies of the new republican leadership. But that same leadership, somehow, as I have seen time and again, evokes respect and admiration among Russia's other Muslims. Ground zero has been built over; a bright future has arrived. So where does the truth lie?

The picture of normality is an alluring one. In the company of two Chechen acquaintances, Salman and Abu Bakr, who accompany me around Grozny for five days, I try at first to put my finger on what this "normality" consists of. Even in this short period, though, I am relieved that they don't overdo it with the banality, and that at certain turns in the conversation, cracks into the past open up which give a vista onto what may lie beneath the surface constantly projected on Russian TV screens. In the Channel One presentations of Grozny, the city is more shimmering symbol than reality: the downtown skyscrapers and glittering tower blocks make it look like the cutting edge parts of Moscow. I imagine a vast glittering city, whose hub, the enormous pristine Ahmed-Hajji "Heart of Chechnya" central mosque ("the biggest in Russia, the biggest in Europe") seems like a distant miracle. And so, as we chug around in a 1990s Volga sedan on my first evening, I am relieved to see that Grozny is not so much Eurasian Mecca as another preening provincial small town, a good deal smaller than Mahachkala and a good deal tidier than Tver or Ivanovo, but still comfortingly anticlimactic. And its normality is, in part, the normality of small-town Russia.

The apartment prices are obscene, I am told—"no one knows where the money comes from or what Chechens live on"—and, when I ask whether mortgages might ease the way up the property ladder, the answer "all deals are done in cash here" is accompanied by throaty laughter. One of my new acquaintances is a Syrian Chechen: his grandfather left in the early 1920s and his father was born in a village in the Golan Heights. The 1967 war with Israel pushed them to Damascus. And now the Syrian war has pushed Abu Bakr here, to the joy of his family, who have welcomed him back three generations later. He is in the hotel business, and that too is all normal: "Chechens don't know how to do business. It's all backroom coffee deals, but meanwhile everyone else in the country is on WhatsApp and internet advertisement sites. The central hotel only escapes bankruptcy because they have a deal to put up all visiting football teams, even opposing teams, which goes against all professional etiquette."

Local football, incidentally, is running as normal: "It's a disaster. Instead of cooperating with other teams in the Caucasus, like Mahachkala and Nalchik, all our Caucasian teams try to undercut each other constantly, and are getting filled with Russian instead of local players. If anyone here understood management they would create a strong all-Caucasian team." Permitting myself a wry thought, I invent a name for the team: Caucasian Emirate, the self-adopted name of the remaining two hundred-odd fighters still shivering it out in the mountains, while furious rebuilding goes on down here. Abu Bakr's football talk has me thinking, though: if people cannot get together a good all-Caucasian football team, what chance is there for the Islamic revolution?

So: all this corruption, incompetence, graft and exaggeration is par for the course, in the provinces at least, where there is still a lot of catch-up to play with the big cities. A relative Russian-style daily normality is still the order of the day, then. It's all about cutting corners rather than cutting off heads. And I am even treated to a small bathetic miracle on that first evening: an electricity outage means that the Central "Heart of Chechnya" mosque is clothed in plain old ordinary night darkness, barely visible, off duty for a while from its never-ending task of symbolizing the triumph of moderate, traditional Islam in the Caucasus. My companions gawk at its invisibility: "But what can have happened?" they cry, before darkened shop windows and extinguished street lights point them to the truth. Even the casual aside as we dip into an underpass that "some of the heaviest fighting took place here in the first Chechen war", while suggestive, is to be expected. It is only when we are nosing our way through various suburbs, that a pebble is thrown into the calm surface: my friend now proposes that, before turning in, we "go for a cup of tea on Putin."

In the privacy of the car, before we go into the public space of the café, hoping I am on the right side of nosy, I have to ask: "Don't you find it odd— this name for your main street?" "It was odd at first," Salman says. "It even jarred, produced a bad feeling. Now, though, we don't even notice it." And so we take a spin down "Putin", looping back at the end where a Soviet monument depicts the crouched bulky figures of an Ingush, a Chechen and a Russian in frozen embrace against an incipient snow flurry. As we pull up outside the café, the driver takes his key out of the ignition, and it occurs to me: "Wasn't that monument destroyed in the fighting?" "It was," he says. "But they rebuilt it."

Still, the seams show: this deliberately resurrected Soviet monument of an Ingush and a Chechen made more sense when Victory Avenue was the main thoroughfare in the capital of the Chechen–Ingush Soviet republic. Now, though, the whole symbolism of a purposely rebuilt Soviet sculpture emits an uneasy ambiguity, encouraging one to re-imagine the past in different ways.

Chechen Avatar

Still, these are weak ripples and the flat surface of normality is restored, oddly enough, by a dose of highly standard Russian eccentricity the next morning after breakfast.

I am in the kitchen of the Sheikh Deni Arsanov School for Languages on Sheikh Deni Arsanov street, about ten minutes drive from "Putin". Here to greet me is Ibragim Arsanov, the great-grandson of the *sheikh*. In the next couple of days, he will take over some of the duties of hosting me. Forty-six years old, with an easy smile, a ready wit, and a tall loping form made taller by his astrakhan hat, he is the director of the school and also a well known public figure in Chechnya. He is fluent in English and French, and studied in both Paris and London. On this first day, he leads me to the kitchen where the company settles down for tea, bread and cheese and new people come in and out to join the conversation. Straightaway, the man opposite stretches out his hand and introduces himself as Ruslan Zakriev, and then proceeds to monopolize the conversation with a tale that at first seems far from the Chechen realities I am trying to sniff out. More and more, though, it comes to seem strangely germane to what is going on here.

"I am suing James Cameron," he declares proudly with a toothy smile. "You know: the director of *Avatar*." He whips out his iPhone and shows me a clip of Channel One news. The camera zooms in on Zakriev standing outside the courtroom in Stavropol, while the voice-over recounts his story. Zakriev goes over it in person with the air of one who will tell his tale to whoever will lend an ear. "He stole the *Avatar* plotline from me. I wrote a fifty-page story in 1996 and published it in 2002, several years before the film came out. There are about thirty striking similarities between our plots and ideas. It 's all quite easy to prove. And that Cameron is like the class cheat. He's nicked someone's else's test paper and writes all the answers down correctly, but when you quiz him orally, he doesn't know what to say. Have you ever wondered why he just can't come up with the sequel? It's been years, hasn't it? I am owed millions, billions maybe." I look over at Ibragim and the others: are they just keeping a polite silence, or is there something to this? "It's true," Ibragim nods, detecting my skepticism. "I have read the story." Stranger things have been known to happen.

We discuss the details of this odd affair further, and are joined by three young film directors who are looking to break the monopoly of Russian film in post-Soviet cinema by trying to set up their own film festival in Kazan, which will draw Kazakh, Tatar and Chechen artists. Ruslan is off again: this time, he wants to persuade the newcomers to make the sequel of *Avatar* following Ruslan's own ideas. "It'll make millions," he gushes. "People will come just to see what it's like, even if it's made on the cheap with low technology." When they are gone, Ruslan turns to me: "You see," he resumes his tale, "Cameron missed the whole point. The whole story depends on a deep Sufi mystical meaning."

It is only two days later that Ruslan finishes off this thought, but already at this point, though I do not know it, I have been initiated into the story of Sheikh Deni Arsanov, the man who has given his name to the street and the school we are in. Dazed by Ruslan's nonstop chat, it takes me all this time before I ask him to explain this "Sufi meaning". In Cameron's film, the avatar is a creature without a consciousness; the astronaut climbs into the pod and is wired up so that his thoughts can be transmitted to the slumbering creature. Ruslan tells me that his story contained a similar idea, and it was based on a story concerning Sheikh Deni.

One day a disciple saw the *sheikh* lying on the veranda and called across to his wife: "Is the *sheikh* in?" The wife called back: "No." "But I can see him," protested the disciple. "Come and try to wake him then!" was the wife's reply. The *sheikh* was present physically but his spirit had left his body and was roaming the land helping people in need. Ruslan's point is that the situation does not work without a knowledge of Chechen Sufism. It is all rather charming: the idea that millions watching this blockbuster around the world owe their inspiration to a remote Chechen spiritual master. Over the coming days, though, it is not the image of the avatar that will linger with me, but rather the idea of the *sheikh*'s body, temporarily deprived of his spirit.

For this is the impression that grows on me as I get to know Ibragim Arsanov and his circle. It is not merely my judgment, but the sober and brave assessment of Arsanov himself. For it is a plain fact that while the Sufi orders exist and play a central role in Chechen society now, there are no *sheikhs* left to head them. As a result, much of the Sufi spirituality that should permeate the Sufi orders is absent; all that is left is the body of the sleeping *sheikh* and a set of rituals, awaiting the return of the spirit to give them living meaning again. Spiritually, of course, this is a far from "normal", and as I get to know better the story of Arsanov's *vird*, I begin to get a different angle on what is normal and abnormal in Chechnya.

Arsanov's own *vird*, or Sufi brotherhood, is a case in point. Unlike other *virds*, they had a *sheikh* for longer than most; most of the other *virds* lost their leaders in the 1960s and 1970s. This crop of Sufi leaders had been born before the Revolution and survived the dislocations of persecution, war, deportation to Central Asia and return to Chechnya. Before they died, they did not manage to raise true disciples and so left behind them sheikhless *virds*. Some saw this as a punishment for the bad times they were living in. But Sheikh Ilias Arsanov, the last of Sheikh Deni's ten sons, survived up until 2002. Like Sheikh Said Affandi in Dagestan, on the surface he led an unprepossessing life as a driver and shopworker. But he led an active life of prayer and had a demanding ascetical routine.

"But nowadays," says Ibragim Arsanov, "it is difficult for many of us to observe even the simplest rules of our order." Of course, in living so long Sheikh Ilias survived all the above-listed woes, as well as the two fierce

Chechen wars of the 1990s. For that reason, perhaps, he too did not manage to rear a spiritual heir. And his followers are too dazed as yet to produce one. This leaves the *vird* open to all sorts of political manipulation that is far from the original intention of a *vird*, which is usually translated into Russian as "spiritual brotherhood". Of course, as I discover soon, the same goes for Chechnya's now politically dominant *vird*, the Qadiriyya: it is headed by Ramzan Kadyrov, but despite occasional gestures, his leadership is not that of a *sheikh*.

Once more of beards and veils, Sufis and Salafists

Still, Ibragim is lining the nest in which a future revival may occur. During several meetings in the kitchen of the Sheikh Deni Arsanov School for Languages, he explains a bit about himself and his background. Rather than taking part directly in politics, he prefers to engage in behind-the-scenes cultural revival. The school for languages owes its name to Ibragim's own passion for philology: French and English are taught here by, among others, his own nephew, who tells me later that he first became passionate about foreign languages when listening with fascination to Ibragim translating Radio Svoboda for the assembled family in the 1990s. Ibragim himself attained his fluency at Pyatigorsk University, followed by stints in England and France. But the school is far more than just a language college. Set in an impressive honey-colored building topped by an Arabic-engraved cupola and crescent, it is actually the restored *medrese* first built by Ibragim's famous ancestor, Sheikh Deni, in 1904. But this is not its first restoration: the *medrese* was rebuilt in the early nineties. Then came the two Chechen wars, and Ibragim's family only managed to rebuild it once again in 2003. Since then the number of students attending it has been steadily growing.

The story of the *medrese*'s double revival illustrates something else about Chechnya's peculiar fortune. Ibragim tells me that Sheikh Deni also included the study of language in his study program more than a century ago. This was rather peculiar for the Caucasus at the time, where religion and secular studies did not usually mix. But Sheikh Deni had a Tatar neighbor who was close to the *jadid* movement, and one of the reasons why he wanted to create such a mixed program was so that his neighbor would have somewhere to study. Thus the Sheikh Deni *medrese* was an important instance of the *jadid* movement in the Caucasus in those days. "In that sense," laughs Ibragim, "I have inherited my ancestor's spirit. I firmly believe in combining secular and religious knowledge. Like Sheikh Deni, I too have contacts with today's Tatar *jadids*." He is referring to the young scholars of the Gaynutdin muftiat, whose conferences he attends regularly. Most striking of all, however, is that fact that the descendants of Sheikh Deni's Tatar neighbors still live on the same street and are friendly with Ibragim.

This constant springing up of Sheikh Deni's *medrese*—on the same street, and with the surrounding neighbors miraculously intact—has something of a fairy-tale air: it might not be too strong a word to call it a resurrection, and it puts one in mind of Rinat's irrepressible minaret in Bulgar, which so captured the imagination of his listeners in Siberia and the Volga region. It is a tale of resilience, but, as with the sleeping avatar, it cannot but hold a sadder side: after every re-founding, the ground has been pulverized; much has been lost. An ugly word has entered Russian recently: *retraditsionalizatsia* or re-traditionalization. The idea behind this paradoxically un-Slavic word seems to be that pre-1917 traditions can simply be revived after a 70 year hiatus. But, as with the Soviet statue on Prospect Putin, while tradition is usually a case of slow evolution, these revivals are often unpredictable leaps into the past. The result can be incongruities and odd puzzles.

One such little puzzle, which I am not encountering for the first time, is that of beards. As we are standing in the hall one evening, and students are coming in through the doors, Ibragim and I are talking about what happened in the nineties, when the first nationalist Chechen war was hijacked by Wahhabis and took on a violent religious coloring. "We have had it up to here with those beardies," Ibragim recalls with distaste. While I am having dinner with another acquaintance who is close in age to Ibragim, and connected to his *vird*, I hear the same complaint: "All these beardies and their hadiths: it's so pernickety. It's not manly, it's not Chechen. I am practically an Arabophobe nowadays, you know: not because of the language, which I like, but all these pointless medieval hadiths with their slavish imitation and regimented behavior." Typically, he goes on to parse the Qur'an as endorsing alcohol in small amounts. However, at the very moment that (the clean-shaven) Ibragim is making his anti-beardie remark, I observe a male student behind him, who is hopping out of his boots and changing into slippers. Like all the other male students in Ibragim's school of language/*medrese*, he has a long bushy beard and is wearing a broad cotton skullcap. If length of facial hair is the criterion, then it is a mystery why the anti-beardie Ibragim's neo-*jadid* revival is turning out "beardies" at such an alarming pace.

So what is going on? Human rights groups have often reported that Chechen authorities used to seize the regime's critics and dress them up as militants, leaving their corpses to be discovered later after framed shoot-outs. But the odd thing is that the stereotype of Wahhabis as "short-trousered freaks with shaved lips" as Farit had phrased it so solidly in Kazan (or as Sirozhidin in Fergana might have put it) is being undermined now: nearly all of the young men I meet while with Ibragim and my acquaintance have long beards and shaved lips. If they had to be framed up as extremists, it would simply take a spare pair of combat trousers to complete the picture. Indeed, in Chechnya the hair symbolism has hit a serious glitch: in reply to my perplexed queries about beard-styles (and later veils), another man around the kitchen table offers his interpretation: "It's all pure imitation. If Kadyrov cuts his hair short, those in his close circle cut it short too. If he grows his beard, their beards are long too. In fact, no joke, they all go to the same barber. And then every kid in the street imitates the elite, and so it works its way down." Since the time I was in Fergana, Karimov has died, but his beard-phobia has outlived him there, and one wonders how long Chechen visitors to the Valley might survive intact or what mutual compromise adherents of these different strongmen could come to.

But are Ibragim's students only muddying the symbolic waters with their beards? Is Ibragim's condemnation of "beardies" while surrounded by "beardies" just an odd little anachronism? Perhaps Ibragim's hirsute students have beardless hadith-hating, *jadid*-loving souls? The answer to this question might lie in the painful dialectic between Chechenization and Islamization. Ramzan Kadyrov's father Ahmat was given a remit by Putin to pursue a policy of Chechenization: this was intended to put Chechens back in high administrative posts and to allow the region's native oil wealth to be retained in greater part by the republic (something that other sidelined regions have also tried to extract from Moscow). As such it would address some of the grievances that lay behind the first Chechen war. Chechenization would also reverse the internationalist foreign-funded Wahhabism so favored by the Chechen leaders who had fought Russia in the Second Chechen War, men such as Doku Umarov, Shamil Basaev, and Ibn al Khattab.

Part of the Chechenization packet was to be "moderate, traditional Sufi Islam"—that elusive construct that has heads being scratched in Kazan, too. Ahmat Kadyrov had resisted the creation of shari'a courts under Mashkhadov in 1998, and as the second Chechen war started, he had declared continued jihad against overwhelming Russian forces to be pointless and self-defeating. All this is why he was chosen by Putin to foster a Chechnya that would provide a solid, patriotic southern border for the Russian Federation. However, this vision of Chechenization relied on a naive and typically dualistic view of Chechen Sufism, and of Sufism in general. For like beards, Sufism has its own logic of growth, which may have been forgotten by the Kremlin politicians. It was imam Mansur in the 1800s who first used the Naqshbandiyya *tariqat* to mobilize weakly Islamic Chechens against the Russian colonizers (a pattern seen at the same time in Sudan and West Africa). His efforts were brought to a climax by imam Shamil, whom I had been chasing around Dagestan's mountains a year earlier. During his thirty-year long imamate, the great Sufi leader had come down heavily on both Dagestani and Chechen Muslims who did not toe the shari'a line. Thus Chechen Sufism, or *muridism* as it was dubbed by the tsarist and then Soviet authorities, was the Wahhabism of its day. The famous 1990s Wahhabi, Bagauddin Kebedov, a Dagestani Avar who launched the "invasion" of Dagestan in 1999 (so reversing imam Shamil's line of expansion), in effect setting off the second Chechen war, was one of many who forgot this: part of his critique of "Sufism" was that it heretically rejected the idea of jihad![1]

A contemporary Islamic scholar, Jonathan Brown, drives home this point with his comments about an influential Indian Sufi whose heritage was also used by anti-colonial fighters in later years: Shah Wali Allah.[2] In short, Brown points out that Wali Allah was a Salafist (or a proto-Salafist) and a Sufi. He was a Salafist because he insisted that if investigation reveals that a practice advocated by the four *madhabs* (traditional medieval Islamic law schools) contradicts the Qur'an or hadiths, it must be rejected. And his Sufism in fact deepened this Salafist tendency, as it encouraged an Islamic universalism that went beyond the agreed upon parochial division of the Islamic world into four schools.

In Russia and even elsewhere today, this notion of a "Sufi Salafist" has come to seem like a bizarre oxymoron. But the universalism of Sufism, which united Dagestanis, Chechens and other Caucasians in a trans-ethnic *imamate* under Shamil did indeed, as with Wali Allah, go hand in hand with a deep shari'a revival that even transcended *madhab* difference. Perhaps this is the key to why Ibragim's students so resemble the defeated Wahhabis of independent Ichkeria, and why Ramzan's beard is getting to be so much longer than his father's stubble and/or mustache. The more that students are given access to Islamic sources, including "pernickety Arab hadiths"—on which, of course, half of Sunni Islam rests—the less chance Ibragim's eclectic, beardless and Astrakhan-crowned Avicennan "traditional Sufism" has of retaining a hold.

There is simply no guarantee that Sufism can be fitted into the box that Soviet-born Russian Muslims and non-Muslims want it to fit into.

In Dagestan, much mirror-image name-calling ensures that Sufis and Salafists never mistake each other's identities, even though anomalies constantly threaten to disrupt this simplistic consensus. A good example of this is respected Sufi *sheik* Abdul-Jalil Affandi's somber pronouncement in 2016 that the Mahachkala concert of Maher Zayn, a popular Arab Islamic-themed singer, violated the shari'a prohibition against listening to music. As one admiring commentator wrote on the YouTube video of the speech: "If we said this, people would immediately scream that we are Wahhabis." In other words, strict and pietistic observance that can seem socially odd in the atmosphere of modern Russia is often not judged according to meticulous religious logic: rather the labels Sufi and Wahhabi have degenerated into name-calling labels. Similarly, the practice of removing photographs from relatives' tombstones is said to be evidence of Wahhabi extremism; a better explanation would see it as a perfectly legitimate ("non-extremist") Islamic rejection of creeping Russian Orthodox influence on popular burial customs.

Here the dynamic of Chechenization slipping mysteriously into Islamization, to the surprise of the older generation, and the horror of some Russians who did not foresee such developments on their soft (and much bruised) southern border, can be stopped by fiat from above. However, it is not as if this slip into Islamization is accidental; Ramzan himself has not just forgotten to shave his beard. He too is under the influence of Islamization, it seems, and also heeds shari'a norms, albeit in a highly erratic and selective way.[3] After all, in treading the new path of Islamic traditionalism, he has to take into account what the broader Islamic world outside Russia is up to. One evening I am in the kitchen with Vahid Akaev, one of Russia's leading scholars of Caucasian Sufism, who began writing seriously about Islam in the Caucasus in the late Soviet period. I raise this very question of the new (post-Wahhabi) "religious turn", this time with regard to veils. And he tells me an instructive story.

Sometime in the early 2010s, Ramzan and his uncle were at the Press House in Grozny at an exhibition of women's fashion. The display featured women modeling traditional Chechen headscarves and women modeling Middle Eastern hijabs. Ramzan, it is said, leaned over to his uncle, Ahmat-hajji, and commented: "I prefer our traditional costumes." His uncle disagreed and chose the hijab. Shortly afterwards Ramzan left, seemingly in disapproval. But the decree from above had been given: hijabs were preferable to headscarves.

Akaev relays another story from memory: a visiting Russian dignitary was set to address some students. In the front row he noted three girls in full-face veils: "And who told you to dress like that?" he remarked loudly.

The details are not fully precise in the retelling, but the overall message is: somehow under the guidance of various internal and external impulses, the post-war Putin-sponsored leadership lurched in favor of a light (hijabs but not face veils) Islamic gloss on the Chechenization campaign. Recently, Kadyrov gave a televised speech in front of his ministers mocking the full-face veils of two women that he personally stopped on the street, quizzing them as to where they had got the bizarre notion of dressing like "Beduins". He then seized one girl's mobile phone and was outraged to discover that all of her contacts had Arabic names. Of course, this was not an invitation to discuss the niceties of shari'a law, evolving Islamic tradition and the balance between Arab and Chechen customs in North Caucasian Islam; like the Russian minister's curt observation, it was a spontaneous act of "retraditionalization", dictating what is and what is not acceptable in the Chechen republic nowadays by iron fiat.

Of course, this Islamization was not a complete "lurch" into the dark. After all, Ramzan's father, mufti Ahmat Kadyrov, had declared a *gazavat* against the Russians in the supposedly "secular" first war, and his reasons for rejecting shari'a courts in 1998, like the other *alims*, were not final; he simply believed that people's level of religiosity made shari'a courts premature. The nod of Ramzan Kadyrov's uncle in favor of the hijab was then simply a continuation of his brother's beliefs: now, maybe, the people are ready.

The minister who looked askance at the fully veiled students is not alone, and the Russian gaze is, after all, important. Veiling in Chechnya—even of the "light" Ramzan-approved sort—is now causing a ruckus in the broader national media. While I am in Grozny, the new education minister Olga Vasilieva, a controversial conservative Orthodox figure, exchanges heated tweets with Kadyrov. She points out that the High Court has upheld the local ban against girls wearing the hijab at school when appealed to in cases arising in Stavropol and Mordovia. Kadyrov debonairly denies that a High Court ban on wearing veils at school in Russia makes the practice illegal, and then, this time wrapping himself in the mantle of the law, appeals to the clause concerning religious freedom in the Constitution. "My three daughters," he tweeted, "study at school, wear the hijab and are getting excellent grades.... Should I remove them from school and look for a place where they are allowed to be Muslims?" In Stravopol, an imam who campaigned vigorously for the hijab in schools was assassinated in 2013, some believe by Federal forces.[4]

Stavropol is a buffer zone between southern Russia and the Caucasus; it seems some people are now very anxious that Chechnya's surprise re-Islamization does not leak into "Russia proper".[5] (And I note that, despite protests by the leadership, people here reflexively say "in Russia" when talking about the country outside Chechnya).

I have followed all this news in Moscow, but after talking to Ibragim and my other acquaintances, I begin to see how all this looks from inside of Chechnya. From Moscow and the Slavic heartlands, this top-down Islamization can be read differently: for a minority, it is indeed an enviable "retraditionalization"; for most, it is another sign of how the Chechen tail seems to be wagging the Kremlin dog, extracting unprecedented concessions through the implicit threat of new violence and shattering the universal, impartial rule of law. But is everything homogenous in Chechnya itself? And how do these top-down decisions get to be implemented with a curt efficiency and anticipatory mimicry that would be the envy of "normal" Russian bureaucracy? Some of the answers come to me on my trip to the Sheikh Deni mosque, and then the following day when we travel to Ibragim's native village of Shalazhi.

A licensed free-thinkers' club

The Sheikh Deni mosque is ten minutes drive from the *medrese* and is a six-pointed honey-stoned building that bears more resemblance to Oxford's Bodleian library than a conventional mosque. It lies about five minutes beyond the "Heart of Chechnya" mosque in the center, where a steady stream of people is already gathering for Friday prayers as our car pushes through the crowds. We pull up outside the mosque and as Ibragim goes off to perform his ablutions, I stand in the snow chatting to Salman. He explains to me a bit about the role this mosque plays in Chechnya today. "It's a sort of free thinker's club," he says with a wry laugh. "People here generally all belong to the Naqshbandiyya *vird*. Kadyrov and his circle are Qadiriyyas. The people here are a sort of mid-way opposition. We are not anti-Russian, obviously, but we do not blindly support everything Kadyrov does. Nowadays, the muftiat are just yes-men. They want you to sing their praises constantly whatever they do. For example, we will refuse to go on those mass demonstrations. Usually, it's very dangerous not to take part in them. You can lose your job if you are in government, or worse... But we have forged a certain position for ourselves."

At this point, I am urged to find a place inside the mosque before the spaces are all taken, and our conversation is broken off. As we come in, the preacher at the front is rounding off his *khutba*. There are twenty-five more minutes until the *azzan* begins, and the preacher, speaking in Chechen, continues to talk. His tone is intimate, calm, at times joking. Once or twice he singles people out; smiles break out on faces at certain of his comments. Evidently, in this small mosque, where the worshipers cannot exceed a hundred and fifty in number, nearly everyone knows each other. As the time for the *jum'a* prayer draws closer, a frail white-bearded old man on a raised platform in the center of the mosque rises and sounds the *azzan*; the prayers begin.

Afterwards, I carry on the interrupted conversation by asking what the Chechen-language *khutba* was about. "Basically," Salman summarizes, "he was saying that you should not follow your leaders blindly... and also that you should not just blindly copy your ancestors. Instead you should think for yourself." Given his own tongue-in-cheek remarks about the mosque being a free-thinkers' club, I hazard that this might be code for not blindly following Kadyrov. "Something like that," laughs Salman. "Everyone can make their own interpretation..." Pausing for a bit, he then adds: "But I am not sure I liked what he was saying about not following your ancestors... I should speak to him about that." No doubt, this sounds all too much like an invitation to engage in *ijtihad*, or personal interpretation; around here, the fear is that this sort of total free-thinking might end up in the forests and mountains again...

The licensed and careful dissent practiced at this mosque once again goes back to the figure of Sheikh Deni Arsanov. The Naqshbandiyya *vird*, in which Sheikh Deni was an important figure, in fact dominated Chechen life in the tsarist and Soviet periods, as I learn from Vahid Akaev, who himself belongs to the *vird*. When he recounts the history and meaning of his *vird*, he is not merely retelling past history. He was himself one of the first scholars in the post-Soviet period to try and give an objective account of Islam in the Caucasus, and he gives me an original copy of his 1994 book on Kunta-Hajji, the Sufi (Qadiriyya) *sheikh* so admired by Tolstoy and now, due to the attention of Ramzan Kadyrov, the main spiritual figure from the past in the republic today. As Akaev explains, although the Naqshbandis were a minority in Chechnya compared to the Qadiriyyas, they always dominated intellectual and political life. After the Revolution, the Soviets persecuted them due to the leadership roles they occupied under the tsars; they tried to portray the Qadiriyya *vird*, who did indeed count a large base among the peasant population, as more "proletarian". But the attempt to undermine the

Naqshbandis never succeeded. It was only with the Kadyrovs that the Qadiriyyas have come to dominate Chechen political life. Nonetheless, Ramzan shares the common Chechen respect for the Naqshbandis, and Sheikh Deni in particular, and this explains why Ibragim Arsanov and other members of his *vird* can carry on this moderate opposition.

I talk to other members of the Naqshbandiyya *vird* after the Friday prayers, and get a mixed picture of what it is exactly in Chechnya today that they are opposed to. One man laments the politicization of religion that Kadyrov is engaging in; he calls it bluntly "a mixture of Leninism and Islam that is not at all healthy." It is easy to see what he means: most official buildings round Grozny are hung with pairs of portraits of the "great leaders": either Ahmat and Ramzan Kadyrov, or Ahmat and Putin, or Ramzan and Putin. One building is decked with a dual portrait of Putin and Kazakh President Nazarbaev, in a sort of nod to the broader Eurasian friendship of peoples. At intervals, billboards by the road or on high buildings declaim the wise sayings of Kadyrov senior. He goes on to shake his head in irritation: "We need a different way forward. Our society is so militarized. I don't just mean Chechnya, but Russia in general."

I could not agree more. But then I wonder whether these criticisms, which so echo my own liberal mindset, are not a little tailor-made for my sensibilities: later that afternoon, when sitting around the table with the same man, someone starts showing a short documentary about Turkmenistan on his phone. Everyone round the table is full of wonder at the prospect of this post-Soviet paradise, where apartments are subsidized and huge luminous buildings are being thrown up left, right and center in the capital. My erstwhile liberal of the morning joins in the general adulation, and continues to express joy as the conversation turns to praise of Karimov in Uzbekistan and Rahmonov in Tajikstan. I don't want to rain on everyone's parade by pointing out that Turkmenistan's last president was a monumental kleptocrat who imposed his bizarre views on his population, and insisted mosques give as much respect in displaying the Ruhnama, his own book of spiritual wisdom, as the Qur'an. If there is a gold standard for Leninism mixed with quasi-Islam and local Turkic paganism, this was surely it.

Meanwhile, another member of the *vird* complains that Kadyrov has filled political positions with his own members. But then someone else objects: "When we were in power, we did the same thing. And in fact, the Qadiriyyas did invite Sheikh Ilias to take part in government, but he turned them down. To give him his due," he continues, "Kadyrov has been fairly inclusive. I would say that we Naqshbandis have lost our energy recently. I would put it like that. And we are suffering for that. But I too do not like this manipulation of Sufism to build solidarity. I would say that Kadyrov has been very successful on the practical level, rebuilding Grozny, getting us back on our feet that way. But his ideology leaves a lot to be desired." (In passing, he adds angrily: "I don't understand why Russians begrudge us this success. They complain that we are doing it with their taxes; but they were happy enough to fund our destruction with those same taxes.")

The same man goes on to point out that the Sheikh Deni mosque was actually funded with money that Kadyrov set aside from government funds, and when I get back to the *medrese* I notice a little certificate hanging on the wall which commemorates the legal renaming of the street on which the *medrese* lies; it used to be named in honor of Patrice Lumumba, the archetypal Soviet African hero whose name still graces the People's Friendship University in Moscow, where many Caucasians study. I also find out that government money was behind the *medrese*'s rebuilding. Looking up at the building from outside, I now notice that there are two large portraits of Kadyrov junior and senior on the upper wall. The "free-thinkers' club" is thus most certainly a licensed opposition; it is evidence that not all dissent is suppressed, but it is a dissent which has to claw out a space between Patrice Lumumba, Ramzan Kadyrov and a Turkmenistan-style propensity to venerate leaders as spiritual heroes. Indeed, the Syrian–Chechen Abu Bakr had indicated that this search for mentors was even more widespread: "I try not to comment on religion, partly so as not to get into trouble, but partly, too, because as a native Arabic-speaker, people hang on my every word and idolize me as some kind of *ustadh*. I could set up my own sect if I wanted to!"

Channeling the Deportation

While the going is good, and there is a mood of frankness, I decide to quiz Salman and the others about the commemoration of the 1944 Deportation in the republic today. After my experience in Dagestan with the benign Stalinophile Bagaudinovich, I wonder whether Stalin may not be popular in Chechnya too. An al-Jazeera documentary had recently covered the arrest and prosecution of Ruslan Kutaev, head of the assembly of the Peoples of the North Caucasus, on the absurd charge of possessing heroin. The elderly academic was behind a conference called "Deportation of the Chechen people: what was it and can it be forgotten?" The mind-boggling impression given was that Kadyrov, whose father was born in exile in Kazakhstan, had banned commemoration of the Chechen holocaust, seemingly out of a desire not to ruffle Russian feathers.

"Kutaev was using the commemoration... for political purposes," Salman tells me cautiously. "Commemorating the Deportation is not banned here. And Kadyrov recently denounced Stalin in no uncertain terms. Still, you know, the Chechen people do not love Stalin, but they do not hate him either; they bear no ill will. And since the return in 1957, things went quite well for us, so that, yes, many are nostalgic for Soviet times."

My hosts offer no further comments on the commemoration issue, and so I have to find out further details online from the *kavkazr* dissident site. Ramzan Kadyrov has not banned commemoration of the Deportation, rather he has channeled it into his vision of Chechen history by changing the date from the actual deportation of February 23 to May 10, the date of his father's burial, and transferring the Stalin Deportation Memorial Complex, which was originally set up by the force behind the first Chechen war, General Johar Dudaev, to Ahmat Kadyrov Prospekt. Thus the hot and potentially divisive issue of Russia's ill-treatment of the Chechen people has been re-scripted and subsumed under the Kadyrov family ideology. May 10, the day after Russia's Victory Day commemorating the Great Patriotic War, has also been made the date of general national mourning for all victims of Chechnya's tragedies, again removing any possible separatist meaning that might be ascribed to them. Whether the Naqshbandiyya "licensed opposition" finds this distasteful I do not discover, not wanting to press the issue, but during another conversation, one man lets slip that "if changes are not made, if more conversation is not allowed, the situation will get explosive."

Ruslan Kutaev is evidence of this: not only was the elderly man sentenced to four years in prison (later commuted to two months), but he was tortured and his family threatened. This seems to be the price of viewing the world in other than Kadyrovite terms. Thus an odor of fear emanates from Kadyrov and his guard: to put it mildly, it discourages dissent and makes the religious symbolism surrounding the Islamized Chechnya look dismayingly hollow— even, or especially, to certain Muslims who care about their faith. In Moscow, I was on friendly terms with a high-ranking figure in the muftiat who, when in Chechnya, made the mistake of voicing his belief that Ramzan's prayer-beads do not combine very well with his cheerful embracing of female pop divas. An immediate explosion of hate clouded the Russian Muslim social networks: people with Chechen hashtags outbid each other to engage in vicious playground mockery of the Muscovite's surname; Kadyrov himself swiftly declared the offender *persona non grata* in Chechnya; and the person's activities have since been subject to similar mockery and abuse.

The Muscovite's point is a good one. Whatever else is going on, Kadyrov also seems to have become swept up in the Putinite post-modernism that afflicts Russia. In this post-modernism symbols, religious or otherwise, often have no reality behind them, or else they are linked by violent fiat to the reality power ascribes to them. Kadyrov likes fashion. On one occasion, he appeared at the launch of his daughter's new label in a finely coutured suit lightly patterned in a blue camouflage motif. The famous gangsta rap artist Timati, who has also had an audience with Putin, was standing in all his muscley tattooed glory next to him for a photo-op. A quick Google search reveals the spectacle of a leader who fought real and bloody conflicts in camouflage combats, relaxing in an Armani-style suit that echoes the colors of Russian special forces combat clothing. Round his neck were the prayer-beads that irked the Muscovite, replete with a miniature Qur'an nestling at chest-level. Religion and war, and it seems Truth—one of the Islamic names for God—have become fashion accessories. Is this irony? Double bluff? Hiding in plain sight? In the world of politicized crony capitalism, it is hard to tell who is the gangsta-rapper and who the president. Another brief scandal flared up some months later, when Timati carelessly posted an Instagram picture of himself reclining in what was allegedly Kadyrov's luxury private jet; the rapper quickly removed this sinister reminder of the Islamic leader's grotesquely disproportionate wealth.

This intra-Muslim dispute is only one of several more high-profile social media instances where the Chechen leadership has acted as if all sanctity and justice emanated from its house. A similar baying for blood occurred when the Olympic boxer Fedor Emelianko criticized unprotected children's fight competitions in Grozny in September 2016, and was seconded by other heads of sports organizations in Russia. Pictures of a bruised Emelianko losing one of his fights were posted on Chechen social media and insults heaped on him. Ultimately, sensing that national and even international rules and perceptions were making this position look bizarre, Kadyrov backed down and called for peace with the "Russian knight" Emelianko. The reconciliation had a role-playing air: "Chechen warrior" and "Russian knight" in the new re-traditionalized Russia kneel to each other in chivalric peace for the glory of the great Motherland. It is another blast of bluff: rearrange the facts and photo-ops; if they swallow it, good. If not, issue a theatrical denial.

So when I express a desire to meet a member of the official muftiat, Salman looks at me pitifully: "I don't think you will get anything from it. My advice to you as a foreigner is to stay away, and as someone with your Moscow connections." Still, I cannot help asking Salman and his friends why Kadyrov acts in such a manner, and the answer is obvious, though sometimes obscured by the dry ice wafting across the stage: "It is in our blood. After all we have suffered at the hands of the Russians, we sometimes still want to tell them what's what." Putin's long and probing hand reaches right up to the "Heart of Chechnya" in the name of the capital's central street, and can never be expelled from the body politic. The official line is that Kadyrov is content with this: the hand is reaching out in embrace, after all. And yet the hand at the same time produces unexpected paroxysms, grimaces and flashbacks. For a moment the warm embrace begins to look like the last throes of a to-the-death wrestling match. It is another variation on the Hadji-Murad allegiance-switch, or Rasul Gamzatov's self-revision, except that now Kadyrov junior is praising the Russians for having "brought banners of happiness and friendship", this time not to Gunib but to Grozny. And there is the odd proviso, too, that this paean of praise to Russia is being yodeled, while the yodeler is bit by bit putting on the costume and unrolling the dusty banners of the old Shamil...

Shalazhi: taips *and* virds, *war and peace*

On Saturday, I travel with Salman, Ibragim and a new companion to Shalazhi, Ibragim Arsanov's native village. The addition to the group is Muhammad, a Tajik from Khujond. A year ago, he was appointed imam of the central mosque in the industrial Urals town of Kurgan, which lies near the border with Kazakhstan. Like Abdollo, the Moscow Tajik teacher and preacher, he has worked most of his life on the building sites of Russia, and is also the product of Tajikistan's informal network of Islamic teachers, who are soaked not just in Islam but in the classics of Persianiate civilization (he is proficient in Turkish and Arabic and has a deep knowledge of Persian poetry.) During our trip to Shalazhi and then back in Grozny, he is adopted as an *azzan* by Ibragim and the Shalazhi imam and constantly nudged to the front when a prayer-leader is needed: his Qur'anic recitation is so resonant and lilting that it captures the hearts of whoever hears it. Muhammad has a short salt-and-pepper beard, wears dark-framed glasses that give his soft face a serious air, and has a habit of softly exhaling at frequent intervals: "*Alhamdullilah*," a sigh of satisfaction at God's constant bounty in the universe.

Muhammad had been working in Chechnya for three years before getting his appointment at Kurgan. His presence is a reminder of how the different parts of the Russian-language Muslim world interact, how they are slowly reaching out to each other. His new Kurgan congregation consists mainly of Kazakhs, some Tatars, and a large representation of North Caucasians. Muhammad is familiarizing himself with Chechen traditions, which is why he too is keen to see Shalazhi, where he can meet the families of some of his Kurgan congregants.

As we climb the gentle gradient to Ibragim's village, conversation in the car turns to the situation in Muhammad's home country. The new Russian imam comes from the Leninbad region of northern Tajikistan, which escaped the worst of the Tajik civil war that raged from 1992 to 1997. Like others in his area, he supported their local boy Emomali Rahmonov, the current president, who belonged to the Soviet clique that had ruled the country since 1937. For him, deep Islamic faith has always dovetailed unproblematically with respect, or even veneration, of neo-Soviet authoritarianism. And Islamic extremism has always conveniently been defined, at least in part, as expressions of the faith that engage in criticism of that leadership. He voices praise of the recently deceased Karimov, as well as his own leader, and joins in admiration of the marvels of Turkmenistan. For him, Chechnya and the Kadyrov father–son leadership, fit neatly into this paradigm, and getting to know Chechnya, its buildings festooned with the portraits of the local great leaders, is really just picking up a different dialect. Surprisingly, though, the Chechens in the car are less familiar with Tajikistan than he is with their realities, with Ibragim opining that "the war there was a fairly short-lived affair." Muhammad patiently explains that one tenth of the country's population perished in a half-decade of fighting.

At one point on the road, as if to accompany this reminiscence of war, a large convoy of military trucks thunders past us on their way down to Grozny. The obligatory jokes about the hunt for an English spy are cracked, and we stop off at Gekhi, our driver's village, to pick up some supplies. As we wait to be met, the driver finds a station on the radio and turns the music up. The silence is distilled by the high-pitched notes of a boppy love song. Everyone sits back in silence, seemingly to enjoy. Five minutes pass: the car idles, and I am reminded that in addition to war, stern leadership and struggles over the meaning of Islam, there is the ever-present threat of cheap Russian pop music seeping out of every communication portal, from Central Asia to the Caucasus. Somehow it is a discreet reminder that true shari'a is just out of reach in the steppes of the post-Soviet space. Where Muslims elsewhere have to make a careful case for the use of music in religious celebration, taking its prohibition for granted elsewhere, here the conversation has not even begun—and with Kadyrov frisking around with a rap-artist, it is hardly likely to either—except perhaps among the so-called "Salafists" and those austere Dagestani Sufis like Abdul-Jalil Affandi. I cannot see the Tajik builder-imam's face, but I wonder if he, too, is tapping a beat on one knee while clicking the orange prayer-beads that he holds constantly in his right hand.

We start up again, and the driver tells us a little about his town as we leave it behind us. As with other towns on the road, most of it is all hard red brick edges and concrete shops. The old village was destroyed in the wars, the driver explains: forty percent was leveled in Special Forces operations. In 1993, there were 27,000 people; now there are 1500 people. The rest have been killed or emigrated. Many of his friends who remain have gone into the police and government service to make a living. With a grimace, the driver remarks: "I avoid them, though, even if they are relatives. Policemen are always hungry."

Next, he shares a story that happened a bit further up this road. A group of his friends were driving up to the hills to go for a swim in a local lake. Some militants stepped out ahead, and they promptly did an about-turn, not wanting to be get near enough to them to fall under suspicion. The next day, they were pulled over at the same spot by Russian special forces, who hauled them out of the car and accused them of going off to join the fighters. Probably through knowing the right people, they were released eventually. The point of the story seems to be that the so-called militants were in fact the Russian Special Forces trying to lure locals into letting slip their true sympathies. I have heard similar stories recently from Ingushetia, where many people find themselves caught between the Scylla of angry militants and the Charybdis of corrupt local "law" enforcement.

It is not long before we pull into Shalazhi. Our first stop is the mosque—the first to be rebuilt after the Soviet period, once again by Sheikh Deni's descendants. After that, it is time to explore the village, which is more of a town in fact, given its size. It stretches gradually up a gentle slope into the distance. Thick-walled houses, each with their own spacious courtyard, face each other across broad streets that seem to go on forever. We park outside one house to pay our respects at a wake: for three days, the elders in their grand astrakhan hats sit in the far corner, their breath billowing onto the frozen air, and preside over the stream of visitors tramping across the enormous courtyard to pay their respects. The plunging temperatures are offset by two concrete pipes that run along the front row of their chairs; each one is glowing from within with some slow-burning fuel. Here the Islamic custom of putting one's hand to one's heart is a bit more elaborate: the men lower their torsos towards each other and half hold each other in a bowed embrace.

Further up the village is Ibragim's house. The top room is being refurbished to make room for Ibragim's bride. With a builder's professional interest, our Tajik imam pokes around among the fittings and asks about the provenance of the wood; Islamically, his heart is rested too, it would seem. For it was only in our stop-off in Gekhi that he had discovered that Ibragim was not married. "But you must marry. It is an obligation!" he had said in shock. In another culture, this would be a rude breach of etiquette. But the Chechen had understood the Tajik's ejaculation in the right spirit as a mere statement of religious fact. The two young bearded and skull-capped youths hauling packages into the boot also smiled: one had four children, the other five already. "Perhaps I'll take two wives," Ibragim had rejoined with guilty humor, "to make up for lost time."

When the future marital nest has been sufficiently appreciated, we walk outside and I admire Ibragim's orchard, which trails down towards a fast-flowing stream. On the other side is a tall hill covered with bare trees: hunting and fishing opportunities at a stone's throw. As we shiver in the cold, Ibragim recounts a bit of the village's history. "Up there," he gestures northwards, where the land rises even higher, "is where the mountaineers live." The houses he is pointing to do not seem that much higher than where we are standing, but Ibragim explains that the term "mountaineer" refers to their *taip*, or Chechen clan. All Chechens preserve the distinction into lowlander and highlander *taips*, even though these geographical terms may have long ago become of merely historical relevance. Ibragim explains that his own *taip* consists of fifty people who trace their provenance back to a village a hundred and fifty miles outside of Grozny.

While *taip*-affiliation is important in terms of choosing a marriage partner, he goes on to say, *vird* affiliation is much more important, and *virds* bring together many people of different *taips*. Vird-affiliation explains a lot more about Shalazhi, it turns out. Ibragim's Naqshbandiyya *vird* took a stance against fighting the Russians as far back as the first Chechen war. "We were branded traitors," Ibragim recalls. The mountaineers who lived at the far end of Shalazhi had close blood and *vird* connections with Dudaev, and so took a stance to resist the Russians. As a result, their end of the village was bombed heavily. A while later, we get into the car and drive down to meet

Ahmad, Shalazhi's young imam, who returned from studying in Syria five years ago, and he fills me in on more of the village's story: "Our *vird* was caught between the mountaineers and the Russians. We set up our own civilian militia to fight off the militants, and we came to an agreement with the Russians that they wouldn't bomb or attack us. We also took in refugees fleeing Grozny. At one point, there were thirty people living in our house!" The situation in a big village like Shalazhi was not unique: the mixture of *taips* and *virds* meant that several towns were divided by the fighting. Today, a few of the "mountaineers" have come back to their houses and they keep their heads down, well out of politics.

Ibragim speaks more about the notion of a *vird*, with a mixture of an academic's cool objectivity that alternates uncomfortably with the pain of one for whom this is a personal reality. "The *tariqats* started out as spiritual brotherhoods," he says, "but they have degenerated because of all this politics. From a brotherhood of spirit, the *virds* turned into an economic mafia in the late Soviet period. People joined the *virds* for material benefit. Now they are measured by material and worldly measures: how many people do you have in government, how many in 'business'. Sufism is about love and tolerance. And if people really did act that way, society would indeed change. But the *tariqats* today are incapable of change, unfortunately," he concludes grimly.

Ibragim himself was chosen two years ago as the leader of his *vird*. As a prestigious and impressively educated descendant of Sheikh Deni, the elders found him a natural choice. But the appointment had to be officially confirmed by Ramzan Kadyrov in a ceremony, and now Ibragim's job is to mediate between his *vird* and the republican government. In all there are twenty *virds* in Chechnya today, with five dominant ones. Ibragim's explanations make it clear how the government can mobilize people so quickly onto the streets or on social networks: in theory there is a tight chain of command going from Ramzan to *vird* leaders and downwards to the rank and file. Of course, Chechnya is a deeply mono-ethnic society in a way that is not true of neighboring Dagestan, still less of Russia as a whole. With its tight *vird*-system in place, Chechnya is potentially "united" in a way that Putin's eponymous "United Russia" party can only dream of. No wonder that for some "Eurasianists", Ramzan and Chechnya are symbols of the perfect political order. That hand that reaches down into the body politic can also take something back for its own spiritual–political benefit.

However, I cannot help thinking of Sheikh Deni and Ruslan Zakriev's tale of the Chechen avatar: all body, no spirit. When we get back to Grozny the following day, Ibragim invites me to attend a council of his *vird*. It takes place in a classroom at the *medrese*. About twenty men in astrakhan hats and velvet skullcaps listen to Ibragim talk for half an hour, and then a discussion begins. As usual, the conversation is all in Chechen: unlike in Dagestan, the mosques and *virds* can bypass the Russian language. So I wander in and out, catching only snatches of suggestive Russian seasoning: policy, government, representation. When it is all over, I press Ibragim to give me the low-down, expecting more insight into the *vird*'s vision of the future, its alternative spiritual program for Chechnya. But Ibragim shakes his head sadly: "It's all very boring, I'm afraid. People only seem able to discuss ritual matters. This time we got stuck on the details of our burial ritual. Everyone holds stubbornly to their position and refuses to compromise. It all has to be black and white."

The same evening I go out for dinner with Muhammad and Ibragim, and he tells me more details. It all boils down to whether there should be a pause for prayers before the final soil is scattered on the coffin. Ibragim was trying to persuade his elders that this is how he remembers it and this is the correct way. The hour-long discussion, with voices getting louder and hoarser, consisted of their resistance to this view. Muhammad now tells us that Ibragim's view actually accords with how the burial ritual is performed in his hometown by his Naqshbandiyya *tariqat*.

"We pause and read *tabarak*," he says, "and then recite the prayer that praises Allah as giver and taker of life. It is a moment to focus the mourners' minds on death. Death should always be the focus of the believer's thoughts...." Ibragim chuckles delightedly, and says: "I wish I had brought you into the discussion. I felt certain that I was right. Your experience would have given an important confirmation." It is an interesting moment: one feels that the terrible wars and repressions have damaged Chechen historical memory; people are clinging desperately and stubbornly to the pieces that they know. As they rarely meet outsiders, their views are not often tested. Muhammad's explanation not only confirms the form of the ritual, but gives spirit to its body. Muhammad and Ibragim find a further link, too, when the Tajik tells us that Ahmat Kadyrov, although belonging to the Qadiriyya *vird* in Chechnya, became a student of a Naqshbandiyya *sheikh* when he was studying alongside Ravil Gaynutdin in Bukhara in the late Soviet period.

We do not stay long in the village, pausing only for a quick lunch and a short tour of Ibragim's childhood house. The room where he used to study as a boy is hung with portraits of Sheikh Deni and his son, and Ibragim's brother tells us more about how the Sheikh preached to Ossetians and converted three villages, whose descendants still revere him to this day. Later, curious to find out more about the "last *sheikh*", I track down some more information about him from the memoirs of his grandson. I discover that he was a well known peacemaker in Chechnya before the revolution, resolving blood-feuds between highlander clans, as well as between other Muslim ethnicities as far afield as Stavropol. In 1917, he was appointed executive head of Chechnya and attempted to make peace between Chechens and Cossacks when the Revolution came in 1917; later, he lost his life in a skirmish with Cossacks in the main square of Grozny.

Sheikh Deni's son, Yakub, was shot by the Bolsheviks, but his other son Bagauddin, following the peace-making ways of his father tried to reconcile himself and his people to the new order. In 1944, he was instrumental in persuading Chechens who had fled the Deportation order for the mountains to come down legally and join their families in Central Asia. The last of Deni's ten sons, Sheikh Ilyas Arsanov, continued his father's policy in the 1990s: it was he who called on his *vird* not to fight the Russians, predicting that "tragedy would strike the homes of every single person" if the Chechens should take up arms. During the siege of Grozny, Ilyas was captured and held in a pit in the mountains. He was only released due to the efforts of the President of Ingushetia and some Ingush businessmen. He was lucky: twenty-nine other members of Deni's family were shot by the anti-Russian militants.

The Damascus–Grozny–Moscow axis

Back in Grozny, one of the last conversations I have is with Ahmad, the young imam of Shalazhi, who has travelled back with us. I am curious to hear his impressions of Syria and of life since he returned.

Potentially, the Syria connection is a dangerous one: after Saudi Arabia and Tunisia, Russia has the most people fighting for ISIS in the world, and Chechens make up a large proportion of those Russians.[6] The border with the Middle East and its politics is very porous here. But Ahmad's story demonstrates the other side of the Damascus–Grozny–Moscow axis. "I studied in Syria for five years," he tells me, "mainly at the Abu Nur Islamic center in Damascus. I attended the talks of Ahmad Kuftaro, the famous Naqshbandiyya preacher who called on Andropov to come to Islam in the 1980s. I was the senior student among a group of twenty-eight Chechens. When the first shots were fired in 2011, our teachers hurriedly brought our exams forward from May to March and then it was decided that we had better leave."

The name of the center and Ahmad's main teacher is a give-away: Kuftaro, like Ayatollah Khomeini, may have called upon Andropov to renounce Soviet atheism for Islam, but he was also a personal friend of President Assad and an early supporter of the secular–nationalist and Soviet-sponsored Ba'ath revolution in the 1950s. As a result, while other Islamic movements and institutes were severely repressed, Kuftaro became the Grand Mufti of Syria and his activities were energetically promoted by the Assad regime. I am reminded of Vladimir Popov in Kazan: "If only Lenin had been religious, then the Soviet Union would have been perfect." Or, as one might speculate: "If only Andropov had become Muslim..." But in a sense, in Chechnya that odd counterfactual has come to pass: there is certainly a congruity between Syrian and Russian authoritarianism, no doubt in part due to the Soviets sharing certain tricks with their client. It is not just our Tajik imam, or Chechen Sufis, who have made their peace with stern leadership: the soft, open Islam of Kuftaro, who supported women's rights and interreligious dialogue (as well as belonging, like the Shalazhi imam, both to the Shafi'i *madhab* and the Naqshbandiyya *tariqat*), seemed to find the hard, cruel soil of Assad's dictatorship quite conducive to its flourishing. In a sense, this deal with autocracy has been a feature of Sunni Islam since its early days.

Now, of course, Putin has helped Assad claw back control and reestablish his rule in parts of Syria. And Ramzan Kadyrov has sent some of his crack Chechen guards to help Russia do it. For his supporters this is a matter of pride. But it does not take much imagination to see why there are also Chechens fighting against Assad, some of them for ISIS and some of them for other "moderate" Islamic groups supported by the West. The number of militants may have dropped drastically in Chechnya, but the fragile logic of Kadyrov's ideology and Putinite support leaves plenty of space for resistance and discontent. However, my time with the Naqshbandiyya "free-thinkers' club" points to another path between these options. The earlier comment of one of my new acquaintances that the Kadyrov ideology was a mix of Leninism and religion showed that there is at least some hope for a way out of the dichotomy between neo-Soviet authoritarian Islam (whether Syrian, Chechen or Tajik) and anarchistic–eschatological Salafism-Wahhabism— with the latter the only form of resistance that can be imagined by those trapped within authoritarian systems.

To begin with, the idea that Kadyrov's Islamic ideology is Leninist was for once meant, refreshingly, not as nostalgic praise but criticism, and a consciousness that this is not the only way Islam should function today. Kadyrov's Islamic ideology stands condemned in its own terms by those who hold this view. Among the reasons, one might speculate, is this: one pillar of Kadyrov's top-down Chechen Islam depends on a cult of his father and his martyr's death; and the other is the public promotion of Sheikh Kunta-Hajji, the founder of Kadyrov's own Qadiriyya *vird* in the mid-nineteenth century.

But one of the core elements of Sheikh Kunta-Hajji's position was the idea that "a Sufi should hold in his hand prayer-beads and not weapons." Kadyrov appears often in the presence of his heavily armed associates. In 2014, he filled a stadium with 20,000 of his security apparatus, all dressed in green camouflage and toting rocket-propelled grenade-launchers and submachine guns.[7] Kadyrov waltzed briskly through the midst of them, with his hallmark prayer-beads worn round his neck and his *tariqati* skullcap on his head, so standing Kunta-Hajji's dictum on its head. Likewise the characteristic "loud *zikr*" introduced by Kunta-Hajji was meant to encourage asceticism and pacificism; now, as Kadyrov's men gather to perform it in the center of Grozny, it is a tool of political theatre, almost like a tribal war dance: an explicit display of the implicit monopoly on violence and, indeed, Islamic orthodoxy claimed by his mini-state, and a clear warning shouted against would-be dissenters.

Ironically, Kunta-Hajji's pacificism was initially rejected by Imam Shamil, who had shifted the focus of the "quiet" Naqshbandiyya *tariqat* to mobilize Dagestanis and Chechens in the *gazavat* against the Russian colonists. Shamil thought that the other-worldly asceticism of "zikrism", as Kunti-Hajji's new Qadiriyya movement was soon dubbed, would blunt jihadi passions. By the 1990s, though, the situation had reversed: Arsanov's Naqshbandiyya *vird* now occupied a pacificist position from the outset of the war. Ousted from their Soviet-era dominance, the Naqshbandis in Chechnya continue to occupy a quiet, critical position behind the scenes, skeptical of the loud Qadiriyya revival, though in many ways as dependent on Kadyrov's (Putin-derived) beneficence as everyone else in Chechnya.

The question that I take away is: will their quiet critical resistance last long enough and be coherent enough for the spirit to return to the sleeping *sheikh*'s body? It is true that Kunta-Hajji's original pacificism was also very quickly turned into a political tool by the "naibs", or secular leaders of Ingushetia and Chechnya then, and the hyper-politicization of the Islamic message is nothing new in modern history. However, at least some of the original non-political message of "zikrism" was retained by the *sheikhs* in the nineteenth century. Today, this sheikhless "Qadiriyyism" looks in danger of replacing content with form forever: externally, the muscle-pumping *zikrs* contine to swirl in the public spaces, especially for the cameras; but crack the fruit open, and there seems to be an incongruous pulp of jets, rap and shady dealing. Perhaps it is an Islamic dilemma that is not just confined to Chechnya.

I have reason to ponder this question again on my last day. Before leaving for the airport, I have a final meeting with Vahid Akaev, the historian, in the company of Ibragim, Salman and Muhammad the Tajik. We talk more about the bloody nineties, and Akaev and Salman tell me about how they survived the violence and the paradoxical effect it had on them. For Salman, "funnily enough, the war cured me of my Russophobia. When I was growing up, I blamed the hypocrisies of communism on the Russians. Then I went to study in Stavropol and I actually mingled with real Russians and my feelings became more natural. After I had seen so much destruction in Grozny, that also helped me feel sympathy for people, regardless of their nationality." Akaev adds: "After you have seen so many dead bodies, so many miserable homeless people, you begin to understand human suffering. Before, I can say, I was indifferent to strangers. Now, when I see a person, my heart reaches out to them. When I see humiliated and deprived people, I feel guilty: what can I do to help them? We all have the same blood in our veins..."

Such sentiments give cause for hope, hope that parts of Chechnya are already healing inwardly. However, the thought of the Syrian connection is still fresh in my mind after my talk with Ahmed. While for some, the violence has led them to search for peace, or *salaam*, for others violence and the constant threat of violence—such as Kadyrov's black-uniformed guards patrolling the downtown areas, leading Salman to remark: "And they want tourists to come here?!"—only deepens their anger and resentment. During our conversation, Ahmed had shown me a video of the powerful Syrian anti-Assad preacher, Qa'qa, on his phone. Qa'qa ranted in that soul-stinging frenzy-inducing way that only Arab rhetoricians can, and Ahmed smiled quietly as his words thundered out of the little gadget. "Won't you get in trouble for accessing that?" I asked. "Only if I put a 'like'," replied Ahmed with a smile.

For Ahmed and Muhammad, himself a master of Arabic, who is also sitting nearby and enjoying the rhetorical performance, Qa'qa's words do not go to the heart. But Salman's next remarks seem to me more ambiguous: "What is happening in Syria," he explains his view now, "is the same as what happened here. A simple case of colonial divide-and-rule. Russia is playing the same game with the Syrians that they played with us, down to covertly helping extremists." Salman belongs firmly in this Naqshbandi free-thinkers' club, and offers his opinion with the detached, if dejected air of a distant observer. Ibragim, Salman, Vahid Akaev, Muhammad in his way, are fighting a different fight: to coax the *sheikh*'s spirit back into his body. But it is common knowledge that Chechens, Dagestanis and other North Caucasians have been slipping off to Syria in the thousands; others have decided to continue the fight by joining the Ukrainians in the Donbass. So violence is still breeding violence, and things are far from settled.

But it is also an interesting fact, as Huseyn Aliev has pointed out,[8] that most of the Syria-bound jihadis do not come from the ranks of the Caucasus Emirate in the mountains of Chechnya and Dagestan. While some famous figures such as al-Shishani may have been fighters in the two Chechen wars, continuing unfinished business on a larger stage, the foot-soldiers even here seem to be unpredictable recruits. These are people who are unaffiliated with the old organizations. In other words, as in the rest of Russia, the new Caucasian jihadis are "self-recruited" internet converts to eschatological Salafism. They are, one might say, darkly fermenting souls who refuse to accept the iron-fist logic of Kadyrov's traditional Qadiriyya Checheno-Islamization, and who watch Russia's shifting allegiances, first allied to Sunni Turkey and then its bitter enemy, and opt for a more timeless logic that will shortcut these fickle switches.

These anonymous young men who slip off to Syria to engage in jihad are the continuing nightmare of Russian Muslims. Their actions, as I have seen time and again, are scrutinized by Islam experts as well as by ordinary Muslims, who look to their own souls to see whether perhaps there is really not something in their religion that they might need to suppress. But when I get back to Moscow, I fall into conversation with an Orthodox seminary student, who tells me about a provincial parish in central Russia. Several of the young men in the parish make good money as mid-level managers. But they like to spend their summer holidays and their money by buying the latest ammo and combat gear. Then, instead of heading off to the dacha with the wife and kids, they board a train to the Donbass in Eastern Ukraine to fire off rounds at the despised enemy state that is murdering good Russian men and women. These Orthodox militants are a small minority, of course; but Salman's comment that Russia is too "militarized" is a truism for anyone who has lived through the increasing tempo of aggression in the last few years since the Crimean debacle. Is die-hard holiday mercenary fighting the new "normal" for Russia as a whole?

It might seem so sometimes. The orange-and-black St George's victory ribbons that used to be pinned to cars and lapels only on Victory Day a half-decade ago have now become all-year-round tokens of a seething animosity. There is a constant whiff of testosterone in the air, and a lurching urge to know where the next Berlin might be. Two Russian citizens cross their country's border. One man is heading to the Donbass; the other to Syria. Can the increased military budget that is swallowing up pensions and healthcare really content itself with little ribbons? Won't some people finally take the rhetoric at face value? In Grozny, Victory Prospect has been renamed Putin Prospect. Given the hysteria about Victory in the country, one can only conclude that even the great 1945 victory must take second place to the 2000 victory that saw Russia crowned with a new president. But again, the old letters can still be read under the revamped sign: victory, defeat, revenge—but whose and where? The questions have been released like a poisonous suggestive gas.

As our conversation draws to a close, Vahid Akaev lets drop a remark that reminds me of another obvious issue: as in Dagestan there is a lurking problem which plagues all the Islamic houses in the Caucasus, regardless of stripe: the failure of agriculture, construction and industry, and massive nepotism and corruption. I am reminded of the quiet remark of Bagaudinovich's daughter again: "They need to build schools, not mosques." In this sense, Ibragim Arsanov's school is remarkable: they really do seem to be turning out students who will be able to cross borders with their linguistic talents, while learning their religion. Akaev, too, takes me to task when, trying out the theory I had coined in Mahachkala, I suggest that maybe nepotism is too ingrained in Caucasian culture and the *taip*-system to eradicate:

"I wouldn't agree," he insists. "That was a 'gift' we got from the Russians. They bought out the highlanders with gold and silver, and the rot started there. Our culture, in fact, values individualism. A son must even criticize his father if the truth is at stake. In that sense, our culture is compatible with your Western values."

"What does it all mean?"

On my way to the airport, we pass a brick-walled settlement. The driver tells me it is a military village, where most of the Russians who still live in Chechnya are housed. On Sunday morning, I had had breakfast alone in town, and then taken a stroll down Putin Prospekt, where four burly Russians in fur-hats were taking a selfie against the blue street sign bearing the President's name. Somehow, for all the heated mutual adulation between Putin and Kadyrov that lights up the nation's screens, the "friendship of the peoples" that is going on here still seems a bit ersatz. It was hard not to see this "selfie" as another sort of victory pose.

But, as elsewhere, what I had been most interested in investigating was not so much shifting political alliances as the state and prospects of Islam, and Muslims' ideas of themselves and their religion. In the end, I boarded my plane back to Moscow with a feeling of sadness, the same feeling that seizes a certain kind of person when they consider Russia's Orthodox revival: as many even high up within the church have begun to realize, the great religious boom has been oversold; the Soviet-style statistics on rebuilt churches and the long televised services with the Patriarch and Putin standing shoulder to shoulder conceal a world in which ritual and—re-appropriated but little-understood— Tradition have come to drown out the spirit, leaving many people confused, disunited and disappointed. Religion has become a blunt tool, not a bridge. How else to explain why religious people are as rigid as the unconverted, or more so?

Chechnya is where Putin's reputation was made; it is the bloody womb from which he emerged as a successful leader who publicly and violently reversed the disorder that Russia suffered under Yeltsin. Different commentators differ as to whether Putin made today's Chechnya, or whether Chechnya may not have made Putin. Whatever the answer, the fates of Moscow and Grozny are closely connected, strange mirror images of each other. In both places, the pulse of raw power can be felt, even in the quietest corner of the mosques or churches.

In St Petersburg, a few months before going to Chechnya, I had met an Ingush student of Arabic and philosophy. He belonged, like Kadyrov, to the Qadiriyya *vird*. He had taken part in many "loud" *zikr*s, and I was curious to know how he conceived of them, what they gave to him. "It's a question I have often asked myself," he said, "and I have to say, I am still not sure what its exact spiritual meaning is. Sometimes it is just physical exercise. I work myself into such a sweat, I run so hard around the circle, that it is like a workout at the gym. But as for its effect on my life, my prayer, it is more difficult to gauge. I am still trying to work out what it all means."

A few months after my visit to Grozny, I was visiting friends in Mahachkala, when I heard a far more risqué opinion of what was going on in

Chechnya. This time, there was no backtracking talk of "good totalitarianism." Rather a man, whose business took him regularly to the neighboring republic, told me: "Chechens are leaving the republic. It's empty. They secretly hate Ramzan. He's like Stalin. Oh, the mosques are beautiful, the roads are even. But it all has a touristy feel. All these glittering buildings are standing empty." The words chimed with my own impressions; and I could not help comparing the two places. Dagestan, too, was split by the angry Salafi–Sufi dichotomy, but somehow the sheer number of religious leaders, of *sheikhs* who could trace their lineage, their *silsala*, back to the Prophet, was smoothing this angry wound over with its genuine link to the pre-Soviet past (albeit intimately, sometimes too intimately, intertwined with that past). In Chechnya, the *sheikhs* had long departed; only costumes, it seemed sometimes, and gestures had remained, whipped this way and that by a harsh wind.

For Abdo Haireddin in Moscow, Chechnya and Ramzan Kadyrov are the answer to the problem of "Salafism". For some Russian Muslims, Chechnya is simply the answer *tout court*: a wondrous moderate-Islamic republic arising on the ruins of extremism, inside of Russia, and all with the say-so of Russia's great leader. Here the question of beards and veils, the great Question of Tradition, can be solved with the blinking of the leader's eye, and the questions can cease. Everyone can get back to blind obedience and doing their own thing in private. The Russian Islam expert, Denis Sokolov, has come to a similar conclusion: for Russian Muslims, now, as he sees it, the choice is between ISIS and Kadyrov.[9] He did not even mention the Moscow or Kazan muftis with their *wasatiyya* as a possible third way.

But when the questions cease, *rigor mortis* sets in, and it is doubtful that the avatar will be reunited with his consciousness. The Ingush student, the quiet Naqshbandiyya descendants of Sheikh Deni Arsanov, and no doubt many others in the quieter spaces of their mosques and homes, sat round their "kitchen tables" (that great forum for muttered dissent in Soviet times) are still asking questions. One can only hope they outlive the monochrome answers offered all too readily sometimes by those at the top, and the dismal Kadyrov–Isis dichotomy.

PART FIVE

MOSCOW RETURN

7.

MOSCOW: BRAIN OF ALL THE RUSSIAS

United Russian Islam: a mosque and an ideology

And so it is back to Moscow again, both my personal Moscow and Muslim Moscow—though the two of them have been drawing closer and closer together.

In the last three years I have traveled to Kazan, Kyrgyzstan, Fergana, Dagestan, and Chechnya. And each time I come back, the visits to the muftis' offices in the new Cathedral Mosque off Prospekt Mira have become more frequent. In fact, I seem to have been accidentally adopted by the Moscow muftis. A conference is being planned in London: what themes would the British like? A last minute press release in English: can you just polish it up? Should we call our new organization the International Muslim Forum or the International Islamic Forum? Perhaps "Islamic" sounds a bit extremist? And I am being paid quite nicely for translating various books and articles into English. I have moved from sniffing around on the outside and leaping in for occasional interviews to becoming another part of the furniture. Moscow, with its great pulsing gravitation beams, has that effect.

The Cathedral Mosque has been up and running for almost two years now, and it is a machine that is trying to absorb and digest not just me, but all the Islams out there in the post-Soviet space that I have been gallivanting around. The future, the "bright future", of Russian Islam is being forged here in the

225

humming offices of the Spiritual Board of Muslims of the Russian Federation. And before I get dissolved entirely in its bright beams, I have to finish off interviewing the figures behind this new ideology.

Damir Muhetdinov: Russian Muslim culture, or Muslim Eurasianism

Perhaps the man doing more than anyone to draw all these Muslim spaces together is Damir Muhetdinov, now the first assistant mufti of the Russian Federation, chief mufti Ravil Gaynutdin's right-hand man. Like many of the other Moscow team, he is from Nizhny Novgorod. Nizhny Tatars, caught between Kazan and Moscow, have usually voted with their feet and their hearts in favor of Moscow. So if any ethnic Muslim group is going to try and develop the idea of an all-Russian Islamic identity that can transcend regional allegiance, it will be them.

In 2015, Muhetdinov published a short book called *Rossisskoe musul'manstvo*, loosely translatable as "Russian Muslim culture". The front cover bears a jauntily angled photograph of the restored Cathedral mosque, its tallest minaret reaching up to spear the bold block letters of the title. The subtitle reads: *A call to understanding and contextualization*. The main essay is followed by several responses written by Russian scholars of Islam. Muhetdinov's office in the Cathedral Mosque is hung with portraits of venerable past muftis from Ufa, Orenburg and Moscow: like the architecture of the mosque (blending Russian–Muscovite and Kazan–Tatar designs) this is an aesthetic attempt to create a new tradition by blending old ones, rather as the local cults in ancient Israel were merged into the single Jerusalem cult under David and Solomon. Or, to take a more recent analogy, rather as Moscow claimed to replace Kiev, and indeed Rome and ancient Jerusalem, as the main city of Christianity on earth.

The latter analogy is, actually, far more than analogy. In some ways, the Russian muftiat is, consciously, trying to do for Russian Islam what the Muscovite tsars and then emperors did for Orthodox Christianity and its patriarch in the region. If one looks more closely at the title of Muhetdinov's book again, this becomes clear. The word "rossisskoe" in the title derives from "rossiya": the latter only became the term for Russia in the time of Peter the Great, replacing the older terms Rus and Muscovy, and is associated with Russia as an imperial state—an echo that will not entirely go away, given post-Soviet Russian political realia.

In English, it sometimes appears in translated phrases such as "tsar of all the Russias". There is something appealing about that translation: all the places I have travelled to were once units in this imperial Russia, they were once themselves little "Russias" making up one larger Russia; Tsar Nicolas II was, after all, "lord of Turkestan". Gradually, the Moscow patriarchate began to see itself in correspondingly grandiose terms: the head of the church is by title the patriarch of Moscow and all Rus, but his authority extends into dioceses that are now situated in the lands of the former Russian empire, such as Uzbekistan, Ukraine or Lithuania. Even the term Rus has now acquired imperial overtones.

Gaynutdin, Muhetdinov and their team are implementing a dual strategy. On the one hand, there is an external agenda. The new muftiat is heavily funded by Putin's government and has a job to do: make Russian Islam organized, presentable and government-friendly ("traditional"). On the other hand, there is an internal agenda: as citizens of Russia, they naturally want to shape their country in accordance with their own beliefs, and as Muslims they naturally also see Muslim unity as a desirable goal. So there are three elements: government requirements; citizens' ambitions; and Muslim goals. They are not always compatible and the muftis are walking a dangerous tightrope carrying out this task.

It is sometimes difficult to untangle what is government propaganda in this new all-Russian Muslim ideology, and what is genuine content. Moscow, in general, often functions like a brain without a body: all decisions are taken internally without the body being told what is happening. Sometimes the body is even dispensable. In the Muslim case, this leads to the odd situation whereby muftis of regional cities live permanently in Moscow: Muhetdinov himself is from Nizhny Novgorod but lives in Moscow. In 2015, however, he was appointed mufti of St Petersburg, though the mosque there already has a mufti. It is easy to see how this Moscow-centric arrogance, which turns "all Russia" into a mere phantom limb, is sometimes viewed with skepticism in Kazan, Mahachkala, and even smaller cities like Samara.

Still, the view from Moscow produces an interesting perspective. In his various publications, Muhetdinov skillfully synthesizes Russian Muslim thinkers and Russian Christian thinkers.[1] Russian sources include classic Silver Age religious thinkers who are also referenced by the Orthodox church and the Russian government (notably Ivan Ilin, Putin's favorite thinker), as well as the contemporary neo-Eurasian thinker Alexander Dugin—another Kremlin favorite. Muslim sources include a range of nineteenth and twentieth century

Tatar *jadid* thinkers, as well as Central Asian medieval mystics like Naqshbandi and Yassawi. Muhetdinov's claim is that the sensibility of the Russian Christian and Muslim thinkers converges: Naqshabandi and Ivan Ilin, for example, both preached a mysticism of the heart and a vision of the religious life where the secular was fully absorbed into the sacral. This is one sense in which, for Muhetdinov, Islam is "all-Russian": it shares a sensibility with the other traditional religions of the region, primarily Orthodoxy. He claims that his own version of the Russian Idea merely corrects the narrow Christian provincialism of the original version.[2]

However, some ambiguity remains; Muhetdinov alternates between calling this sensibility "Russian" and "Eurasian". After all, Naqshbandi was from Bukhara in present-day Uzbekistan, and Yassawi from present-day Kazakhstan. While before 1917 these lands were mere administrative districts in the Russian empire, to claim them as Russian today would obviously be inappropriate, and, indeed, provocative. Hence the term Eurasian comes in handy,[3] and maps more easily onto the Eurasian Islamic space that was coextensive with the area held by the Golden Horde in the Middle Ages. (Indeed the Golden Horde era is now celebrated in different muftiat publications: a 2016 book about Crimea's mosques is suggestively subtitled: "in commemoration of the 750th anniversary of the Golden Horde").[4] On the other hand, Muhetdinov needs to define a Russian Islam for the Russian state, and Eurasian is too vague for that. The term *russky islam* also does not fit: *russky* (rather than *rossiskii*) implies ethnic Russian. Unlike "Eurasian" it is too narrow—for Tatars, Avars or Chechens. So when referring to Islam within the present boundaries of the Russian Federation, Muhetdinov has to settle for *rossisskoe*.[5]

Echoes of Gasprinsky: the Crimea then and now

But the term *rossiskoe*, with its buried echoes of Peter's expanding imperial state, also comes with its own oddities and dangers. In 2014, Muhetdinov wrote a 118-page booklet chronicling—and celebrating—the incorporation of Crimea and its Tatars into the Russian Federation. He called it an event of not just a "regional nature, but rather of a federal and even international nature" that signified Russia's ability to maintain fruitful cultural relations with its Muslim minority, and symbolized Russia's key role as a bridge to the larger Islamic world. He especially praised the central role of Gaynutdin's negotiations with Crimean mufti Ablaev in assuring the peninsula's smooth transition into Russian political structures, and sought to allay Turkish fears about the mistreatment of Crimean Tatars by showcasing Russian Muslims' harmonious existence within the Russian state and underlining cultural links between Kazan and Crimean Tatars. Unfortunately, within two years, several of the Crimean Tatar activists Muhetdinov had praised for wisely acceding to Russia's demands (including Mejlis head and spiritual leader, Mustafa Jemilev, and new deputy prime minister, Lenur Islamov) had been expelled or imprisoned and Russia was in a furious dispute with Turkey over a downed Russian plane. In other words, there are problems in hitching one's ideological wagon to passing political vagaries. A conference planned to take place in Istanbul in 2015 likewise had to be canceled and London was hastily selected as an alternative venue.

Muhetdinov's approval of Crimea's incorporation was not unique: it caught the mood of many Russians, Muslim and non-Muslim, in celebrating the annexation of Crimea. Nor are the ambiguities inherent in the term *rossiskoe* of Muhetdinov's making, of course: they are part and parcel of modern Russia's not fully post-imperial or post-Soviet history. There is also no doubt an element of flattering the state in order to create a space where one can pursue one's own less bombastic goals.

Nonetheless, the "return" of Crimea had more than coincidental import for his theory of *rossiskiy* Muslim identity. This is because one of the main lynchpins of Muhetdinov's all-Russian synthesis is the thought of Ismail Gasprinsky (1851–1914), who is considered the founder of jadidism as a movement. Gasprinsky himself was from the Crimea, and developed a theory of imperial Russian Turkic–Slavic symbiosis. He saw Russia as the key to the reform of Muslim life and believed that Russian Muslims, having absorbed European progress through the medium of Russia, could in turn lead the rest of the Muslim world out of their backwardness. The Russian empire would then become a Slavic–Turkic joint project. Gasprinsky was friendly with the Slavophile, Mikhail Katkov, and in his vision he makes clear that the Russian element would continue to dominate the Turkic–Muslim component.[6] A hundred years later, the return of Crimea, for a modern-day Gasprinskian Turkic–Slavic conservative ideologue, was bound to resonate with exciting symbolism. For the non-Russian world, though, such a hitching of Muslim identity to Russian politics will naturally seem less persuasive.

However, Muhetdinov is going beyond Gasprinsky in his modern-day Turkic–Russian synthesis with shadings of empire. While Gasprinsky saw Russia as the "elder brother" and teacher, Muhetdinov hints that Russian

Muslims may in fact embody the destiny of Russia even better than Slavic Christians. This is the Russian Idea Islamized. A mix of neo-Eurasian and conservative Orthodox thinkers close to the Kremlin have been advancing a vision in which Russia is the preserver of traditional values and a bastion of Christian traditionalism against a degenerate Europe. Often they bolster this ideology by seeking right-wing allies in Europe and America. Patriarch Kirill has also linked this discourse to claims of the incompatibility of Western notions of human rights with Orthodox holism. Muhetdinov, ignoring the irony that this conservative vision is often Islamophobic, boldly argues that Russian Muslims are in fact the best upholders of such conservatism. He names the main enemies of Russia as European ultra-liberalism and individualism, whose rotten fruits are militant secularism; profit-seeking and enrichment; the erosion of gender identity; the "problematization of gender identity"; and the destruction of the traditional family.

Muhetdinov then contends that it is Russia's Muslims who best embody "family values" and a traditional religious lifestyle. He points to statistics that show the higher fertility of Russia's Muslims compared to the ailing Slavic population, favoring statistics that put Russia's Muslims at almost 25 per cent of the population by 2050. He then argues that sidelining Russian Muslims' voices will lead to an explosive situation, pushing Muslims to adopt more isolationist ideologies as a means of self-expression. He believes that this can be avoided if powerful politicians incorporate a specifically Russian Muslim discourse into Russian identity now. That way the demographic shift will be cushioned by an earlier ideological shift. All this is very much in the spirit of the Eurasian ideology, which believed that it is an intellectual elite that shapes a country. The notion of an elite doing people's "ideological" thinking for them also, of course, has a thoroughly neo-Soviet feel.

One can see, too, that this is another exercise in explicating that multi-valenced term, "traditional Islam". Batrov in Kazan gives the term a pluralistic meaning, and links it to canonical notions of Muslimness. Professor Ramazanov in Mahachkala is, in fact, not far off from Muhetdinov in his notion of Muslimness as incorporating "traditional families", conservative values and loyalty to an autocratic state. Muhetdinov might be said to fuse both of these opinions: he also references canonical Islam (Hanafism and so on), and he is careful not to alienate Russia's remaining atheists and secularists. He is not aiming at a theocracy. But he lays even stronger emphasis on the currently fashionable notion of Russia's "traditional values".

There is much in this vision that echoes the mood of Muslims around Russia and its fluctuating near abroad, as I have seen. But there are also deep tensions. Muhetdinov describes his ideology as "moderate conservatism", though in the Western context it looks more like ultra-conservatism: in fact, Muhetdinov's essays are scattered with quotes from Pat Buchanan, the American paleoconservative. The reaching back for pre-revolutionary Russian thinkers also seems archaic. At least one of those thinkers, Konstantin Leontiev, was an ultra-conservative who advocated ritualism and stasis in politics and religion, and Muhetdinov's attacks on liberalism seem very close to that vision. The Orthodox Leontiev saw the hierarchical Ottoman empire as a more natural ally for Russia than liberal, individualistic Europe, as did Gasprinsky. Muhetdinov is close in spirit to this position. History holds a warning, however: contrary to Leontiev's equation of stasis and longevity, the Ottoman and Russian empires—in reality—collapsed.

This is problematic, because Muhetdinov also diagnoses the problems of modern Islam as archaization and lack of education. But then it is not clear how his own paleoconservative ideology can be a beacon for world Muslims seeking to solve their problems. In personal conversations, Muhetdinov concedes that Russian Muslims need to look not to the Arab or Iranian world for education—his time studying in Saudi Arabia left him severely underwhelmed—but to England, the U.S. and Germany. This closet pro-Western position, which cannot be expressed in the public arena, is found quite often among Russian conservatives. In other remarks that I pick up on in my various visits to the Spiritual Board headquarters, he and his colleagues also admit that while there is much that is positive in Russian Muslim history, Islam is still regarded as a second-rate religion by most non-Muslim Russians. The Crimean episode is further evidence of this: in his Crimean pamphlet, he had praised the Crimean Tatars for their resistance against Soviet persecution and stressed the human rights aspect of the Crimean Tatar movement in the Soviet and post-Soviet period. This, too, makes it a somewhat dark irony that he should so laud the current Russian government at a time when its promises to uphold Crimean Tatar rights turned out to be so fickle.

Muhetdinov's attempt to Islamize the Russian Idea is fighting talk. In one sense his Islamic–Christian synthesis is simply a more sophisticated expression of the natural interaction of Volga Islam with Christianity (I have seen a copy of John of Kronstadt's "My life in Christ" on his desk; an acquaintance tells me he reads it regularly, and that his nanny was a Russian Christian.) But how much chance it stands of success in "*nasha* Russia",[7] as Muhetdinov once expressed it ironically to me, is highly debatable, and he himself seems to recognize this in private. The continued favor of the government is never guaranteed, for one. And Muhetdinov also has to be careful not to offend Russian Muslims with more fundamentalist views, as can be seen with the reception of his project of "Qur'anic humanism".

Qur'anic humanism rests largely on the work of the Russian–Syrian scholar Tawfik Ibrahim. Recently the muftiat's publishing house issued a full-length book of that title by Ibrahim, where the scholar attempts to derive the continued legitimacy of Judaism and Christianity from an inclusivist reading of the Qur'an. However, Ibrahim's presentations are badly received by the Arab participants in the muftiat's conferences, and after one recent conference a Chechen delegate even called up the governor of the city to complain that the conference was promoting heresy. The government, whose favor the muftiat is bending over backwards to retain, can always use these divisions for its own ends. In Putin's Russia, nuances and hyper-intellectualism are not favored: Muhetdinov recently got into trouble again for combing through arcane shari'a sources that suggest the hijab may not be obligatory; Rustam Batrov in Tatarstan came under angry fire in 2017 for unearthing a source that talks of the possibility of *namaz* being recited in a language other than Arabic. After this, he put in a plea to retire from his position in the muftiat in order to concentrate on scholarly work: there are limits, it seems, to how clever a government mufti ought to be.

Thus, the humming Moscow headquarters of a future united Russian Islam, is not assured of victory quite yet.

Forging a Russian Islam: the converts' perspective

Nonetheless, the desire to create a genuine Russian Muslim discourse that converges on the larger Russian discourse and so helps Russian Muslims to find a voice in the society they inhabit is surely genuine. Interestingly, among Muhetdinov's team there are several prestigious Russian converts to Islam, whose life experience is shaping this Russian Muslim discourse. There are also secular Russian Orientalists and secular Russian Muslim scholars, who have their own reasons for taking part in this project: "my team of Orthodox atheists", as Muhetdinov once jokingly described the former.

Three converts whose life stories illustrate the new religious, cultural and political fusion of Russianness and Muslimness are Iman Valery Porokhova, Vyacheslav Ali Polosin and Sergei Jannat Marcus.

Iman Valeria Porokhova: a Slavonic Qur'an

Porokhova is less directly linked to the muftiat, but her story overlaps with the other two. She married a Syrian in Soviet times and with his help recently completed a Russian translation of the Qur'an and a collection of hadiths—the same collection Gulnara had used for spiritual inspiration in Bishkek. Like Vladimir Popov, whom she helps decipher the Arabic script, her Arabic is reputedly superficial; her Russian though is stunning. Her Qur'an translation is melodious and lilting, and resonates with literary echoes, including echoes of the Russian Old Testament. Some have criticized her for this Slavicized Qur'an and the audacity of taking up the task at all, given her background. But for many Russian converts, it is a natural point of reference. In 2016, the muftis produced an updated edition of an older Russian translation of Yusuf Ali's famous English translation and commentary, which is intended to be Russian Islam's "authorized" version of the sacred book. One can see the many places where they have also borrowed a melliflous turn of phrase from Porokhova.

Porokhova is also, like Ramazanov and Sodik Yusuf, another Qur'anic miracle-hunter. Despite the fact, or because, she has no scientific background, she waxes lyrical in public talks about embryology and mountain pegs and oceanic currents. On the other hand, more like Bishkek Gulnara than Kazan Gulnaz, she has no time for the hijab, making appearances, instead, in a broad-brimmed hat. Recently, boldly claiming that the hijab is not Qur'anically sanctioned, she appears without any headcovering at all.

Sergei Jannat Marcus and Vyacheslav Ali Polosin also illustrate the phenomenon of the Russian intellectual convert. I meet them together at a Moscow Muslim event that illustrates the general environment in which they move.

It is January 2015, and Marcus has chosen a Tajik *chaikhona* (tea-house) popular with the Central Asian intellectual diaspora in downtown Moscow to hold a *mawlid* for the Prophet's birthday. The gathering consists of academics, diplomats (the Tajik deputy ambassador), journalists, lawyers and other public figures from the world of Moscow Islam. Among them are Leonid Syukaiainen, Russia's leading academic expert on shari'a law, and Mikhail Silelnikov, a renowned poet who often attends Islamic events. Born in Soviet Uzbekistan, Silelnikov has a sympathy for the East that recalls Vladimir Popov and writes poems and edits anthologies with Eastern or Islamic motifs.

A blind Tajik *qurra'* recites the Qur'an as guests occupy their seats at the tables. Sergei Marcus, the host, takes the microphone and talks the audience through the Islamic history of the locale where the *chaikhona* is situated, and praises the Muslim component in Russian history. He then asks the guests to come up and say some words about the recent Charlie Hebdo shootings. All but one of the speakers ignore the deaths of the journalists and focus on the Islamophobic reaction of Europeans in the aftermath. They urge restraint against anti-Islamic and anti-religious provocations and highlight the solidarity of Russian Orthodox and Russian Muslims in the face of European secularism. This is a message that Patriarch Kirill will reiterate in the following weeks; a million-man strong rally in Chechnya protesting Islamophobia and demonstating love for the Prophet takes place the following week, too, showing the mood here is representative. The rally, according to my Chechen acquaintances, is—for once—actually spontaneous, rather than organized from above.

Ignoring Islam, the former head of the armed forces under Yeltsin gives a neo-Soviet take on the matter: it is all the result of a certain cosmopolitan nation ganging up on Russia over the Ukraine. Syukaiainen is the only one to express sadness at the death of the cartoonists. Round the table, Silelnikov and Syukaiainen engage in jokes with the Tajik and Uzbek guests. There is an atmosphere of Russo-Muslim neo-Soviet bonhomie and banter similar to the wedding in Mahachkala.

Afterwards and in several other meetings, I talk to Marcus and Polosin to discover the motives for their conversion and their present views. The theme of Muslim–Christian interaction has been a recurrent one in this book, but it takes on a different meaning in this case. Both men spent many years as engaged Orthodox Christians in the liberal wing of the church, and both of them turned to Islam in a way that suggests that Islam was actually a continuation of their spiritual quest.

Vycheslav Ali Polosin: the rationalist

From the end of the Soviet period and throughout the 1990s, Polosin worked as an Orthodox Christian activist and priest to create a democratic Christianity in the new post-Soviet Russia. He always combined serious academic study, journalism, and political activity. He was one of the authors of the 1990 Law on the Freedom of Conscience, which put all religions and denominations on an equal footing before the law. With Gleb Yakunin, a disciple of Father Alexander Men (Russia's most famous dissident priest of the Soviet period) and two others, he founded the Russian Christian Democratic Movement. But evidently, as the nineties progressed, Polosin was becoming more and more disenchanted with the growing statist face of Orthodoxy and the retreat from religious equality of the 1990 law. He was also working on a doctoral dissertation that developed a rationalist, Weberian approach to monotheism, and soon this spilled over into his faith convictions. He withdrew from public life towards the end of the 1990s and then in 1999 he travelled to Dagestan to meet with Said Affandi for a spiritual consultation. The *sheikh* took him on as a disciple, and later that year Polosin publicly announced his conversion to Islam. He broke his ties with the Moscow Patriarchate and began instead to work for the muftiat in Moscow.

The conversion of a prominent Russian to Islam disturbed the comfortable consensus among Tatars and Russians that Islam is traditional for the former, Orthodoxy for the latter. What made it worse is that Polosin began publishing Islamic apologetics that were well-seasoned with his insider knowledge of Christianity. He also engaged in public debates with Father Daniel Sisoev, a conservative Orthodox priest who was later killed by a Muslim—though some maintain the motive was to evict him from expensive church real estate. Sisoev, too, had ignored the "consensus" and preached openly to Tatars and Caucasians. Although the Poloson–Sisoev debates involved each slinging verses at the other, for the Russian context they were energetic and innovative.

Naturally, Christians criticized Polosin's new religion and apologetics. Andrei Kuraev, a famous Orthodox activist, accused him of recycling Soviet anti-Christian propaganda. But an accusation that is sometimes leveled more generally at the "new jadidism" of the muftiat came from Georgy Fares Nofal, Polosin's mirror image: an Arab who converted to Orthodoxy and now writes Christian apologetics against Muslim critiques. He contends that Polosin, who does not know Arabic, does not have a very solid grasp of Islamic sources, and implies that his Islamic faith is a sort of "Russian liberalism of the seventh century", suggesting that Polosin's rationalistic version of the faith is his own reformist concoction which has little in common with Islam as traditionally practiced. For someone who grew up in the Middle East, he might have a point; but then it all comes down to the hoary question of how wide your definition of Islam is.

When I meet him, Polosin seems to have mellowed a bit from his Christian-baiting days. "Nowadays, I don't do disputes. They were a bit hair-raising," he says. "We had to hold some of the brothers back." Instead he seems to have shifted to the muftiat's more peaceable approach: "I am much more interested in interpretation now.... My aim is not to get a one up over people, but rather to show that there is no contradiction between our texts, between the Qur'an and the Bible. I no longer believe the prophecies in the Bible are so clear-cut. Jesus is only vaguely foretold in the Old Testament. I try to take a more academic approach now. I have also changed my view about the validity of gentile Christianity. I used to go along with Ahmad Deedat in saying it was a pagan invention. But now I believe that the Eucharist was not pure paganism. The mission to the gentiles filled pagan rituals with Biblical content, and in this sense they were successful and providential."

The retreat from Ahmad Deedat's views also shows a growing maturity: a famous preacher, Deedat is popular on Russian YouTube, and his views are on the unscholarly and fundamentalist end of the spectrum. They also have an anti-Western and anti-modern slant that is often lapped up in Russia. Polosin insists, though, somewhat in contradiction to his public writings that "I am a Western person essentially. I condemn the Eurasian idea that Russia's destiny must be Eastern. Russia is not Eurasia. It's Europe! I have mixed blood, I'm part Mordvin, Russian, Jewish..." He even tells me that he considered converting to Judaism and visited a rabbi who was a friend of his when his monotheist leanings began to get serious (like Marcus, he has a Jewish grandparent).

He assures me that he prays the five *salat* prayers regularly, but to some extent Nofal is right: he is looking for a more Western- or Russian-friendly Islam. "I am a northerner by mentality," he says. "And that goes for the question of covering women too. I don't understand that." (By chance, however, I meet his second wife at a conference, and she is a young Dagestani woman veiled in the now fashionable Middle Eastern style). Like several of the muftiat workers, he also finds the ritualistic or behavioral hadiths unattractive, and even laments the primacy of the "five pillars of Islam": "When did they develop?" he asks. "It's dangerous even to ask that question. Some hadiths talk about three or four pillars! *Namaz*, daily prayer, is a pillar. Fine: but what about the hadith that says that whoever takes interest will have Allah as an enemy? Or take all the hadiths condemning gossip. Why isn't gossip one of the pillars? ... We perform all the five pillars, but then we are quite prolix about breaking all the ethical commandments! But that's fine. Ethics is pushed into the shadows... Compared to Islam, in fact, Christianity is much better with this. And the Torah, too, has the Ten Commandments. But in Islam, it wasn't formulated so well. No one formulated it, in fact..."

Sergei Jannat Marcus: the romantic

Polosin is a former Christian liberal whose outlook is decidedly rationalistic. Marcus, by contrast, is a romantic. In Marcus, the Russian Muslim and Russian Christian story converge in a remarkable way. Like Polosin, Marcus was involved in underground Christianity in the 1980s. He became an "elder" in Father Alexander Men's ecumenically-inclined Orthodox Christian brotherhood. Men was a priest of Jewish origin who wrote about Christian culture and philosophy and established contacts with Western Protestants and Catholics, believing that the "walls of different confessions do not reach to heaven". Unlike some dissidents he was not actively anti-Soviet, but his non-political ministry was so popular among the Soviet intelligentsia that he and his group were perceived as a threat by the KGB. When the Soviet Union collapsed, Men's followers went in different directions: one became a Christian nationalist, one founded an institute for interfaith dialogue, and others founded liberal parishes in Moscow (to one of which the Tatar Christian Askhat now belongs). These stories are a well-documented part of post-Soviet Christian history (or Judeo-Christian history, if one counts those "Menians" who returned to their Jewish roots and emigrated to Israel).

However, Marcus' story can also be seen in this light. His Christianity contained all the elements of the Menian synthesis: it was intellectual, dissident, universalistic, and had strong Jewish–Christian overtones (Marcus' grandfather, from whom he gets his surname, was Jewish). Marcus stumbled into Islam, but once inside he came to see it as continuing and even expanding these elements: there is a Jewish–Christian foundation to Islam, but Islam, especially in its mystical Tatar–Turkic manifestation, seems more open even than Christianity to the sort of Gnostic, Indian and Eastern religiosity that Marcus was also interested in. He also came to believe that Islam could offer something to Russia that Christianity could not.

This more political aspect of his Islamic identity goes back deep into his Christian period. Unlike Men, Marcus actually was arrested by the KGB for religious activity and served two out of three years of a prison term in Siberia. During his sentence, he came to feel that dissidence just for the sake of dissidence had no meaning; it was unhealthy to see oneself as a perpetual victim: one should also create. Besides, when he was released it was 1988 and *perestroika* meant that religion was now permitted. Marcus, like Polosin, thus decided to go into Christian politics. One event, however, dismayed him and ate away at his Christian convictions. This, strangely, was the decision to canonize Nicolas II. Marcus was disgusted: in his view, the last tsar had reneged on his responsibilities to protect the Russian nation and had facilitated the Bolshevik destruction of Russia—which to his regret, his own grandparents contributed to (his grandmother was friendly with Lenin's wife, Krupskaya). Thus it was actually a romantic–royalist vision of Russia that turned Marcus away from the Orthodox Church and opened him up to other paths.

This other path surprised him by turning out to be Islam. During his public Christian activity in the 1990s, he presented Russia's first religious radio show. The Islamic affairs presenter left and Marcus, adopting the pseudonym Andrei Hussein, began to fill in for him part-time. The more he covered Islam, though, the more sympathetic he became, and one day he had a dream that he was standing up from praying *namaz* in a mosque. A year later, he found himself in the mosque of his dream in Egypt. His Islamic reporting also took him to Iran, and he found himself bewitched by the country and the Islamic lifestyle. Marcus had always flirted with beliefs in reincarnation and he toyed with the idea that there was some Iranic aspect to his past to which he was now responding. The Iranian story has often attracted mystically-inclined Russian intellectuals (such as Gumilev and Roerich), and it is historically the case that the Scythians and other Iranic peoples were widespread on the territory of ancient Eurasia that is now part of the Russian Federation. Christian Eurasians ignore this, of course. But in the new type of more universalist Eurasianist sensibility that was opening up to Marcus, the possible Turkic and Iranic layers beneath Slavic Russian identity were preserved in the Islamic culture of Russia's modern Muslim peoples, such as the Tatars and Bashkirs.

Marcus eventually converted officially to Islam in 2002, with help from Polosin, who helped crystallize for him some of the final intellectual details of his decision. He did not see it as turning his back on his Christian past, even though he had taught iconography and church architecture for two decades. For, as he explains, "when I first came to God, I came to what I call the nameless God, and the only option open to me for expressing that in this period was the church."

Marcus is referring to his experience as a student in the 1970s: a close girlfriend had committed suicide and Marcus, like so many others, felt suffocated by the darkness and cynicism of Soviet life and ideology, of which "the worst part was not the outer darkness but the inner darkness." He contemplated suicide as a rational option. One night, though, he fell asleep, and in his sleep he heard a voice quite clearly answering this despair at the darkness:

"There is light. And you must be light too," the voice said. The following morning, his despair had lifted. "It was strange to walk down the street, knowing I was now a believer. But a believer in what? In the Unknown God without sound, without name, is how I saw it for a long time." In becoming Muslim, Marcus believed he was returning to that original revelation.

As a Muslim, Marcus has continued his public cultural activities. To begin with he was burning with his old liberal dissident fire. I read an old article of his where he criticizes interreligious dialogue in Russia for being cynically controlled by the patriarchate, which limits the options artificially to the "four traditional religions" and excludes Catholics, Baptists and others. New religious movements like the Russian Krishnas, or Shi'ites, are not allowed to contribute and this is all a continuation of the Russian state's war against so-called sects. All this is pleasing reading for a Western liberal, but nowadays, Marcus (like Polosin) has had to recognize that there are things which it would be counter-productive to say. As a result, he now pours his efforts into providing Muhetdinov's team with the intellectual baggage needed to forge a Russian-compatible Muslim identity.

Muhetdinov is aiming at *rossisskoe musulmanstvo*. The term *rossiskoe*, as we saw, is meant to be broad enough to include non-Russian ethnicities who have lived for centuries on the territory of what is now Russia. However, in addition to the Tatars and Avars, one can say that Marcus is trying to forge an ethnic Russian, or *russkoe, musulmanstvo*, which will be another shade in this broader canvas. Marcus writes Islamically-themed poems in Russian and articles exploring the attitude of the Russian literary greats to Islam and Muslims. "There can be no true religion without culture," he tells me, unintentionally echoing French Islamic scholar Olivier Roy.[8] The references in Gaynutdin's or Muhetdinov's speeches to the compatibility of *sobornost'* (Russian Orthodox conciliarity) or Berdyaev's Russian idea with Tatar philosophy owe some of their origins to Marcus (and others like him). He is injecting an ethnic, cultural and linguistic Russianness into what has until now been primarily non-Russian Islam in Russia. Of course, not all his suggestions are welcome, and Tatars continue to be somewhat wary of public displays of Russian converts, as it compromises their position with an already mistrustful government.

As for the conservative "traditional" aspect of Muhetdinov's *rossiskoe musulmanstvo*, Marcus' own views on the family dovetail. He has four children of his own and several grandchildren and the patriarchal lifestyle, which he sees endorsed in both the Old Testament and the Qur'an, appeals to him. Being a royalist, he also imputes a mystical dimension to families and genes, rather like Ramazanov in Mahachkala. As with Polosin and many Russians, he has mixed roots, in his case Polish, Jewish and Russian: though rather than rejecting any aspect of his identity, his broad interpretation of Russianness and Muslimness allows him to celebrate them. And he sees his conversion to Islam as a form of penitence for his family's role in Bolshevism, and in general for Vladimir the Great's decision to choose Orthodoxy over Islam in tenth-century Kiev on the grounds, as the early Chronicles put it, that "it is merry for Rus to drink". In one of our meetings, he tells me a long story about how he and a group of friends who also had Polish ancestry were contacted by the spirit of the fifteenth-century Polish king, Vladislav III Yagelon. Due to their common origins, they shared an astral body with the king, which is why they could "see" him. The king's spirit had become trapped in Bardo, the Tibetan name for purgatory, and ultimately the group found a renowned Russian Sinologist who contacted Tibetan monks expert in the exorcism of such spirits. Marcus' friends traveled to Tibet for the ceremony and the visitations ceased.

The more eclectic aspects of Marcus' Islam do not make it into the public sphere, of course. However, he is an energetic figure who works to bring together all the many strands of Islamic and near-Islamic belief from the different corners of Russia and the former Soviet East. Along with Polosin, and figures like Ahmad Makarov, another convert[9] who has made a film called "Muslims Russia is proud of", he is working hard to shape a specifically Russian type of Muslim identity.

Russian Islam: the Muslim scholars' perspective

There is another group of people contributing to the new all-Russian Muslim "ideology": ethnic Muslim academics. They too can be found in the corridors of the Spiritual Board or at their conferences. In Soviet times, Oriental Studies was politicized and had strong links to the government. Conglomerates of scholars would often work on large projects that championed one or another view of ethnic origins or formation (the popular theory of "ethnogenesis") in order to shore up current political arrangements.[10] This is not to say that there was no objective work, and often the study of Arabic or old Turkic manuscripts was a way for non-Russian nationalities to covertly study religious and cultural material and create a resilient identity. Nowadays, Russian Oriental Studies is not as organized, and many leading scholars have since died. But in the minds of some, the revival of academic Oriental Studies is connected to a rediscovery of their own place in the post-Soviet order. At conferences held by the muftiat, the genre of the presentations is oddly mixed: an academic talk can segue mid-way into a call to "revive the Russian '*umma*".

Alikber Alikberov: European Dagestani

Alikber Alikberov's work on the ancient Albanian kingdoms is a case in point and affects modern Lezgin self-perception. In 2012, Alikberov helped draft a document that was read at the Organization of Islamic Cooperation, officially acknowledging the Islamic component in Russia's formation. Alikberov was optimistic that this high-level policy was seeping down to the popular level: "Putin began speaking about Russia's Islamic identity in 2010, and I noticed the difference in everyday life. For example, there was a boxing match between Klichko and Suleimanov. Klichko's Ukrainian, Suleimanov's Dagestani. Ten years ago, people would have rooted for the Slav, regardless of nationality. But then people started supporting Suleimanov: he's Dagestani, a Caucasian, yes—but he's Russian. People finally get it!" His hopes, since Crimea, have wilted though.

Still, he takes part in the Moscow muftiat's conferences and even acts as an advisor to the authorities on Islamic issues. Once he was summoned to Tobolsk and asked to talk to some Dagestani Wahhabis who were getting into trouble with the law. Alikberov sat down opposite them and poured himself a dram of vodka, then knocked it back swiftly. Then he gave his pep-talk: "You see: I am free to drink, and you are free to practice your religion. Remember, this is something that Muslims in Arab countries don't have. We should consider ourselves lucky here." Their shared Lezgin ethnicity meant that the boys listened to him. And Alikberov understood them, too: as he sees it, Wahhabism in this case, with its simple norms of dress and ritual was a way to weld disparate Caucasians and Central Asians into a fraternity that can powerfully resist the depredations of skinhead gangs. As they talked more, the group boasted that one skinhead had even converted to Islam, he was so impressed by their "code". So far, the group had only been caught engaging in petty acts of vandalism: they had torn down of a cross in response to a nationalist assaults on immigrants. Alikberov feels that his intervention can stop them moving onto something more sinister.

Aidar Habutdinov: fitting in with the Russians

Another telling example is that of Aidar Habutdinov. Along with Aidar Yuzeev, he is one of the leading scholars of Tatar history, philosophy and theology. His books provide useful support for the effort to recreate a "new traditional" Tatar, and more broadly, Russian Islam. And yet, oddly, Habutdinov is not religiously observant. Rather like Battaeva in Mahachkala, the old Soviet mentality is too strong in him: "I once tried to fast," he says in his delicate voice, "but half way through giving a lecture, I realized it was simply impossible. I had to excuse myself and go and get a glass of water to drink."

Still, in a way that will not percolate into the ideological pamphlets of the muftiat, he has his own specific sense of Muslim identity: "It was in the eighties that I first began to understand that I am a Muslim, what it means to be a Muslim. My grandfather died. My father was a card-carrying communist all his life. But when he buried him, he performed the Muslim ritual, and he knew it perfectly. It was such a revelation to me. And then I began to understand about my grandparents and relatives: they were all imams, *mudarisses*, they studied in *medreses* in the twenties—that link was never broken. In Kazan it was weaker, but in the villages of Tatarstan it survived all the way through Stalin up to Khrushchev. There were tens of thousands of Sufi *murids*, they supported the mosques and *sheikhs* with their contributions, and it was only when Khrushchev offered payment to them that they were weaned off this underground alternative economy and existence. But, still, all the rituals were transmitted. The most important ritual, I would say, is the burial ritual, the one that opened my eyes. All this survived, it was impossible to crush it."

Habutdinov has not managed to incorporate any of these rituals into his own life. However, if one defines ritual more broadly, there is one facet of the Islamic message that he does consider himself a practitioner of: "I became an academic," he says, "and our Muslim duty is to transmit knowledge to our younger generation. That is what Islam tells us to do." He seems to have in mind the hadith that encourages believers to go to China to seek knowledge; the Qur'an too has been read as encouraging science and knowledge by many Muslims down the ages. For most Muslim returnees, the ritual aspects that define their identity are *namaz* and *oraza*: these are highly discrete and homogenous behaviors that can resist the erosion of time in their transmission; they are also heirlooms connecting the practitioner not just to God but to ancestors. Habutdinov seems to have chosen a different sort of "discrete behavior" that is for him just as Islamic: scholarship, learning, and most importantly, teaching. It is a revival in different form of what his recent ancestors practiced in the *medrese*s of Tatarstan through the twenties.

And yet, there is a twist. "I decided to become an academic... but when you become an academic in Russia, you have to join the Russian way. For example, you have to drink, you have to get drunk. It's a way of being accepted. In drink is truth, you do not hide anything. If you refuse to drink, you are an outsider. When you drink, everyone knows you are not going to harm people, you are not holding a dagger behind your back." Thus the trajectory from the old to the new is not direct: the ancestors taught in the *medrese*s and kept the shari'a strictly; the descendants teach in the university, keeping the spirit of the ancestors alive, but having to adapt to the demands of modernity and Russianness.

From the "ideological" point of view of the new "Hanafite–Naqshbandi Russian Muslim culture", Habutdinov's Muslimness is too secular. The framework of "traditional" values would seem to demand a fuller return to archaic patterns of living. But perhaps Habutdinov's Muslimness already exemplifies a legitimate type of secular Muslimness and, like Ildar Abulzyarov, he can plead the Hanafite get-out clause about having faith in his heart. Likewise, Alikberov and several other scholars are studying and publishing Caucasian and Central Asian Sufi manuscripts. These publications are all fodder to demonstrate the existence of a specifically Russian, or Eurasian, Muslim sensibility. The irony, though, is that the scholars responsible for this work have a purely academic interest in the different Sufi schools and approaches. One seeming exception proves the rule: the young Ukrainian scholar of Sufism, Mihaylo Yakubovich, who has just edited a fourteenth century Sufi text by a Crimean Turkic theologian, is, in fact, a practicing Muslim: an ethnic Ukrainian, he converted when he was nineteen, and then completed the only Ukrainian translation of the Qur'an. But even he looks upon Sufism as a set of abstract theories, constructing his own Muslim life on different grounds. Perhaps, the treasures of Sufism being translated and analyzed await a future generation who will bridge the gap from secular scholarship to communal religious practice.

Ilshat Nasyrov: "I don't fully understand myself..."

Occupying intermediate ground is Ilshat Nasyrov, the Bashkir scholar of Arab philosophy and Sufism mentioned earlier. He is another cell in the Moscow

Muslim brain and his scholarship also feeds the muftiat's revival. Originally from Bashkiria, he was part of the first wave Islamic revival in the early nineties. Having studied at a small *medrese* in the Bashkir town of Oktyabrskoe, the muftis had plans for him to become an imam. Nasyrov, though, had bigger ambitions and he went abroad to study in Sudan during its civil war. Then he moved to Saudi Arabia, where he befriended some Sudanese and Saudi Uzbeks, whose roots went back to pre-revolutionary Turkestan. Amazingly, in the Wahhabi capital of the world, he was thus invited to secret Uzbek and Sudanese *zikrs* and even found an Uzbek Sufi manuscript to translate.

Thus his connection with Sufism is partly academic and partly spiritual. Like Habutdinov, he was born into a family whose connections with Islam were hanging by a thread. As he makes clear, the destruction of Bashkir Islam was even more tragic than what the Tatars underwent. Bashkiria was the first region after 1917 to be given independence, but then things turned sour: famine, typhus, civil war, and the hostility of Russian communists meant that 50 per cent of Bashkirs perished in the twentieth century. The traditions of Bashkir Sufism were destroyed. Nasyrov recounts some of his own family's history:

> I'm from southern Bashkiria, and belong to a certain clan. We know our ancestry. We still have clans. Of course, it's not like in Chechnya, say, where this still has a real social–political meaning. With us it's more formal now. But up to 1917, our 'tribes' owned certain parts of the land; that's what clan belonging meant. There was also an ancient tradition of Bashkiri cossakdom, of Bashkiris serving in the Russian army. One of my mother's ancestors was a mullah–chaplain; he got to Paris with the Russian army in 1814. Though, before that, the Bashkiris had been fighting against the tsar for two hundred years.

> My father was a history teacher in a small town. I get my love of history from him. But it was my mother who was responsible for my interest in religion. Her grandfather was also a mullah; he died in 1942: he was repressed by the Soviet authorities. In the nineties, we saw his NKVD file. They said he was a senile trouble-maker. Even on my father's side, my grandfather was Islamically knowledgeable. He knew many *suras* of the Qur'an by heart. Even in Soviet times, he performed many Islamic ceremonies for people: naming, burial, and other rituals. He could read Arabic beautifully. My father, though, had lost it all. He was a completely Soviet person. But that loss was widespread in Bashkiria. Sufism, and other forms, were not preserved like in Dagestan....

Nasyrov fasts and prays *namaz* (not entirely consistently) but like Yakobovych, this has only an indirect connection to the Sufi theosophy that he writes about. The closest he managed to real Sufism was when he became a *murid* of Said Affandi of Cherkesk. As he says, Dagestan was the only place where the communal structures survived which could make Sufism something other than an academic exercise. For some years, he worked for the Dagestani muftis and translated several Dagestani works. His links with the Dagestani muftis started when they discovered he had translated Rasulev, who was a link between Tatar–Bashkir Sufism and Dagestani Sufism, and whose disciple, Saipulla Qadi, was Said Affandi's own spiritual leader. Still, Nasyrov found it difficult to work with the Dagestanis: "They were very inflexible, very set in their ways," he says. Then he confirms my own impressions when he adds: "That's a problem in Dagestan. Maybe it's a product of their Soviet underground training, that they only saw one path, one truth. It's true on both sides, among the Salafists and the Sufis."

Although Nasyrov does not feel comfortable with the "common peoples' Sufism" of Dagestan, he still firmly believes that the esoteric and the exoteric must go together. He is not comfortable with the idea of Rustam Sabirov's *shahada*-less Sufism: "There's a lot of historical experience in the established religions. I don't think it's good to merely have the esoteric without the exoteric. One can get lost. However, of course, some people have become disillusioned with the exoteric aspect, seeing it as established for political reasons. And then "neo-Sufism" is an option. I am not against it necessarily. In Bashkiria, there's a well known politician who has become a Buddhist. He talks about Shambala all the time. But he knows our people well, he knows our traditions, and I respect him—even if I find some of his Shamabala talk a bit, well, funny."

Nasyrov recognizes that Russian Islam is in a state of choppy transition now. His hope is that it will find its way back to an intelligent rather than fanatical rediscovery of tradition, and he feels his translation work is helping in this endeavor. But doubt and testing are necessary stages on this path. He phrases it as follows:

> There's a famous Turkologist, a Bashkir who emigrated to Turkey after the Revolution, called Zaki Balidi Togan. He was the founder of the Bashkir Republic. In his youth, he passed through the crucible of doubt. He read all the Russian and Western books. But at the end of it all, despite it all, he still came to the opinion that it is impossible to break with tradition; one must observe tradition—the universe, after all, is founded on reason, and Islam is a spiritual path to understand this. But

he also insisted: religion must never make you a spiritual slave. The purpose of religion is to help you in times of desperation. One mustn't get bogged down in meaningless theoretical disputes, nor hurt people who might be offended by your views. Perhaps that's advocating double standards, but I don't think so. I agree with Togan's approach. It's about freedom of thought. I have often wondered: Why did the gates of *ijtihad* close? How did we lose that freedom of thought? In my opinion, it was partly the Mongols; but also the closing of the Silk Road after the Portuguese discovered an alternative sea-route. Traffic of goods *and* ideas stopped.

He is cautiously optimistic about how the Islamic rediscovery process has evolved since the nineties. All the muftiats, he believes, are getting more sophisticated. He also notes that many returnees from the nineties later left Islam again (a case I encounter with Atiya). This was partly due to the conflict in the North Caucasus. Now, a second wave is forming. He observes:

> Strangely enough, it's the Russian-speaking youth who are being drawn to the religion, and quite often they are highly educated. In Bashkiria all sorts of *jamaats* are springing up, informal gatherings in people's apartments. This is in the towns; in the villages there's very few successful people left, they've all gone to the towns. I was at a wedding a while ago. There was lots of drink put on. The old Soviet types were having it. But absolutely none of the young people touched it!

It is an interesting observation and raises a question: if the new wave consists of people who are mainly Russian-speaking, the need for a specifically Russian-language Muslim sensibility becomes all the more urgent. The works of Marcus, Nasyrov, Habutdinov, Alikberov and others is laying the ground for this, assuming the Russian government carries on its present attitude of partial tolerance towards Muslims.

The Russian Islamic revival is thus being stoked in part by secular Muslims, and in part by partially "returned" Muslims. Their aims sometimes coalesce with Muhetdinov's grand vision, and sometimes they diverge from it. The result is that sometimes the muftiat's claim to be describing, reflecting and developing real Muslim instincts on the ground have some basis; at other times, they seem more like flights of rhetoric: there are no structures in place to ground them.

An example of such a discrepancy between ideology and reality can be observed in the Moscow Islamic university.

The Moscow Islamic University

Damir Khairetdinov: "This is my native city"

Damir Khairetdinov has been head of the Moscow Islamic Institute for four years. He studied in Saudi Arabia in the nineties with Damir Muhetdinov, and worked for a number of years at the Saudi embassy in Moscow. Opponents of the muftiat like to use these facts to link him with Wahhabism. This is a favored device to give credence to personal grievances; Khairetdinov compares the charge to the equally inflated one of pan-Turkism that fulfilled the same function before 1917 and at a recent conference called on his fellow Muslims to step away from such mud-slinging. In Khairetdinov's case, the charge is particularly spurious: he was born into a fourth-generation family of Moscow Tatars. His main academic work to date is a book about the history of the Moscow Muslim community since the fourteenth century,[11] and he is also deeply involved in rediscovering Tatar theological traditions, both *jadid* and Sufi. All this has a personal angle for him, as his own family preserved Islamic commitment through the Soviet period.

"My grandfather," he tells me, "was very involved in the committee of the Cathedral Mosque. He was close to the imam-khātib who was killed in 1980, the year of the Moscow Olympics. The imam died in mysterious circumstances. Some people said it was because he had been stealing money, but in fact there were political reasons. There were plans to knock down the Cathedral Mosque, to make space for the Olympics events. As usual, there were two parties in the Kremlin. One was hard-line Communist and wanted to get rid of all vestiges of religion. The other was pragmatic: they wanted to keep the mosque to show the Arab countries. The imam had been campaigning vociferously for the mosque, appealing to the pragmatists. The pragmatists won. And the imam was killed, as we saw it, in revenge. I remember KGB agents coming to our flat and questioning my grandfather: he had been very active in the campaign to keep the mosque. So I definitely had this very strong sense of religious involvement from my grandfather's side of the family." Khairetdinov's grandfather was born in Moscow (so that his grandson considers himself a true Muscovite dedicated to the study of its history), but took his family to his Nizhny village in summer. There, at an underground mosque, the young Damir learned how to do *namaz*, but was warned: "On no account tell your friends in the Komsomol about this." His Islamic lineage on his mother's side was even stronger: his mother's aunt was married to the mufti of Ufa, Abdurahman Rasulev, the son of the famous Tatar theologian, whose works Nasyrov translated and whom Magomedov had mentioned admiringly in Mahachkala.

Thus Khairetdinov, far from being a neophyte Wahhabi, is an old acolyte of "Russian Muslim culture", who knows the ins and outs of negotiating a place for Islam in a Russia that waxes ambiguous about the religion. For him, his Tatar and Muslim identity are comfortably intertwined and he accepts that most of his fellow Tatars are highly secular and live as a minority in a non-Muslim environment. He himself has settled on a non-ostentatious form of Islamic observance ("I am not going to pray *namaz* in the street if I miss the time like they do in Saudi Arabia"), and feels comfortable with all Islamic denominations.

He is also used to living under less than free conditions: he openly admits that the money for his Islamic University comes from the government and the security services, and that their every move is scrutinized. He also admits that the situation has become even more oppressive since the nineties: back then Russian Muslims could study abroad, but now it has become much harder, albeit for good reasons.

Khairetdinov, however, also lays the blame on Russian Muslims themselves, contrasting them with Finnish Muslims. Helsinki is home to a small Nizhny Tatar community whose roots go back to before 1917. In 1960, the community built its own four-story Islamic center with a mosque on the top floor. The center was funded by shops on the other floors. "When I got back to Russia, I wrote about this," Khairetdinov says. "I tried to get our own Tatars to do something similar. But they don't want to. Our Tatars are very conservative. We don't need a minaret, as I said, but they won't hear of it. 'Why can't we have a big beautiful mosque like the Christians have their churches?' And so we are stuck with this problem of the low number of mosques."

Khairetdinov admires Moscow Jews for doing something similar, and recalls a moment of Jewish–Muslim cooperation: "In the Danilevsky Muslim Cemetery, there's a whole part of it for Jewish graves. You'd never get something like that with Orthodox and Muslims. Any dialogue there is, is always government-initiated; it's not genuine. But with Jews and Muslims, it's possible. A couple of months ago," he continues, warming to this theme, "I was invited to an event at the new Jewish Museum in Marina Roscha. I thought I'd stick my head in and stay for a bit, to show my face. But I ended up staying for two hours. I couldn't tear myself away. The parallels were so striking! For every picture, for every display unit, you could have changed the Jewish names to Tatar names. It was the same movements, the same aims, the same problems. It was incredible!"

Khairetdinov is thus a self-confident Russian Muslim who understands his environment and its possibilities. What was striking, however, is the contrast between the rector and some of his students, which brings home the difficulties of communicating a very personal Tatar experience to an audience of a different background.

Hussein: the lonely Shi'ite

A picture of student life emerges from the stories of Ildar and Hussein. Hussein was born into a family of emigrants from Azerbaijan in a provincial Russian town. He grew up with hardly any religion and, after a series of crises and disappointments, became religious in his late teens. His secular father initially opposed his son's choice but when Hussein was accepted into the Moscow Islamic University, he was proud of him, and Hussein too could not believe he was going to study in the capital.

But his time at the institute turned into a series of spiritual crises. In his first year, the administration invited Turkish teachers who brought Naqshbandiyya practices with them. "We were doing Naqshbandiyya rituals all the time, even in the dorms," Hussein recalls. "It was so regular, so intense, we didn't even have time to finish our homework. They took over every waking minute." Ildar chips in: "They would hang a picture of the *sheikh* in the prayer room. And then everyone would do *zikr* in front of it. The more *zikrs* a *murid* (pupil) does, the more reward he builds up. And according to the Naqshbandis, you can also transfer merits. So the *murid* recites extra *zikrs*, and dedicates them to the *sheikh*: it's like a payment for what the *sheikh* is giving him. The *murid* in effect is paying the *sheikh*, so the *sheikh* will take him to a higher *maqimat*, or Sufic level, closer to God. So our students were being forced to do *zikrs* all the time, as 'pay-back' to the *sheikh*."

Obviously, the administration had decided that the Sufi influence would be the best way to banish any possibility of Wahhabi influence. But the irony was that by this time, Hussein had already become a Salafist. It is a crisis often found among new Muslims. When he first became religious he did not even know that there were different *madhabs*. This discovery set his mind reeling, and through reading and chance conversations he eventually decided that *madhabs* were a late invention and he needed to get back to the pure, original

Islam of the Qur'an and the Companions. In other words, he turned himself into a Wahhabi. Hussein tells me that he was not the only one who went down this path, and a decent fellow student from a few years earlier, a Russian convert, went through the same thought process. However, he ended up leaving to fight in Chechnya and was killed.

But the irony piles on. "In the second year," Hussein continues, "the Turks were taken away. A new era began: a Salafist era." The administration had brought in Russian Muslim teachers who had studied in Egypt. "But what they didn't realize is that their time in Egypt had turned them into clear Salafists. I'll tell you how it works: we had a good student, a Sufi, and he went to Egypt for three months. And in just those three months he came back a Salafist! Anyway, these new professors were teaching *Aqida*, Principles of Faith. A whole new group of students appeared in the Institute as well, most of them Salafist too. Where they came from, we had no idea. It looked like they had been gathered artificially."

However, Hussein's life did not improve because—with almost comically bad timing—he had now started to rediscover his Azerbaijani Shi'ite roots by Skyping relatives back in Baku. As a result his next year was one of unmitigated persecution, with friends dropping him and accusing him of being a *kafir* and Shi'ite recruiter. Things got so bad that he considered emigrating to Iran. Hussein has now graduated. Despite his roller-coaster ride, he feels that overall his studies were positive and gave him much-needed knowledge. He mentions Khairetdinov as a good teacher who put Salafists in their place with soft but stunningly accurate one-liners. Nonetheless, it is clear that Khairetdinov's own "traditional Islam", an heirloom from decades of family experience, could not substitute for students making their own discoveries and mistakes. These young students are maturing in an atmosphere of turmoil that engulfs both Russia and the Arab world. Sufi fanaticism and Salafist fanaticism, familiar to me from Dagestan, both made their appearance in the institute. And even now, some of Hussein's words seem disturbing, as he ponders the reasons for radicalization:

> Well, it's an attractive notion, it's very romantic. In the forest, you can escape from all your sins. You hunt for your food, there are no women, there's no temptations, nothing *haram*. If the FSB comes, there's a bit of shooting. Yes, I really had a strong desire to die as a martyr like that. But I have gone through that phase. First of all, only Allah knows where the real jihad is today. Maybe Israel: I could go there. But even that we don't know. I think now that the notion of suicide bombing is flawed. Who are the real suicide martyrs: it was the ones who ran against the crowds of

attackers to defend the Prophet. You could therefore make the analogy that suicide bombing is right. But, and there are several big buts... it's like this: if I want to do a good deed, say, like build a mosque. Would it be right to build it on money from drugs or prostitution? That would be a cursed way to do it. Because someone who commits suicide goes straight to Hell, they're a *kafir*. So you can't attain a good end by a bad means.

When I ask for more precision about his analogy, Hussein assures me that he does not think that killing *kafirs* is "a good end". Still, it is a surprising way to be thinking, especially at an institute funded entirely by the Russian government.

Ildar: healing Christians in Latin, Muslims in Arabic

Ildar's story is completely different. He is a Tatar from a large city in Tatarstan and far more confident than Hussein. In fact, it was Ildar who kept his friend from running off to Iran or giving up on Islam entirely. As a Tatar, Ildar is far closer to the mentality of Khairetdinov, Marcus, Farit and Ruslan from Kazakhstan. He tells me he has the powers of healing and interpreting dreams. Then he pulls out a New Testament and reads various verses to me: he carries it everywhere and has the highest respect for Christ. Ildar also reads the Lord's Prayer in Latin when he is performing healings over Christians and knows it by heart. (It is not often that a Muslim recites the *Pater Noster* to me from memory). He is interested in Eastern religions, and points out the similarities between Sufism and Yoga: the former talk of *hijama* or energy points on the body; the latter talk of chakras. Then there is Kabbalistic *gematria*, which can also be used to extract secrets from the Qur'an. Ultimately, though, he says: "For me, Islam unifies all the branches of knowledge from different areas of the world. I read the Old Testament, the New Testament and the Vedas, and put them side by side with the Qur'an. I see nothing new in Islam, just old things absorbed and given their place."

Given this Tatar eclecticism, the Salafist and Naqshbandiyya "revolutions" were water off a duck's back. Nonetheless, he was angered by the Salafist phase, and says that when he saw a copy of a book by Abd al-Wahhab circulating, he was highly distressed: "I just couldn't tolerate the idea of Salafism getting a hold in Russia. I even thought of writing a denunciation to the FSB about the fact that there were copies of Abd al-Wahhab's book, in Arabic, circulating in the institute." It is another odd moment that points to a strained and mistrustful atmosphere: would not the most sensible course of action be to consult with the rector? Might not a better solution be to read, understand and deconstruct Abd al-Wahab's books? However, it also reveals the devout Russian patriotism of a Tatar, something lacking in Hussein, a first-generation immigrant.

Ildar's thought bubbles with a typical blend of scholarship and YouTube hearsay. He, too, mentions Ahmad Deedat and quotes his views about Christianity. However, Ildar is an independent thinker. I put it to him that if he is so keen on the Gospels, he must see that their narrative structure leads to the Crucifixion—a fact denied by orthodox Islam. He talks around the subject, but concludes: "Rationally speaking, I would say it's highly likely he was crucified. Isaiah talks about three days away from the world of the living. So, it's certainly possible, rationally. But this isn't what Islamic doctrine teaches."

How then does he square his rational conclusion with his Islamic commitment? "Well, I try to combine rationality and Islam, as I believe Islam is the true faith," he answers thoughtfully. "Sometimes I don't always understand a question. But then I wait and hope that the conflict will be resolved. Our minds are too limited to understand everything at once. So for a certain time, with some questions, I live in doubt. In my life I have lived with things that were a mystery, but then when I went on I found the answers. Some things are not given straight away. It can depend on many factors: age also plays a big role."

This acceptance of doubt as a key ingredient in mature religious faith is attractive and reveals a self-confidence that probably not all the students feel. It contrasts with Hussein's own hungry quest for absolute certainty. Interestingly, Ildar then mentions Yahya Haroon, the Turkish creationist with whom Professor Ramazanov in Mahachkala was so enamored. Talking to two other professors at the Moscow Islamic University, I get the impression that they, too, adopt the Qur'anic miracle-hunting approach. Ildar comments:

> "Some people try to show that all science is in the Qur'an. There's a Turkish scholar who says that the seven heavens mentioned in the Qur'an are the seven layers of the atom. But that just strikes me as silly. There's no good analogy there at all. Making such comparisons is bad for the reputation of Islam as well."

Ildar and Hussein are both Russian citizens. The institute also has quite a few Tajiks and Uzbeks studying there. However, it seems that several of them are mostly there for more worldly motivations: to get Moscow residency. The Central Asians I speak to are cagey and mouth the usual platitudes about peace and harmony. A post-doctoral student doing some part-time teaching at the institute tells me that the students do not accept the permissibility of returning a greeting of *salaam* to a non-Muslim. This all indicates that the "Russian Muslim culture" being discussed in journals and conferences is, once again, often very far from capturing the far more riven, anxious reality on the ground, even right beneath their noses in the very heart of Moscow.

Maverick philosophies: millionaires and militants in turtlenecks

The Moscow muftiat is good at talent-scouting and drawing different figures into its projects, as I have found out myself. But many Muslims in Moscow lead their lives outside of its sphere of influence, and many distrust it intensely. Three influential figures who demonstrate an alternative Muslim way of life are Shamil Aliutdinov, and Gulnar and Gaidar Jemal.

Shamil Aliutdinov: upwardly mobile Islam

Aliutdinov is the imam at the Victory Park mosque. He is the only Russian Muslim to have graduated from the prestigious al-Azhar university in Cairo. His brother, Ildar Aliutdinov, works as an imam at the Cathedral mosque, and Shamil Aliutdinov has friendly relations with the team there. However, he is an independent, and the brand of Islam that he is promoting is deserving of attention in its own right. In many ways it is a sort of American-style televangelism. Aliutdinov writes popular books explaining Islam and linking it to the message of American self-help gurus (including somewhat antique ones like Dale Carnegie). Islam comes out in this version as a religion of upward mobility and aspiration. He has written a series of "Trillionaire" books ("A trillionaire listens", "A trillionaire speaks" and so on), encouraging everyone to aspire to be a "trillionaire", not just in terms of wealth but in terms of realizing one's potential. The books contain stories of his own successes: the decision to order his day to achieve more, to take up a new sport, learn a new language, read a new book. Stories of other Muslim achievers are included too, and self-help advice is dispensed.

Aliutdinov travels round Russia, as well as appearing in Crimea and Kazakhstan, speaking to packed auditoria. He is dressed in an expensive suit and tie and projects an image of success and middle-class acumen. His audience is also composed of wealthier Muslims; while the Historic mosque draws less well off Caucasians, and the Cathedral mosque is a magnet for Tajiks, Uzbeks and Kyrgyz, many of the parishioners at the Victory Park mosque will be Chechen or Dagestani businessmen who arrive in expensive jeeps. Of course, there are young students in the audience like Rifat Mustafin, and Moscow Tatar business people—but the demographic is still the upwardly mobile.

In addition to the aspirational, self-help messages, Aliutdinov hosts question-and-answer sessions on Islam after the Friday *jum'a* prayers and at other times. He has also published popular books for new and not-so-new Muslims clarifying aspects of Islamic ritual: fasting, *namaz*, marriage and so on. Another book is a compendium of recent convert tales, and still others take up theological questions like the difference between Sufism and Salafism, and whether a new Muslim can carry on performing music or doing art (he has a detailed discussion grounded in a wide range of classical sources about what a Muslim artist can be permitted to draw in *How to see paradise*; the mention of drawing without shadows makes me think of Farit). Aliutdinov has, additionally, been working for several years on a commentary of the Qur'an, and in 2012 all four volumes were combined into one massive tome called "The holy Qur'an. Meanings. A theological translation", which contains comments on nearly every verse. It is a prodigious achievement for the world of Russian-language Islam.

Gulnar Jemal: *hijabistas* and inferiority complexes

Gulnar Jemal is the editor of a Muslim woman's magazine. On the cover of one of their 2015 editions is a glossy picture of Shamil Aliutdinov and his wife. This shows the overlap in aims between Jemal's magazine and Aliutdinov's projects, but Jemal puts it into words, revealing the presence of a collective inferiority complex (Askhat was not the only one to suffer in this way, it seems): "In general, Muslims in Russia are very backward and uneducated. Islam is quite barbaric here. It's stuck in the Stone Age, and it needs a lift. So this magazine is an attempt to give Muslims something sophisticated and contemporary. Someone needs to portray Islam in its pure form, to strip it of all these ethnic accretions which have covered it. We have to change that; we need to make Islam first-rate, not some poor second-rate relative." The magazine includes articles on topics like Iranian film; the British Muslim pop-singer Yusuf Sami; the experience of Russian Muslim women who have married Arabs; how to raise children; orphans; charitable organizations; human rights in shari'a; and various women's and fashion issues. It is professionally produced and aims at a wide readership, including non-Muslims.

Jemal's glossy magazine and Aliutdinov's self-help gospel and smart suits might appear banal in the European or U.S. context. But for Russia, and especially Russian Islam, they are a radical innovation. The attendees of Aliutdinov's conferences and talks, and the readers of Jemal's magazine will not be satisfied with shoddy pamphlets or naïve sermons. Many of them have university degrees and professional qualifications, and, for better or for worse, they are fully immersed in modern Russian capitalism. In Soviet times, the state often made sure that priests and imams were not too talented; it was a way to discredit religion. This new "glossy" Islam attempts to undo that damage.

While Aliutdinov and Jemal may not be directly involved in the muftiat, they both share this aspirational quality. In the old days Islamic teachers and muftis would have been unconcerned about dress; but Khairetdinov, Muhetdinov and other "Islamic professionals" now wear stylish suits under their ceremonial gowns. They too are projecting a modern, middle-class image for Muslims. Another comment that Jemal makes draws comparisons with the West: much Muslim socializing, she says, is devoted to charitable projects— helping Chechen or Syrian refugees, the Palestinian cause, flood victims and so on. Again, this is par for the course for the West: but this sort of self-organizing civic action is still relatively new for Russian society; in Soviet times, independent initiatives would have been crushed by the state and seen as subversive. Many secular Russians, especially in the poorer provinces, still display a brutal attitude to charity; more than once I have heard the sentiment that orphans are worthless rejects who should be left to die.

I talk at some length to Gulnar Jemal, and through her I also meet her more publically famous husband, Gaidar Jemal, when she invites me to their downtown Moscow flat. Gulnar tells me that the community of Moscow Muslim activists is quite tight-knit: "We know them all," she remarks. The reason this is interesting is that in a game of six degrees, one would find it odd to link Aliutdinov and Gulnar's husband. This is because Gaidar is a notorious firebrand and provocateur, who often appears on national TV offering support for Chechen resistance fighters or championing the cause of Islamic fighters in some part of the world. With his shaven head, chiseled half-Azeri looks, and Italianate clothing, he looks more like a mafia don.

Gaidar Jemal: "... and the darkness shines brightly"

In person, though, Gaidar is charming and he and his wife are an affectionate couple. I listen to both of their stories, as well as receiving a personal insight into Gaidar's Islamic worldview that serves in many ways as a fitting coda for all my conversations and travels.

As I talk a bit more to Gulnar, I find out that, despite her Turkic name, she turns out to be a Russian convert who, a bit like Marcus, stumbled into Islam by chance in the 1980s. "I converted really just in order to marry Gaidar," she says. "I went from being a sort of hippy girl with jeans and long hair into a Muslim activist. I helped Gaidar in the Islamic Renaissance Party. He was one of the founders. Probably I first got a real taste for Islam when we traveled together to Tajikistan. We went once in 1984, I think it was, and then in 1986. It was like discovering some lost purity: the lakes, the mountains, it was like an uninhabited island. In the Pamir mountains, we met with real dervishes: Soviet life had hardly touched those isolated parts."

Gulnar speaks a bit more about the reasons for her conversion and her hopes for Islam in Russia nowadays. She comments that "the biggest contribution of Islam to our days now is in reconstructing the family. The family in Russia, in the modern world, is falling apart." She also talks about how they raised their own daughter, and there is a typical Russian mix of influences. On the one hand, wanting the best for her education, they sent her to a Jewish school (an irony considering some of Gaidar's public anti-Jewish insinuations). On the other, a Tatar nanny helped raise her: "She was a good woman, but fanatically Salafist after her studies in a Naberezhny Chelmy *medrese*. She insisted on sewing little silver eyes onto all the animals on the girl's sheets. Somewhere she had read a hadith that animate images must look alive if they are to be halal. It was quite spooky! But she had a good heart and we learned a lot from her."

Gaidar, who has come into the room by this time, seems to be getting restless with this trivial conversation and soon he takes over, injecting some heavy philosophical input. He gives me a brief sketch of his early years. He was born to an Azeri father and Russian mother in Moscow, and read voraciously in his Russian grandfather's philosophical library in his teens. Despite having one "Muslim" parent, and despite being such a public Muslim figure, it bears remembering that, like Gulnar, he is effectively a new Muslim who joined a flux of post-Soviet Russian intellectuals looking for meaning in "Eastern" philosophies. As Gulnar says: "We were not unique: Bykov [a T.V. personality] and Pelevin [a writer] looked into Buddhism, but there were many Russian intellectuals who explored the Islamic option."

Gaidar helped found an Islamic political party in Astrakhan in the late eighties, the well known Islamic Renaissance Party. Later it sprouted affiliates around Russia, and in Tajikistan it mobilized people against the communists and fought a losing battle against them in the civil war. After a stint in the oil industry, he moved to Sudan, and worked with al-Turabi, before the latter's defeat. For a while he had some contact with Kalim Saddiqi, founder of the Muslim Parliament of Britain. He has thus always been a believer in the political role of Islam, and to this day he firmly and unabashedly sees Islam as an unambiguously political program. As Gulnar has hinted, he went through a Sufi phase, but now rejects this as mystical nonsense (in contrast to the muftis and their academic collaborators).

"Islam is not a mystical religion," he opines. "The notion of *wahdat al-wujud*, the unity of being, is really not Islamic. In Christianity you have the liturgy, where matter is transformed into divinity. Hinduism has something similar, something sacramental. But Islamic prayer, *salat*, is called *'ibadat*, service. It is an entirely social ritual, a military ritual, it is the raising up of a flag by a military unit. The serried ranks of worshipers in the mosque are a potential army, strict, ready for fighting. For Islam, God is in no sense within the world, the world cannot be mystically transformed into God—ever. Belief comes when a person believes in something outside of his experience. Belief is an act of will, of assertion. One cannot believe in facts; facts are. You can't believe in a teapot."

He is in good provocative form, throwing the idea that "Islam is peace" back in the face of what he sees as the state-sponsored *munafiqun*, or hypocrites, of whom the muftis are his prime example. "The muftiat is a pressure-cooker," he continues. "It's strictly controlled by the security forces, and they receive money from the FSB. It's all *haram*. That's particularly true of Moscow. It's not true all over, though. In Saratov it's better. That's because the Moscow muftiat is obsessed with occupying some sort of position as the center of Russian Islam. But nobody believes that except the muftis themselves. And they kick up this fuss about not having enough mosques. What do you need more mosques for: the more mosques you have, the more FSB agents there'll be! You can have prayer-houses—though they are probably crawling with agents as well. We don't go to the mosques, except for a big event or a holiday sometimes."

But although Gaidar rejects the "distraction" of Sufism and the idea of a state-sponsored "Russian Muslim culture"—whose claws, as he would see it, have been removed—his current brand of political Islam is more Leninist than Salafist (if one overlooks the Leninism inherent in much political Salafism). "A lot of people want to bring back the Caliphate after ninety years," he explains. "They see it as a revival of a space where the shari'a will rule. But I think that's a bad idea. For me, Islam has a different meaning. Islamic politics was started by Muhammad as resistance to the global society. It reveals the metaphysical evil of society, and challenges it. The history of monotheism is a history of confrontation with power: Abraham against Nimrod, Jesus against Caesar, Muhammad against Byzantium and Persia. The global system is a projection of the shadow of Iblis. You don't need a naïve demonology to understand this. The root of the word Iblis makes it clear: its etymology is in the Greek god Apollo, who is connected with the gods of Olympus. Iblis refuses to bow to Adam. All he can see in Adam is clay, materiality; he cannot see God's breath in man. He cannot see the apophatic point of Spirit. Nowadays, Russia just engages in an imitation of resistance to the global system, whereas in reality it is enmeshed in the same game of Iblis."

His analysis of capitalist materialism includes a critique of the modern lifestyle: "People pay their lifetimes into the system," he believes. "The system takes energy from them. One hundred to two hundred years ago, people lived in bare corners, they lived simple lives. One hour of life cost them nothing. But the grandson of the man who lived so spendthriftly is office plankton working all hours to pay for the education of his son, a rat in a wheel, occasionally jumping out to charge up in a fitness club: every hour costs more for him than the entire life of his grandparents. Satan is the landlord taking the rent regularly: today he takes a dollar, tomorrow he'll take two dollars..."

"ISIS is a step in the right direction," he continues cool-headedly. "It is a better form of resistance. Before people just went off to the Caucasus to die; victory didn't interest them. What do we need victory for? I just want to leave this life. That was the reasoning. That's just a form of desertion. But ISIS is organizing space, economic life, the legal field, the extraction and sale of oil. It has some clear goals: to liquidate the threat of the Kurds as the Western arm in the region; the destruction of the Saudi dynasty. Their third goal is to save Egypt from Sissi...."

But globally, "ISIS will have failed if they just create another Islamic ghetto somewhere. We saw the Ottoman caliphate and that collapsed; it is over. Rather, an Islamic state should serve as a rallying-point for a more widespread resistance to the Western capitalist system." And that is where he sees his own role. Though he could have left Russia many times, he stays in Moscow out of a belief that Islam in Russia will be able to play a key role in this resistance.

"Russia has a special meaning for me. Or rather, the territory that Russia encompasses means something to me, not necessarily Russia *per se*. It's important to keep the Russian language—not for the Slavs, but for all who come here and will come here. I believe in renovating the human material of Russia. We need immigrants. Those who live here now are too imprinted with the clichés of past life, they are incapable of engaging in a passionate search. A new project requires new people. With a new project people will come here en masse, from Indonesia, Pakistan, England—all over. They will come for self-realization, and to build an opposing pole, an anti-system. Political Islam will provide the network for those who come here. Not everyone can become Muslim but the masses need a mystical basis for their struggle. The church cannot help here. Liberation theology is marginal, no one in the church speaks about it. The church is by its nature on the side of the rich and of tyranny. If you ask me, they are a reception committee for the anti-Christ. This is the role of the world government... But we shall greet the Mehdi and the Messiah."

Gaidar's account of the future is spiced up with some heavyweight metaphysical terminology, but in essence his vision is close to that of Ismail in Zelenodolsk. The same could be said of his criticisms of the muftiat: while couched in harsh language, they echo common criticisms among other Muslims, and even the self-criticism of the more self-aware muftiat workers.

Gaidar, though, is more revolutionary than Ismail and he sees his own speeches and writings as fomenting the coming of an imminent cataclysm: "Your contemporary Muslim today hates the modern world, but he doesn't understand it. There's a lot of Islamology[12] but no 'kufrology', that is, a systematic philosophy of the doctrines that oppose Islam in the modern world today. There is no Islamic philosophy of evil. Marx proposed a simple model: the appropriation of interest by the capitalists. It was simple, but it worked. You can build congresses around it. Muslims cannot describe today's world without some 'kufralogical' terminology. There's Ali Shari'ati, of course, who is interesting, but he's too general. He doesn't give the specifics....

"I don't appear much in public nowadays. I just do enough to keep the public aware of the message. What's the message? The message is that there's a crisis looming. I don't want to be like Lenin, making speeches from the balcony to an unprepared audience. I want the public to be ready... So I go on this talk-show, that talk-show. Everyone is expecting the regime to collapse as a result of sanctions, everyone expects that there will be chaos and a chance to seize possibilities like the Bolsheviks did. I also think this will certainly happen. We have reached the end of the road, it's very close."

It is a cold snowy night as I leave their apartment and tramp through the winding allies and courtyards that surround their block. Echoes of Gaidar's philosophy buzz around my mind. I grapple with his "philosophy of darkness", which is another rejection of optimistic Sufism: "They always talk about light. But I say that any light radiates light and slowly loses its strength in the infinite primal darkness. How can this attrition of the light be overcome? What is the true symbolism of the divine? One needs to find the darkest part of the darkness and make it shine. If you put dark ink on the surface of less dark ink, the dark ink shines forth. If you take a black page and put even blacker ink onto it, the blackness begins to shine. It's a strange phenomenon! Darkness is overcome by darkness! And that darkness cannot be diminished. One must free the lightness of the primal darkness: ontological light, the light of Plato, the Sufis and so on, is doomed."

There is something Mephistophelean about Gaidar's worldview, but also undoubtedly something bold, seductive and original. After all, there is a dark edge to modern Russian life, there is a constant seething anxiety, and it is a relief to hear it articulated, for once, by a representative of the usually complacent intellectual class. Gaidar's philosophy may seem implausible, and there are definitely elements of *ressentiment* and hatred in it. Its support of the Wahhabi forest-fighters, not to mention the Islamic State, is grotesque. And like other Russian Muslim philosophies, it is still stiffly "ideological", for the concept of "ideology" is a Marxist holdover that will not go away. But at least it does not try to justify an evidently rotten system. Dugin, Putin's neo-Eurasian philosopher, is a long-time friend of Gaidar Jemal and had been sitting on the same sofa where I had sat a week earlier. The two used to share a similar revolutionary fervor. But Gaidar now dismisses him as a gray cardinal, a man who has sold out to Putin and to the "philosophy of light". He is waiting for a different revolution, which Trotsky-style, will herald an unending series of further revolutions: it will be resistance all the way down. Islam in this vision is like "an iron rod, come to strike the world". In Jemal's version of history, it originated with Abraham's father Azar in the depths of the ancient Caucasus mountains, and then descended onto the Babylonian plains to destroy tyranny.

Russian Muslim culture: an exploding dialectic?

My shoes are drowning in slush as I finally emerge and hail a taxi. Will the Islamic revolution come soon to Russia? Will Gulnar Jemal's glossy magazine for Muslim women still be permitted? And what about Gulnar Jemal's upwardly mobile bourgeois Muslim lifestyle? What about the muftiat, assembling bit by bit their new modernist–Sufi Russian Muslim culture? Or is Gaidar just another voice of a marginal intellectual indulging in far-fetched rhetoric, while the future belongs to his wife?

Jemal's questions return to me several times in the coming year. Whenever I catch him on TV or the Internet, I tune in to read or watch a new interview. For all his darkness and belligerence, I cannot help remembering our meeting fondly. And then, one day, towards the end of 2016, I see a picture of him on the internet. He is looking weary and emaciated. A couple of months later, he is dead. The burial takes place quickly in Kazakhstan, where he had been speaking at a conference, his last, it turned out.

But this is not the last time Jemal's name comes up. It is when I am in Chechnya, again after his death, that a chance conversation makes me go over our talk in a different light. Vahid Akaev, the philosopher and writer on Caucasian Sufism, is telling me about how Maskhadov finally caved in to the demands of Basaev and Umarov to introduce a shari'a constitution in the semi-independent Republic of Ikhkeria.

"What does that mean exactly, a shari'a constitution?" I ask. "Maskhadov modeled it almost exactly on the shari'a constitution that Hasan al-Turabi introduced in Sudan," Akaev replies.

I do a double-take: al-Turabi? Sudan? And I put it to him that this idea can only have come from Gaidar Jemal, who worked with al-Turabi in the 1990s. Akaev knew Jemal, but he had not known of his association with al-Turabi. Akaev ponders out loud, and eventually deduces that this is the best explanation of the Sudanese choice: "Jemal, Yanderbiev, Adam Khalif, and Kibidov all knew each other. They were all present at the founding of the Islamic Renaissance Party in Astrakhan in 1990, and they kept in touch with each other. So I think that's right: Jemal must have been the link...."

Yanderbiev was a Soviet poet and playwright, who then became president of Ichkeria during its "shari'atization". Khalif was to become the self-styled emir of the Caucasus Emirate after Ichkeria was pounded out of existence. And Kibidov, expelled by the Dagestani muftis from the republic in 1996, was the Dagestani Salafist who first took refuge in Chechnya–Ichkeria, and then in 1999 led a small force of Islamists back into Dagestan with the aim of setting up a shari'a enclave. It was this incursion that triggered the Second Chechen war and the final destruction of Ichkeria, followed by the rise of the Kadyrovs.

The Russian Muslim world is, after all, a small world. I had not known, as I sat opposite him, that such a direct line plummeted from this small Moscow apartment to the bombsites of Grozny and the shari'a enclaves of the Caucasus mountains. The little band of Soviet writers and philosophers who met in Astrakhan a quarter of a century ago are all dead now. Most of them died violent deaths. Only Gaidar continued through it all to preach the Islamic revolution so blatantly on Russian television.

Jemal, after all, was what would be called elsewhere a Wahhabi, plain and simple, despite all the philosophical trappings. Indeed, maybe he was more "radical" than Kibidov, Khalif and the remaining "emirs" in the mountains today. After all, their grievance has mostly been with Russia, the "Mongolian" oppressor of Muslims (and how odd, that they use the same moniker as the muftis; the only difference is that for the muftis, the Mongolian element is parsed favorably). And that grievance has interfered with the Emirate focusing exclusively on creating an international Islamic state or Caliphate. As with the anti-Karimov Islamic Movement of Uzbekistan, the element of international anti-Zionist jihadism has always had a slightly half-hearted feel; perhaps it's an involuntary hangover from too much cosmopolitan Soviet "friendship of the peoples" rhetoric.

But Jemal had told me that the Caucasus Emirate was not revolutionary enough. In his vision, they came off as mere Leninists, or indeed mere Stalinists, one might say. Stalin had confined the revolution to Russia; Jemal's Trotskyite Wahhabism, it seemed to me that night, was about lighting fires internationally—or, rather, spreading wells of deepest divine darkness.

Reviewing our talk, I saw other Chechen links as well: Jemal's talk of Azar, the idea that Abraham had been a Caucasian, all put me in mind of Ruslan Zakriev. In between suing James Cameron, Zakriev pens multiple articles showing the link of the Chechen language and people with the Biblical Noah. I had been an audience to these eccentric genealogies and etymologies myself.

But there was another thing: I had to admit that while Ruslan's banter had been slightly comical, Jemal's deeply intelligent, ponderous and sincere talk had been seductive, persuasive. The "Salafist" question had dogged me for the last three years, from the moment I set out to ignore it. How could people embrace such a simple and stupid version of Islam? How could they turn to violence? "How can people blow themselves up?" as Akaev had asked me in Chechnya, just after telling me that the effect of all the bloodshed he had seen was to humanize him. And why would anyone assume that, with my sheltered experience, I had the answer to questions like that?

Now, in my own intellectual arrogance, I had a partial answer: Jemal, the dark cardinal, now deceased, had mesmerized me for some time at least with his vision of social justice, his bold critique of the Russian state, and his brisk dismissal of armchair academic Sufism. By overhearing a particular dialect of Salafism—the intellectual dialect: the language of the explosive intellectual dialectic—I had caught a glimpse of how it can inspire action. And perhaps I was not the first Western liberal to be bewitched by this dialectic: there are enough Western commentators on the Caucasus who seem to take a vicarious pleasure in the continued Islamic resistance and the threat it poses to Kadyrov's Putinite mini-state, just as in the 1980s, it seemed like a good idea for Western powers to support political Islam in Afghanistan and elsewhere.[13] Gaidar Jemal had died a natural death. But his ghost lives on. The Moscow muftis have been assembling a synthesis, a new all-Russian Muslim ideology. The Marxist dialectic, stolen from Hegel, had talked of thesis, antithesis and synthesis. In private, very private conversations, I had now heard several people among their number tell me that they too had been "Salafists", "anti-government" in the 1990s. "In Saudi, we even pretended to be Chechens," one person reminisced. "All the doors would open then. They loved us!" But now, the same people have rejected this anti-government view: "It was naive. It was youth. It was based on emotion, on pure silliness." Now the old Salafism has been reworked dialectically into what Muhetdinov in one article aptly calls the "rational Salafism" of jadidism, thereby trying to reclaim the mantle of the Salaf for less exclusivist purposes.

Putin, it seems, is going to stand for election in 2018 again. Just when it seemed as if the neo-Soviet was going to evolve into something else, history is on the point of freezing again. And I think of Jemal rejecting the synthesis, rejecting the thesis even, calling people eternally to engage in permanently explosive antithesis.

The sort of antithesis that plummets down into the heart of the Caucasus mountains, perhaps, and puts everyone and everything else off balance.

EPILOGUE: MULTIVERSE OR HALL OF MIRRORS

My attempts to understand Islam in Russia are at an end. The process could go on indefinitely, but it is time to stop when I feel myself dissolving into the object of my investigation. For nearly four years, I have tried to add layer upon layer to my understanding of Moscow. My trips have been in the nature of "rain checks", quick explorations of the soil in different locations. But it is in St Petersburg towards the end of 2016, on a somewhat different trip, that I am struck by another thought, a thought that provides a temporary conclusion.

I am on a minibus, acting as translator and guide for a group of Muslim visitors from England and Germany. It is another attempt by the muftis to find Islamic groups outside of Russia to collaborate with: the Middle East is dangerous nowadays; America is not quite the Great Satan, but it is under a haze of suspicion. Europe, especially Germany, is just about all right, sometimes. It's a tough call avoiding the roadblocks that Russian politics throws up, while also negotiating the ones thrown up by international Muslim life.

The tour has started in Russia's northern capital, Peter the Great's "window to the West". St Petersburg is the first stop on the itinerary: the idea is to acclimatize the group gradually, let them climb through this window before entering deeper into Russian culture. The first evening there had been a reception in the muftiat headquarters. A mixed audience of Russian Muslims had fired questions at the delegate. Now, I share impressions with the foreigners, and one visitor tells me: "I was surprised at the variety: Uzbeks, Tatars, Kyrgyz... somehow I had always thought of them as existing in isolation, never coming together." And it is a true observation: to some extent, gradually the all-Russian synthesis is taking place. Muslims from all parts of the former Russian–Soviet empire are coalescing in post-Soviet Russia, sharing a single space and language. But is it enough to counteract the deadweight of Gaidar Jemal's explosive anti-thesis?

Up here, in the northern stratosphere of Petersburg's crumbling imperial architecture, is a good place to think about thesis and anti-thesis, and insuperable dualism. The Russian philosopher Yuri Lotman believed that Russian culture thinks in binary oppositions: charity versus justice, holiness versus politics, and above all, us versus them.[1] Here one might add Petersburg versus Moscow, which are like the two heads of the Russian imperial eagle, looking East and West, or perhaps tugging the body in different directions so the bird cannot fly. And this is what sets me thinking.

It occurs to me that Moscow's triumph is, of course, far from complete. It has not yet managed to forge a "united Russian Islam" for a United Russia. Instead of a universe, this Russian pattern has been replicated: there is a multiverse of questions and different answers, and a multiverse of regions and interpretations, each one locked in a quizzical dualistic tangle with Moscow. At least four regions see themselves as the true center of the Russian Islamic universe: Chechnya, Dagestan, Tatarstan, and lastly, Moscow. I had seen this self-centeredness best expressed each time in the conviction that Grozny, Mahachakala, Kazan and Moscow all boast the biggest mosques not just in Russia, but Europe. (And now that there are plans to build another massive mosque in Crimea, the plot thickens.) Underneath it all was a growing layer of migrants, also coalescing into another separate and omnipresent center. Perhaps I was back to the metaphor I had started out with: that of the shattered mirror.

The day after the tour of St Petersburg sites, the delegation visits the Ingush cultural center in the north of the city. We pile into the bus again. First stop is the old Oriental Institute on the Neva, where the group is mildly disturbed by the crumbling stacks and undigitized state of the famous manuscript collection. Then we cross the choppy waters of a canal, and then another. A stop-off at the famous St Petersburg mosque has been promised, though I know it is going to be a very brief one. The old Soviet-era mufti is not on good terms with the new Moscow-run Petersburg muftiat, and using his chummy relations with the Leningrad region governor, he keeps his mosque and dwindling community to himself. In all, the group is allowed ten minutes to gawp from the outside at this dazzling slice of Bukhara that holds its own nicely amid the Italianate palaces of the Venice of the north. Again, there are perplexed questions: but why can't we go in? True, there is building work going on, but the real reason—far harder to explain—lies in the fact that it is the Hegelian synthesis that is still very much under construction, and not all the sharp angles have been smoothed away. So it's back on the bus again.

The Ingush are more welcoming, a piece in a corner of the all-Russian mosaic that has been completed and is ready to show to visitors. Everyone takes part in a loud Qadiriyya *zikr*, and then gathers upstairs for a meal. One of the English group belongs to the Naqshbandiyya *tariqat*, and when questioned about what he thinks of the Ingush *zikr*, he politely, Britishly, Islamically, offers that both the "quiet" way and the "loud" way of worship lead to Allah. So far, so good. But then the topic of the August 2016 anti-Wahhabi conference in Grozny comes up and one of the hosts boasts of how Wahhabism has now been defeated thanks to the conference. There is a self-satisfied murmuring of general assent down one end of the table and we are down a wormhole and into another self-contained reality again.

A few weeks before the arrival of the foreign visitors, on 25–27 August, Kadyrov had arranged the conference in Grozny (though he did not partake in it). It was called "Who are the people of the Sunna and Consensus?", and such was its importance that it was timed to coincide with the 65th anniversary of his father's death. It resulted in a printed *fatwa* that identified those who had "strayed from the righteous, true path... of the Ahl as-Sunna wa al-Jama'a and joined themselves to innovation and error" and who must thus "repent of [their] sin and abandon the error in which [they] dwell." Righteous Muslims included those who follow the founder of the Qadiriyya and Naqshbandiyya *tariqats* and held to the familiar Maturidi–Asharite package. Sinners and the lost included Wahhabis, Salafists and a few others. Shortly after the conference, Kadyrov boasted to his Interior Ministry personnel that the conference would have "the same effect as a bomb exploding" on the heretics.[2] The text of the *fatwa* also made it clear that it was "the unanimous decision of the Muftis and scholars of Russia and its implementation is obligatory for all Muslim organizations on the territory of the Russian Federation...."

Our non-Ingush muftiat host keeps quiet, as do the English and German Muslims, and the self-congratulatory laughter goes on before dying a natural death in the silence. For the fact of the matter is that the main Spiritual Board of Muslims of Russia has refused to accept the legitimacy of the conference, and has since condemned it as divisive. The rector of Cairo's al-Azhar University, Ahmed al-Tayeb, who attended the opening session, later distanced himself from the heresy-hunting and divisive tone of the *fatwa*, and

267

among the Moscow muftis there are rumors that the Arab delegates who agreed to the *fatwa* had in fact put their names unwittingly to a different Arabic version. Even worse, the Saudis later criticized the conference in categorical terms and there were even rumors that Kadyrov had to apologize to them in person.

Some commentators highlighted the irony of Kadyrov, with his Christmas trees and Kunta-hajji veneration, getting to define orthodox Islam. But the point is not this so much (Christmas trees were long ago secularized into New Year trees by the Soviets, and there is nothing in principle suspect about Kunta-hajji): rather, it is the sincere and extraordinary conviction that Grozny can act as the center of Islamic Russia, and one feels, even of the entire Islamic world. After all, the Grozny *fatwa* not only condemned Salafism but also the Muslim Brotherhood, which is widespread in the Arab world and has many different forms. The claim to Russian centrality is more obvious and can be seen in the condemnation of two other groups besides the Salafist-Wahhabis: the Habashites and Hizb at-Tahrir. The former are an obscure movement with Sufi-style eccentricities, now enjoying growing popularity among anti-Russian Crimean Tatars.[3] The latter used to be the bugbear of Central Asian rulers and had long thrived in Crimea under Ukraine's laissez faire rule; now they are being ruthlessly tidied up out of existence as a threat to the new Russian "order". Where Muhetdinov had intellectually wooed the Crimean mufti Ablaev with his pamphlet, Kadyrov with the takfirizing *fatwa* issued on his territory was acting as brawn to Moscow's brain and dangling the threat of serious violence against Crimean Tatars who might not have shaken their old anarchic Ukrainian-era habits. But whether Arab or new-Russian, the message seemed to be: heretics of the world unite, and come to Grozny to offer your repentance.

And so a better question would be: how has the tiny city of Grozny come to see itself as the center of the world? And the answer seems to me, in part, to be a Russian one. Kadyrov, you might say, is channeling Putin. Putin's vision is of a post-US multi-polar world; the rhetoric proclaims that there are now many equal powers. But the message for home consumption is that Russia is the new civilizational center and savior of the world. This messianic self-love is a beam emanating from Moscow, and it is reflected and refracted in the souls of Russia's multiple Islamic centers, as I saw most clearly in Dagestan and Chechnya.

The situation is, however, more akin to a hall of mirrors. For Kadyrov also reflects Putin's light back to himself. The shimmer coming from a world-shaking Islamic conference in one of his cities, the city that bears his name in its very heart, gives Putin the reflected glory of being, in part, an Islamic ruler who has a natural (rather than merely colonial) right to intervene in Syria and negotiate with Iran. And the hall of mirrors continues, going down the line to Russia's other "traditional religions". Metropolitan Hilarion Alfeyev,[4] chairman of the Department of External Church relations, and widely billed to be the next Russian Orthodox patriarch, now quotes the Qur'an on religious tolerance in his speeches in Egypt and to Iranian delegations in Moscow. A careful reading of these speeches would suggest that Alfeyev is not channeling Kadyrov so much as Muhetdinov and his Qur'anic humanism.

With this blinding beam of light flashing from mirror to mirror, it is hard to know where the light originates. And perhaps that is the point: each one can think that they are the veritable source of light. Political pundits even doubt whether Putin himself is the source of it all, and not himself a shimmering mirage, the composite reflection of jockeying Kremlin clans.[5] After all, while Metropolitan Hilarion quotes the Qur'an to Russia's nuclear guests from Iran, his writings and the writings of other church hierarchs make it quite clear that there can, after all, be only one light: the light of Orthodox Christianity. And Islam, despite Muhetdinov's Eurasianist dreams, will have to play the role of diminished crescent moon to Russian Christianity's blazing sun. Similarly, within the Islamic panopticon, each location tries to eclipse the other. The universe of united Russia refracts into a multiverse of Russias. This, then, is the key to Grozny's peculiar pan-Islamic pretensions.

Of course, the light of religious ideology conceals some underlying and persisting geo-political and economic realities. After the blazing Grozny conference, there was some reparation work to be done with the Saudis, whose oil companies are mooting cooperation on Chechen energy projects. Nor are other Islamic regions as keen as Kadyrov to become self-effacing mediums for the Kremlin's power pulses. This became clearest after the downing of the Turkish jet in 2015: Kadyrov and his entourage erupted into vicious condemnations of Turkey, not just channeling but amplifying Kremlin rhetoric, to the extent of denying any Turkish contribution to the Chechen republic—even though the same Turkish team of architects who built the Moscow Cathedral mosque also built Grozny's Ahmad-hajji "heart of Chechnya" mosque. Dagestan's president Abdulatipov preserved a dignified neutral silence. Ravil Gaynutdin in Moscow tried to argue that ties should not be decisively cut, a position the Kremlin later came to on their own. And Tatarstan's Minnikhanov, more sure of his republic's economic independence from Moscow, loudly declared that it would continue to foster its friendly relations with the Sunni republic and its Turkic cousin.[6]

After the visit to the Ingush center, the foreigners returned to bed down in their four star hotel on Millionaire Street near the Hermitage museum. The next day the muftiat's representative, who had a background in national security, sat at the front of the minibus and directed the driver to an Uzbek restaurant-cum-hotel in the St Petersburg suburbs. From the Ingush to the Uzbeks was an hour's drive, and it all evoked a sense of déjà vu, causing me to revisit in my mind my own various trips of the last few years.

On the way, I quizzed the young muftiat worker about Petersburg Islam, and my theory of a multiverse received further grist. The national media usually shows Moscow's Muslims on national screens come Ramadan, and that was the iconic image I had absorbed; but now I was being informed that Petersburg itself boasted a 20 per cent Muslim population, which was thus proportionately higher than Moscow's. Again, the owner of the halal restaurant had been brought into the pan-Russian orbit of the Moscow-based muftiat, so creating the impression that there are no black holes between the little Ingushetia and little Uzbekistan of the northern capital. But, of course, the reality was messier.

I was not thinking of the (by now) tedious problem of extremism: Ildar Abulzyarov's novel, *Khush*, a story set in the St Petersburg mosque about suicide bombers, was after all fictional.[7] More to the point was the Fergana-style "Eastern" hyperbole of the halal hotel, which left the visitors nonplussed once again. Though the food in the restaurant was exquisite, the halal profile of the hotel boiled down to the rooms having an arrow on the floor indicating the *qibla*. And the cheerfully bawdy demeanor of our hotel guide gave the distinct impression that this last-minute halalification was more a device to divert foreign Muslims' capital than to raise levels of God-consciousness. While "Easternness" could pass as a good substitute for Muslimness against a post-Soviet Russian background in the case of Sirozhidin, when measured against the more canonical ideas of Muslim identity held by the Europeans, it began to look somewhat tattered and eccentric.

What's more, this was high-end "Easternness", and what the bus ride had not taken in was the lives of the guest-workers slowly reshaping this and many other Russian cities—lives that I had all too briefly dipped into in Fergana. As we left the restaurant, I thought again of how the Moscow muftis had managed to arrange this slice of Uzbek life into their all-Russian Muslim culture. But a few years ago, Haidar Hafizov, a Tatar mufti in the Siberian region of Yamalo–Nenetsk, had stated a simple demographic truth that also threatened this worthy synthesis: "The era of Tatar Islam and Tatar mullahs has gone...." he wrote, to widespread outrage.[8]

Hafizov was referring to the situation in his own oil-rich region where the Muslim population has increased one and a half times in the last twenty years, as labor in the energy sector—including workers such as the younger son of Sirozhidin from Fergana—moves from temporary to permanent migrant status. The Tatar–Bashkir population is now outnumbered at a rate of 2.4 to 9.4 in different areas by Caucasians and Central Asians, a statistic that must also take in the shifts in Moscow and St Petersburg. On the one hand, the new permanent ethnic Muslim population is switching to Russian for inter-ethnic communication. This feeds into the sort of all-Russian Muslim culture that the Moscow muftis are trying to encourage. On the other hand, local conflicts are being brought to the region: militants fleeing Dagestan will hide out in small Siberian towns and even plot local attacks there. Caucasian Salafism will push out local Tatar "*babai* Islam", and there have been several cases of imams or assistant imams either being pushed out by Caucasian Salafists or else "going over" to the Salafists. How, then, can a handful of Tatar muftis shape this burgeoning Russian Islam, into which they are so rapidly being dissolved?

But another difficult reality lies behind Hafizov's words. Hafizov, after all, was merely stating that Siberian mosque congregations are now predominantly non-Tatar and so need non-Tatar imams. Slowly, in fact, the Moscow muftis are responding to this demand, as I saw with Muhammad the Tajik, with whom I had travelled in Chechnya. The other black hole, though, can be seen in the statement of another Siberian mufti, Tagir Samatov. When accused by unhappy locals of not doing enough to prevent hooliganism and extremism among the region's new Muslim population, he pointed out that his Khanti-Mansk Autonomous District is home to up to 50,000 Muslims. Only 5 per cent of them go to the mosque, though. The other 95 per cent go elsewhere, or are not religious and not even particularly well-informed about their own ethnic history (one researcher found that Dagestani youths hanging out on the small-town streets did not even know who Imam Shamil was).

The last black hole, then, on our whisk around "Muslim St Petersburg" and elsewhere was this: not only is the established ethnic leadership of Russian Islam being slowly undermined from below by migrants, so making everything topsy-turvy, but, in fact, only a tiny percent of Russia's new Muslim population is truly observant anyway. And among these, it might be said, if Abdollo is to be believed, that for some populations a majority are covertly "Salafist", or else belong to communities that do not come under any umbrella, be it the various Russian muftiats, or the *mahallas* of their hometowns and countries. The rest are a mass whose sympathies are unpredictable and are open to manipulation of different sorts (I had seen a smattering of such unaffiliated, or loosely affiliated, ethnic Muslims in Fergana, Kazan, Mahachkala and Moscow.)

Uneasily, I continued to ponder these gaping lacunas as our delegation of Western–Russian Muslim rapprochement boarded the overnight Sabsun express train from Petersburg to Moscow to continue its tour there. The lingering image was now one of chaos and disintegration, putting me in mind again of V.N. Kalinin's finding that Russia has more Muslim organizations than any other country in the world, bar one. The variety, as I had seen amply now, can be boiled down to two factors: the fluid definition of contemporary Islam, which no one can quite yet pin down; and the landscape onto which this shifting Islam is being projected, which is like the crinkled terrain of a 3D map. The deepest valleys are the wells of traditionalism that survived the Soviet period: they are found in Margilan or the high Pamir mountains, where the rhythm of people's lives is almost as archaic as their co-religionists in neighboring Afghanistan; and the highest peaks, looming in the airless atmosphere of secularism, can be found in some parts of the cities of Tatarstan or Moscow itself, where the only thing that remains of Islamic rhythms is an Arabic-derived surname. But in Russia today, both the thinly Muslim native and the (sometimes) densely Muslim immigrant are living side by side, and sometimes swapping places as they seek to change their identities.

And yet, perhaps all this was becoming too pessimistic. Perhaps, after all, I pondered, if one draws away to a higher plane, there is some unity, and the Islam sweeping over the gnarled terrain imbues the landscape with its own type of unity, of *tawhid*. After all, in its essence Islam is an individualistic religion. The Qur'an banishes intermediaries and calls the individual, regardless of his ancestors, family or background, to enter into direct contact with the Creator. On my journeys, I had encountered scores of people who had turned to their Creator in submission, who had become *muslimun* to God. Undoubtedly, with such immense variety, I had missed much in my overambitious desire to understand the whole of Russian Islam; there is, inevitably, much that must have streaked past the window unobserved. But those points of light that I had seen could not be denied. I played with this metaphor of light, as the train hurtled through the night towards Moscow—Moscow again.

At the macro-level, the highest political level, between the self-appointed multiple centers of Russian Islam there is a veritable light-show going on, with beams slashing left and right. This is the top of the pyramid. Below it is the Moscow muftiat and other organizations that enter into the consciousness of observers in the form of the clumsy acronyms beloved of Russian political life: DUMRF, TsDUM, SADUM, and all their varying permutations, each one wrapping itself in a label: Hanafite, "traditional Tatar", Sufi, Habashite, Hizbi, or even 'the people of *wasatiyya*'—though the labels often only roughly correspond to people's true intents and capacities. And this is often what attracts the chroniclers of Russian Islam.

Then there are the lacunas, the black holes, that separate Power from the People, and the People from each other, that had me in the throes of a Raskolnikov-type despair. But at the bottom of the pyramid, a vast, extended and chaotic space, there are the individuals who come and go in their practice of Islam, the individuals I had been chasing. Some of them drift in and out of organizations and labels. In the last twenty-five years, many have embraced Islam, hurtled on an intense trajectory, and then fizzled out, either in explosion or exhaustion, sometimes under pressure from Power, sometimes under pressure from within. A few have survived the course and reached maturity, often—due to the atmosphere of mistrust—without the luxury of a community or mosque to give a deeper dimension to their faith. And, I comforted myself, this movement of light particles in the obscurity constitutes another history, a history of Russian Islam in the individual sense, in the metaphysical sense, where difference can be put aside for a higher unity.

This light, seething amid a Jemalian darkness, is also surely part of the history of Russia's Muslim heartlands in the time of Putin. These particles of light, sometimes coalescing into bundles, sometimes hiding in their own darkness, look like the seventy-three sects of Islam mentioned in Rustam Batrov's favorite hadith. They may or may not be pieces in an Islamic State of the sort advocated and dreamed of in very different ways by Geidar Jemal in Moscow, Kadir Malikov in Kyrgyzstan, Ramzan Kadyrov in Chechnya, the Caucasus Emirate, the escapees to Syria, the Crimean Hizbis, or the Moscow and Tatarstan muftiats. But, trapped between the weight of the Russian government at the top and the horizonless chaos of Russia at the bottom, they do constitute a state of Islam, a state of being in submission, or at least struggling against the odds, to be in submission to God. Without this light from below, the light-show above would cut out. You can't build on emptiness. And you can't take the light-show for the light itself. This state of Islam, with its seventy-three sects awaiting judgment, shades off beyond human vision. Regarding its fate one can only say, as the Muslims say: "And Allah knows best"!

And with this thought, the train pulled into Moscow.

APPENDIX ONE

For readers whose speciality is more in Russia than Islam, or vice versa, the following glossary clarifies Islamic and Russian terms.

GLOSSARY OF TERMS AND NAMES

Abu Hanifa (Abu Hanifa an-Numan ibn Sabit al-Kufi, 699-767) — Islamic theologian and legal scholar of Persian origin, founder of one of the four Sunni legal schools, the Hanafite.

al-Azhar — the most prestigious Islamic university in the Sunni Islamic world, in Cairo; founded in 970.

al-hamdulilla — Arabic: "praise be to God!"

Al Ghazali, Abu Hamid (1058–1111) — Islamic theologian, philosopher and Sufi. Author of hundreds of critical and apologetic works. In his fundamental work *The Revival of the Religious Sciences* he made an attempt to reconcile different tendencies in Islamic thought on a united Sufi foundation. A key thinker newly translated into Russian by Ilshat Nasyrov and referenced by various Russian muftis today.

adab — Arabic: morality, manners.

Ali Shari'ati (1933-1977) — the ideologue of the 1979 Iranian revolution, whose writings combine political (Shi'ite) Islam with Marxist undercurrents.

'aqida — the branch of Islamic theology that studies the principles of faith.

275

ayat — Arabic: sign. The name for a verse of the Qur'an.

adhan, azzan — the Islamic call to prayer.

bairam — Turkic: holiday. In Eurasian Islam, it refers to the two main Islamic festivals: Kurban bairam (Arabic: Eid al-Adha), the festival celebrating the end of the hajj pilgrimage; and Uraza bairam (Arabic: Eid al-Fitr), the festival marking the end of Ramadan.

Bashkir — (formerly nomadic) Turkic people, also with Finnic and Iranic roots, living near the Ural mountains, speaking a Kipchak language closely related to Tatar. Incorporated into Russian empire from 18th century onwards.

Bigiev, Musa Jarullah (1875-1949) — Russian Muslim philosopher, one of the leaders of the *jadid* (renovationist) movement in nineteenth–twentieth century Russia. Popularizer of the idea of the all-inclusiveness of the divine mercy, critic of *kalam* (Islamic scholastic theolgy) and *ishanism*. One of the key thinkers referenced in the Russian muftiat's formulation of "traditional Russian Islam".

barakat — Arabic: blessing

Bashlarov, Saipulla kadi (1853-1919) — Dagestani scholar, doctor, *jadid*, and *sheikh* of the Naqshbandiyya, Shadhiliyya and Qadiriyya tariqats.

bid'a — innovation, heretical departure from tradition.

bismillah — Arabic: "in the name of Allah". A short prayer uttered by Muslims before starting an endeavor.

Caucasus Emirate — the name of the *jihadi* movement launched by anti-Russian separatists after the second Chechen war. Also the self-described name of the state claimed to exist by separatists who continue to resist Russian rule in the North Caucasus. Its existence was officially announced by former President of Ichkeria, Doku Umarov in 2007, and included the Republic of Ichkeria, with ambitions to include the entire territory of the North Caucasus, as well as other Muslim territories in Russia. It claimed the 2012 assasination of Tatarstan mufti, Valilulla Yakupov.

chaikhona — the Uzbek and Tajik term for a tea-house.

Collectivization — Stalin's policy of modernizing agriculture in the late 1920s and 1930s, which resulted in the deaths of millions.

dar al-harb — Arabic: "territory of war". In medieval Islamic jurisprudence, this was the term used to refer to non-Islamic states with which the world of Islam (= **dar al-Islam**) was considered to be at war. The other terms in this classification are: **dar al-silm** = region of peace (a territory that is non-Islamic but is deemed to be at peace with the Islamic state), and *dar al-'ahd* = region of agreement (a non-Islamic territory that has made a treaty with the Islamic state). Reformist shari'a scholars claim that these terms cannot be applied straightforwardly in the modern world. For the Russian context, cf. *al-Qaradaghi.*

dervish — Arabic: "poor". The term for a wandering Sufi mystic, often used in Central Asia, Persia, and India.

dua — Arabic: invocation, supplication. Personal prayer, outside of the obligatory *salat* prayer.

dawa — Arabic: invitation. Islamic missionary work.

dekulakization — part of the bloody process of *collectivization*, it involved stripping so-called kulaks (theoretically, exploitative richer peasants) of property and livestock and exiling them.

Eurasianism — the intellectual movement that sees Russia as a civilization that combines the best of Europe and Asia. It had three waves: the anti-Communist émigré movement in the 1920s, the work of *Lev Gumilev* in the Soviet period, and its revival by Dugin and others in the post-Soviet period (the "neo-Eurasianist" phase, which has a political and economic addition).

Faizkhanov, Husain (1823-1866) — early *jadid* thinker, pedagogue, historian, Turkologist and Orientalist, archeographer, calligrapher. Played a significant role in the development of the religious culture of Tatar society in the second half of the 19th century. Another key figure in the modern Russian Muslim revival.

fajr — dawn prayer.

al-fatiha — the "opening" prayer, the first seven verses of the Qur'an, recited in every cycle of Muslim *salat*, and memorized early by observant Muslims.

fatwa — legal verdict or opinion formulated by an Islamic scholar of jurisprudence, or *mufti.*

Filioque — Latin: "and through the Son"; the key phrase in the Nicene Creed that is present in the Catholic version and absent in the Orthodox version, a locus of theological dispute, with the Orthodox maintaining that the unsanctioned Catholic addition diminishes the status of the Holy Spirit, and thus removes the divine status of the Spirit-filled Church through which Christians are mystically deified.

fitnah — Arabic: sedition, transgression. Used to refer to unethical behavior that divides the Islamic community.

Gasprinsky, Ismail (1851-1914) — Crimean Tatar intellectual, enlightener, publisher and politician, who won fame and recognition among the entire Muslim population of the Russian empire. One of the pillars of the *jadid* movement and pan-Turkism. Another key figure in the modern Russian Muslim revival.

gazavat — Arabic: military expedition, Islamic war. Used (in preference to *jihad*) by the first Caucasian leaders as the term for the retaliation against the Russian invasion. They also chose the title *ghazi*, one who leads a gazavat.

Golden Horde — also called Ulus Jochi: the empire of Genghis Khan's successors on the territory of modern Central Asia, the Caucasus, the Crimea, and Russia. It lasted from c.1240-1500, and then disintegrated into various Muslim khanates that were in turn absorbed into the expanding Russian empire. Both contemporary Eurasianists and modernist Russian Muslims look to it as a positive precedent, rejecting the negative interpretation of the "Tatar-Mongol yoke".

guberniya — tsarist administrative district.

Gumilev, Lev (1912-1992) — Soviet historian, translator from Persian, adherent of a Eurasian version of Russian history, who embraced eccentric theories of the biosphere's influence on the origin of peoples and nomadic movements in the Eurasian steppes. His influence has revived in the various neo-Eurasian ideologies circulating now in Putin's Russia.

Habashites — a spiritual movement supported by Ukrainian-oriented Crimean Tatars in Crimea after the Russian annexation in 2014, as an alternative form of anti-Russian identity to *Salafism* and *Hizb ut-Tahrir*. The movement was popular in religiously pluralist countries like Lebanon and Ethiopia and mixes the Shafi'i *madhab* with many Sufi practices.

Hadd, pl. **hudud** — Arabic: "limit, prohibition". Corporal and capital Qur'anic punishments proscribed for six crimes. Generally rarely applied in Islamic history, with the exception of modern fundamentalist Islamist governments and groups, who see it as the prime symbol of Islamic government.

Hadji-Murad — an Avar leader (c.1816-1852) who acted as **Imam Shamil's** main naib for some years. Before that he supported the pro-Russian Dagestani khans, and towards the end of his life, offended at not being chosen to be Imam Shamil's successor, he again went over to the Russians. Leo Tolstoy wrote a novella about him (published posthumously in 1912).

hadith — reports or accounts of the sayings and behavior of the Prophet Muhammad gathered in six classic compendiums. A crucial part of Sunni Islam: the decision over which are genuine and which not, is highly influential in shaping Sunni Muslim observance.

hafiz — a person who has memorized the entire Qur'an.

hajj — the pilgrimage to Mecca, done in fulfillment of the fifth religious obligation incumbent on Muslims; one who has completed the pilgrimage is called *Hajji*, or *Hojji*.

haram — forbidden, unclean, opposite of *halal*.

hijab — Islamic head covering for women. See also *paranja*.

hijra — Arabic: journey or migration of the Prophet Muhammad and his companion Abu Bakr from Mecca to Medina; also used for the migration of Muslims from unfriendly zones to friendly ones.

Ibn Hanbal Ahmad al-Shaybani (780-855) — early Arab jurist, ascetic, theologian and hadith scholar, whose disciples went on to found the Hanbalite *madhab*, which today is prevalent mainly in Saudi Arabia. As such, it is associated with the Wahhabi–Salafi interpretation of Islam. However, as with Ibn Taymiyya, it can be argued that the Wahhabi interpretation and use of Hanbalism is selective and the connection between them is contingent.

Hizb ut-Tahrir — a pan-Islamic movement founded in 1953 in Jerusalem that spread from the Middle East to the West, South East Asia, and then to Central Asia in the post-Soviet period. Its declared goal is the gradual, peaceful creation of an international Caliphate; its critics claim its followers tacitly support violent means. It is illegal in Russia and Central Asia, but legal in Ukraine and in Crimea, before its annexation by Russia. After the annexation, Hizb was a rallying-point for anti-Russian Muslim identity. *Hizbi*: a member of *Hizb ut-Tahrir*.

hojji — see *hajj*.

Iblis — the name in the Qur'an for Satan, the Devil.

Ibn Taymiya (Takiuddin Abu Abbas Ahmad ibn Abdulhalim al-Harrani) 1263-1328 — Muslim theologian, jurist of the Hanbalite *madhab*. A theologian often referenced by modern *Salafis* as the founder of an anti-traditionalist rational reading of the Qur'an and opponent of Sufism, partly due to his call to open the gates of *ijtihad*. The reality is that Ibn Taymiyya only opposed "non-canonical" Sufism and argued that the recognized Sufi scholars and schools were an intrinsic part of full Islamic faith. Russian neo-*jadids*, like Muhetdinov, reference him as a forebear of their own reformist "rational", rather than radical, Salafism.

Ibn Sina (Avicenna) 980-1937 — medieval Muslim polymath, philosopher and doctor. Born near Bukhara, he is seen as a "national" hero by both Uzbeks and Tajiks. His rational philosophic approach and scientific medical fame make him an attractive figure for both Central Asian secularists, the religious and those in-between.

Ichkeria — the Chechen name for Chechnya, and used between 1994-1999 as the name for the quasi-independent Chechen republic that existed between the two Chechen wars. After that, the Independent Republic of Ichkeria has existed unrecognized by anyone except the Taliban in Afghanistan.

Idil(-Ural) — the Tatar-Turkic name for the Volga river. The Idil-Ural Republic (the Ural part referring to the mountain range) was also the name of the Tatar-Bashkir republic that existed briefly after the Russian revolution, before being dissolved by the Bolsheviks. Referenced by Tatar nationalists today.

iftar — the evening meal that follows the breaking of the Ramadan fast.

ijaza — license or permission granted by a higher authority to teach a certain Islamic subject

ijtihad — Arabic: "exertion". The effort used to deduce a law that is not self-evident; legal reasoning. Also used by *jadids* and reformers to mean "original thinking" in religion, and contrasted with *taqlid*.

APPENDIX ONE

imam — leader of an Islamic community or mosque.

(Caucasus) **Imamate** — the name given to the Islamic state set up to resist the Russian conquest of the Caucaus; it existed in Dagestan and Chechnya from 1828-1859.

inshallah — Arabic: "God willing".

ishan — Central Asian and Volga term for a Sufi *sheikh*, or leader. *Ishanism* is also the term used by *jadids* and the Soviets to denigrate fake Sufism, in which Sufi leaders took advantage of their followers.

Islamic Movement of Uzbekistan (IMU) — an anti-Karimov movement formed in 1998 by two Fergana valley Uzbeks that morphed into an al-Qaeda linked Islamist organization.

jadid — Arabic: "new". The name given to the Russian branch of the Reformist movement that spread through the Islamic world in the nineteenth century. In Russia, the movement tried to combine Islamic observance with participation in Russian and then early Soviet modernity. Famous early jadids included *Ismail Gasprinsky, Musa Bigiev, Hussein Faizkhanov, Shihabuddin Marjani* and *Qayyum Nasiri*. Contemporary Russian–Tatar theologians such as Damir Muhetdinov, often draw on this legacy today, and can be called "neo-jadid" thinkers.

jahiliyya — Arabic: the term used to refer to the time before Islam, to pagan Arabia, the time of ignorance.

jamaat — Arabic: "community", the term used to refer to Muslim communities.

jihad — Arabic: "struggle, striving." In Islamic tradition, the "greater jihad" refers to striving with the *nafs*, or ego; the "lesser jihad" refers to war in the defense or expansion of Islam. In modern political Islam, jihad is associated with the political and military fight for an Islamic state. Derivative terms: *jihadi*, a person or movement that engages in political Islamic fighting.

jum'a — Friday congregational prayers at the mosque.

Ka'aba — the sacred black stone in Mecca which is central to *hajj* pilgrimage rites.

kafir — Arabic: "heretic, infidel".

Kolkhoz — Russian: "collective farm", a result of Stalin's and later Soviet leaders' collectivization policy.

khātib — Arabic: "preacher". Reader of the *khutba*, or sermon at Friday *jum'a* prayers. The imam-khātib is a central and influential figure in the life of a mosque community.

Krashen — baptized Tatars living mainly in the Volga region, whose roots go back to the Christianization of the region after the conquest of the area by the Russians in the sixteenth–seventeeth centuries.

Kunta-Hajji (1830-1867) — Chechen Sufi religious leader and mystic, who brought the *Qadiriyya* order to the North Caucasus, and introduced a pacifist form of Islam. Founder of *zikrism*, the "loud" version of *zikr* practiced to this day by Chechens and Ingush. After his arrest, some followers of zikrism advocated violent resistance to Russia again.

lezginka — a solo male or pair dance performed by the Caucasian Lezgin people, which is popular among all Caucasian peoples.

madhab — Islamic school of law. In early Islam, there were dozens of madhabs (pl. madhahib), but eventually they narrowed down to four main Sunni schools: the Shafi'i, Hanafite, Hanbalite and Malikite, named after their founders. (The fifth Ja'fari madhab is Shi'ite). The Hanafite school is common in the Volga and Central Asia, the Shafi'ite in the Caucasus. Simple differences concern the postures followed in prayer, so that madhab differences are immediately noticeable when adherents of different madhabs pray *salat* next to each other.

mahalla — (Central Asia): neighborhood, quarter

mahdi — an eschatological figure in Islamic tradition: the "guided one", who will come at the end time to guide humanity before the Day of Judgment.

Manas — hero of the Kyrgyz Epic of Manas, much admired in modern Kyrgyzstan.

Marjani, Shihabuddin (1818-1889) — Russian Muslim, philosopher, historian, educator, sheikh of the Naqshandiyya Sufi brotherhood. Also famous as an ethnographer, archeographer, orientalist, and pedagogue. One of the most authoritative Russian Muslim thinkers, and another key figure in the modern Russian Muslim revival, whose books are being published again today.

APPENDIX ONE

al-Maturidi, Abu Mansur (870-944) — Islamic thinker, founder of the eponymous school of *kalam* (Islamic theology) known as Maturidism. Today seen as one of the key thinkers in "traditional Russian Islam", though his emphasis on *kalam* goes against the *jadids'* critique of it.

Mawlid (al-nabi) — celebration of the birthday of the Prophet Muhammad. Also: a song composed in honor of the Prophet's birth.

Mishar — a subgroup of Tatars from the Nizhny Novgorod Volga region, who speak a different dialect of Tatar from Kazan Tatars, and have slightly different ethnic origins (including a greater admixture of Finnic–Mordvinian).

medrese — Islamic seminary.

mudarris — student in a medrese.

mufti — technically an Islamic jurisconsultant who can issue juridical decisions (fatwas); but in Russian and Ottoman usage, a government-appointed leader of a Muslim community.

murid — Arabic: disciple; used for disciples of Sufi sheikhs.

munafiq(un) — Arabic: hypocrites; the term used in the Qur'an to refer to those who accepted Islam insincerely for worldly advantage.

Mutazilite — early Islamic philosophers known for putting reason above revelation; their rationalist orientation is admired by several post-Soviet Muslim intellectuals.

namaz — the Turkic terms for the *salat* prayer.

al-Naqshbandi, Bahuddin (1318-1389) — great religious figure, born near Bukhara, founder of the most widespread Sufi order, the Naqshbandiyya, which is still dominant in the North Caucasus, Volga region, and Central Asia today (as well as in Turkey and India).

nashid — Islamic religious song with theological content, usually sung without musical accompaniment.

Navruz — Persian or Turkic new year day. Its celebration is considered heretical by fundamentalist Salafi Muslims.

nikah — marriage, the Islamic marriage ceremony.

otincha — wise woman (in Central Asia).

paranja — traditional Central Asian robe for women and girls which covers the head and body. Known as the *burqa* in neighboring Afghanistan.

Petlura, Simon (1874-1926) — Ukrainian nationalist leader who fought for Ukraine's independence after the Russian revolution.

al-Qaradaghi, Ali Muhiddin (b.1949) — Qatari shari'a scholar of Iraqi-Kurdish origin, who founded and heads the Qatar-based International Union of Muslim Scholars. Qaradaghi has strong ties with Ravil Gaynutdin and the Spiritual Board of Muslims of the Russian Federation, and has visited Dagestan, Ingushetia and Kabardino-Balkharia. He issued a *fatwa* in 2012 declaring the North Caucasus *dar al-Islam* and *dar al-silm*, in other words declaring the anti-Russian jihad of the Caucasus Emirate Islamically illegitimate.

Qayyum, Nasiri (1825-1902) — early Tatar *jadid*, instrumental in developing the modern written Tatar language and modern Islamic education.

qibla — the direction a Muslim faces when praying salat; it is ascertained by lining oneself up with Mecca.

Qur'anic humanism — the name of the modernist Islamic project being developed by the Spiritual Board of Muslims of the Russian Federation. It tries to combine classical Islamic scholarship, Western academic Islamic studies, and the Russian *jadid* heritage. One of its main figures is the Syrian-born Tawfik Ibrahim.

qurra' — a reciter of the Qur'an.

Ramadan — ninth month of the Islamic calendar in which Muslims fast from dawn to sunset.

Rasulev, Zainulla (1833-1917) — renowned Bashkir Sufi *ishan*, whose religious authority was respected in the Volga and Ural regions, as well as in the Caucasus. His son, Abdurahman Rasulev, was head of the Central Spiritual Board of Muslims of the USSR, and collected money for a tank division in the Second World War.

Roerich, Nicolai (1874-1947) — artist, theosophist, who depicted ancient Eurasian and Tibetan landscapes in a modernist spiritual, icon-like style.

Rublev, Andrei (c.1360-1427) — the greatest medieval Russian icon-painter, whose icons include the "Trinity", or the "Hospitality of Abraham".

Salafism — a modern, reformist version of Islam, originating in different versions in Egypt, India and Saudi Arabia, which advocates return to the practices of the pious ancestors, or Salaf. In ignoring the diverse and nuanced classical Islamic tradition of jurisprudence and textual interpretation, it can produce highly literalistic readings and practice and encourage an anti-modern, exclusivist behavior among its adherents; certain forms of Salafism have blended with political Islam, or Islamism, to produce violent movements that see suicide-bombing and military struggle against non-Muslims, or those considered by *takfiris* to be non-Muslims, as legitimate. Other versions reject such violence. Salafism is considered to be "non-traditional" and extremist by the Russian government, and elided with *Wahhabism*.

salat — Arabic: prayer, used to refer to the five-times daily canonical prayer of Islam. The Turkic equivalent is *namaz*.

samizdat — underground dissident literature that circulated in self-published format in the Soviet period.

shahada — the Islamic declaration of faith which is pronounced in Arabic before witnesses to convert to Islam: "I testify that there is no god but God, and I testify that Muhammad is the messenger of God."

Shaimiev, Mintimer — President of Tatarstan from 1991-2010. Achieved increased autonomy for his republic.

Shafi'i — one of the four main *madhabs* of Sunni Islamic law, founded by al-Shafi'i (767-820); prevalent in much of the North Caucasus.

shari'a — Islamic law, based on the Qur'an and hadith, and in Sunni Islam, also the legal reasoning (by *ijma* [consent] and *qiyyas* [analogy]) of traditional *madhab* scholars.

shaytan — Arabic: Satan, the devil.

Shadhiliya — a Sufi order founded by the medieval Moroccan Sheikh al-Shadhili (1196-1258); one of the Sufi orders present in Dagestan.

sheikh — Arabic: "old man, elder, respected teacher", used commonly in Russian Muslim discourse to refer to respected religious leaders.

silsila — unbroken chain of transmission of spiritual authority from the Prophet Muhammad to sheikhs of Sufi tariqats.

Slavophilism — the conservative intellectual movement initiated by thinkers like Alexei Khomiakov and Ivan Kireevsky after the defeat of Napoleon in Russia; it saw Russia's uniqueness in its Eastern Orthodox heritage, which was to be a guide for Russia's cultural and social future.

sobornost — a key concept in Khomiakov's *Slavophilism*, often translated as "conciliarity": the idea that Eastern Orthodox Christianity steers an ideal holistic middle path between Catholic papal authoritarianism and Protestant hyper-individualism.

Solovki — a Soviet Gulag prison-camp in the Arctic north.

subhana Allah — Arabic: praise be to God.

Sufism — the mystical tradition of Islam; in Arabic, Sufism is called *tasawwuf.*

sunna — the tradition of the Prophet Muhammad; Sunni Islam is the mainstream form of Islam that bases itself on the Qur'an as supplemented and interpreted through the lens of the Sunna.

Qadiriyya — Sufi order founded by Abdul-Qadir Gilani of Baghdad (1077-1166). Widespread in Chechnya and Ingushetia, brought to the region by Sheikh Kunta-Hajji.

Tablighi Jamaat — a fundamentalist revivalist Islamic organization founded in India in 1927 which aims to bring nominal Muslims back to true Islamic observance. Banned in Central Asia (apart from Kyrgyzstan) and Russia.

tafsir — Arabic: exegesis. Interpretation of the Qur'an.

taip — Chechen word for clan.

Tajuddin, Talgat (b.1948) — head mufti of the Central Spiritual Board of Muslims; known for his patriotic comments about "Holy Russia"; one-time rival for leader of Russian Muslims, a position since 2015 generally agreed to be occupied by Ravil Gaynutdin. Active in Ufa, Bashkortostan.

tajwid — the canonical rules governing the correct recitation of the Qur'an.

takfir(i) — Arabic: denouncing someone as a kafir, i.e. a heretic or non-Muslim. The term also refers to exclusivist and extremist interpretations in modern political Islam, which use takfir to "render Muslims non-Muslim" and apply to them the rules of jihad.

taqlid — Arabic: "imitation". The recommended practice of shaping one's Islamic observance by following a recognized legal opinion or school; also used negatively by jadid-reformers to denigrate blind obedience to fossilized past authorities.

Tarkovsky, Andrei (1932-1986) — renowned Soviet film director, whose films include Andrei Rublev and Solaris.

tariqat — Arabic: "path". The name for a Sufi order or brotherhood.

tariqatist — Russian-based word for member of a tariqat.

Tatar, Tatar-Mongol — the Tatars were a Turkic tribe in Southern Mongolia at the time of Genghis Khan. After the conquests of Genghis, the Tatars were fused with the Mongols in the popular imagination of conquered peoples (including the Arabs), and after the Golden Horde period the term "Tatar" was applied more and more widely, eventually denoting simply "Muslim" in Russian (Azeris and even non-Turkic Chechens could be called Tatars). The term "Tatar" today continues to refer to disparate groups, such as Crimean, Polish, Kazan, Meshar, and Lithuanian Tatars. These groups emphasize their non-Mongolian origins, mostly Turkic but also Finnic and Iranic, and reject the equation of Tatarness with the misfortune of the "Mongol yoke".

tawhid — Arabic: divine unity, monotheism.

Tengrism — worship of Tengri, the supreme God of the Turkic tribes. This type of native paganism has enjoyed a revival among some groups in Kyrgyzstan and Kazakhstan, and is seen as an alternative to Islamic revival, though sometimes combined with it.

tugra — an Arabic-Turkic calligraphic heraldic sign used by Ottoman and other Turkic rulers.

al-Turabi, Hassan (1932-2016) — Islamist leader of Sudan, who introduced shari'a law in the north of Sudan. The only political Islamist to gain power, he turned Sudan into an ideological center of international Islamism.

'ulema (singular: alim) — Arabic: "scholars". Used to refer to the traditional scholarly class in classical Islamic civilization.

'umma — Arabic: "people, nation". The term used to denote the worldwide Islamic community, or nation. It can be given a political, social or mystical interpretation.

Uraza (Oraza) — Turkic word for Ramadan.

ustadh — Arabic: "teacher". In the Islamic context, an Islamic teacher or mentor.

vird — the Chechen term for Sufi brotherhood or tariqat.

Wahhabism — the movement associated with Arabian reformer Muhammad ibn Abd al-Wahhab (1703-1792). An austere, ultraconservative, often exclusivist form of Islam that is the official doctrine of the Saudi kingdom, and promoted by it internationally. In Russian political discourse, the term is synonymous with Islamist extremism, and suspicions of anti-state violence.

wasatiyya — the "middle way" recommended for Muslims in the Qur'an, and used by Uzbek and Russian muftis today as a "native" equivalent of "moderation".

wudu — ritual washing performed before the salat prayer.

Yassawi, Ahmed (1093-1166) — founder of the Yassawiya Sufi order, Turkic mystic and poet, whose ziyyarat is in modern-day Kazakhstan.

Yusuf, Muhammad Sodik Muhammad (1952-2015) — influential Muslim thinker in late Soviet and post-Soviet Uzbekistan. As first mufti of independent Uzbekistan, he defended Muslim rights and was dismissed by the Uzbek government in 1993. Worked in Libya and Saudi Arabia, returned in 1999. Author of numerous publications that influenced Islamic thought in the entire post-Soviet space. Frequent participant in Russian Muslim events; friend and fellow-graduate from Mir-i Arab medrese of Ravil Gaynutdin.

zikr (dhikr) — Arabic: literally "remembrance". A term used to refer to prayer, and especially the sessions of communal chanting of prayer, possibly to musical accompaniment, that is found in Sufi culture.

ziyyarat — the graves, or mausoleums, of saints which have become pilgrimage destinations, common in North Caucasus, Central Asian and Volga Sufi culture.

APPENDIX TWO

A NOTE ON THE INTERVIEWS

All interviews were conducted in Russian between July 2013 and January 2017. The total number of interviewees was eighty-eight. The shorter interviews lasted for 45 minutes to 1 hour; the medium interviews from two to three hours. Longer interviews continued for upwards of six hours, and as can be seen in the text, sometimes for several days if I was staying with an individual or family. I took written notes during interviews, and shortly after the interviews, transcribed the long-hand version. Most transcripts were on average 6-7 pages long. Out of these eighty-eight transcribed interviews, twenty-five or so have made their way into the present book in some detail; the rest of the material formed an important informational backdrop, however. Having conducted almost one hundred interviews, I began to encounter repetition in people's accounts of their views and experience, a sign, as I took it, that I was getting a good general sense of the issues and problems at hand.

Interviewees were from a wide range of employment: guest-workers, builders, couriers, journalists, academics, engineers, translators, students, cleaners, drivers, sportsmen, restaurant-workers, concierges, professors, businessmen, muftis, imams, artists, and so on. Early on in the research, I met people simply by approaching them on the street, at work, in mosques, or through neighbors and friends. As time went on, I became more involved with the various government muftiats and was given contacts around Russia through them: I was aware that this type of contact was susceptible to expressing "pro-government" views, but I tried to counter this bias through accessing other sources, and drawing on my own experience with people outside those circles. Nonetheless, in this project I was not interested in trying to develop a profile of anti-government Salafis, but rather of "mainstream" Muslim life (though, of course, this might beg a question that could be further investigated in more systematic work).

Interviewees' ages ranged from teens to mid-70s (and one five-year old in Mahachkala). As regards gender, there was some imbalance: only twenty three of my interviewees were women. In Moscow, my interviewees came from places I had not visited: Crimea, different parts of Bashkortostan, Ukraine, Tajikistan, Turkmenistan, and Kazakhstan, as well as other cities in Tatarstan (e.g. Naberezhniy Chelmy), Dagestan (e.g. Khasavyurt), Chechnya (e.g. Gudermes), Uzbekistan (e.g. Tashkent, Bukhara) and Kyrgyzstan (e.g. Osh). As such, my base included representatives of all the main Muslim regions of Russia and its "near Muslim abroad". Another tool to put people's words in context, of course, was by comparing them to the views of Russian Jews and Orthodox Christians, as well as secular Russians, with whom I have extensive contact in my professional and everyday life.

In some places, I have changed the names of minor figures in order to protect them from possible repercussions; in a few places I have attributed more controversial views to such minor anonymous figures.

APPENDIX THREE

A NOTE ON THE USE OF THE TERMS 'SECULAR' AND 'MUSLIM'

a. The term 'secular'

This book does not try to reach theoretical conclusions; its main purpose is to convey the experience of being Muslim in Russia today. Nonetheless, the question of levels of religiosity in modern Russia keys into academic debates about the relationship between religion and (post-)modernity, with the formerly widespread belief that religious practice and belief are ultimately incompatible with modernity ("secularization theory") slowly being replaced by the idea that religion can, should and will make up some of its losses and thrive in modern societies (Peter Berger's "desecularization theory", Habermas' "post-secularity"). There is a lot of material in this book that could contribute to such debates, but in the interests of writing for a broad readership I have avoided them and merely drawn on terms that are in broad circulation, without rigorously (re-) defining them for present purposes. Nonetheless, the following observations may be in order for those wanting to use materials presented here for more theoretical purposes.

'Secularism, secularity, secular'

The term 'secular' and its derivatives have acquired several meanings; the following are the three main senses that I have in mind:

1. Soviet secularism. This was an aggressive, anti-clerical form of the Enlightenment idea that religion should be excluded from the functioning of the state, and ultimately starved of oxygen or actively eradicated, out of the belief that (rational) modernity and (irrational) religion are incompatible. In principle, according to the different Soviet constitutions, all religions were protected. In practice, propaganda in the media, schools and the public arena aimed at undermining and eradicating religion. This aggressive secularism has left traces in post-Soviet religious practice and belief.

2. Post-Soviet secularism. This is based on a 'neutral' view of religion, and focuses mainly on the relationship of religion and the state. The 1993 Russian constitution assured equal treatment of all religions, while the (technically non-binding) preamble to the 1997 "Federal law on freedom of conscience and religious organizations" singled out four traditional religions (Orthodoxy, Islam, Judaism, Buddhism) as having special historical ties in Russia; in practice, this has led to 'non-traditional' religious groups, such as Jehovah's witnesses, or Salafists, either receiving unequal treatment at the hands of the state, or being banned. It also enables a situation whereby the state is increasingly attuned to the interests of the Orthodox church, so compromising this form of neutral secularity, or leading into post-secular approaches (see 4). The resulting secular model puts Russia somewhere uneasily between Britain, with its state church headed by the monarch, and the U.S., with its strict legal separation of church and state. An uneasy division of Russia into traditional Muslim and Christian regions seems to be the growing practice, with tolerance and sponsorship of religious practice shaped by historical geography.

3. I then use 'secular' to mean the general post-Enlightenment Western-origin worldview widespread in industrial and post-industrial nations (both within and beyond the Western world), in which explanations of the world are generally justified by reference to science rather than traditional religious texts. In the Russian context, 'secular' individuals are

shaped by the more specific experience of both Soviet and/or post-Soviet secularism. Secular individuals, broadly speaking, are characterized by the belief that religion should be active mainly in the private sphere; by skepticism with regard to tradition; sometimes by a this-worldly, materialist worldview; as well as by autonomy and individualism in interpreting and applying the norms of religion, rather than unquestioning obedience to living or dead religious authorities. Such individuals have usually grown up without a religious upbringing; if they are religious they have rediscovered religion for themselves. As individuals 'find religion', they may be attracted to 'post-secular' options (see 4).

4. Post-secularism. This terms is associated with the theories of Jurgen Habermas and Charles Taylor, but also keys into Peter Berger's thesis that secularization is being replaced by desecularization. The term revises the earlier (descriptive and prescriptive) separation of religion and modernity, and sees a legitimacy in various forms of synthesis between the two. In Russia, the growing involvement of 'traditional' religions in political ideology and cultural policy would be an example of this, as would the growing involvement of religious individuals in shaping a religious vision for their communities and country. Post-secular visions are sometimes visceral reactions against aggressive Soviet secularism.

b. The term 'Muslim, Islam'

Again, I have used the term 'Muslim' rather pragmatically and heuristically without giving the rigorous definitions appropriate to a more formal academic work. Here I can offer a little more clarity. There have been many definitions of who is a Muslim across history, ranging from highly exclusivist (the Kharijites, contemporary *takfiris*) to highly inclusivist (e.g. the Hanafite dictum that one's Muslimness can never slip after pronunciation of the *shahada*). More exclusivist groups insist that Muslimness be defined by continued adherence to specific beliefs and practices, less exclusivist groups adopt the lowest common denominator of "one Qur'an, one *qibla*", or else believe that a child born to a Muslim parent is Muslim, while others believe an affirmation of one's Muslimness should be made when the child reaches the age of discernment. In addition, there is the widespread notion in Russia of being a "nominal" or "ethnic" Muslim: a person raised in a "Muslim-heritage" culture and region (such as Tatarstan or Dagestan), whose Muslimness may consist of no more than an Arabic surname or Turkic first name. In short, combining these possible definitions would yield a broad array of different types of Muslimness, and could be a worthy topic of investigation in itself. My underlying method in the book, however, was merely heuristic, i.e. sufficient for the immediate goal of an initial survey of different types of Muslim self-identification and self-definition. The goal was then to engage in a narrative phenomenology, i.e. to convey the lived experience of a self-identifying Muslim rather than to explain it, or "translate it", in terms of a theory drawn from outside the experience of the subject.

At points, I have combined these two multivalent terms, as when I refer to "secular Muslimness". As indicated, such a term could yield different meanings, depending on initial meaning of each term. For example, as applied to Zuleyha—who was told fairly late by her mother that she was a Muslim and chose consciously to be married in the *nikah* ceremony, but adheres to none of the five pillars or other ritual practices—this could take the form of identifying with her Muslim-heritage linguistic and cultural (Tajik) roots, while claiming the autonomous Enlightenment prerogative to shape this heritage for her own private, "spiritual" rather than "ritual-religious" use. Further investigation would require a different and stricter academic genre and analysis of the materials presented in the book.

APPENDIX FOUR

POSTSCRIPT: A VISIT TO A SALAFI SHEIKH IN INGUSHETIA, OCTOBER 2017

As the book was going to press, I made a final trip to Ingushetia; one important interview that I include in this appendix was with Sheikh Isa Tsechoev. It throws further light on the discussion of Sufism and Salafism in chapters 5 and 6. The young man who was my guide in Ingushetia was called Magomed Bekov. He runs a successful business in Ingushetia, as well as organizing a circle for a number of Ingush intellectuals seeking to build a better future for their republic.

Sheikh Isa Tsechoev

Isa Tsechoev is a Salafi sheikh from Ingushetia with a large following across the North Caucasus. He has been accused, groundlessly, by Kadyrov of being a Wahhabi and supporting terrorists. A bomb was placed beneath his car recently. During our interview, the sheikh's son patrolled the courtyard nervously with a gun over his shoulder. A fellow sheikh with a similar outlook, Hamzat Chumakov, has also been 'takfirized' by Kadyrov (proof that there can be violent "*takfiri* Sufis" too). Recently, a car-bomb crippled the latter, depriving him of his legs. Rumors of the identity of the attackers vary: one version points to Kadyrov, the other to members of the Ingush Qadiriya Batal-hajji *vird* (an Ingush sub-group of Kadyrov's *tariqat*). It seems one of Kadyrov's motives for denouncing and attacking these Ingush Salafis is to stop

Chechen youth moving to Ingushetia to join the *jamaat*s of Tsechoev and Chumakov; any departure from the Kadyrovite party-line is punishable with violence. These attacks are the tail-end of the much more frequent killings that raged from the late 1990s until recently between Salafis and "traditionalists" across the North Caucasus, with "moderate" Salafis often morphing into "jihadi" Salafis when pushed underground by government bans or denunciations by tariqatists. I had a long talk with Sheikh Tsechoev at his mosque in the village of Ali-Yurt a half-hour outside of Nazran, the capital of Ingushetia, in late October 2017.

We started by discussing Tsuchoev's early life, so that I could gain an idea of how an Ingush from a traditional Sufi background could end up in the "anti-Sufi" camp. While in Ingushetia, I met several people from so-called Salafist *jamaat*s (for which there is now more tolerance from the authorities) whose stories generally reflected this trajectory, and so explain the *sheikh*'s broad appeal. Born in exile in Kazakhstan, Tsechoev moved back to Ingushetia in 1957. In exile, all Ingush belonged to *virds*. However, even though Tsechoev's grandfather was the prestigious sheikh Bamat-Girei-hajji Mitaev (1838-1911), who was a direct disciple of Kunta-Hajji, he himself was not initiated by oath into any *vird*.

"The reason," he explained, "is that my father died when I was only one and a half. In exile, *murids* would gather in people's homes. But because my father was not alive, that didn't happen in our home. The first time I saw Bamat-Girei Sufis was on the platform at Jambile when the train was pulling in to take us home. My mother pointed them out and I wept, feeling my father would have been among them if he had been with us." Other members of his *taip* belonged to the Naqshbandi *tariqat*, while his mother's relatives were Kunta-Hajji *murids*. This multiple *vird*-belonging had a disorienting effect on him: "When I was getting into my teens, all these family members made their claims on me. They were each pulling me in a different direction. 'Join this *vird*, it's better because of this reason, or this one, and so on.' It actually seemed to me that all this contradiction could not be true and I decided to find out what real Islam was.... at the age of fifteen, I started reading the Qur'an and learning Arabic grammar and *tafsir* with a teacher. He was a weak teacher, the knowledge had not been well preserved in Kazakhstan, but still, it was a start... I also learned the Shafi'i *madhab* from old books printed before the revolution."

At this time, Tsechoev had finished university, graduating in mathematics, and he began teaching in a school; his Islamic studies were all carried out in secret (though people in his village knew and respected his learning), and part of his dedication to these studies was the result of a promise he had made to Allah that if he finished his secular studies successfully, he would dedicate himself to the study of the religion.

In the 1970s, a colleague who had studied in Jordan smuggled some books about Islam back into the Soviet Union. Tsechoev read one about the Muslim Brotherhood and the thought of Hassan al-Banna. Tsechoev recalled: "It was at this time that I found out about political Islam, and I understood then what Islam really is." Tsechoev expressed to me his continued support for the idea that political Islam was the true Islam and that "any true Muslim should be a Salafi, yearning for the status quo at the time of the Salaf when politics and religion were guided by the same *usul* (legal principles)." However, a bit later he qualified this, explaining that his views on the means to attain that status quo had changed after his four years studying Arabic and *fiqh* in Algeria from 1990-1994. "I lived through the troubles in Algeria in the early 1990s when the Islamic Salvation Front briefly gained political power and set up a mejlis to implement shari'a. The bloodiness of the conflict was devastating, and I swore that I would never support such a movement." Instead, "I now try to spread Islam through education. That is my fight."

Thus one could call Tsechoev a "moderate Salafi", a term often used by Islam experts. Still, one of the issues I was trying to probe in talking to Tsechoev was the helpfulness of such a term. After all, Tsechoev's position was similar to that of Kadir Malikov in Kyrghyzia, who eschewed the term "Salafist" for himself. But the situation became still odder. I asked Tsechoev what school of Islamic law and theology is taught in his *medrese*: is it "Salafist", and what is Salafist law and theology? "We teach Shafi'i *fiqh*, but we also supplement it with other *madhabs*." We discussed the example of distributing grain or money to the poor on Ramadan, and Tsechoev on the spot opined that the Shafi'i preference for grain should be modified rationally to fit in with the Quranic verse that the poor should be fed and satisfied, a condition that grain-distribution would obstruct. In this case the Hanafite preference for money should prevail. But this was the same as the "traditionalist" position of government mufti Rustam Batrov in Kazan, and hardly constituted the strictly "anti-*madhab*" position associated with Salafism; rather it was a pluralist "multi-*madhab*" position. Regarding theology, Tsechoev answered my question about God's attributes by saying that "unlike Asharites" (again, the theological school of the "traditionalists"), he takes the "Salafist" position that God does indeed have "a face" (and hands, a throne etc) as described in the

Qur'an, but that one cannot know what this really means. Again, I put it to him that this is not a "Salafist" position (which is an anachronism for the medieval period when these discussion took place), but rather the traditional Asharite position of *bi-la kayfa* (accepting literal statements but "without asking how", i.e. not digging into unknowable details). In sum, on doctrinal and legal questions it seemed that there was little, if anything, to distinguish Tsechoev the "Salafist" from educated and thoughtful, and indeed self-described "traditional" Muslims in other parts of the post-Soviet space.

I finally, teasingly, ask Tsechoev whether he could imagine a "good Sufism", that is, the gathering of Muslims for *zikr* which increased their devotion to God and did not result in abuses. I mentioned that Ibn Taymiyya himself only criticized pseudo-Sufism, rather than Sufism per se. "Probably in the time of al-Ghazali, there was some such true Sufism," pondered Tsechoev. "But I have never seen it. When I was in Algeria, I asked if there was real Sufism, but I was told that it no longer existed. And what I have seen with my own eyes here is sheikhs demanding strange rituals and contributions at funerals and further impoverishing poor people." Even here, then, Tsechoev's "Salafism" did not, in principle, exclude all forms of Sufi devotion.

In this respect, another conversation in Ingushetia allowed me to imagine a different outcome of Tsechoev's own critique of Sufism. Two evenings before our meeting, I had had dinner with an ex-bureaucrat who had turned to farming, and his brother, who worked for the state treasury. Like Mogamed, and like Tsechoev, both of them had become disillusioned with their Qadiriya upbringing: the running round in circles as children, then teenagers, at crazed *zikr*s seemed mechanical, pointless. The treasury official had been doing some reading, and in his own much less tutored way had come round to Tsuchoev's point of view that Ingush Sufism was not satisfactory. He, too, identified with "Salafism" (proof that this "post-tariqatist" movement exists across the board, and indeed is often more common among the educated and middle-class). However, the day before I had encountered similar "*zikr*ism-fatigue", only this time the outcome was different. Ibragim, too, had concluded that Ingush Kunta-Hajjism was "dead Sufism", a case without anything inside it, form and no content (I was amazed by how closely, down to the very metaphor, his analysis overlapped with my own feelings for the matter, inspired by Arsanov). However, during the visit of a famous Cypriot Naqshbandi sheikh to Russia, Ibragim had falteringly asked what a person was to do if he felt his *tariqat* was not sustaining him. He received the answer that a dead or absent *sheikh* (such as Kunta-Hajji) is no *sheikh* at all, and that such a person should seek a new *sheikh*. Ibragim is now one of the very few followers of the Yemeni Sufi Sheikh, Umar Habib, in Russia. For him, a true connection to a disconnected past, turned out to be not some form of (Shafi'i Asharite) "Salafism", but a living Sufism with an unbroken *silsala*.

My conversation with an influential Salafi sheikh had thus added more detail to a recognition many have arrived at: "Salafism" and "Sufism" in Russia and its near-abroad were somewhat arbitrary labels, and the opposition between them was sustained by political reasons (in this case the official Ingush muftiat's monopoly on distributing *hajj* funding seriously compromised the respect felt towards it by many in the republic). I asked Magomed for his views on Tsechoev and this highlighted another problem with the Sufi-Salafi dichotomy. Earlier, Mogamed had described himself to me as "a bit of a Salafi, a bit of a Sufi, a bit of a Shi'ite even" (labels that now seemed less contradictory), and generally sympathetic to Tsechoev. But now he pondered: "He's a mathematician, and a high-school teacher, you can see that. Everything's one plus one equals two. I'd go mad with that." For Magomed, both North Caucasus-style Salafism and Sufism were, one might say, on the same side of a single wall, two simplistic provincial approaches that ignored the broader world. Magomed was keen for Ingush Islam to find its place within a larger Russian Islam, and within a multi-religious world (he had recently come back from a trip to Israel and asked me to address his group on the history of Judaism). It seemed clear that Tsechoev's remit did not so much oppose such pluralism as simply not comprehend the need for it.

Under Ingush President Yevkurov, "moderate Salafis" like Tsechoev are being given the protection of the law (much to Kadyrov's annoyance). If this continues, then perhaps Tsechoev and Salafi *jamaat*s like his will be left unbruised by violence and defamation long enough for the free action and thought of questing Muslims to finally allow the Salafi–Sufi dichotomy to break beyond the wall and move into another dimension. Then the grim mutually limiting embrace of the two bugbears could gently be released. To some extent this is happening: Ingushetia is more Islamically pluralist than Chechnya, and this pluralism extends to public commemoration of the Deportation, and the appearance of art and novels by young creative intellectuals interpreting that past. This is a source of optimism for Magomed, and those working for a less fractured future in Ingushetia and elsewhere in the North Caucasus. But, of course, non-theological factors like unemployment, corruption, inflated federal funding, weakening ties with "mainland" Russia, a failing economy, vested interests, and so on, continue to be powerful hindrances along this way.

BIBLIOGRAPHY

Afandi, Said al-Chirkavi, *Sokrovishchnitsa blagodatnix znanii* [The treasury of blessed knowledge], Mahachkala: Nurul Irshad Publishing House, 2012.

Ahmed, Leila, *The Quiet Revolution*, New Haven: Yale University Press, 2011.

Ahmed, Shahab, *What is Islam? The Importance of Being Islamic*, Princeton: Princeton University Press, 2015.

Akaev, Vahid, *Sheikh Kunta-Hajji* [Sheikh Kunta-Hajji], Grozny: Ichkeria, 1994.

Alfeyev, Hilarion (Metropolitan of Volokalamsk), 'Musul'mane i khristiane v sovremennom mire' [Muslims and Christians in the modern world], Cairo speech, 2011, http://www.pravmir.ru/musulmane-i-xristiane-v-sovremennom-mire/

Aliutdinov, Shamil, *Svyashcheniy koran. Smysly* [The sacred Qur'an. Meanings], Moscow: Dilya, 2012.

— *Kak uvidet' ray* [How to see paradise], Moscow: Dilya, 2013.

Berger, Peter (ed), *The Desecularization of the World: A Global Overview*, Grand Rapids: Eerdmans, 2005.

Bobrovnikov, Vladimir, 'Izobretenie islamskikh traditsii v dagestanskom kolkhoze' [the creation of Islamic traditions in a Daghestani kolkhoz], in *Dagestan i musul'manskii vostok* [Daghestan and the Muslim East], Moscow: Izdatel'ski dom Mardzhani, 2010.

Brown, Jonathan, *Misquoting Muhammad. The challenges and choices of interpreting the Prophet's Legacy*, London: Oneworld, 2014.

Bustanov, A.K, 'Nozhnitsy dlja sredneiasiatskoi istoriografii: "vostochnie projekty" leningradskogo vostokovedenija,' in *Orientalizm vs. Orientalistika* [Scissors for Central Asian historiography: the "Eastern projects" of the Leningrad school of

Oriental Studies], A.I. Miller i L.S. Perepyelkin, Moscow: Fond issledovanii islamskoi kultury, 2016.

Epstein, Mikhail, *Posle ateizma. Novie vozmozhnosti teologii* [After atheism. New possibilities in theology], Moscow: Ast-Press, 2013.

Gasprinsky, Ismail, *Russkoe musul'manstvo* [Russian Muslim culture], Bakhchiserai, 1896.

— *Russko-vostochnoe soglashenie. Mysli, zametki i pozhelaniya* [Russian-Eastern harmony. Thoughts, notes and desires], Bakhchiserai, 1896. Publisher?

Gaynutdin, Ravil, *Vvedenie v shariat* [Introduction to shariah], Moscow: Medina Publishing House, 2014.

Habermas, Jürgen, 'Secularism's Crisis of Faith: Notes on Post-Secular Society', *New Perspectives Quarterly*. vol. 25 (2008) pp. 17-29.

Ibragim, Tawfiq, *Koranicheskii gumanizm* [Qur'anic humanism], Moscow: Medina Publishing House, 2015.

Jemal, Gaidar, *David protiv Goliafa* [David versus Goliath], Moscow: Izdatel'stvo 'Sotsial' no-politicheskaya MYSL, 2011. Publisher?

Kemper, Michael. "Shariatski diskurs imamata v Dagestane pervoi poloviny XIX v" [Shariah discourse about the imamate in Dagestan in the first half of the 19th century], in *Dagestan i musul'manskii vostok* [Daghestan and the Muslim East], Moscow: Izdatel'ski dom Mardzhani, 2010.

Khairetdinov, D.Z, *Moskovskaya sobornaya mechet'* [The Moscow Cathedral mosque], Moscow: Medina Press, 2015.

— *The Muslim community in Moscow: from the 14th century to the beginning of the 20th century*, Nizhny Novgorod: Medina Publishing House, 2008.

Khalid, Adeeb, *Islam after Communism*, Berkeley: University of California Press, 2007.

Kofanova, E. N. and M.M Mchedlova, 'Religioznost' rossian i yevropeitsev 2010' [Religious practice among Russians and Europeans in 2010], http://wciom.ru/fileadmin/file/monitoring/2010/96/2010_2(96)_10_Kofanjva.pdf

Kurbanov, Ruslan, *Fiqh musul'manskikh men'shenstv. Musul'manskoe zakonodatel'stvo v soveremennom musul'manskom mire* [The fiqh of Muslim minorities. Muslim jurisprudence in the modern Muslim world], Moscow: Medina Publishing House, 2011.

Lewis, David, *After Atheism. Religion and ethnicity in Russia and Central Asia,* Surrey: Curzon, 2000.

Lotman, Yuri, *Besedy o russkoi kul'ture. Byt i traditsiya russkogo dvoryanstva (XVIII-nachalo XIX veka)* [Conversations about Russian culture. Daily life and tradition of the Russian aristocracy (XVIII-beginning of the XIX century)], Moscow: Azbuka, 1997. Publisher

Makarov D.V. and A.N. Starostin, *Migratsia i antropotok na yevraziiskom prostranstve* [Migration and human movement in the Eurasian space], Moscow: Medina Publishing House, 2013.

Malikov, Kadir, *Sotsial'naya aktivnost' musulmanskogo soobshchestva Kyrgystana na sovremennom etape* [The social activity of Kyrgystan's Muslim community in the present], Bishkek: Tsentr sotsial'nyx issledovanii Amerikanskogo universiteta v Tsentral'noi Azii, 2011.

Muhetdinov, Damir, *Rossisskoe musulmanstvo. Prizyv k osmysleniu i kontekstualizatsii* [Russian Muslim culture. A call to understanding and contextualization], Moscow: Medina Publishing House, 2015.

— *Islam in the 21st century: a program for renewal. (Selected papers),* trans. by D. Rubin, Moscow: Medina Publishing House , 2016.

— 'The dilemma of our age: pseudo-Salafism or intellectual Salafism?', in Muhetdinov, 2016.

Muhetdinov D., S.R. Kashaf et al., eds, *'Bigievskie chteniya'. Musulmanskaya mysl' v XXI veke: yedinstvo traditsii i obnovleniya* [Bigiev memorial lectures. Muslim thought in the 21st century: unity of tradition and innovation], Moscow: Medina Publishing House, 2016.

Novitsky A.I, *B.I. Urmanche* [B.I. Urmanche.], St Petersburg: Morskoi Peterburg, 2015.

Olcott, Martha, *In the Whirlwind of Jihad,* Washington D.C.: Carnegie Endowment for International Peace, 2002.

Pomerantsev, Peter, *Nothing is True and Everything is Possible. Adventures in Modern Russia,* London: Faber and Faber, 2015.

Popov, Vladimir, *Zhivopis' Grafika* [Paintings. Graphic art], Kazan: Zaman, 2015.

Rashid, Ahmed, *Jihad. The Rise of Militant Islam in Central Asia,* London: Penguin, 2002.

Rubin, Dominic, *Holy Russia, Sacred Israel. Jewish-Christian encounters in Russian religious thought,* Boston: Academic Studies Press, 2010.

BIBLIOGRAPHY

BIBLIOGRAPHY

BIBLIOGRAPHY

—'Musul'manstvo v russkom i britanskom filosofsko-religioznom prostranstve: ot inakovosti k konvergentsii' ['Islam in the Russian and British philosophical-religious imagination: from otherness to convergence'], in *Islamskaya mysl': traditsiya i sovremennost'. Vyp. 1*, ed. T. Ibragim and V. Naumkin et al., Moscow: Medina Publishing House, 2016.

Sagitova, V., 'Musulmanki-migranty v Tatarstane: stsenarii adaptatsii v prinimayushchem obschestve' [Female Muslim migrants in Tatarstan: scenarios for adaptation in the host society'], in Makarov and Starostin, 2013.

Shmelova A.P. and Y.S. Potapova, 'Problemy vospriyatiya migrantami rossiiskogo islama', ['Problems with migrants' reception of Russian Islam'], in D. Muhetdinov, S.R. Kashaf et al ed., 2016.

Skobelev, Denis, 'Demografiya kak politika. Korennoe nasilenie Sibiri v sostave rossiiskoi imperii i SSSR: dinamika chislennosti kak otrazheniya politiki tsentra' ['Demographics as politics. The native population of Siberia in the Russian empire and the USSR: the dynamics of population as a reflection of the politics of the centre'], in *Istoricheskie esse o Sibiri*, ed. Sergei Glebov, Moscow: Ab Imperio, 2013.

Starostin, Alexei, 'Vzaimosvyz' islama i migratsionnykh protsessov na severe Tyumenskoi oblasti v 1990-2000 gg' [The link between Islam and migration processes in the north of Tyumen oblast in 1999-2000"], in Makarov and Starostin, 2013.

Yakubovich M., V. Rubtsov, N. Husainova and V. Bikchentaev, *Svyashcheniy koran. Smyslovoi perevod s kommentariami* [The holy Qur'an. A translation of its meanings with commentary], Moscow: Medina Publishing House, 2015.

Yusuf, Muhammad Sodik Muhammad, *Iyman, islam, kur'an* [Iman, Islam, Qur'an], ed. Ali Vyacheslav Polosin, Moscow: Hilal, 2010.

— *Vasatiya — put' zhizni* [Wasatiyya: the path of life], Moscow: Hilal 2011.

Zaitsev et al. *Mecheti kryma na staryx fotografiyax* [Crimea's mosques in old photographs], Moscow: Medina Press, 2016.

Zygar, Mikhail, *All the Kremlin's men. Inside the court of Vladimir Putin*, New York: Public Affairs, 2016.

Web resources

Barrett, Richard, 'Foreign fighters in Syria', June 2014, http://www.soufangroup.com/foreign-fighters-in-syria/

Bzarov, Aslan, 'Zhestoko ubit za zaschitu hidzhaba: ocherednoi imam rasstreljan neizvestnymi na stavropole' ["Brutally murdered for defending the hijab: another imam is shot by unknown assailants in Stavropol"], 27 September 2016, http://onkavkaz. com/news/1271-zhestoko-ubit-za-zaschitu-hidzhaba-ocherednoi-imam-rasstreljan-neizvestnymi-na-stavropole.html?fromslider, accessed 30 March 2017

Florida, Richard, 'The Economic Power of Cities Compared to Nations', Citylab, 16 March 2017, https://www.citylab.com/work/2017/03/the-economic-power-of-global -cities-compared-to-nations/519294/?utm_source=atlfb

Florinskaya, Yulia, 'Mashtaby trudovoi migratsii v Rossiyu' [The scale of labor migration to Russia], http://russiancouncil.ru/inner/?id_4=2342#top-content

Fuller, Liz, 'Grozny Fatwa On "True Believers" Triggers Major Controversy', 14 September 2016, RFE/RL, http://www.rferl.org/a/caucasus-report-grozny-fatwa-controversy/27987472.html

Hazir, Ümit-Nazmi, 'The Significance of Russian Muslims in Turkish-Russian Relations', 11 February 2017, http://www.kafkassam.com/the-significance-of-russian-muslims-in-turkish-russian-relations.html

Heathershaw, John and Montgomery David, 'The Muslim Radicalisation of Central Asia is a dangerous myth', 29 December 2014, openDemocracy, https://www. opendemocracy.net/od-russia/john-heathershaw-david-w-montgomery/%E2% 80%98muslim-radicalisation-of-central-asia%E2%80%99-is-dangerous-1

Huseyn, Aliev, 'Conflict-related Violence Decreases in the North Caucasus as Fighters go to Syria', The Central Asia-Caucasus Analyst, 4 January 2015, https://www. cacianalyst.org/publications/analytical-articles/items/13171-conflict-related-violence-decreases-in-the-north-caucasus-as-fighters-go-to-syria.html

Sokolov, Denis, 'Putin's savage war against new Muslims', 20 August 2016, http:// europe.newsweek.com/Putin-savage-war-against-russia-new-muslims-490783

— "Vybor mezhdu Kadyrovym i al-Bagdadi, [The choice between Kadyrov and al-Baghdadi]", accessed 13 September 2017 at https://www.vedomosti.ru/opinion/ articles/2017/09/05/732320-mezhdu-kadirovim-i-al-bagdadi

Tatar-zade, Ali, 'Four lions of the Crimean Savanna', Media Krym, 5 July 2011, http:// risu.org.ua/en/index/studios/studies_of_religions/45605/, accessed 6 March 2017.

Vatchagaev, Mairbeck, 'Qatari Sheikh Becomes Tool for Kremlin in Struggle Against North Caucasus Militants', Eurasia Daily Monitor, Issue 11, 203, http://jamestown. org/program/qatari-sheikh-becomes-tool-for-kremlin-in-struggle-against-north -caucasus-militants-2/

BIBLIOGRAPHY

'Number of Migrants in Russia for 2016', Top Migrant, http://topmigrant.ru/migraciya/obshhaya-informaciya/migranty-v-rossii.html

"Spetsnaz Kadyrova po trevoge dal klyatvu Prezidentu Rossii!" ["Kadyrov's special forces on high alert swear allegiance to the President of Russia!"], https://www.youtube.com/watch?v=IGflZYJe8Yg

SUGGESTED BACKGROUND READING

The following are some basic English-language works that treat Islam in the Russia and Central Asia region (the one exception is Khalid Abu El Fadl's book, which I include as a compelling and engaged statement of the parameters of the extremist-moderate debate in Islam today); I have omitted a large contingent of books in Russian, which inform my own book, assuming that most readers will not know Russian, and that if they do, they can track down the relevant works independently.

Balzer, Marjorie Mandelstam, ed., *Religion and Politics in Russia*, London: Routledge, 2009.

Bennigsen, A. and S.E. Wimbush, *Muslims of the Soviet empire*, Bloomington: Indiana University Press, 1986.

Brower, Daniel and Edward Lazzerini, *Russia's Orient. Imperial Borderlands and Peoples, 1700-1917*, Bloomington: Indiana University Press, 2001.

Bukharaev, Ravil, *The model of Tatarstan under President Mintimer Shaimiev*, New York: St Martin's Press, 1999.

Crews, Robert, *For Prophet and tsar. Islam and Empire in Russia and Central Asia*, Cambridge MA: Harvard University Press, 2006.

Fadl, Khaled Abou El, *The Great Theft. Wrestling Islam from the extremists*, London: Harper One, 2007.

Gammer, Moshe, *The Lone Wolf and the Bear. Three Centuries of Chechen defiance of Russian rule*, London: Hurst, 2014.

Heinrich, Hans-Georg, Lobova Liudmilla, and Alexei Malashenko, *Will Russia become a Muslim society?*, Frankfurt: Peter Lang GmbH, 2010.

Hiro, Dilip, *Inside Central Asia*, London: Overlook Duckworth, 2009.

— *War without end. The rise of Islamist terrorism and the global response*, Hove: Psychology Press, 2002.

Hunter, Shireen, *Islam in Russia. The Politics of Identity and Security*, New York: M.E. Sharpe, 2004.

Kefeli, Agnès Nilüfer, *Becoming Muslim in Imperial Russia. Conversion, Apostasy, and Literacy*, Ithaca: Cornell University Press, 2014.

Olcott, Martha, *In the Whirlwind of Jihad*, Washington D.C.: Carnegie Endowment for International Peace, 2002.

Rashid, Ahmed, *Jihad. The rise of militant Islam in Central Asia*, London: Yale University Press, 2002.

Roi, Yaacov, *Islam in the Soviet Union*, New York: Columbia University Press, 2000.

Rorlich, A.A, *The Volga Tatars. A profile in national resilience*, Stanford: Hoover Press, 1986.

Ware, Robert Bruce, *The Fire Below. How the Caucasus shaped Russia*, London: Bloomsbury, 2013.

Yemelianova, Galina, *Russia and Islam. A Historical Survey*, Basingstoke: Palgrave, 2002.

Zenkovsky, Sergei, *Panturkism and Islam in Russia*, Cambridge MA: Harvard University Press, 1967.

NOTES

ACKNOWLEDGEMENTS

1. I have changed Sirozhdin's name, as well as those of his family members, to protect their anonymity.

1. MOSCOW: MELTING-POT AND WOULD-BE MECCA OF RUSSIA

1. This is to phrase it somewhat provocatively: the Europeanness of Russia is a constant matter for dispute, and if one counts Turkey as Europe, then Istanbul's Muslim population dwarfs Moscow's.
2. Quoted in D.Z. Khairetdinov, *Moskovskaya sobornaya mechet* [The Moscow Cathedral], Moscow: Medina Press, 2015, p.29.
3. Ibid., p.63.
4. Cf. Denis Sokolov, 'Putin's savage war against new Muslims', Newsweek, http://europe.newsweek.com/Putin-savage-war-against-russia-new-muslims-490783
5. Cf. http://topmigrant.ru/migraciya/obshhaya-informaciya/migranty-v-rossii.html. Novosti Mail.Ru, accessed 5 November 2016.
6. 'The Economic Power of Cities Compared to Nations', City Lab, https://www.citylab.com/work/2017/03/the-economic-power-of-global-cities-compared-to-nations/519294/?utm_source=atlfb
7. The bulk of the money for the new mosque came from a Dagestani businessman called Suleiman Kerimov, Russia's 21st richest person. A member of Putin's inner circle, he was arrested in France in November 2017 for tax-evasion and money-laundering.
8. Lack of knowledge of Arabic is the norm for non-Arab Islamic cultures and is not a hindrance to Islamic observance, but after the boom of the 1990s, Rais evidently

feels a little self-conscious about not reaching a level of Arabic reading, which his wife went on to achieve after her classes.

9. Cf. John Heathershaw and David Montgomery, 'The Muslim Radicalisation of Central Asia is a dangerous myth', Open Democracy, https://www.opendemocracy.net/od-russia/john-heathershaw-david-w-montgomery/%E2%80%98muslim-radicalisation-of-central-asia%E2%80%99-is-dangerous-1

10. In the case of Yakupov, however, it soon became clear that extremists were involved: a group calling themselves the Mujahedeen of Tatarstan, and swearing allegiance to Doku Umarov of the Caucasus Emirate, claimed responsibility for the attack. But the following FSB clean-up operations netted people whose links with extremism were dubious at best.

11. Peter Pomerantsev, *Nothing is true and everything is possible. Adventures in modern Russia*, London: Faber and Faber, 2015.

12. Leila Ahmed, *The Quiet Revolution*, London: Yale University Press, 2011.

13. Cf. Mohammed Arkoun and Yves Lacoste, "L'Islam et les islams: Entretien avec Mohammad Arkoun," quoted in S. Ahmed 2015, p.130. S.Ahmed's monumental "What is Islam? The importance of being Islamic." convincingly refutes the notion of "islams" but proposes a theory of one pluralistic Islam resulting from different interpretations of the "text", "pretext" and "context" of the Qur'anic revelation, which could usefully be applied to "Russian Islam".

14. Cf. Jonathan Brown, *Misquoting Muhammad. The challenges and choices of interpreting the Prophet's Legacy*, London: Oneworld, 2014, p.48: "The [new Sunni] movement's doctrine of political quietism, based in the belief articulated by Ibn Hanbal and others that Muslims should never rebel against their ruler regardless of his heresies or iniquity made Sunni Islam eminently acceptable to the rulers of the Muslim empire as well. The combination of popular and state support proved unbeatable."

15. As quoted by A.P. Shmelova and Y.S. Potapova, 'Problemy vospriyatiya migrantami rossiiskogo islama', in D. Muhetdinov, S.R. Kashaf et al., (ed), *'Bigievskie chteniya'. Musulmanskaya mysl' v XXI veke: yedinstvo traditsii I obnovleniya.* [Bigiev memorial lectures. Muslim thought in the 21st century: unity of tradition and innovation], Moscow: Medina Publishing House, 2016, p.264.

16. See Appendix two for comments on the interviewing process.

2. SEARCHING FOR THE MIDDLE WAY: BETWEEN KYRGYZSTAN AND MOSCOW

1. Martha Olcott, *In the Whirlwind of Jihad*, Washington D.C.: Carnegie Endowment for International Peace, 2002.

2. See, for example, Ahmed Rashid's *Jihad: the rise of radical Islam in Central Asia*, London: Penguin, 2002.

3. The irony is that the authorities quoted here by Yusuf, Ibn Taymiyya and Ibn Hanbal, are both frequently referenced by self-styled Salafis; cf. glossary for more detail on these Islamic scholars.

4. D. Muhetdinov, 'The dilemma of our age: pseudo-Salafism or intellectual Salafism?', International Islamic Conference, Grozny, 26 August 2016.

5. Muhammad Sodik Muhammad Yusuf, *Vasatiya – put' zhizni*. [Wasatiyya: the path of life], Moscow: Hilal, p.140.

6. Ruslan Kurbanov, *Fiqh musul'manskikh men'shenstv. Musul'manskoe zakonodatel'stvo v soveremennom musul'manskom mire* [The fiqh of Muslim minorities. Muslim jurisprudence in the modern Muslim world], Moscow and Nizhny Novgorod: Medina Publishing House, 2011.

7. Personal communication, Professor Timothy Winter, September 2016.

8. Kadir Malikov, *Sotsial'naya aktivnost' musulmanskogo soobshchestva Kyrgystana na sovremennom etape* [The social activity of Kyrgystan's Muslim community in the present], Bishkek: AUCA, 2011.

9. See Appendix 4 for the interview with Ingush *sheikh* Isa Tsechoev.

3. BETWEEN MOSCOW AND FERGANA: CHASING THE GHOST OF ISLAM

1. The aunt commented a little venomously: "I know those people in Margilan still wear the *paranja* now behind closed doors." Pondering on this, it seemed to me like an odd accusation: after all, the *paranja*'s purpose is to conceal a woman in the street, not in her own house! What's the point being made?

2. Like his friend in Andijan, Sirozhidin too is addressed as Hojji—a title Asmira constantly uses to refer to her husband.

3. I met up with Asmira in Moscow in October 2017, and she told me suspicions about Islamism in Fergana had increased since Karimov's death. At Shuhrat's university they have snap security checks; recently an all-A student who tutored his peers after class was arrested for allegedly recruiting for ISIS. This information confirmed to me that the anxiety I had encountered in Fergana was not exceptional, or entirely due to my presence.

4. V. Sagitova, 'Musulmanki-migranty v Tatarstane: stsenarii adaptatsii v prinimayushchem obschestve', [Female Muslim migrants in Tatarstan: scenarios for adaptation in the host society], in D.V. Makarov and A.N. Starostin, *Migratsia i antropotok na yevraziiskom prostranstve* [Migration and human movement in the Eurasian space], Moscow: Medina Publishing House, 2013.

4. TATARSTAN: AMONG THE ARTISTS

1. Farit speculates that his family was "probably pushed out of the Kazan area by the Russians, like other Tatars." But after the eighteenth century, there was no expulsion of Tatars by Russians; Siberian Tatars are often descendants of those who moved voluntarily as merchants, teachers and so on. Farit's speculative narrative seems to assimilate his own family story to a general history of Tatar suffering at Russian hands.
2. *Alif* is the first letter of the Arabic alphabet, and consists of a single vertical line.
3. One thinks of Berger's rejection of his own secularization thesis in Peter Berger, ed., *The Desecularization of the World: A Global Overview*, Michigan: Eerdmans, 2005, as well as Jürgen Habermas' 'Secularism's Crisis of Faith: Notes on Post-Secular Society', *New Perspectives Quarterly*, vol. 25 (2008), pp. 17-29.
4. Cf. Denis Skobelev, 'Demografiya kak politika. Korennoe nasilenie Sibiri v sostave rossiiskoi imperii i SSSR: dinamika chislennosti kak otrazheniya politiki tsentra', [Demographics as politics. The native population of Siberia in the Russian empire and the USSR: the dynamics of population as a reflection of the politics of the centre], in Sergei Glenov, ed., *Istoricheskie esse o Sibiri*, Moscow: Ab Imperio, 2013.

5. DAGESTAN: SHEIKHS, STALIN AND THE SPIRIT OF THE MOUNTAINS

1. Bagaudinovich is Ramazanov's patronymic, which all Russians, non-Muslim or Muslim, have. Addressing someone by first name and patronymic is a sign of respect. Referring to someone by their patronymic alone, especially in abbreviated form, can be a term of familiarity or affection.
2. As in other parts of Russia, it is not always clear that such assassinations have been the work of Salafi-Wahhabis; in a conversation from another trip to Dagestan, Ramazanov expressed the opinion that 'government forces' may have been behind many of these killings—the aim being to sow dissension among the ranks of the Islamic revivalists. The fact that the perpetrators have not been found in many cases adds fuel to this hypothesis in the minds of many. Both the Federal government and the republican authorities could have an interest in weakening Islamic revival: the former due to fear of Islam's growing role in Russia, the latter out of a general neo-Soviet distrust of the role of religion in the state.
3. Trofim Lysenko (1898-1976) was a Soviet biologist who, for ideological reasons and with Stalin's encouragement, disseminated the idea that acquired characteristics were heritable. He thus seriously damaged Soviet biology (and agriculture).

4. E.g. Muhammad Sodik Muhammad Yusuf, *Vasatiya – put' zhizni* [Wasatiyya: the path of life], Moscow: Hilal, p.255: "In this stage of the embryo, like a leach it is nourished by suction. This scientific phenomenon is recognized by the Qur'an and Western scientists, who have often referred to it in their scientific works."

5. Vladimir Bobrovnikov, 'Izobretenie islamskikh traditsii v dagestanskom kolkhoze'[the creation of Islamic traditions in a Daghestani kolkhoz], in *Dagestan i musul'manskii vostok* [Daghestan and the Muslim East.], Moscow: Izdatel'ski dom Mardzhani, 2010.

6. Abdullaeva, who also goes under her maiden name Ainu Gamzatova, put herself forward in December 2017 as a candidate for the March 2018 presidential elections. She gave a speech outlining her pride in a multi-faith and multi-national country where a Muslim woman can stand for President. Eventually, she was barred on technical grounds.

7. Mairbeck Vachgaev (Vachgaev 2012), a former official in Mashkhadov's independent Ichkeria, and now living in exile in Paris, is one example of someone who questions al-Qaradaghi's authority, claiming that Russia's support of the Qatari mufti only compromises his authority among Russian Muslims. However, al-Qaradaghi's credentials (a PhD in Islamic law from Al-Azhar) and his position: that the medieval division of the world into a *dar al-Islam* and a *dar al-harb* are antiquated and dangerous, are necessary if Islam is to be harmoniously integrated into the Russian space.

8. Early Soviet ideology aimed to create Soviet literatures and ethnic identities that would be "socialist in content, national in form"; but under Stalin, the ideal changed into fusing all pre-Communist ethnicities into a greater Soviet people, or *narod* in Russian. Often, in this model, Sovietization took place through Russification.

9. This unpleasant portmanteau combines the words "liberal" and "pederast", and says much about how the West and liberalism is perceived today in Russia.

10. This is based on Michael Kemper's analysis of the Arabic manuscripts of Shamil's main legal consultant al-Urudi. Urudi very carefully answered all criticisms of Shamil's Islamic legitimacy stemming from Dagestani and Cherkassian *'ulema* (religious scholars) who opposed him. Kemper shows that scholars of the Shafi'i school in Medina, to whom these opponents wrote, also took Shamil's side. Cf. Kemper, 'Shariatski diskurs imamate v Dagestane pervoi poloviny XIX v' [Shari'a discourse about the imamate in Dagestan in the first half of the 19th century], in *Dagestan i musul'manskii vostok* [Daghestan and the Muslim East], Moscow: Izdatel'ski dom Mardzhani, 2010. One of the issues concerned the legitimacy of Shamil calling himself a caliph when there was already an Ottomans caliph: the answer was that if one caliph is not doing his job in protecting Muslims, it is legitimate for several caliphates to exist.

11. The Nogais are spread over Dagestan, Chechnya and two other Russian regions, and had a harsh history in tsarist and Soviet times; some of them do indeed want to "cut loose" and be granted their own republic.

6. CHECHNYA: THE AVATAR IS SLEEPING...

1. For Kebedov's critique of the non-jihadi and so non-Islamic character of modern North Caucasus Sufism, cf. https://www.youtube.com/watch?v=6ZZvqjd1iI8, 'Bagauddin o sufistakh nyneshikh' [Bagauddin on present-day 'Sufists'].
2. Brown, *Misquoting Muhammad*, 2014, p.65.
3. See below for his friendship with the rapper Timoty: a canonical "shari'a" beard in his case goes hand in hand with an endorsement of music that one would be hard pressed to justify Islamically. The point, again, is that what the leader approves becomes synonymous with what is Islamic; while what he disapproves of is best not disputed.
4. Cf. Aslan Bzarov 'Zhestoko ubit za zaschitu hidzhaba: ocherednoi imam rasstreljan neizvestnymi na stavropole', [Brutally murdered for defending the hijab: another imam is shot by unknown assailants in Stavropol], 27 September 2016, http://onkavkaz.com/news/1271-zhestoko-ubit-za-zaschitu-hidzhaba-ocherednoi-imam-rasstreljan-neizvestnymi-na-stavropole.html?fromslider, accessed 30.03.2017
5. Another instance of the significance and symbolic manipulation of the veil in Russia today can be seen in the picture on the front cover of this book. It shows the Ingush Dzakhiev family, one of the sixty families hosted by Putin in the Kremlin to pick up their awards in the 2016 Family of the Year competition. The picture of Putin standing small amid a posse of four hijabed women might alarm some: this Islamic Ingush couple with nine children certainly ticks the "traditional" "clean-living" box that Russian conservatives want, but it could also be seen as a graphic illustration of the demographic victory of Muslims over ailing Slavs (touted by Bagaudinovich). However, the Kremlin's iconography of the event was very precise: the young girls are veilless and wearing sleeveless dresses, so no "Salafism" or "extremism" there; more importantly, father Maksharip is a retired law-enforcement officer and war veteran, which in Ingushetia very likely means he took part in the war against separatists and Wahhabis.
6. Cf. Richard Barrett, 'Foreign fighters in Syria', The Soufan Group, June 2014, http://www.soufangroup.com/foreign-fighters-in-syria/
7. This event can be viewed at: https://www.youtube.com/watch?v=IGflZYJe8Yg The clip is titled: 'Spetsnaz Kadyrova po trevoge dal klyatvu Prezidentu Rossii!' [Kadyrov's special forces on high alert swear allegiance to the President of Russia!].

8. Aliev Huseyn, 'Conflict-related Violence Decreases in the North Caucasus as Fighters go to Syria', The Central Asia–Caucasus Analyst, 4 January 2015, https://www.cacianalyst.org/publications/analytical-articles/item/13171-conflict-related-violence-decreases-in-the-north-caucasus-as-fighters-go-to-syria.html

9. Cf. Denis Sokolov, 'Vybor mezhdu Kadyrovym i al-Bagdadi, [The choice between Kadyrov and al-Baghdadi]', accessed 13 September 2017 at https://www.vedomosti.ru/opinion/articles/2017/09/05/732320-mezhdu-kadirovim-i-al-bagdadi

7. MOSCOW: BRAIN OF ALL THE RUSSIAS

1. Tatar thinkers include the *jadid* classics: Hussein Faizkhanov, Musa Bigiev, Ziatdin Kamali, and Ismail Gasprinsky. Russian thinkers include: N. Berdyaev, P. Florensky I. Ilin, and K.Leontiev. The latter are proponents of the "Russian Idea". The overlap with Askhat Vafin's Islamo-Christian synthesis is clear.

2. This non-Christian universalization of the Russian Idea bears a strong resemblance to the attempts of pre-1917 Jewish adherents of Russian religious thought to give a non-Christian meaning to Russian Platonic ideas; this is especially vivid in the work of Mikhail Gershenzon and Aron Steinberg (cf. Rubin 2010 for detail). Dominic Rubin, *Holy Russia, Sacred Israel: Jewish-Christian encounters in Russian religious thought*. Academic Studies Press, Boston: 2010

3. He also prefers the term *musulmanstvo* to *islam*, arguing (as Patimat Abdullaeva had pointed out to me) that there cannot be a Russian Islam, merely a Russian cultural incarnation of a single underlying Islam.

4. Zaitsev et al., *Mecheti kryma na staryx fotografiyax*, [Crimea's mosques in old photographs], Moscow: Medina Press, 2016.

5. Not that Muhetdinov, glancing over his shoulder at his sponsors, does not try occasionally to drag these medieval Central Asian Sufis into the orbit of modern Moscow. In a speech at the First International Forum of Sufis held in Delhi in March 2016, he speculates about whether the hand of London can be seen in the choice of a former British colonial capital for the venue (cf. Muhetdinov 2016). Dismissing this as "conspiratorial thinking", he still ends his speech: "We entreat Allah that in the near future a serious international forum on questions of *tasawwuf* [Sufism] will convene in Moscow." Sufism is presented as an option to contain extremism and develop the Islamic world: Moscow should thus be at the forefront of this effort.

6. It is an odd philological fact that Gasprinsky refers to Russian Muslims as *russkoe musul'manstvo*: that is, he uses the narrower ethnic-linguistic adjective "russkoe" rather than his heir Muhetdinov's broader *rossiskoe*. Perhaps the early hopes

that Russia's Muslims could be so Russianized as to merit the narrower epithet have since dissolved. For more on this, cf. Dominic Rubin, 'Musul'manstvo v russ-kom i britanskom filosofsko-religioznom prostranstve: ot inakovosti k konver-gentsii', [Islam in the Russian and British philosophical-religious imagination: from otherness to convergence], in T. Ibrahim and V. Naumkin et al. eds., *Islamskaya mysl': traditsiya i sovremennost'*, *Vyp. 1*, Moscow: Medina Publishing House, 2016.

7. '*Nasha* Russia' ('Our Russia') is a popular comedy show which spoofs the surreal realities of modern Russia, including corruption, illogicality, police, guest-work-ers, and so on.

8. Olivier Roy, *Holy Ignorance: When Religion and Culture Part Ways*, London: Hurst, 2010.

9. Makarov's background is more complex: his father was a Cossack, his mother a Tatar—both strongly traditional ethnicities in the Russian empire.

10. Cf. A.K. Bustanov, 'Nozhnitsy dlja sredneiasiatskoi istoriografii: "vostochnie pro-jekty" leningradskogo vostokovedenija,' in *Orientalizm vs. orientalistika*, [Scissors for Central Asian historiography: the "Eastern projects" of the Leningrad school of Oriental Studies], A.I. Miller I L.S. Perepyelkin. Fond issledovanii islamskoi kultury: 2016.

11. D.Z. Khairetdinov, *The Muslim community in Moscow: from the 14th century to the beginning of the 20th century*, Nizhny Novgorod: Medina Publishing House, 2008.

12. The term 'Islamology' belongs to Ali Shari'ati. Shari'ati argued fiercely for the idea of Islam not as a culture that collaborates with power, but as a revolutionary 'ide-ology'. These elements and the fact that Jemal identified as Shi'ite in the early 1990s indicate that Shari'ati must have had a considerable effect on his thinking, as well as on other post-Soviet Russian Muslims close to Jemal.

13. Keenan (2012) is a good example of this. He writes that "diversity must be embraced to curb the alienation of Muslims" and then later (far less persuasively) that Doku Umarov, the leader of the Caucasus Emirate, has shifted to a more "peaceful" approach that requires reciprocal tolerance from Russia. It is easy to see how such support of a leader of the Caucasus Emirate could be taken by many Russians, on the street and in power, as "anti-Russian", especially given Umarov's claims of responsibility for the 2010 Moscow metro bombings and the 2011 attack on Domodedovo airport, not to mention his declaration that "there are no civilians in Russia". Tolerance for a separate Islamic state on Russia's southern border, which is the goal of the Caucasus Emirate, is unlikely to be a persuasive position for Russia at large.

EPILOGUE: MULTIVERSE OR HALL OF MIRRORS

1. Yuri Lotman, *Besedy o russkoi kul'ture. Byt i traditsiya russkogo dvoryanstva (XVIII-nachalo XIX veka)*, [Conversations about Russian Culture. Daily life and tradition of the Russian aristocracy (XVIII-beginning of the XIX centrury)], Moscow: Azbuka, 1997.
2. Cf. Liz Fuller, 'Grozny Fatwa on "True Believers" Triggers Major Controversy', RFERL, 2016, http://www.rferl.org/a/caucasus-report-grozny-fatwa-controversy/27987472.html
3. Cf. Ali Tatar-zade, 'Four Lions of the Crimean Savanna', Media Krym, 5 July, 2011, http://risu.org.ua/en/index/studios/studies_of_religions/45605/ accessed 6 March, 2017.
4. Hilarion Alfeyev, 'Musul'mane i khristiane v sovremennom mire' [Muslims and Christians in the modern world], Cairo speech, 2011, http://www.pravmir.ru/musulmane-i-xristiane-v-sovremennom-mire/
5. Cf. Mikhail Zygar, *All the Kremlin's men. Inside the court of Vladimir Putin*, New York: Public Affairs, 2016.
6. Cf. Ümit-Nazmi Hazir, 'The Significance of Russian Muslims in Turkish-Russian Relations', 2016, http://www.kafkassam.com/the-significance-of-russian-muslims-in-turkish-russian-relations.html
7. Some months after I wrote these lines, the world once again had to sit up and parse Islam through the lens of extremism in St Petersburg, when a terrorist set off a bomb on the city's metro on 3 April 2017. The suicide bomber, Akbarzhon Jalilov, was a young and fresh-faced Kyrghyz waiter with Russian citizenship, an ethnic Uzbek who was born in the southern Fergana valley Kyrgyzstan city of Osh, and worked in a Sushi bar. In nationality, ethnicity, city, and profession he was identical to my neighbor, Dima, whom I mentioned in chapter 2.
8. Alexei Starostin, '"Vzaimosvyz" islama i migratsionnykh protssessov na severe Tyumenskoi oblasti v 1990-2000 gg' [The link between Islam and migration processes in the north of the Tyumen oblast in 1999-2000], in D.V. Makarov and A.N. Starostin, *Migratsia i antropotok na yevraziiskom prostranstve* [Migration and human movement in the Eurasian space], Moscow: Medina Publishing House, 2013. The following paragraph draws on this article, too.

INDEX

INDEX

Aliutdinov, Shamil, 14, 30, 253–4, 255
Almush, ruler of Volga Bulgaria, 125
Altai, Siberia, 110
al-Alwani, Taha Jabir, 43
American University of Central Asia, Bishkek, 50
Amman, Jordan, 50, 87
Andijan, Uzbekistan, 56, 82, 89, 92, 93, 104, 105
   massacre (2005), 87–8
Andropov, Yuri, 215, 216
anti-Christ, 52, 259
anti-Semitism, 21, 70, 75, 77, 256
anti-Wahhabi conference (2016), 267–8
anti-Western sentiment, 55, 96
aqida, 135, 250
Arab nationalism, 128, 130
Arabic, 31, 62, 309–10
   Bashkirs, 29, 31
   calligraphy, 22, 29, 112–22
   Dagestan, 159, 163, 168, 174, 175, 187
   Kyrgyzstan, 56
   Moscow migrants, 16, 19, 29, 309–10
   namaz, 232
   Oriental Studies, 240
   Russian converts, 233
   Soviet suppression, 62, 104
   study abroad, 22, 23, 26, 31, 143, 297
   Tatars, 10, 11, 13, 14, 29, 31, 71, 112–22, 131, 133, 143
   Uzbekistan, 30, 86, 89, 90, 92, 94, 96, 100, 101, 104–6
Arabistan, 102–3
Arkoun, Mohammad, 33
Armenia, 178
Arsanov, Bagauddin, 215

Arsanov, Deni, 195–8, 204, 205, 211, 213–15, 219, 222
Arsanov, Ibragim, 194–215
Arsanov, Ilias, 196, 205, 215
Arsanov, Yakub, 215
asceticism, 196
Ashʿarism, 135, 267, 297, 298, 299
Ashkabad, Turkmenistan, 26
Ashkenazi Jews, 21, 179
al-Assad, Bashar, 173, 216, 218
astrakhan hats, 154, 194, 200, 211, 214
Astrakhan, Russia, 256, 261, 262
Ataturkism, 51, 120
atheism, 11, 21, 27, 35, 50, 56, 60, 71, 73, 91–2, 104
   Soviet Union, 27, 35, 50, 60, 91–2, 104, 117
Aushev, Maksharip Magometovich, 314
Australia, 54
Avars, 155–89, 200
Avatar, 195–6, 213–14, 262
Avicenna, *see* Ibn Sina
ayats, 158, 168
Azar, 260, 262
Azerbaijan, 12, 17, 19, 20, 81, 110, 249–51
Azeris, 169, 188, 255, 256
al-Azhar university, Cairo, 253, 267, 313
Azimov mosque, Kazan, 110, 114, 139
azzan, 156, 158, 174, 204, 209

Baʾath Party, 216
babais, 134
Babur, Mughal emperor, 97–8
Baibekov, Hussain, 6
Bakiev, Kurmanbek, 45
Baku, Azerbaijan, 250
al-Banna, Hassan, 297
Baptists, 63–5, 239

INDEX

Malikov, Kurban Nichbek, 50
Mansur, Imam, 200
March of Peace, 68, 69, 73–7
Marcus, Sergei Jannat, 232, 233–4,
    237–40, 246
Mardani, Shaykh, 93
Margilan, Uzbekistan, 82, 87, 93, 94,
    97, 99, 102, 106
Marina Roscha, Moscow, 248
Maris, Mari-El, 28, 138
Marjani mosque, Kazan, 132
marriage, 17, 31, 47
    arranged, 13, 82–3
    in Dagestan, 167–8, 176
    homosexual, 55
    inter-faith, 71–2, 111, 130, 138
    nikah, 32, 294
    polygamy, 46, 51, 53, 174–5
    in Uzbekistan, 82–3, 84, 91, 93, 94,
        96, 98
    virginity, 82
marshrutka, 82
martial arts, 114, 115
Marxism, 259, 260, 263
Mashkhadov, Aslan, 199, 261, 313
maslaha amma, 52
al-Maturidi, Abu Mansur, 135, 136,
    159, 169, 267
mawlids, 163, 168, 233
Maximov, Georgy, 140
Mayakovsky, Vladimir, 142
Mecca, 21, 29, 36, 75, 96, 117, 136,
    144
Medina, 132, 313
medreses
    Cathedral mosque, Moscow, 133
    Mir-i-Arab, Bukhara, 8
    Muhammadiya, Kazan, 112, 117,
        118, 143, 144
    Naberezhny Chelmy, Tatarstan, 256
    Oktyabrskoe, Bashkortostan, 244

Said Affandi Institute, Dagestan,
    163
Sheikh Deni Arsanov, Grozny,
    194–203, 206
Tatarstan, 27, 112, 115, 117, 118,
    242–3, 256
Uzbekistan, 8, 30, 87, 91, 104
Medvedev, Dmitry, 134
Men, Alexander, 235, 237
Meshket Turks, 100
middle way, *see wasatiyya*
Millionaire Street, St Petersburg, 270
Minnikhanov, Rustam, 269
Mir-i-Arab medrese, Bukhara, 8
Mira Prospect, Moscow, 5, 225
miracles, 101, 133, 142, 145, 159, 165,
    166, 233, 252
mishars, 11
Mitaev, Bamat-Girei-hajji, 296
Mogomaev, Muslim, 19
Moldova, 67
Mongol empire (1206–1368), 3, 70,
    106, 114, 125, 164, 246, 262
Mongolia, 3, 29, 110
Moonies (Unification Church), 30
Mordvins, Mordovia, 110, 202, 236
Moscow, Russia, 3–36, 67–77, 225–63
    Bolshaya Ordynka street, 3
    Bolshaya Tatarskaya street, 3, 4
    Butovo, 12
    Cathedral Mosque, *see under* Cathe-
        dral Mosque
    Cherkessovskaya mall, 76
    Conservatory, 29
    Danilevsky Muslim Cemetery, 248
    Domodedovo airport attack (2011),
        316
    Halal Expo exhibition, 68
    Higher School of Economics, 19
    Historic Mosque, 4, 6, 16, 30, 253

INDEX